The
220 Best
Franchises
To Buy

The
220 Best
Franchises
To Buy

The Sourcebook for Evaluating the Best Franchise Opportunities

REVISED EDITION

Constance Jones
Special Consultants: Andrew J. Sherman, Esq., and Robert Perry

The Philip Lief Group, Inc.

BANTAM BOOKS

NEW YORK · TORONTO · LONDON · SYDNEY · AUCKLAND

THE 220 BEST FRANCHISES TO BUY
A Bantam Book

PUBLISHING HISTORY
Bantam edition published 1987
Bantam revised edition / April 1993

Library of Congress Cataloging-in-Publication Data

Jones, Constance.
  The 220 best franchises to buy / Constance Jones and The Philip
Lief Group, Inc.—Rev. ed.
    p.   cm.
  ISBN 0-553-35155-9
    1. Franchises (Retail trade)—United States.   I. Philip Lief
Group.   II. Title.   III. Title: Two hundred twenty best franchises
to buy.
HF5429.235.U5J66   1993
658.8'708—dc20   92-28438
                                                     CIP

Published simultaneously in the United States and Canada

PRINTED IN THE UNITED STATES OF AMERICA

BVG   0 9 8 7 6 5 4 3 2 1

Contents

PART III

Appendices and Index

Preface to the Revised Edition

In recent years, franchising has consistently grown at a rate outstripping the American economy. Franchise businesses employ over 7.2 million people in more than 60 different industries, according to statistics released by the International Franchise Association.

If you are considering buying a franchise because you want to own your own business but would like the support of a known name and a tested marketing system, this revised edition of *The 220 Best Franchises to Buy* will provide you with an excellent overview of the best opportunities available today, from automotive products and services to restaurants, retailing, and the business services industry, among many other fields.

Many people think only of fast-food establishments when they hear the word "franchise," and while restaurants are at the forefront of business growth, industries in areas from home construction to education are leaders in franchising. The revised edition of *The 220 Best Franchises to Buy* provides over 100 new profiles of businesses in new franchises and growth industries. All of the franchises profiled in the first edition have been carefully reviewed, and those still providing good value to their franchisees have been retained and updated.

You'll note that this revised edition also includes a number of new franchises that can be started as home-based businesses, an important trend in both franchising and entrepreneurship. Starting up a franchise as a home-based venture allows for a lower initial investment, with the potential to grow and expand into a commercial setting as the business develops. Home-based franchises are growing in popularity, and often are a strong draw to women entrepreneurs, many of whom seek out opportunities that allow them greater flexibility to manage child-care responsibilities while they work.

Overall, franchised businesses—both traditional opportunities in commercial settings and home-based options—are growing in appeal to women and minority entrepreneurs as well as to the general community of investors who seek out small business enterprises. Prospects for franchising are bright even through rough economic times because companies that don't have the capital to expand with company-owned units will make more desirable franchises available to franchisees. Of course, as more and better opportunities arise, growing numbers of entrepreneurs will turn to this lucrative market, and competition will be stiffer. Naturally, franchised businesses also stand to thrive in an improving economy, as increased consumer confidence provides for a healthier and more active customer base for products and services.

Part I of this book provides you with important insights into choosing and buying a franchise, while Part II provides you with a helpful overview of the 220 franchises we feel represent some of the best opportunities available to you today. Two new appendices will help you better evaluate the opportunities you choose to explore further. The careful legal review of the 23 categories of the Uniform Franchise Offering Circular will give you a more complete understanding of that crucial legal document, and the review of "red flags" will enable you to pinpoint an aspect of a franchise that may be headed for trouble.

Whether you are just beginning to explore franchising or are on the verge of making some key decisions, the revised edition of *The 220 Best Franchises to Buy* is a vital resource to guide you to successful entrepreneurship and investment.

Introduction

Franchising now accounts for more than one-third of all retail sales. Total sales by franchised retailers climbed to an estimated $758 billion in the early 1990s. According to the International Franchise Association, franchising will sustain—or better—this annual 8.5 percent rate of growth in sales for years to come. As greater numbers of enterprising businesspeople recognize the profits to be had through franchising, they purchase franchises in every field from automotive services to videocassette rental. The number of franchised units in operation expands at a rate of 6 percent annually, which is good news—for close to 2,500 franchisors, who reap a percentage of their franchisees' gross sales; for half a million franchisees, who cash in on franchisors' trademarks and experience; and for over six million people directly employed in franchising. And new franchisors enter the arena every day, opening up even more opportunities for ambitious people who dream of owning their own businesses.

The 220 Best Franchises to Buy contains descriptions of franchising giants with histories of phenomenal success and of young companies with fresh ideas and aggressive strategies for growth.

A Little Bit of History

The term "franchise" comes from the Old French word *franc*, meaning "free from servitude." Its Middle English form, *fraunchise*, meant "privilege" or "freedom," and today *The American Heritage Dictionary of the English Language* defines "franchise" as a "privilege or right granted a person or a group by a government, state, or sovereign, especially . . . suffrage . . . the grant of certain rights and powers to a corporation . . . authorization granted by a manufacturer to a distributor or dealer to sell [its] products."

Since the 1850s, when the Singer Sewing Machine Company became the first to employ franchising as a method of distribution, independent businesspeople have been enjoying unique privileges and freedoms as franchisees. In the first half of the 20th century, franchising took the forms of automobile and truck dealerships, gas stations, and soft drink bottlers. These franchised businesses still make up three-quarters of total franchise sales, but ever since McDonald's came on the scene in the 1950s, companies in virtually every industry have adopted franchising as a way of business. As the economic scene changes, franchising finds new and wider applications. And because franchising can be used to distribute just about any product or service, its potential seems almost unlimited.

What Is Franchising?

Though often referred to as an industry, franchising is actually a method of doing business. In fact, nearly 90 different industries are represented in the franchising community. Franchisors use franchising as a marketing technique in order to expand their market share more rapidly and less expensively. Three distinct types of businesses make up the larger category known as franchising. The first, distributorships, involves the simple granting of the right to sell a product or products originated or owned by the parent company. The second, trademark or brand-name licensing, gives licensees the right to use the company's trademark or brand name in conjunction with the operation of their businesses. This book is primarily concerned with the third type of business, the full business format franchise.

In a full business format franchise, the franchisor (licensor) offers to franchisees (licensees) the license or right to sell its goods or services and/or to use business techniques the franchisor has developed. Franchisees generally pay an initial fee to start up and thereafter forward a percentage of their gross sales to the franchisor at agreed-upon intervals throughout the term of the franchise contract.

In return for these payments, franchisees gain a combination of privileges, which may include the rights to sell a proven, recognized product, to use a set of business practices based on the parent company's experience in the field, to receive initial training, and to benefit from an assortment of ongoing support services. But franchisees also have responsibilities to franchisors—which go beyond the payment of fees and which they are contractually obliged to meet. Among these might be requirements to meet a variety of quality controls for products and services sold, restrictions on what they can sell or how they can operate under the company's name, specifications for their business location and site appearance, and prohibitions on the operation of any similar businesses during or after the term of the franchise contract.

Franchisees have a range of tools at their disposal that their small, nonfranchised competitors rarely have. Brand names, trademarks, copyrights, trade secrets, and even sometimes patents allow them to offer customers what no one else can. Uniform logos, storefronts, and interiors make their businesses more immediately recognizable to potential clients. By following the company's business practices and offering products that meet the company's standards, franchisees can consistently provide customers with quality goods and services.

Many franchisors are corporations with purchasing power that can save franchisees money. They often operate research and development divisions, which constantly test and improve products; marketing departments, which conduct regional or national advertising in a variety of media; and franchisee educational and training programs, which offer comprehensive initial and refresher training to franchisees. And the franchisor's ongoing support system can supply franchisees with assistance in organization, site selection, construction, store opening, merchandising, management, sales, purchasing, and employee recruitment and training, among other things. As long as they keep up their own end of the franchise bargain, franchisees can reap the many advantages of operating their own businesses under the guidance of an experienced and recognized company.

Better Odds

As a franchisee, you can have the satisfaction of being in business for yourself, of making your own business decisions, and of seeing your own hard work pay off. But you need not feel that you're all alone out there. Before they franchise their businesses, good franchisors thoroughly test their products and methods. They make the mistakes, work the kinks out of the business, and establish a reputation. So if you're willing to work hard, pay a few fees, and conform to the franchisor's system, statistics show that you are more likely to succeed with a franchise than if you open a nonfranchised business on your own.

According to the Small Business Administration, 30 to 35 percent of small businesses fail within the first year of operation. But less than 5 percent of all franchise units fail each year, says the U.S. Department of Commerce. Clearly, franchising increases your chances of success—but no one can guarantee your success. "The biggest problem with people getting into franchising is that they think it's easy," notes Linda Serabian, a Subway sandwich shop franchisee. "They think that they don't have to do anything. But it doesn't work like that. It takes a lot of hard work."

No franchise can offer instant wealth, and you should steer clear of any that make get-rich-quick promises. Most franchisees see very low income in the first couple of years of operation—indeed, some even lose money during the first year or two. But with enough elbow grease, the well-capitalized, motivated franchisee can expect to earn an excellent income after the rocky opening period.

A Franchise versus Your Own Small Business

Though owning a franchise may involve just as much work as running an independent small business, you can gain two advantages through franchising: When you operate a franchise, you generally offer an item or a service that people may buy more readily because of its recognized name, and you use previously tested and proven operating systems and business methods. It is easier to maintain a good reputation than to establish one, and you will save your energy and money by following established procedures rather than having to figure out, by trial and error, how best to run your business. As a franchisee, you receive ongoing support and assistance from experienced professionals, but as a small business owner-operator, you have to figure out how to do everything yourself.

Why, then, doesn't every hopeful entrepreneur rush out to purchase a franchise? Because franchising involves two trade-offs that not everyone is willing to make: fees and conformity. Many successful, satisfied franchisees, like Sherridan Revell, who owns an AAA Employment franchise, feel that "the only disadvantage to owning a franchise compared with running your own business would be giving up the royalties each week to the home office." While the vast majority of franchisees consider the security of a franchise and the expertise of the franchisor well worth the added expenses, some resent the requirement that they must continue paying royalties even when they no longer need the constant support or assistance of the franchisor.

The initial franchise fee, the franchisor's requirements for the size and location of your facility, and its specifications for the equipment and supplies you must use can add up to higher start-up costs for franchisees than for businesspeople who open similar businesses on their own. When it does, however, Sherridan Revell still feels that the advantages far outweigh the disadvantages. "It is well worth it to be part of an established company."

Franchisors have carefully determined what makes their businesses work, and therefore require franchisees to make the investment needed to implement their methods. In some cases, this results in a larger initial investment by the businessperson, but not always. Because the company's research and experience can decrease or eliminate some expenses that you would have to bear if you struck out on your own, and because many other costs (like those for advertising and product development) are spread over many franchisees, buying and operating a franchised business can end up costing you less.

Despite this, some prospective franchisees decide that the rights to sell a patented product or process or use prepackaged procedures, or the intangible benefits of an established company name, are not worth the amount they would have to pay in order to have access to them. All hopeful business owner-operators must decide: "Could I do just as well on my own?"

The second perceived disadvantage to being a franchisee is that "in exchange for security, training, and the marketing power of the franchise trademark, you must be able and willing to give up some of your independence," as Bruce Weldon, a Coustic-Glo franchise owner, puts it. Your own success depends in great part on the company's reputation, which in turn depends on your ability to maintain the company's standards. In order to succeed as a franchisee, then, you must follow company guidelines for offering uniformly high-quality products or services.

For mavericks, tinkerers, and incurable nonconformists, franchising can be a frustrating experience. Franchisees give up some of their business autonomy in exchange for the use of the franchisor's name, products, and techniques. "Only a fool would pay for tried-and-true methods and then not use them," says an AAA Employment franchisee. Purchasing a franchise eliminates some of the risks associated with starting a business only if you take advantage of the franchising system—which means submitting to some controls. If you don't mind turning in reports, purchasing from designated sources, or allowing company personnel to check up on your operation, then you won't mind the relatively minor constraints involved in being a franchisee. But if you like to do things your own way, you may not be satisfied with reproducing someone else's success.

Should You Buy a Franchise?

Only you can determine if franchising is right for you. Deciding whether you should buy a franchise, which one to buy, and how to go about buying one is a complicated, sticky business. Part I contains detailed information on what you should consider when making what could be the most important investment of your life. Guidelines and checklists, arranged in a logical, step-by-step manner, will provide you with a starting point for your decision-making process.

The
220 Best
Franchises
To Buy

Part I

Choosing and Buying a Franchise

Introduction to Part I

An Overview

Choosing which—if any—franchise to buy can be confusing, time-consuming, and a little overwhelming. But you can make the process a lot easier by carefully determining what you need to know and do and then conducting your investigation in an organized way. A decision based on a thorough, sound evaluation of your franchising opportunities will make good financial sense and will match your personal and professional goals and abilities.

No one can give you better advice on buying a franchise than a franchisee, who has gone through the experience of evaluating and selecting a franchise. Curt and Candy Holstein, who own a Merry Maids franchise, summarize what most franchisees have to say about choosing a franchise: "Compare the available franchise opportunities. Look at the company's track record on training, marketing, start-up support, and continuous growth and development support. Understand the contract with respect to royalty fees, contract renewal, and other short- and long-term commitments." Part I is, in effect, a step-by-step breakdown of the many details involved in analyzing yourself and the franchises in which you are interested. Clearly, each person and each situation is a little different, so you should adjust these guidelines to fit your specific needs and objectives.

Organizing Your Investigation

Your franchise will probably be the biggest investment (except, perhaps, your home) that you will make in your lifetime, and it will also entail an enormous legal commitment. As a career, a franchise will demand the lion's share of your time and energy for the next several years, if not for the remainder of your working life. Because of the significance of your franchising decision, you should do everything in your power to be thoroughly informed about your opportunities and obligations as a franchisee. Before you invest, you should:

1. Know yourself
2. Know the product and its market
3. Know the franchisor
4. Find out about fees, expenses, and financing
5. Learn about training programs, support, and assistance
6. Know your legal rights and the terms of the contract

Step by Step

You can find out what you need to know by following a straightforward, step-by-step process. Chapters 1–6, based on the list that follows, will guide you through the stages of investigating a franchise opportunity.

- Before you contact franchisors, you should analyze your interests, abilities, and weak points, as well as your financial goals, capacity, and limitations.
- Take a look at the product you would be selling as a franchisee. Analyze the market for the product in your region and determine if you can find a viable location for the franchise in your area.
- Determine which franchise programs might suit you (based on your self-analysis) and contact the franchisors for further information.
- After you receive the information you have requested, narrow down your list of possibilities to two or three companies, using a preliminary evaluation of the franchisors, their products and services, and their franchise programs.
- Check outside sources of information—publications, government agencies, consumer groups, etc.—for more background on the franchisors.
- Contact the companies you've singled out and indicate your interest to them. Submit the preliminary franchise applications to establish yourself as a serious prospect.
- If any of the companies have not yet provided it, request detailed information on the financial and legal particulars of owning one of their franchises. Ask for a list of currently operating franchisees that you may speak with.
- Consult with your accountant and lawyer to determine the feasi-

bility of investing in the franchises in which you are interested. Check franchisors' earnings claims (if they make any) and prepare profit projections for your potential business.

- Speak with some of the companies' franchisees regarding their experiences with the franchisors. Learn all you can about the kinds of support the companies provide.
- Meet with the corporate staff of each of the companies you are considering. Ask any questions you might have, and give the company an opportunity to interview you. Make your decision.
- Have your accountant and lawyer review the standard franchise agreement that the franchisor has given you. Negotiate favorable terms, where possible, before you sign the contract.

If you follow these steps, you should be able to make a wise decision regarding your investment in a franchise. Though franchise fraud has become relatively rare since the 1979 passage of a federal law that requires all franchisors to disclose certain basic facts to potential franchisees, you can never be too careful. Don't rely solely on the information the company gives you, and verify financial data and earnings claims whenever you can. And remember: Franchise owners can be a most valuable source of information. Keep in mind also that in 15 states, there are laws governing franchises.

The hints and checklists that follow in Chapters 1–6 will help you make the most of the information contained in Parts II and III. Because you, your region, and each of the franchisors you are investigating have unique characteristics, you may want to tailor the guidelines to fit your situation. The checklists should simply provide a framework for your research and evaluation.

1. Know Yourself

Before you contact franchisors, analyze your interests, abilities, and weak points, as well as your financial goals, capacity, and limitations.

Although most prospective franchisees know it is wise to evaluate franchisors' performance and learn about a franchise before investing in it, many never think to sit down and take a good look at themselves. But self-analysis must play a vital role when making the right franchising decision. No matter how good an investment a given franchise might be, it can only bring headaches if you are ill-suited to the business itself, to franchising in general, or to running your own business in any form. As Gary Sollee, a Chem-Dry franchisee, puts it: "You will not succeed in any business unless you have a positive attitude and are willing to work your tail off and sacrifice for a few years. You'll only get out what you put in." And if you don't have an honest understanding of your financial capabilities, or realistic financial goals and expectations, you could get in over your head. To avoid making a costly mistake, determine whether or not you are cut out to be a franchise owner—both temperamentally and financially.

Franchisors frequently point to the following characteristics as key to the success of a franchisee: a willingness to work hard, take risks, and work within the franchisor's system. Your business and educational background, your financial capability, your management and sales abilities, and the support of your family will also play significant roles in your business. True, no two franchise owners are alike, but those who prosper share certain traits: enthusiasm, ambition, energy, organization, the ability to get along with others, adequate capitalization, and clear, realistic financial goals.

Are you suited to a career as a franchisee? You're the only one who can make that determination through an honest self-analysis.

Can I Succeed in Franchising? 10 Key Questions

1. Do I enjoy hard work?
   Am I willing to work long hours?
2. Am I willing to forfeit days off and vacation time?
   Am I motivated to succeed—whatever it takes?
   Do I have a lot of physical and emotional stamina?
   Will my family tolerate my long hours?
3. Am I ready to take the responsibility of being my own boss?
   Have I ever been self-employed? Did I like it?
   Am I enthusiastic about running my own business?
   Would I resent taking business problems home with me?
4. Would I like to make my franchise my career?
   Can I dedicate years—or a lifetime—to my franchise?
   Will I run my franchise myself?
5. Will I be able to get the money to finance my business?
   Do I have sufficient resources to tolerate low or negative returns
   for the first year or so of operation?
   Could I live with temporary financial uncertainty?
   Am I willing to forfeit income now to gain income later?
   Am I looking to get rich quick?
6. Do I enjoy taking risks?
   Do I prefer the security of working for someone else?
   Do I enjoy making decisions?
   Am I self-reliant and self-motivated?
   Am I willing to accept responsibility for my actions?
7. Do I have any business management experience?
   Am I an organized person?
   Can I handle lots of detail?
8. Am I a good supervisor?
   Can I recruit and hire the right employees?
   Do I enjoy working with others?
   Can I deal effectively with customers?
   Do I enjoy sales?
9. Am I willing to conform to the franchisor's system?
   Will I mind giving up some of my independence?
   Can I take orders and follow instructions?
   Can I deal effectively with authority?
   Can I accept help from others when I need it?
10. Do my friends and family think I can succeed?
    Would they provide encouragement and support?

Have you been able to answer *yes* to these 10 questions? Affirmative responses indicate that you have the balanced combination of independence and team spirit, ambition and realism, and experience and flexibility to explore the franchising option further.

The next question is, What kind of business would I like to own? Consider the following points to help you focus your interest:

- Do I have hobbies or interests that could become part of a business — a love of children, an interest in fashion, etc.?
- Do I have any special skills or talents that might be useful in my business? Can I repair cars, operate a computer, etc.?
- Do I have any pertinent work experience or education?
- What are my dislikes — do I hate paperwork, sales, or manual work, for instance?
- Do I have any particular weaknesses that might be a disadvantage in running my business; e.g., am I afraid of public speaking, am I bad with numbers, do I have a short temper, etc.?

The next step in your search for the ideal business opportunity is to research the market demographics in your region.

2. Know the Product and Its Market

Take a look at the product you would be selling as a franchisee. Analyze the market for the product in your region and determine if you can find a viable location for a franchise in your area.

Your livelihood as a franchisee will depend upon your ability to sell your product to customers within your region. If you can't sell the product in your area—no matter how successfully it might sell somewhere else—you won't make any money. Do an honest evaluation of the sales potentials of the franchises that you are considering purchasing: Do they offer high-quality products that will appeal to your customer base? Will the products sell five years from now? What kind of competition can you expect? Can you find an appropriate location for your business in your area?

Check sales data of similar or related businesses in your region to get a feeling for how your franchise might do. Your Chamber of Commerce, local banks, and trade associations might be helpful in this regard, as will the Small Business Administration and the Department of Commerce. Consult national and regional business or trade publications to determine how the particular type of business—whether franchised or independent—has performed historically, both in your area and as a whole. Find out what industry analysts and government experts have to say about the future: industry trends, economic forecasts, and projections of future demand for the product you would sell as a franchisee.

As they recognize the potential profits of catering to the special needs of the baby-boom generation, people purchase franchises designed to appeal to that market, especially those in the service industries. New business areas now being tapped by franchising include timesaving home and personal services (like maid services and lawn maintenance); child-care services; health/beauty/fitness goods and services; convenience stores; and business services like banking, consulting, and financial planning.

9

Increasingly, small independent businesses convert to franchising to gain an extra edge in the marketplace, especially in the areas of home repair and improvement, business services, and nonfood retailing. These areas all promise to remain hot markets for some years to come, not only for conversion franchises but for franchisees starting from scratch. In today's economy, service businesses are hot, and demand for recreation, entertainment, and travel-related products, as well as for automobile and truck rental and aftermarket services, will continue. Management consulting, tax services and accounting, computer-support services, and financial planning promise to be big sellers among the business service industries.

These forecasts provide only a general idea of where some of tomorrow's opportunities may lie. Use your own specific knowledge of your region when analyzing the local market for a given product. Note regional trends and tastes and the economic condition and outlook for your area. If location will play an important role in the success of the particular franchise in which you are interested, check to see if you can find any viable locations available in your area. But most of all, make sure that the franchisor distributes products and services of the highest possible quality. As you consider the franchisor's product and its market, ask yourself the following questions:

- How long has the product been on the market?
- Is it a proven seller or a brand-new innovation?
- Could it become obsolete?
- Is it a fad or gimmick product?
- Will it sell a year from now? Five years? Ten years?
- Is it a necessity or a luxury item?
- Is the product's appeal seasonal?
- Does the product have broad appeal or a specifically defined market, e.g., tourists, children, senior citizens, the wealthy?
- Is the product manufactured by the franchisor or by a third party?
- What is the reputation of the manufacturer?
- Are the materials, products, and techniques I use and sell as a franchisee of a good quality?
- Are there warranties or guarantees on the product or service? Who backs them up?
- Who is responsible for the repair or replacement of faulty merchandise?
- Who pays for such repairs? Who is responsible for refunds?
- Are there government standards or regulations for the product or service?
- Are there any restrictions on its use?

- Is the product or service patented, copyrighted, or otherwise protected under federal or state intellectual property laws?
- Is the product exclusive to the franchisor?

- From whom do I purchase merchandise, materials, and supplies?
- Will I get a fair price?
- Can I count on reliable delivery and ready availability?
- Will I be able to sell the product at a competitive price?
- Who sets the price of the product to my customers?
- Who in my territory will buy the product?
- Will demand be strong enough to support my business, net a healthy profit, and meet any sales quotas the franchisor might set?

- What kind of competition will I face in my region?
- Do numerous companies already compete for the same business in my area?
- Do I know of any major competitor planning to enter the market in my territory?
- What is the franchisor's competition now, and will it change in the future?
- What is the franchisor's strategy for dealing with competition?
- What are the franchisor's views with regard to product diversification? Advertising and marketing?
- Will the franchisor's name attract customers to my business?

- Is the location of my franchise important?
- What kind of location will my franchise require?
- Are there any such locations available in my area?
- Is the purchase or lease price affordable?
- What kind of construction or improvements would be required?
- Would the franchisor approve the site I have in mind?

Many franchisors will conduct a demographic analysis of your region and study the traffic patterns of possible franchise sites once you make a formal application for a franchise. These studies can provide you with further information that you can use in evaluating your franchise opportunities.

Once you have taken a look at yourself and evaluated your region's marketplace, you should find out everything you can about your potential business partner—the franchisor.

3. Know the Franchisor

Determine which franchise programs might suit you (based on your self-analysis) and contact the franchisors for further information.

Do you have extensive sales experience? Do you enjoy working with children? Do you have an interest in fitness? Find out what franchising opportunities exist in your area of interest or expertise; then call or write to the companies that offer franchises that appeal to you. Most franchise departments will send you a package of materials containing information on the company, the franchise itself, requirements for becoming a franchisee, the estimated initial amount required to invest in a franchise, and the franchisor's training and support programs.

After you receive the information you have requested, narrow down your list of possibilities to two or three companies, using a preliminary evaluation of the franchisors, their products and services, and their franchise programs.

In order to conduct a meaningful investigation of your choices as a potential franchisee, you should explore more than one company in great detail. But you should limit your comparison shopping to no more than a few prospects. You don't want to be overwhelmed by a multitude of details. You may have sent an initial request for information to 10 or 15 companies, but you can't do an in-depth evaluation of all of them—and you won't need to.

In most cases, you can tell right off the bat whether or not you are really interested in knowing more about a given franchise program. By answering the following basic questions about each franchise that has immediate appeal for you, you will be able to pinpoint two or three real possibilities from among those you initially thought might interest you.

- Would you enjoy making a career out of running this franchise?
- Do you have the skills—or could you learn them—to operate this business?
- Do you have the resources to invest in and operate this franchise?
- Does it seem as if the returns of your investment in this franchise might be in line with your financial needs and objectives?
- Does the franchisor seem to be reputable, forthcoming, and the type of company with which you would enjoy a partnership?

Checking off the points on this list will help you decide which franchisors you would like to know more about. As you continue your investigation, don't rely solely on the information companies send to you.

Check outside sources of information—publications, government agencies, consumer groups, etc.—for more background on the franchisors.

Find out what the business press—newspapers, magazines, etc.—has to say about each company you are considering. Is it financially strong, well managed, and reputable? Are its officers well regarded in the business community? Has performance been good in the past year, and does it promise to remain so? What is the outlook for its franchise program? Does the company have good relations with its franchisees?

Government agencies like the Federal Trade Commission, the Department of Commerce, state consumer protection and securities divisions, and the Small Business Administration can be valuable sources of information on individual franchisors and franchising in general. They may keep on file disclosure statements of registered franchisors, which contain detailed information about all aspects of the companies' franchise programs.

Since 1979, when the Federal Trade Commission promulgated its disclosure rule, the law has required most franchisors to provide disclosure statements (also referred to as "offering prospectuses" and "offering circulars") to prospective franchisees. Additionally, 15 states have laws requiring the registration of companies that offer franchises for sale within their boundaries and the disclosure of certain information to prospective franchisees. You should contact your state's securities division or consumer protection division. The Department of Commerce publishes a number of useful pamphlets and booklets on franchising, and the Small Business Administration can also provide you with information.

Check with consumer protection groups like the Better Business Bureau to find out if any complaints have been lodged by franchisees or customers against any of the companies you are investigating. Try to get a sense of how the public at large perceives each company and its products. Does the company provide high-quality goods or services? Does it make good on warranties and live up to its promises? Is there any indication that it might be fraudulent—a fly-by-night organization?

Franchising organizations can also provide background information on many franchisors. The International Franchise Association (IFA), located in Washington, D.C., is a membership organization for franchisors. The IFA can provide a list of its members, all of whom have pledged to abide by a strict code of business ethics. The IFA also makes available various other publications useful to prospective franchisees. For information on franchisor/franchisee relations, and to get an idea of how franchisees feel about various franchisors, you can contact the National Franchise Association Coalition, a membership organization of franchisees from many companies.

You may also go to credit agencies or investor service firms like Dun & Bradstreet, Standard & Poor's, or Moody's for more detailed financial information on a franchisor. Does the company pay its creditors promptly? Is its operation highly dependent on debt financing?

Once you've gathered all the information you can about the franchisors and their operations, do a detailed analysis of each one:

- In exactly what type of business is the company engaged?
- What do its franchisees do?
- Does the company have a reputation for honesty and fairness?
- What can the franchisor do for you that you would not be able to accomplish on your own?

- How many years has the company been in business?
- How many years has it been franchising?
- How many units are in operation?
- How many of those does the company own?

- As a franchisee, would you be getting in on the ground floor of the business or joining an established network?
- Would you be working within a highly structured system, one that is more loosely organized, or one that is still being developed? Which would you prefer?

- Is the company publicly held?
- Is it a corporation, a partnership, or a proprietorship?
- Is the company a subsidiary of any other company?
- What is the parent company's reputation and condition?
- Does the company have any business relationships or structural

peculiarities that might have an adverse effect on its franchise program?

- What is the experience of the company's officers?
- Is the company's management stable, or is there excessive turnover among corporate staff?
- Does the company's success appear to depend on the efforts of a single person, or does the company employ a dedicated, well-trained, knowledgeable staff?
- If the founder, chairman, or other individual left the company, would its ability to function and thrive be materially affected?
- Is the company or its officers engaged in any lawsuits or bankruptcy proceedings?

- Has the company's rate of growth been healthy?
- Can the company support all of the new franchises it sells?
- Does the company seem to sell too many units in the same region?
- Is the company more concerned with selling franchises or with offering to the public quality products and services?

- Does the company have a good relationship with its franchisees?
- What are the company's plans for its franchise operations?
- Has the company been buying out franchisees? Has another company or individual?
- Does the company compete with its franchisees for business?

- Have the company's franchises been consistently successful?
- Can you verify figures for average sales per unit?
- Can you verify figures for the company's system-wide sales?
- Has the company's overall performance been historically strong, and is this performance likely to continue?
- What is the company's financial condition?
- Does the company have a good credit rating?

- Does the company hold patents, trademarks, or copyrights? Can you verify them?
- Is the business based on an exclusive product or process?
- Is the company restricted in any way in its use of its patents, trademarks, or copyrights?
- Will the expiration of these rights materially affect the franchisor or its franchisees?

- Do the company's promotional efforts or image depend upon the participation of a particular celebrity?
- Would the company's marketing strategy be materially affected if it lost the right to use the celebrity name or image in its campaigns?

- Is the company forthcoming with information?
- In its dealings with you, is it employing high-pressure sales tactics?
- Is it complying with laws regulating the offer and sale of franchises?
- Is it eager to investigate you carefully?
- Does the company appear to be ready to help you in every way possible once you become a franchisee?

Find out as much as you can about each franchisor and carefully determine what your findings mean. A poorly managed franchisor can be a franchisee's nightmare. Protect yourself by getting the complete picture of each company that you may one day have as a business partner. After you learn how the business community views each company you are investigating, get in touch with each one and make a more personal judgment.

Contact the companies you've singled out and indicate your interest to them. Submit the preliminary franchise applications to establish yourself as a serious prospect.

Your first meaningful contact with the franchisor can provide you with valuable data on the company—information that goes beyond the usual photos and figures in its promotional booklets and fact sheets. You will be able to get a reading of the franchisor's "personality" through even a short telephone conversation with the executive responsible for recruiting new franchisees. When you call the company, note if it seems well organized and if knowledgeable staff is accessible and willing to answer your questions. Determine if its employees seem unprofessional, uninformed, rude, or evasive. How does the franchisor respond to your expression of interest: With a flashy hard sell or with an attempt to get to know you better? Ask yourself: Would I like to work with this company?

Find out what kind of preliminary application the company requires franchise candidates to complete. Often this form will have been included in the package of information that the franchisor sent in response to your initial request. If the company does not require such an application, find out why. A franchisor that expresses little interest in your background or qualifications, and instead tries to pressure you into making a quick decision, may not be the kind of company that you want as a partner.

Though it may make you feel a little uncomfortable at times, a franchisor's investigation of you indicates that the company licenses only qualified individuals. Such a company will be interested in establishing and maintaining a sound, mutually profitable relationship with you—not in taking your money and running.

Filling out the preliminary application at this stage of your investigation serves several purposes. First of all, it will give you a better idea of what the franchisor seeks in its franchisees. Secondly, by submitting the application, you formally express your serious intention to buy a franchise, thus opening communications between yourself and the franchisor. And finally, the company's evaluation of your application will determine whether you should spend more time and energy investigating the franchise.

Based on the application, the company will decide whether or not it considers you a viable candidate for a franchise. A rejection will free you to devote your time and energy to pursuing other franchises, and you can avoid wasting effort on pointless research. On the other hand, if the company decides that it would like to know more about you, then you should take several more steps to find out more about its franchise program.

If any of the companies have not yet provided it, request detailed information on the financial and legal particulars of being granted one of their franchises. Ask for a list of currently operating franchisees that you may speak with.

The most complete source of information a franchisor can provide you is the disclosure document (offering circular or prospectus), which it has prepared in compliance with the trade regulation rule issued by the Federal Trade Commission (FTC). Some franchisors send this document along with their initial package of information, but most will not release it to you until they feel sure that you are very seriously considering the purchase of one of their franchises.

By law, you must receive a copy of the disclosure statement either at your first personal meeting with the franchisor (or its appointed agent) or at least 10 business days before you either sign any agreement with them or pay any fees in relation to the purchase of the franchise. In addition, if your state regulates the sale of franchises within its boundaries, you must be able to review a copy of the franchisor's disclosure document at the state's consumer protection or securities division offices.

The disclosure document contains the following:

- The general disclosure statement, which includes information on the company and its franchise program: biographical data on company officers, descriptions of training programs, etc.
- A select list of the names, addresses, and telephone numbers of currently licensed franchisees.
- A copy of the company's generic franchise agreement—the contract that contains detailed information on your rights and responsibilities as a franchise owner.

Additionally, some franchisors include earnings claims in their disclosure statements. Earnings claims are statements about the profitability of a company's franchises. The company must fully support these claims with documentation stating exactly how it arrived at the figures. But even when earnings claims appear to be well founded, you should take them with a large grain of salt, because they may be based on assumptions that do not apply to your situation.

While the FTC requires franchisors to release disclosure statements to potential franchisees and indicates what types of information these documents must contain, it does not usually check them for accuracy. The FTC rule states that disclosure documents must be "complete and accurate," but leaves the definition of "complete and accurate" up to the individual franchisor. Remember that franchisors are *not* required to register these offering documents with the FTC prior to the offer or sale. In the vast majority of cases, these documents are legitimate, but you should try to verify on your own any information vital to your analysis of the franchisor.

If a company does not seem willing to provide the hard facts you need to evaluate the franchise opportunity, try to determine if this indicates a genuine concern for the security of potentially sensitive material or if instead the company might be trying to hide something from you. You could probably complete your investigation without the disclosure statement, but that document is by far the most useful tool you can have at your disposal. Now that you have gathered all of the available data that you can find, use it to evaluate the franchise program itself.

4. Find Out about Fees, Expenses, and Financing

Consult with your accountant and lawyer to determine the feasibility of investing in the franchises in which you are interested. Check franchisors' earnings claims (if they make any) and prepare profit projections for your potential business.

In order to make a wise investment, you must have a thorough understanding of the many financial details involved in buying and owning a franchise. The various fees, royalties, and other costs of setting up and running your business, the cash and capital required, the financing possibilities, your sales and profit potential, and your financial liability as a franchisee deserve a close look. After all, profits are what it's all about, and if your franchise doesn't give you a healthy return on your investment—and a substantial reward for the risks you've taken in starting a business—then you'll have thrown away a lot of time, effort, and money.

Unless you have training as an accountant and as a lawyer, you should hire professionals to look over the franchise offering. Someone familiar with balance sheets and contracts can probably sift through the information better, to give you a more accurate assessment of which franchises are wise investments—and what would actually be involved in purchasing and running them.

A good rule of thumb to follow while you investigate the financial aspect of your franchise is that if the franchisor clearly spells out all of the financial details of the franchise, you can be fairly sure of the company's legitimacy. However, you should watch out for any hidden costs of the franchise. Quite often your actual investment can end up much greater than you expected because of miscellaneous added charges, the costs of "optional" items that the company effectively requires you to buy, or other expenses not in fact included in the fees. Make sure that you know exactly what you will have to spend; your accountant can outline the expenses typically involved in starting up the kind of business the franchisor sells. Get specific answers from the franchisor about who pays how much for each item.

When you read through franchisors' disclosure statements or other sales material, you will have to decipher a lot of financial jargon. You will quickly discover that different companies use different terminology to refer to the same items. At the same time, they often use the same words to refer to different things. Carefully determine just what each company means when using terms like "initial investment," "total investment," and "total capital required." In order to make a valid comparison of franchising opportunities, you must make certain that you are, in fact, comparing comparable things.

The third consideration to keep in mind throughout your evaluation of fees and finances is your liability. If you or the franchisor encountered operating difficulties, you would doubtless have some responsibility to customers or to the company for losses incurred by you or the franchisor. Find out exactly what responsibilities you would have, and also what rights you would have as a franchisee. Your lawyer's assistance can prove invaluable in this part of your investigation. Suppose your franchise failed? Suppose the franchisor decided to increase royalty rates? Suppose the franchisor went out of business? You could suddenly find yourself in an untenable financial and legal position. You may want to consider forming a corporation in order to limit your personal liability, but keep in mind that most franchisors will want a personal guarantee. Forming a corporation will help you reap certain tax benefits. In any case, you would be unwise to invest without first investigating the issue of financial liability.

Buying a franchise involves some expenditures that you would not have if you opened a nonfranchised business, although savings in other areas often compensate franchisees for their added expenses. Regardless of this balancing effect, you should find out exactly what tangibles and intangibles you will get for your money. Franchise fees remunerate franchisors for the expertise they lend you, the years of research and development they have put into their products and methods, and your use of the company's brand name.

A large, nationally known franchisor will generally charge a higher license fee than a lesser-known one, simply because of the better recognition its name will afford you. In some cases, a higher fee reflects the lower risk associated with your investment in an established company. Beyond a recognized name, the initial fee may cover the costs of training provided by the company, an opening stock of supplies, consultation on various details associated with opening for business, and other services. The next chapter, "Learn about Training Programs, Support, and Assistance," will help you evaluate these aspects of your franchise.

You may find that the franchisor does not set one standard license fee for all franchisees. If the fee varies, find out on what basis the company determines individual fees. Common criteria determining variable license fees include the characteristics of your territory, the location of your store, and the projected sales volume of your business. Ask how the services provided by the franchisor differ with varying fees.

Keep in mind that you can in a few cases pay the initial fee in installments. While many franchisors require full payment of the fee as a sort of downpayment on your franchise, it may be possible to arrange to pay one third down, one third after six months or so of operation, and one third after a year in business. Some franchisors will finance the fee themselves at a special rate of interest, while others leave the financing arrangements up to you.

Your start-up expenses will include a lot more than your initial license fee. You may have to make significant expenditures for real estate, equipment, inventory, supplies, and opening promotion, in addition to paying further fees to the franchisor for training or other start-up assistance. You should expect to make a substantial total investment—and do not underestimate just how substantial. To protect itself from your possible failure due to undercapitalization, the franchisor may require you to prove that you have a certain net worth or a certain amount of cash or other liquid assets. While this might seem restrictive, the company bases its requirement on its experience of the kind of investment it takes to start one of its units. You would do far better to overcapitalize your business than to come up short.

In calculating your total initial investment—your total start-up cost—take the following things into account:

- Does the franchisor charge an initial franchise fee?
- How much is the fee?
- Is the initial fee refundable?
- What services does the fee cover?
- Does the fee cover the cost of:
    Start-up training tuition, room, board, and travel?
    Site selection and construction aid?
    Signs and fixtures?
    On-site preopening and grand opening assistance?

>   Opening promotional and advertising help?
>   Opening inventory and supplies?
> • How must you pay the fee? All at once? In installments?
> • Will the franchisor finance the deferred balance of the fee?
> • At what interest?
>
> • What will be your additional expenses (if any) for:
>   Purchase or lease of your business location?
>   Construction or remodeling of your facility?
>   Equipment and fixtures?
>   Parts, materials, and supplies?
>   Inventory?
>   Training for yourself or your employees?
>   Opening advertising and promotion?
>   State or local licenses?

Have your accountant calculate your approximate total start-up cost, and compare it with the figure the franchisor has supplied. Once you've determined the probable range of your initial investment, estimate your ongoing operating expenses.

A fundamental component of your operating expenses as a franchisee will be another type of fee charged by the franchisor—the royalty (sometimes referred to as the franchise fee; do not confuse this with the *initial* franchise fee). Royalties both compensate the franchisor for the ongoing support it provides and serve as one of its main profit centers. Most franchisors calculate royalties as a percentage of your gross monthly sales. In other cases, franchisees pay a fixed fee per month or week or per unit sold. Your royalty payments will constitute a significant portion of your ongoing operating expenses, so you should make sure that you consider them equitable in light of the support you will receive in return. In making your judgment, you may want to compare the franchisor's royalty requirements with those of similar franchisors.

Many franchisors charge an additional fee, known as the advertising royalty, which they apply directly to their company's national or regional advertising efforts or to the development of promotional materials that you can use in the operation of your business. This royalty can also take the form of a requirement that you spend a certain amount on your own local marketing campaign. In some cases, you must pay both an advertising royalty to the company *and* spend an additional amount on your local promotions. Look at the company's marketing program to make sure that you'll get what you pay for.

Address each of the following points with regard to both royalties and advertising royalties:

- What royalty payments does the franchisor require?
- How are royalties calculated (as a percentage of gross monthly sales, as a flat fee per month, etc.)?
- If royalties are a percentage of sales, how are sales calculated?
- How often must you make royalty payments to the company?
- How do the franchisor's royalty requirements compare to those of similar franchisors?
- Does the franchisor require you to spend a set amount on your own marketing efforts in addition to paying advertising royalties?
- Will you pay the same royalties as other franchisees? If not, why not?

Some franchisors may not charge royalties in any recognizable form, but might instead require you to purchase certain products or services from them. By taking a percentage profit on everything you purchase from it, a company in effect collects a royalty payment from you. When a company both charges a royalty and requires you to purchase materials or supplies from it, you should adjust your calculation of royalty costs to reflect the additional profit the company may make.

Royalties will be just a part of your ongoing operating costs. As a franchisee, you will have most of the same costs that the independent small business owner-operator has. Some franchisors eliminate some of the direct costs of these items to their franchisees by including them in their ongoing support services. Many provide accounting and bookkeeping assistance free or at a reduced charge, offer insurance programs, or conduct advertising campaigns.

Have your accountant prepare an estimate of the ongoing costs of operating your business. This calculation should include:

- Royalties
- Advertising royalties
- Rent or mortgage payments
- Payroll and your own salary
- Insurance payments
- Interest payments
- Ongoing equipment purchase or rental
- Purchase of materials and supplies
- Plant and equipment maintenance
- Advertising
- Legal and accounting fees
- Taxes
- Licenses
- Utilities and telephone

Once you have an idea of what it will cost to run your business, have your accountant prepare projections of your sales and profit potential—for the first year or two of operation and for when your business has gotten off the ground. Your estimate of sales should take into account current (and probable future) market conditions of your region, demand for your product in your area, traffic patterns of your business location, and prospects for growth. Combine your sales and cost estimates to determine your potential profit, and compare these results with any earnings claims the franchisor may have included in its prospectus or any other sales material.

When looking over a franchisor's earnings claims, make sure you understand exactly how the franchisor calculated the profit projections:

- Are they based on the performance of the company's franchisees in markets similar to yours? On that of independent businesses in similar markets?
- Were the earnings used in the calculations those of longtime franchisees or newcomers?
- Were the calculations made during economic boom times?
- How many franchisees actually earn as much as or more than the amount of the earnings claim?
- Do the figures take into account all operating expenses?

The franchisor must provide written substantiation for its earnings claims. If your accountant's estimate differs greatly from the franchisor's, try to determine why. And once you have actual profit projections in front of you, ask yourself whether or not the projected return on your investment of time and money would be high enough to make owning and operating the franchise worthwhile:

- Will my sales enable me to make enough to meet expenses and make a profit?
- Will I be able to meet any quotas the franchisor sets?
- In order to achieve the required sales volume, will I have to make an excessive investment?
- Do my estimated operating costs appear excessive?
- Will I make enough money to be satisfied?
- Does the risk seem worthwhile—will it pay off?

In your initial self-evaluation, you should have come to a basic understanding of your financial capabilities and goals. Now is the time to do a thorough analysis of your financial status and to compare your financial capability with the total initial investment you will have to make, the operating costs for your first year in business, and your short- and long-term personal and business goals, to determine how much of your operation you will need or want to finance.

Investigate possible sources of financing and determine which lenders would best fit into your business plan. Many franchisors offer limited financing at special rates to their franchisors, and still more offer assistance in securing financing from third-party lenders. Others may actually require that you enter into some sort of financing arrangement with them. Other sources of financing include banks or other financial institutions, relatives, friends, or federal agencies like the Small Business Administration or the Minority Business Development Agency.

In order to obtain financing, you will need to present a personal financial statement and a business plan to the franchisor or other lender. You will need to determine your total net worth and how much of that is in liquid assets. For lenders other than the franchisor, you will also have to develop a business plan outlining the application of borrowed funds and the expected returns of your business. You should present loan applications before signing your franchise contract to find out if the strength of your credit rating and your business plan will allow you to borrow the money you'll need to start your franchise.

Will you be able to borrow enough to help you get started? Do you have the resources to purchase and operate your franchise for a year or more with low or negative returns? Are you likely to get too far into debt? Will a minor setback in your business have major repercussions on your ability to pay back creditors?

When you make any investment, you take a risk. Buying a franchise is no different from buying securities in that you need to decide whether or not to take a risk. It all comes down to one basic question: Is the return on your investment likely to make the risk worthwhile? Your return should be greater than that which you would receive on a less risky investment, like stocks. If you feel that the franchisor you have been investigating can offer the profits you seek, find out more about the franchise program itself: What kind of training and support programs will your license fees and royalties buy?

5. Learn about Training Programs, Support, and Assistance

Speak with some of the companies' franchisees regarding their experiences with the franchisors. Learn all you can about the kinds of support the companies provide.

Find out about the parent company beyond the references it supplies by talking to as many different franchisees as possible and ascertaining what the franchisor will do for you. According to franchisees and franchise experts alike, talking to franchisees should be the single most important aspect of your franchising investigation. No one can give you a clearer notion of what it is like to be a franchisee than other franchisees.

Your investigation of a franchisor will not be complete until you speak with active franchisees—those who have been in business a long time and those new to franchising; those who own many units and those who own just one; and those who have been successful and those who have not. Seek out franchisees who operate in regions with market characteristics similar to those of your region, and try to contact independent business-people or franchisees of other companies similar to the ones you are evaluating. Both during your investigation of franchisors and once you have become a franchisee, you can learn as much from your fellow franchisees as you can from any other source. Take full advantage of this valuable—and free—resource.

Franchisees can supply insight into the real-life financial facts of franchise ownership, and they can advise you about other things to consider when looking at franchise opportunities. "Do not take a pie-in-the-sky approach," warns Robert Bonin, a Ground Round franchisee. "Do an analysis based on realistic sales projections for your location."

Look at more than just earnings, however; talk to franchisees, both successful and not so successful, in person if possible. Determine whether problems lie with the franchisor or the franchisee. Compare yourself with the successful franchisees to see if you could succeed with the franchise. You should speak with as many franchisees as you can, and ask:

- Do franchisees think the franchisor is honest, reliable, competent, and genuinely interested in the success of its franchisees?
- Do franchisees feel that the franchisor exercises too much control? Not enough?
- Does the franchisor give franchisees the freedom to make their own decisions regarding the control of their investment?
- How would franchisees characterize franchisor/franchisee relations?

- Is the franchisor accessible to franchisees?
- Does the franchisor provide enough support and guidance?
- Is the franchisor always willing to help?
- Has the training provided by the franchisor met franchisees' needs?
- Has the franchisor lived up to its promises regarding the training, support, and services it provides?

- Has the franchise been a good investment?
- Are the franchisor's estimations of the initial investment required accurate?
- Are its cost and profit projections on target?

- Can franchisees recommend the franchise to you?

Based on what you find out through your conversations with franchisees, as well as what you have learned by reading the material you have gathered about the franchise, determine just what kind of support and assistance you can expect to receive during the preopening, opening, and later phases of your operation. Between the time you sign the franchise agreement and the time you open your doors for business, you will probably receive some form of initial training—usually a comprehensive introduction to every aspect of your business—as well as assistance in site selection and preparing your premises for opening. Just before opening, you may receive help in ordering inventory, obtaining licenses, recruiting and training employees, and hundreds of other necessary details.

During your grand opening and first few weeks in business—the period that many franchisors consider crucial to the success of your business—a company representative may come to your location to provide general operational support. Once your business takes off, franchisors generally provide a number of services, which may include refresher training, bookkeeping services, periodic visits from company representatives, centralized ordering services (which can result in savings for you because of the company's purchasing power), company publications, and other forms of support. The franchisor's marketing and advertising efforts can also benefit you significantly.

Every franchisor supplies its own unique package of support services, and you will need assistance tailored to your particular needs and abilities. In order to make sure that the franchisor's capabilities fit with yours, you need to find out what kind of help the franchisor provides during each phase of your operation: before you open your doors, during your opening period, and for the term of your contract agreement. Make sure that the details of the training and support that the company will provide are clearly set down in your contract. Your success depends in large part upon whether or not you get the help you need in running your business.

The checklists that follow outline the points with which you should become familiar.

Site Selection and Premises Development

1. Will the company perform an analysis of the demographics within your region to help you find the best location for your business?
2. Will the company require you to use a designated location?
3. Who purchases or leases the site?
4. Are you required to purchase your land and building?
5. Will the company help you negotiate a lease?
6. Will the company purchase or lease the site and then lease it to you?
7. Who is responsible for the construction or refurbishing of your facility? Will the company build your facility for you?
8. Will the company supply you with plans and specifications for your facility?
9. What design or other requirements must your facility meet?
10. Does the company provide any construction assistance?
11. Will the company help you order fixtures and equipment and help you set them up?

12. Are you required to purchase signs, fixtures, or equipment through designated sources?
13. Will you get competitive prices on these purchases?
14. Is there any additional charge for site-selection and premises development assistance?

Initial Training

1. Is initial training available? Required? Optional?
2. Where does the training take place? At corporate headquarters, at your own unit, at an existing unit?
3. Can you train independently using self-study materials?
4. How long is the initial training session?
5. Is there any expense to you for training, e.g., for tuition, supplies, room, board, or transportation?
6. Who trains you? Corporate staff or active franchisees?
7. Who must complete the initial training? You, your management, all of your employees?
8. Does the training take place in a classroom or on the job?
9. Will you get hands-on experience before you open for business?
10. What does training cover? Does it cover:
    Specialized technical/trade knowledge?
    General operations?
    Management and administration?
    Employee recruitment, hiring, training?
    Accounting and bookkeeping?
    Planning and projections?
    Inventory control and merchandise ordering?
    Sales, merchandising, promotion, advertising?
    Customer service?
    Credit accounts management?
    Insurance?
    Legal issues?

Preopening and Opening Support

1. Will a company representative come to your location to provide assistance with your grand opening?
2. Will the company help you hire and train employees?
3. Will the company help you order inventory, materials, and supplies?

4. Will the company supply or help you with grand opening advertising or promotions?
5. Will a company representative accompany you on your first few sales calls (if applicable)?
6. Is there any cost to you for this initial support?

Ongoing Operational Assistance

1. Will you receive regular visits from a company representative?
2. Will support staff be available by phone for assistance?
3. Will field personnel come to your location at your request?
4. Is there any charge to you for these services?
5. Does the company provide you with a comprehensive operations manual?
6. Does the company publish newsletters, bulletins, or updates to your manual?
7. Is there a charge for these materials?
8. Does the company supply you with an accounting system and bookkeeping materials?
9. Does it provide bookkeeping services?
10. What are your reporting requirements?
11. Can you order inventory or supplies directly from the company?
12. Does the company offer merchandise, materials, and/or supplies to you at a savings?
13. Will it extend a line of credit to you for your purchases?
14. Does it deliver orders promptly?
15. Does the company inspect your suppliers for quality?
16. Does it inspect your operation?
17. Does the company provide any other services or benefits, such as tax preparation assistance, insurance plans, legal advice, etc.?

Ongoing Training

1. Is refresher training available? Required?
2. Where does this training take place?
3. Is there any cost to you for participation?
4. What does this training cover?
5. How frequently is such training offered?
6. Will the company train any supervisory or other staff that you hire as the result of routine employee turnover?
7. Will the company charge you for this service?
8. Does the company hold an annual national convention?

9. Are there regional meetings?
10. Can you attend periodic seminars or workshops?

Advertising and Marketing

1. What kind of advertising and marketing policy does the company follow?
2. Does the company conduct national, regional, or local advertising? In what media—television, radio, magazines, newspapers, direct mail, outdoor?
3. Do its efforts benefit all franchisees and company-operated units equally?
4. Is its advertising/marketing program effective?
5. Does the company provide you with promotional material for your own local use—brochures, point-of-sale material, radio spots, yellow pages ads?
6. Does the company provide you with the results of its market research?
7. Will you receive merchandising, promotional, or advertising advice?
8. What will your advertising costs be—royalties only, or significant personal expenditure?
9. Who directs the company's promotional operations—corporate staff or franchisees?
10. Exactly how are your advertising royalties spent?
11. Will you have any additional marketing expenses?

Franchisor-Franchisee Relations

1. Does the company have a realistic understanding of what it's like to operate one of its franchises?
2. Do franchisees have any voice in company policy and/or operational decisions?
3. Does an elected board of franchisees serve in an advisory capacity to corporate management?
4. How does the home office respond to suggestions and complaints from the field?
5. Can franchisees communicate with management through a formal suggestions/grievances procedure?
6. Have franchisees formed an active franchisee association?
7. What is the franchisor's relationship with the association?

If, after completing your research and speaking with franchisees, you feel confident that the franchisor provides the kinds of training and ongoing support that you need, and that franchisor/franchisee relations are good, you can now take the final step toward becoming a franchise owner: negotiating your contract.

6. Know Your Legal Rights and the Terms of the Contract

Meet with the corporate staff of each of the franchisors you are considering. Ask any questions you might have and give the company an opportunity to interview you. Make your decision.

These meetings should allow you to make a final judgment regarding the franchisor with which you would like to do business. A face-to-face meeting can reveal—as no telephone call or letter ever can—the real character of a company and its management. Personal discussion can also raise issues that you might otherwise have neglected. Such a meeting will also provide the franchisor with the opportunity to decide whether or not to accept you as a franchisee.

Finally, if both you and the franchisor have an interest in further pursuing a partnership, the "personal meeting" serves as the franchisor's legal cue to submit to you its disclosure document, if it has not already done so. According to the FTC's 1979 trade regulation, you must receive a copy of this document at your first personal meeting with a representative of the franchisor to discuss the purchase of a franchise, and at least ten days before you sign any agreement with, or make any payments to, the franchisor.

Have your lawyer and accountant review the standard franchise agreement that the franchisor has given you. Negotiate favorable terms before you sign the contract.

In many cases, a franchisor will present you with a standard contract, which protects its interests but not yours. You should not feel pressured to sign this contract, but instead must study it carefully with the advice of your attorney and accountant, and negotiate the most favorable terms that you can with the franchisor. Rarely will astute businesspeople sign a standard franchise agreement without making some changes, so your franchisor should be willing to negotiate with you. It is vital that you get everything relating to your franchise in writing and spelled out in detail.

Although you may feel nervous about demanding certain concessions from a franchisor, any franchisor interested in having you as a franchisee will work with you to hammer out the fine points of an agreement you can both live with. You can negotiate some points of the franchise contract, although terms may be subject to certain state laws. Just as the franchisor may vary fees based on its assessment of your individual franchise, so you can sometimes negotiate more favorable fees based on your evaluation of the franchisor-franchisee relationship. However, some points are virtually nonnegotiable.

Use your position as a potential buyer as leverage in winning concessions. As long as you have the cash, you have a valuable bargaining chip. Beware, however, the franchisor that seems too eager to give in to your demands—if the company easily bargains away clauses that protect its standards, it clearly has a less than complete commitment to maintaining a quality image.

When you consult your attorney and accountant regarding the franchise contract, you should make sure that its terms are both favorable to you and agreeable to any third-party lender that might be financing your venture. Otherwise you might find yourself in the uncomfortable position of being bound to a legal commitment that you cannot honor because you don't have sufficient funds.

You might consider hiring a professional—perhaps your lawyer or accountant—to negotiate your contract for you. A professional has the experience and cool that you may lack, and can often win greater concessions from the franchisor. If you decide to negotiate your own contract, your lawyer should accompany you to the negotiations. During this phase of buying your franchise, you should deal directly with the franchisor. Sales agents or other interested (i.e., profit-taking) parties generally have more to gain from a quick closing than from your satisfaction as a franchisee.

The three most important things to remember when negotiating your contract are:

1. Get everything in writing. Verbal agreements and "understand-ings" are unenforceable.
2. Make sure every detail is spelled out in plain English. Rid your

contract of vagueness and legalese. After all, what does it mean that a franchisor cannot "reasonably refuse" to approve a supplier? What is "just cause" for the franchisor to terminate your contract? Make it clear.

3. Do not pay the franchisor any money until both you and the franchisor have signed the contract. Even if the company assures you that it will refund any down payments if necessary, you will find it very difficult to get your money back after it has left your hands.

The average franchise agreement contains 20 to 25 clauses, covering everything from the initial franchise fee to the disposition of your building and equipment at the end of the contract. When reviewing the document, ask yourself whether or not the franchisor's requirements seem excessively restrictive or lax and whether or not you can live up to your end of the deal. Make sure that the training, services, and advertising support provided are commensurate with the fees and royalties you pay. And make certain that you are protected from the consequences of any mismanagement or poor judgment on the part of the franchisor.

You should be able to answer the following questions when going over the franchise contract:

- Does the contract specify the exact amount of all fees charged by the franchisor?
- What fees does the company require you to pay?
- How does the franchisor calculate fees? Can they be changed?
- How do you pay fees—in installments, as lump sums, etc.?
- When do you pay fees?
- Will the franchisor refund any fees? Under what conditions?
- Can you negotiate lesser fees?

- What rights do you have concerning use of the franchisor's patents, trademarks, and brand names?
- How are you restricted in this use?

- What financial reporting practices does the company require you to follow?
- When and in what form must you submit financial statements?
- Must you follow specific accounting procedures or use certain forms to report to the franchisor?
- Must you meet sales quotas or any other type of performance condition?
- Will the company penalize you for falling short?

- May the company use collection agencies to enforce your payment of fees?

- Does the company require that you actively participate in the operation of your franchise?
- Must you keep certain business hours?
- What products must you offer for sale?
- Are you prohibited from selling particular items through your franchise?
- Must you maintain certain levels of inventory?

- What supplies and/or merchandise must you purchase from the franchisor?
- Does the company maintain a list of other approved suppliers from whom you must purchase?
- Do you receive these goods at a discount?
- Does the company profit from these sales?

- What standards does the company set for your business?
- Must your supplies, materials, products, and services meet standards of quality, uniformity, appearance, or type?
- Will the franchisor give you at least 48 hours' notice before conducting inspection visits?
- What are the company's criteria for acceptable location, premises, equipment, fixtures, and furniture?
- Can it require you to refurbish your facility or purchase new equipment to meet its latest standards?
- How much would this cost you?
- What prescribed operating procedures, bookkeeping systems, and other controls must you follow?
- What kind of insurance must you carry? At what cost?

- Do you receive an exclusive territory?
- What does the franchisor mean by "exclusive"?
- How is your territory defined?
- Do you have the option to expand your territory?
- Do you have the right of first refusal if someone else wants to purchase territory adjacent to yours?

- What are the company's requirements for your location?
- What assistance will the company give you in selecting a site, purchase or lease negotiations, and construction?

- Must the franchisor approve your lease?
- Will the franchisor serve as your landlord? At advantageous terms?

- Exactly what kind of training—initial and ongoing—will the company provide?
- What other management assistance will you receive?
- What start-up assistance does the franchisor include in your franchise fee?
- Will a trained company representative come to your site and stay for as long as necessary during start-up?
- Will you receive a comprehensive operations manual?

- What kind of marketing support will the company provide in return for your contributions to the advertising fund?
- How does the franchisor allocate advertising funds?
- Will you receive advertising support commensurate with your contribution?
- Will the company require you to spend more on advertising than you think necessary or than you can afford?

- What is the length of the contract?
- Can you sell or transfer your franchise?
- What kind of notice must you give the company?
- Does the company have the right of first refusal?
- Does the company have the right to approve your buyer?
- Do you have any liability to the franchisor after you sell your franchise?
- Will the company require you to pay a fee to sell?
- Can your heirs inherit the franchise, or will the contract terminate upon your death?
- How are you protected if the franchisor goes out of business?
- Do you have any liability for misconduct on the part of the franchisor that results in injury to your customers?

- Can you terminate your contract? Under what conditions?
- How much notice must you give of your intention to terminate?
- What are your obligations to the company if you terminate?
- Can the company terminate your contract?
- What is just cause for the company to terminate your contract (e.g., nonpayment of fees, violation of contract terms, abandonment of your business, etc.)?
- What rights do you have regarding contract renewal?
- Can the company refuse to renew your contract? For what reasons?

- If the company terminates or refuses to renew, does the contract obligate it to purchase your equipment and supplies?
- Who would determine the purchase price—and how?

- Does the contract contain a noncompete clause?
- Are you prohibited from engaging in similar business during or after the term of your contract?
- How does the clause define similar business?
- In what geographical areas does the clause prohibit you from competing with the franchisor? For how many years?

These questions outline the issues that you should study when reviewing most franchise contracts. Clearly, contracts differ from franchisor to franchisor, and some franchising opportunities may not fit the typical legal mold. But no matter how individual franchise contracts may vary, each one should set down in writing everything relevant to the franchise. In negotiating your agreement, leave nothing to chance, make sure the document leaves nothing out, and get it all in writing. While you have no guarantees that your franchise will live up to your expectations, your contract can help protect you from the relatively minor risks involved in being a franchisee.

Part II

The Franchises

Introduction to Part II

The 220 franchises described in the pages that follow represent a wide variety of franchise opportunities. Chosen to provide a sampling of the many types of franchises available in diverse industry categories, the franchises listed in *The 220 Best Franchises to Buy* range from industry giants with established track records, to recent success stories that promise to keep right on booming, to younger companies—some with uniquely innovative approaches to franchising—that have identified and begun to tap new markets.

The vital statistics that lead off each entry require some explanatory notes. The terms used in the first part of each listing can be defined as follows:

Initial license fee: The amount you pay to the franchisor in order to become a franchisee. A one-time expense.

Royalties: The amount you pay to the franchisor weekly, monthly, yearly, or at some other interval to cover the franchisor's expenses of maintaining you as a franchisee. Generally calculated as a percentage of gross revenues, but sometimes set at a flat periodic fee or a fee per unit sold.

Advertising royalties: A periodic amount paid toward the franchisor's advertising fund. Sometimes includes a requirement that you spend a minimum amount on your own local promotional program. Calculated as a percentage of gross or as a flat periodic fee.

Minimum cash required: The minimum amount of cash or other liquid assets the franchisor requires you to have available in order to qualify as a franchisee.

Capital required: The amount of capital, as estimated by the franchisor, that you will need to buy and start up your franchise operation.

Financing: Any financial assistance the franchisor provides to new franchisees.

Length of contract: The term of your franchise agreement.

In business since: The date that the company or its parent was founded.

Franchising since: The year that the company started franchising its business.

Total number of units: The latest available figure for the total number of business locations in operation.

Number of company-operated units: The total number of units operated by the company rather than by franchisees.

Total number of units planned, 1995: The company's projection of the number of units it hopes to have in operation by 1995.

Number of company-operated units planned, 1995: The number of units the company plans to operate itself by 1995.

Keep in mind that in most cases, the statistics were obtained from the franchisors themselves and may have changed since the time we surveyed them for the second edition. Whenever the notation "NA" appears instead of a number, the data were not available.

Each of the entries provides a brief description of the company and its franchise program. You should by no means consider these profiles complete—they provide only an overview of each franchisor's operation, which you can use to decide whether or not you would like to find out more about the company. Please note that virtually all franchises provide a training program for new franchisees, often at their corporate headquarters. In most instances, there is no separate charge for the training, although franchisees are expected to cover their own transportation and living expenses during the training period.

7. The Automotive Industry

Contents

Tune-Up and Lubrication

Grease Monkey International, Inc.
Jiffy Lube International, Inc.
Precision Tune, Inc.
SpeeDee Oil Change & Tune-Up
Speedy CAR-X Muffler & Brake, Inc.

Windshield Repair

Novus Windshield Repair

Inspection

Car Checkers of America

Initial license fee: $20,000
Royalties: 5% of monthly gross sales
Advertising royalties: 2% of monthly gross sales
Minimum cash required: $495 initiation fee
Capital required: $70,000 to $80,000
Financing: None
Length of contract: 20 years

In business since: 1986
Franchising since: 1989
Total number of units: 124
Number of company-operated units: 2
Total number of units planned, 1995: 260
Number of company-operated units planned, 1995: 10

Car Checkers provides prospective auto owners with a fast, complete, and objective evaluation of the vehicle they are considering for purchase—a service that has earned them the nickname "Lemon Busters." And since in the United States there are more than 18 million used cars on the road, plenty of wary buyers need the careful survey that Car Checkers provides—an evaluation of more than 3,600 components of a vehicle's electrical, emission, and on-board systems.

Car Checkers franchisees come most frequently from sales and marketing backgrounds, but anyone willing to actively promote and market their services can own and run a successful franchise with Car Checkers. During the two-week training course held at company headquarters in Bridgewater, New Jersey, franchisees learn not only how to perform the inspections, but also how to sell the service to credit unions and banks, Car Checkers' most frequent and regular customers. The founders of the company, Wendy and Lee Geller, are proud of the relationship the home office maintains with franchisees—field representatives are always available to help with any problems or concerns a franchisee might have, and any emergencies can be handled with a phone call to their 24-hour hot line.

One of the most appealing aspects of the service to customers and franchisees alike is the convenience—Car Checkers' white Chevrolet Lumina van contains all of the diagnostic equipment used in the evaluation and goes wherever the vehicle to be evaluated is parked, and then can itself be parked in a regular garage. About 90 percent of Car Checkers franchisees choose to operate the business from home. The specialized equipment used in the car inspections, which include the van, a diagnostic analyzer, a paint-coating analyzer, and a suspension analyzer, is leased to the franchisee. While the company does not finance any part of the investment, the $70,000 to $80,000 capital covers all initial start-up costs and the equipment leasing. Franchisees are also required to have at least six months' personal and living expenses saved. Exclusive territories are granted based on population in an area.

For further information contact:
  Lee Geller, 1011 Rte. 22 W., Bridgewater, NJ 08807, 908-704-1221 or
  1-800-242-CHEX

Muffler Services

Lentz USA Service Centers, Inc.

Initial license fee: $18,500
Royalties: 7%
Advertising royalties: 5%
Minimum cash required: $65,000
Capital required: $90,000
Financing: None
Length of contract: 10 years

In business since: 1983
Franchising since: 1989
Total number of units: 13
Number of company-operated units: 11
Total number of units planned, 1995: 125
Number of company-operated units planned, 1995: 12

Founded and run by a former auto service franchise owner, Lentz USA has a keen understanding of the needs and concerns of its franchisees. Gordon Lentz and the home office staff stress the interdependence of the company's success and the success of each franchise operation, offering operators its services, experience, and support, while at the same time giving them the freedom and incentive of independent business owners.

Lentz USA bases its expectations of rapid growth on its own success thus far and the overall success of the specialty service center business, while the number of full-service auto repair facilities continues to decrease. American car owners have demonstrated their strong preference for professional, rather than do-it-themselves, auto maintenance, and at Lentz centers, they can receive exhaust, suspension, and brake service on their vehicles at highly reasonable prices. In a competitive industry, Lentz stands out as being able to offer, through an agreement with the Exhaust Systems Professional Association, over 10,000 warranty locations nationwide, more than the top three muffler suppliers combined.

Providing franchisees the standard assistance in site selection, Lentz USA goes one step further—it simply won't allow them to make a bad decision. The final location choice is subject to the company's approval, as home office personnel study the demographics, visibility concerns, and traffic patterns as closely as the franchisee. Lentz USA supplies all the fixtures and equipment needed for the facility, from the hoists, air compressors, and storage racks to torch equipment and specialty tools. While the company doesn't extend financing, it does offer finance consultation services.

Training begins with a two-week course for franchisees, covering the vital areas of business, including bookkeeping, customer relations, staff hiring and instruction, product ordering, inventory control, and, of course, product installation and service. Additionally, there are manuals covering day-to-day operations issues, as well as follow-up instruction and ongoing support. The concern, which founder Lentz well appreciates from his own franchisee experience, is that operators aren't "left to fend for themselves." In keeping with that philosophy, the company manages a marketing fund providing a cohesive promotional program that most independent service center operators can't match, including radio and newspaper (and, in some markets, television) advertising and regular consultation.

For further information contact:
  Gordon F. Lentz, President, Lentz USA Service Centers, Inc., 1001 Riverview Dr., Kalamazoo, MI 49001, 616-342-2200

Merlin's Magic Muffler and Brake

Initial license fee: $26,000 to $30,000
Royalties: 4.9% to 6.9%
Advertising royalties: 5%
Minimum cash required: $45,000
Capital required: $155,000 to $160,000, total investment
Financing: Through third parties, subject to individual qualifications
Length of contract: 20 years, renewable without additional fee

In business since: 1975
Franchising since: 1975
Total number of units: 43

Number of company-operated units: 5
Total number of units planned, 1995: 125
Number of company-operated units planned, 1995: 3

In a November 1990 *Success* magazine survey of the 100 best franchises, Merlin's Magic Muffler and Brake ranked lucky number 13 . . . in any business category. The *Success* ranking system was based primarily on "strength of management," and judging from the success and comprehensiveness of its franchise package, it's no surprise why Merlin scored so high.

The management of Merlin recognizes that auto maintenance and repair is a "basic need" business that actually thrives in poor economic times, when consumers are less able to make new car purchases, and that "undercar service" is especially attractive, enjoying the highest growth of the automobile after-purchase market, a tendency for higher profits, and a relative lack of the complexities and headaches that plague high-tech vehicle service enterprises. But this confidence doesn't keep the company from staying on top of an ever-changing, aggressive industry. Its name notwithstanding, there's no wizardry to the making of a successful auto repair franchise operation: the "magic formula" is simply the age-old combination of hard work, high energy, regular contact, constant updating, dynamic marketing, and honing operations until they run at peak efficiency and minimum cost . . . and then perfecting them further.

Merlin shops specialize in the replacement of muffler and exhaust systems, shock absorbers, springs, other suspension components, and brake systems. Some facilities also offer additional services authorized by the company, including lube jobs and wheel alignments. The Merlin management are not believers in small shops, because business tends to come at certain peak periods and customers don't like being kept waiting. Therefore, a facility with at least six service bays is strongly urged as vital to handling the work volume necessary for an attractive return on investment.

Choosing a location for the Merlin shop is a team effort between the franchisee and the company. Merlin has already determined approved locations for new facilities in high-growth areas underserved by the local competition. But a franchisee's own alternative site-location ideas are studied as well, and the final decision is by mutual consent. Without any additional cost, the company will develop and lease the location, in turn subleasing it to the franchisee. Depending on building permits and zoning requirements, construction of the facility can be completed in 120 to 150 days.

The franchisee or his or her designated manager is required to attend and successfully complete a five-week training program at Merlin headquarters. Additionally, a company operations specialist works with franchisees at their facility for a period before and after opening. Continuing guidance is offered as well, through the regularly updated operations manual and periodic visits from Merlin field representatives, who give advice and counsel in such areas as sales methods, installation and repair techniques, and personnel policies.

Marketing is hardly left up to chance. The franchise advertising royalties are placed in a central fund managed by Merlin. The money in the fund is used to create professionally produced materials promoting Merlin shops and services, including TV and radio spots, print media ads, and direct mail coupons. Each new Merlin shop is also specially promoted and advertised during its first five months of operation, using a custom-tailored marketing plan developed, implemented, and funded by the company.

For further information contact:
Mark M. Hameister, Director of Franchise Development, Merlin Corporation, 33 W. Higgins Rd., Suite 2050, South Barrington, IL 60010, 708-428-5000, fax 708-428-8259

Midas International Corporation

Initial license fee: $10,000
Royalties: 10%
Advertising royalties: Included in royalties
Minimum cash required: $75,000
Capital required: $248,000
Financing: Company will help with financing through national lending sources
Length of contract: 20 years

In business since: 1956
Franchising since: 1956
Total number of units: 1,764 U.S., 647 foreign
Number of company-operated units: 118
Total number of units planned, 1995: NA
Number of company-operated units planned, 1995: NA

The elderly gentleman drives his ancient automobile up to the Midas shop and says to the service people: "Howdy, boys." Again he takes advantage of the Midas guarantee on its mufflers: "For as long as you own your car." It's a memorable commercial. The company's slogan "Nobody beats Midas—nobody," also sticks in your mind. Because of advertising like this, according to the company, people in 96 percent of the households in this country think of Midas when they think of mufflers.

Almost 40 years ago this company consisted of one shop in Macon, Georgia. Today there are Midas shops in every state and on four continents. And Midas no longer confines its business to mufflers, having expanded into brake, suspension, and front-end repair. The company's plants in Wisconsin and Illinois turn out the more than 5,900 parts that enable Midas dealers to satisfy their customers.

The company wants enthusiastic, forward-looking franchisees with previous business experience, entrepreneurs who can deal with people comfortably. It looks for people who can control expenses and inventory and keep organized records. If preliminary conversations between you and the company go well, it will invite you to a two-day orientation seminar in Chicago, where you and the company can decide if you make a good match.

If you and the company work well together, you will not have to worry about securing a location. In this franchise, the franchisor picks the spots, builds the facilities, and leases to franchisees for the length of the franchise agreement. You will train at "MIT"—the Midas Institute of Technology at Palatine, Illinois. There, you will take a concentrated two-week course covering shop organization, products and installation, and inventory control. In addition, you will spend at least two weeks in an operational shop to get practical experience for running your own business.

Your franchise agreement requires you to stock and sell Midas parts in your new business. Once you open your doors and wear the familiar yellow Midas shirt, you can expect continued support through the company's district manager and field personnel. The Midas staff will assist with your opening and help you with financial statement analysis, sales training, employee selection, and promotion.

For further information contact:
  Midas International Corporation, Corporate Offices, 225 N. Michigan Ave., Chicago, IL 60601, 312-565-7500

Painting, Detailing, and Rustproofing

Detail Plus Car Appearance Systems, Inc.

Initial license fee: None
Royalties: None
Advertising royalties: Negotiable
Minimum cash required: $25,000

Capital required: $85,000, not including building
Financing: Leasing available if in business more than 2 years
Length of contract: Open

In business since: 1980
Franchising since: 1982
Total number of units: 150
Number of company-operated units: 2
Total number of units planned, 1995: 350
Number of company-operated units planned, 1995: None

Auto detailing, a business previously largely confined to the used-car-dealer market, has flourished over the past decade, as car owners are choosing to hold on to their old autos longer. Growing as an extension of the car-wash industry, detailing centers have become a staple in large urban centers and have recently been expanding successfully into rural markets as well. Burlington, Vermont, Detail Plus co-owner Lexi Gahagen found that within four months of opening, his four-person operation was handling a steady four to five cars a day (each with an average bill of $110) and expecting soon to service an average of 10 vehicles in a given 16-hour, two-shift work day.

Detail Plus has been in the auto cleaning industry since 1980. Sid Yow, who owns several Detail Plus centers in the Southeast, sees that as a big advantage. "Customers don't want a fly-by-nighter to clean their $80,000 cars." The organized appearance and professional design of Detail Plus facilities is another prime selling point, underscoring the meticulousness of the work done there.

Detail Plus centers offer a variety of services, including vacuuming and shampooing upholstery and carpets, custom washing, polishing, waxing, engine cleaning, wheel and wheel-well cleaning, tar removal, paint restoration, and leather and vinyl treatment. The work averages three hours per car, but can be more or less depending on the services rendered. In addition to the general public, customers include new and used car dealers, and the facilities are usually equipped to handle motorcycles, RVs, and boats in addition to autos.

The company supplies owners with its own highly specialized detailing equipment, highlighted by chemical dispensing work stations that place everything at the attendant's fingertips, from vacuums and buffers to cleaners, waxes, polishes, and sealants. The machines eliminate the ubiquitous spray bottles, "a detailer's nightmare," according to Sid Yow, who estimates the handy design of Detail Plus equipment saves him 25 percent in labor costs.

Choosing a two- to five-bay center, owners receive assistance from Detail Plus designers in either converting an existing facility or building a new one. Company technicians then provide training for both management and employees onsite, while the owner can also receive two weeks of instruction at the company's test center. A 200-page operations manual is supplied as well, along with the operating forms needed to run the business. For advertising and promotion, Detail Plus furnishes a complete kit that features proofs for ads, flyers, direct mail pieces and coupons, a sales training video, and professionally produced TV and radio spots.

For further information contact:
  R. L. Abraham, Detail Plus Car Appearance Systems, Inc., P.O. Box 591, Clackamas, OR 97015, 1-800-284-0123, fax 503-656-8553

Flying Colors

Initial license fee: $7,500
Royalties: 6% ($300 minimum)
Advertising royalties: None
Minimum cash required: $12,500
Capital required: $30,000 initial investment
Financing: None
Length of contract: 4 years

In business since: 1985
Franchising since: 1986
Total number of units: 65
Number of company-operated units: 5
Total number of units planned, 1995: 75
Number of company-operated units planned, 1995: 15

Flying Colors, says its young president Benjamin Litalien, "is for the hands-on individual." Indeed, a franchisee can run the entire mobile auto and truck paint touch-up operation himself or herself without any need for additional employees. It's a low-overhead, high-efficiency business that brings its services right to the customer.

Operating from specially equipped vans, Flying Colors not only performs nick, scratch, and paint chip touch-ups on car and truck doors and fenders, but can repair any paint flaw, whether on mirrors, trim, plastic bumpers, or other accessories. Along with its mobile "house call" service, the company's selling points include a particularly quick and cost-effective painting process that offers on-site paint mixing for a superior color match. Flying Colors can hold to its claim of being able to match over 25,000 vehicle paint formulas, metallic or nonmetallic; its special system involves spraying paint over the damaged area and removing the overspray, ensuring better color reproduction and a smooth, glossy finish.

Franchises are currently located in 15 states, mainly in the Southeast and Southwest. The principal client base is new- and used-car dealers as well as any business that maintains a fleet of motor vehicles, from rental agencies to limo services and van lines. While most Flying Colors operators do have some prior experience, no background in the automotive industry is necessary.

The primary property in the operation is, of course, the $20,000 Flying Colors custom van, equipped with built-in airbrush equipment and all the other materials needed for performing a thorough paint·repair job (franchisees can also purchase used vehicles from the company). Prior to starting up, operators receive five days of training at Flying Colors' Houston headquarters, followed by an additional week in their local market. The company also offers its franchisees assistance in establishing regular accounts, initiating effective direct mail programs, and marketing to prospective customers, and the management is currently working to develop a company-sponsored health program. In addition, Flying Colors holds annual franchisee conventions, featuring panel discussions, seminars, and workshops, all underscoring that operators need not have to work harder to "work smarter," with the end result an even bigger array of satisfied clients—and, not incidentally, bigger profits, too.

For further information contact:
  Benjamin C. Litalien, President, International Flying Colors Franchising
  Corporation, 10696 Haddington Dr., Suite 130, Houston, TX 77043,
  1-800-232-1244

Maaco Auto Painting and Body Works

Initial license fee: $25,000
Royalties: 8%
Advertising royalties: $500/week
Minimum cash required: $55,000
Capital required: $89,900
Financing: Third-party financing available to qualified applicants
Length of contract: 15 years

In business since: 1972
Franchising since: 1972
Total number of units: 405
Number of company-operated units: 1
Total number of units planned, 1995: 600
Number of company-operated units planned, 1995: None

Anthony A. Martino, president, chief executive officer, and chairman of the board of Maaco, has made an indelible mark on the automobile aftermarket. In 1959 he founded AAMCO Transmissions, reorganizing it into a franchising operation in 1963. He left AAMCO to found Maaco in 1972.

With consumers keeping their cars longer than they used to, you can make good money in the repainting field. It only takes about 1½ gallons of paint to cover the average car, but you make your profits in the body preparation and the skilled service provided in a professional job.

Your Maaco shop will occupy 8,000 to 10,000 square feet of space, probably in a light industrial or commercial zone. Maaco will offer advice on site selection and will inspect your chosen location for suitability before giving you the go-ahead to build. But finding the site is your responsibility.

Your three weeks of training, at Maaco's headquarters in King of Prussia, Pennsylvania, will stress management skills rather than actual shop work, although the company will familiarize you with the paints, solvents, and thinners you use in your operation. Subjects covered in your training will include sales, advertising and promotion, equipment and maintenance, safety, estimating, inventory control, personnel, customer relations, fleet accounts, record keeping, accounting, budgeting, and insurance. You will also receive on-the-job training at a nearby Maaco shop. The company covers the expense of your training-related transportation and lodging.

Maaco representatives will give you two weeks of assistance, before and during your opening, focusing on hiring and training your staff. Refresher training is available throughout the year at the company's home office and at regional locations. The company will also schedule product update training from time to time.

You can purchase equipment and supplies from Maaco, both for your initial inventory and ongoing operations, although you are free to buy them from other sources. If you buy from Maaco, the company will make a profit on the sale.

Maaco will design and place your yellow pages advertisement for you, although you will pay for the advertisement. The company will oversee a mandatory advertising and promotional campaign at the time of your opening, for which you will be billed $5,000. When you sign your franchise agreement, Maaco will also require you to deposit $10,000 with the company. It will redeposit that sum in your checking account when you open for business, Maaco's way of insuring that you have enough working capital when you begin operations.

All Maaco customers get a company warranty on work done on

their car. You will have to honor the warranty even for work done at another Maaco shop. In that case, however, you will be reimbursed for this work.

For further information contact:
  Linda Kemp, Maaco Enterprises, Inc., 381 Brooks Rd., King of Prussia, PA 19406, 215-265-6606 or 1-800-521-6282

Ziebart Corporation

Initial license fee: $15,000
Royalties: 8%
Advertising royalties: 5%
Minimum cash required: $50,000
Capital required: $50,000 to $60,000
Financing: None
Length of contract: 10 years

In business since: 1954
Franchising since: 1962
Total number of units: 409
Number of company-operated units: 20
Total number of units planned, 1995: NA
Number of company-operated units planned, 1995: NA

When E. J. Hartmann purchased the Ziebart company in 1970, he bought a business that was already well known for its automobile rust-protection service. But by 1975 he felt that Ziebart had to go beyond rust protection and develop a line of products and services that would offer a total appearance and protection package for customers' automobiles. Aware that his was not the only company that would try to develop this market—although Ziebart would be the first—he decided to think big, and rather than slowly building up this new product and service line, he bought an entire chemical company to give Ziebart an instant technical edge on the competition.

Ziebart continually expands its range of automotive protection services. It now sells a rust-eliminator system for used vehicles that already have problems with rust, and a radiator and air-conditioning service, all in addition to its standard line, which includes vinyl top, paint, and interior protection; chip stop; pinstriping; sunroofs; and splash guards.

The company helps you choose a location and advises you on any remodeling or construction that may be required for your Ziebart center. According to Ziebart, "Centers are placed at reasonable distances apart to avoid oversaturation of a given market." But they do not offer you an exclusive, protected territory.

Ziebart offers a three-week training program at the company's headquarters in Troy, Michigan. You pay for travel, lodging, and meal expenses for you and your employees. During the first week you study rust protection; during the second you learn about Ziebart appearance and protection services; and in the last week you deal with the business side of your operation, covering sales, marketing, budgeting, advertising, inventory control, and personnel. Should you choose to include Ziebart's new optional air-conditioning and radiator service in your business, you will take, at an additional charge, two weeks of training in that subject.

Your district sales manager continues to train you during your ongoing operations, instructing you on making outside sales and counseling you on all other aspects of your business. The company's manual will answer virtually any technical question you might have. The manual deals with over 2,000 makes and models of vehicles. You can always consult a company expert if you encounter problems not covered by the manual. In addition, a technical specialist will visit your business periodically to make sure that your operation is up to par and to make specific recommendations to improve any deficiencies.

Your initial equipment and supplies are part of a package Ziebart requires you to buy. Currently, only Ziebart and its authorized vendors supply the products used in your business.

On the national level, Ziebart helps build business for you through its fleet program and national advertising. Locally, Ziebart dealers participate in cooperative advertising.

For further information contact:
  Greg Longe, Ziebart Corporation, P.O. Box 1290, Troy, MI 48007-1290, 313-588-4100 or 1-800-877-1312

Rental Services

Budget Rent a Car Corporation

Initial license fee: $15,000 and up, depending on the population of your territory
Royalties: 5%
Advertising royalties: 2.5%
Minimum cash required: Varies based on the size of the market
Capital required: Varies based on the size of the market

Financing: License fee may be paid in installments
Length of contract: 5 years, renewable

In business since: 1958
Franchising since: 1960
Total number of units: 3,568
Number of company-operated units: 602
Total number of units planned, 1995: NA
Number of company-operated units planned, 1995: NA

The only thing small about this company is the "Budget" in its name. From one lot with twelve cars in 1958, the company has—through Budget Rent a Car International—expanded all over the world, with sites in over one hundred countries. In 1968 it was purchased by Transamerica Corporation, whose headquarters is the huge pyramid building in downtown San Francisco. In 1986 Gibbons, Green, van Amerongen Ltd., an investment bank, bought it in a leveraged buyout. Budget is now third in market share among car-rental companies.

The heart of the rent-a-car industry is the business traveler. Typically, the rental-car customer has just gotten off a plane and is headed for an appointment. Budget Rent a Car does everything it can to see that this traveler heads for the Budget sign first. It has solidified its commercial business with the CorpRate program, which offers car rental packages to corporations. It also customizes pricing plans for companies with frequently traveling personnel. One of Budget's most important customers—whose employees are often in transit—happens to be the biggest consumer of car-rental services in the world: the United States government.

Another strong point of Budget's business is its affiliation with Sears Roebuck. Budget has been operating Sears Car and Truck Rental for over twenty years. This concession is run through regular Budget Rent a Car locations. Budget franchisees thus have an opportunity to tap a market of millions of people who have Sears credit cards.

This company takes maximum advantage of its size and reach. Budget's worldwide computerized reservation center in Carrollton, Texas, is staffed by over three hundred sales agents, who have instant access to any information a customer might need. Patrons may reach one of those agents through one of many 800 numbers. Major airline computer systems display Budget vehicle availability and rates, making travel agents an ally of Budget Rent a Car franchisees.

Many of the decisions involved in opening your Budget Rent a Car business will be your own, with the company acting only in an advisory capacity. You and your general manager—if you hire somebody else for that job—will be trained by the company in the Budget way of doing business. Training will take place either at your business site or at the company offices in Chicago. That training will include instruction on acquiring and maintaining vehicles, as well as standard business practices. You will probably begin business with a fleet of 20 to 50 cars and 5 to 10 trucks.

Budget has a fairly elaborate organization called the Licensee Operations Field Staff, which is dedicated to helping its franchisees. Among the things it is likely to help you with are control and distribution of your fleet, revenue and expense forecasting, market analysis, and handling customer complaints. There is, incidentally, a national toll-free number that any Budget customer can use to register a complaint about any aspect of the company's service.

The company's Fleet Operations Department will help you purchase and sell your vehicles. Its "Fleet Operations Buying Guide" consolidates all relevant data between two covers. Budget will help you establish a line of credit through the company's Budget Vehicle Purchase Program.

Budget Rent a Car management stresses the importance of having up-to-date reports detailing the vital statistics of your business. For example, the company will provide you with figures comparing the performance of your business with that of similar franchisees. Budget will also give you data that will help you develop a profit plan, with forecasts of revenues and expenses. Your participation in these programs— including reporting financial data from your business so it can be included in the company's data base—is mandatory. You can also purchase the company's optional computerized accounting system—Best II—which will further assist you in controlling your finances.

Budget's nationwide marketing program notwithstanding, your local promotional efforts play an important part in bringing in business. Those efforts should generate about a third of your car rentals. The franchisor has extensive marketing capabilities to supplement your local efforts. Its yellow pages department, for example, will work with you to develop your phone book ad. That's a vital place for you to shine, since it's the source for about 80 percent of all rental business on the local level.

A big factor in your business will be Budget's marketing to the travel industry. The company participates in several airline promotions, including Northwest and AmericaWest; joint programs with tour operators; and cooperative activities with hotels, such as Hyatt. Budget Rent a Car has also begun its own promotional program, called Budget Awards Plus.

For further information contact:
Franchise Department, Budget Rent a Car Corporation, 4225 Naperville Rd.,
Lisle, IL 60532-3662, 708-955-1900

Dollar Rent A Car

Initial license fee: $150/1,000 population; $7,500 minimum
Royalties: 8% less up to 5% of credit card fees
Advertising royalties: Included in royalties
Minimum cash required: $75,000
Capital required: $50,000 plus credit line of $500,000 to $2 million
Financing: Company will help franchisees obtain third-party financing or offer
    car leasing through their own company
Length of contract: Indefinite

In business since: 1966
Franchising since: 1969
Total number of units: 740
Number of company-operated units: 10
Total number of units planned, 1995: NA
Number of company-operated units planned, 1995: NA

"The demand for rental cars is virtually unlimited," according to Kermit Whyte, vice president of systems development for Dollar Systems, Inc. "As the population grows and more small- and medium-sized cities open airports, the market for rental cars grows. While our larger metropolitan franchises are sold out, we will keep expanding into midsized urban areas, particularly those served by airports." The Dollar Rent A Car credo is to deliver full-service car rental at a discount. Its commitment to customer savings has allowed Dollar to grow rapidly and offer a nationwide reservations system. Dollar can also offer international travelers confirmed reservations at over 1,700 locations worldwide.

Dollar prefers to sell "master franchises," the right to develop a defined region. The company will help you select an off-airport location or gain entry to airport locations, and will sell you the appropriate indoor and outdoor signs for your business. According to Kermit Whyte, you don't need previous experience in the car-rental business to qualify as a Dollar franchisee, but you should have "any kind of business experience." Because air travel generates most rental-car business, the company is planning most of its expansion at airport sites, but it will approve downtown locations if they can bring in corporate and insurance replacement business.

After the company helps you select and set up your site, it will prepare you through hands-on training at your site. Dollar staff will help you purchase your fleet—they feature Chrysler cars no more than two years old—and will train you in every aspect of rental operations, from car control to accounting procedures. In addition, the company will help you train your counter personnel and plan local advertising and promotions. To supplement your marketing efforts, Dollar conducts a national advertising campaign in airline and hotel magazines as well as newspapers. You may also take advantage of approved co-op advertising.

Periodic reviews ensure that your business operates as efficiently as possible, and the corporate office checks over your revenue reports, profit projections, and operating statements to catch and correct any problems that might crop up. Simplified accounting systems and forms will make your bookkeeping easier. You can puchase these forms from Dollar. With a proven record-keeping system and a detailed operations manual at your disposal, you will be well equipped to run your business. But if you should have any problems or questions, Dollar staff is only a phone call away.

Dollar regularly offers regional training for you and your employees. Through a variety of workshops and seminars, the company addresses the specific needs of its franchisees as well as general topics in car rental. The company meets another of your needs by making business insurance available to you at premium rates based on your revenue. Of particular advantage to you as a Dollar franchisee, though, are the material benefits of the company's nationwide reservations system, through which you can receive reservations from travelers around the country who are planning trips to your area.

For further information contact:
Kermit Whyte, Vice President, Systems Development, Dollar Systems, Inc., 6141 W. Century Blvd., Los Angeles, CA 90045, 213-776-8100

Payless Car Rental System, Inc.

Initial license fee: $30,000 to $150,000
Royalties: 5%
Advertising royalties: 3%
Minimum cash required: $50,000
Capital required: $150,000 to $500,000
Financing: None
Length of contract: 5 years

In business since: 1971
Franchising since: 1971
Total number of units: 150
Number of company-operated units: None
Total number of units planned, 1995: 200
Number of company-operated units planned, 1995: None

Payless serves markets in Canada, the Caribbean, and Europe, as well as in this country. As rent-a-car franchises go, this company does not require a huge investment by its new franchisees. It keeps costs down by specializing in the rental of economy cars at off-airport locations, where site costs are minimized. The lowest franchisee fee secures a location in a market of fewer than one hundred thousand people, while the highest is for major airport markets, such as Chicago and Atlanta.

Franchisees train to run their business at the company's headquarters in St. Petersburg, Florida, during the three-day course. Among the subjects covered in the training are counter and office procedures, sales calls and business development, vehicle procurement and maintenance, staffing, and customer qualification and selection. You can obtain supplementary training on request, for a reasonable fee.

The company advises its new franchisees on site selection, and it works with them to make sure they pick the right mix of vehicles for their beginning fleet. Franchisees can purchase the company's optional computerized accounting system, and they can also take advantage of Payless's volume purchasing of supplies.

One of Payless's strongest points is merchandising, on the local as well as the national level. In fact, as soon as the franchisee's business opens, the company literally walks its franchisee through the process of establishing important local contacts. During that period, a company representative accompanies the new franchisee on visits to insurance adjusters, repair shops, hotels, motels, and major industries to make contacts and drum up business. Payless also promotes itself on the national level with advertising and its Passport Club card, with which businesspeople can rent an economy car at any company location in the country at a special rate. Additionally, Payless has an international tennis champion, Chris Evert, as its national spokesperson for advertising and marketing purposes.

The company obtains even more business for its franchisees through its computerized connection to major airline reservation systems, such as United's Apollo and American's Sabre. Payless's own computerized national reservation system not only links customer needs to available vehicles, it also compiles information on each of its franchisees' operations and comparative data on their competitors, which it supplies to franchisees monthly.

Through the addition of cellular phone and hotel franchising divisions Payless is poised for the future. With its three-pronged strategy, the company is positioning itself to become, as its slogan promotes, "The driving force of the 90's."

For further information contact:
Vice President of Franchise Sales, Payless Car Rental System, Inc., 2350-N 34th St. N., St. Petersburg, FL 33713, 1-800-729-5255

U-Save Auto Rental of America, Inc.

Initial license fee: $6,110 to $17,500
Royalties: Fixed rate per number of vehicles
Advertising royalties: NA
Minimum cash required: NA
Capital required: $52,000 to $135,000
Financing: 24-month
Length of contract: 3 years, with 5-year renewal

In business since: 1979
Franchising since: 1979
Total number of units: 502
Number of company-operated units: None
Total number of units planned, 1995: 750
Number of company-operated units planned, 1995: None

With apologies for the pun, U-Save considers itself a customer-driven company. The company stresses to its over 500 franchisees that understanding the consumer's needs and preferences—and going out of the way to meet them—strengthens not only each operator's own business but the image of the entire company.

And the image is one of a reliable, economical, and rapidly growing car rental service in a competitive field. Focusing on the hometown rental market, the Maryland-based company offers locations throughout the country, with a combined fleet of over 10,000 well-maintained vehicles—trucks, cargo and vacation vans, and station wagons as well as cars of every size and type.

U-Save sells its franchises primarily to new and used car dealers and other auto-related business owners. Usually, they run their rental operation right on the site of their present facility. Some, like Toledo franchisee Paul Wood, find the rental wing of their business so profitable that they abandon their former enterprises altogether.

The company's service begins with a comprehensive training program that teaches new franchisees the intricacies of U-Save's procedures along with critical information for effectively starting up and managing their rental businesses successfully. Constant direct contact between the company and franchisees is maintained through the U-Save's system of state managers, franchisees themselves who have firsthand knowledge of the daily challenges of running a U-Save operation and the skills to furnish operators with the necessary support. The state managers make regular visits, offering training updates, and are always on call to provide assistance.

Back at the home office, meanwhile, U-Save's management is persistently investigating new services to support the operation of each franchise. That has included working with airlines, travel agencies, corporations, and hotel and motel chains to create new business opportunities; negotiating with credit card companies for lower processing fees; contracting with auto manufacturers to provide operators with vehicles more cheaply and efficiently; developing cost-efficient marketing programs that encompass radio and TV commercials and print media ads, from newspapers to the yellow pages; and making available liability insurance—a critical component of the auto rental business—at competitive rates. U-Save also plays an integral role in the lobbying effort in both Congress and state legislatures to help shape the laws and regulations that keenly affect the constantly changing industry.

U-Save franchisees also get assistance from one another at the company's annual convention and state and regional meetings. The agendas are set by the franchisees themselves, who are surveyed to find out what they want to discuss and what issues they want speakers and workshops to address. Also at these conferences, franchisees can get together with their fellow U-Save operators, people like Paul Wood, who will share their advice on effective customer relations, their strategies for working with the insurance replacement business, their experience with new computer systems, and their perspective on the future. As for Paul Wood, "We've seen consistent growth in units and in profitability. . . . We'll be making darned good money."

For further information contact:
  Roland A. Mumford, National Sales Manager, U-Save Auto Rental of America, Inc., 7525 Connelley Dr., Suite A, Hanover, MD 21076, 1-800-272-8728, fax 410-760-4390

Tires and Parts

Champion Auto Stores, Inc.

Initial license fee: $20,000
Royalties: 5% maximum
Advertising royalties: 4%
Minimum cash required: $87,000
Capital required: $175,000
Financing: None
Length of contract: 10 years, renewable

In business since: 1956
Franchising since: 1961
Total number of units: 157

Number of company-operated units: 21
Total number of units planned, 1995: NA
Number of company-operated units planned, 1995: NA

Franchising opportunities with Champion appear most promising in Colorado, Kansas, Illinois, Missouri, Michigan, and Wisconsin. This chain of do-it-yourself auto parts supermarkets, spread over nine states in the Midwest and West, has grown by 39 percent in the past three years. The franchisor claims that its business is immune to dips in the business cycle. In fact, it says it has achieved its greatest growth during recessions.

The automobile parts business got a boost from the oil price shocks of the 1970s. Large numbers of gas stations closed, and many of the surviving stations turned to a self-service, gas-only mode of operation. With repairs less readily available, many car owners finally got up the courage to start fiddling around under the hood. For many people, it started with the feeling that they were capable of changing their own oil. After that, there was no turning back.

Champion store design divides a large expanse of space into neat rows of fixtures, with auto parts either stacked on shelves or hanging from hooks. Radiator belts hang high on the wall. As in a supermarket, numerous signs call attention to sales items or new products. Customers do their shopping with supermarket carts or baskets.

Champion emphasizes that it wants the people who own and run these stores to concentrate on service and sales volume without getting bogged down in details that could be better handled by company professionals. The company notes that many of its franchisees are first-time entrepreneurs. It therefore tries to take on many of the burdens that go with running the business, such as choosing stock. Champion sums up its intent to assist and encourage franchisees in its franchising slogan: "On your own, but not alone."

It's not that you won't be making decisions. You will, for example, have a say in what you stock and how much of it you keep on hand, but the franchisor has a staff of specialists in each product area who buy in quantity at maximum discounts, and you are likely to want to take their advice. Champion also manufactures many parts under its own brand name, which you will stock as a matter of course. You will receive a weekly delivery of your regular stocking order, although anything can be special-ordered at any time. The company fills your orders on a two-day turnaround schedule.

The company will choose your location and lay out your store subject to your approval. You will have to train for eight to ten days in the Minneapolis area, where instruction will take place in one of the company stores as well as in a classroom. Should you desire, the training period can be lengthened. Some of your instructors in Minneapolis will be company store managers, whose knowledge of their field is a good deal more than theoretical.

Champion will help you choose your start-up inventory and put together your first annual sales and expense forecast and monthly budget. The franchisor guarantees that each store, no matter what its size, will pay the same price for all merchandise. The special company computerized accounting system will evaluate how well you do with that merchandise. You can draw on that system at any time for an analysis of any part of your operation.

Champion franchisees must attend the company's semiannual marketing conferences, where they will discuss new products, promotions, and services in a seminar atmosphere. And there will be plenty of promotions to discuss. In fact, Champion runs its own advertising agency. The company does extensive TV and radio advertising, and it will also mail 14 eight-page, four-color circulars a year to your customers. In addition, the circulars appear as inserts in newspapers.

Perhaps the most interesting promotional tool the company uses is its in-store Video Tech Center. This laser disc–based audiovisual device will teach your customers the basics of doing their own repairs. Ordinarily, a programmed sequence of "tech tips" will be displayed on the screen, but customers can interrupt it by using a search control to find the topic most interesting to them. Champion's vice president, Dene Billbe, has observed that customers need a visit or two before they become comfortable with this machine. But, like a video game, it does grab their attention, and "by their second or third visit, they go right to the machine."

For further information contact:
    Earl W. Farr, Champion Auto Stores, Inc., 5520 N. Hwy. 169, New Hope, MN 55428, 612-535-5984

Goodyear Tire Centers

Initial license fee: None
Royalties: 3%
Advertising royalties: None
Minimum cash required: $100,000
Capital required: $100,000
Financing: Long-term note-line and open-account credit available
Length of contract: 10 years

In business since: 1898
Franchising since: 1968
Total number of units: 696

Number of company-operated units: None
Total number of units planned, 1995: 1,000
Number of company-operated units planned, 1995: None

Children growing up in this country in recent years probably think that no important ceremony held outdoors—especially major sporting events—can begin without two rituals: the singing of the "Star-Spangled Banner" and the passing overhead of the Goodyear Blimp. The airship, now something of an institution, to the point where comedians make good-natured jokes about it, has helped Goodyear achieve household-name status. Its franchisees count it among the many benefits of opening their own Goodyear tire center.

As a Goodyear franchisee, you trade a certain amount of independence to use the most familiar name in the tire industry. Goodyear will sublease a location to you and outfit your unit with the equipment and fixtures you need. You lease most of that equipment from the company.

In addition to the use of a heavily advertised brand name, you will also receive some of the most thorough training given by any franchisor. The company picks up most of the expenses for this training, except your transportation. Goodyear requires that new franchisees take 10 weeks of training at its Akron, Ohio, headquarters. The training includes four weeks of classroom instruction and four weeks at an operating tire center. The company takes particular pains to make sure that businesspeople who lack familiarity with the tire industry get a thorough grounding in all that a Goodyear dealer needs to know.

Your Goodyear dealer development counselor and consumer district sales managers call on you regularly at your business to provide merchandising advice and deal with any problems that might arise in your ongoing operation. Your staff can receive supplementary training as needed in regional schools. The company also offers various in-store training aids, including flip charts and videotapes. You will not need a specialized accounting system. Goodyear processes your daily reports, which include invoice, check, and cash records, with its computerized dealer management system, making available to you an analysis of your sales, profits, and expenses. The company's computers also generate your inventory records as well as all other figures that an accounting system usually produces.

Goodyear facilitates customer credit through Goodyear Credit Card. You can also solicit business by direct mail through this credit card operation.

Goodyear knows what it takes to make a successful franchisee. The company seeks people who already have business experience, supervisory ability, and an aggressive sales personality.

For further information contact:
H. M. Harding, Goodyear Tire and Rubber Company, 1144 E. Market St.,
Akron, OH 44316, 216-796-3467

Mighty Distributing System of America

Initial license fee: $13,500 to $55,000, depending on size of market
Royalties: 5%
Advertising royalties: 0.5% (maximum $3,000 annually)
Minimum cash required: $20,000 to $53,000
Capital required: $50,000 to $133,000
Financing: Available (up to 60% of total investment)
Length of contract: 10 years

In business since: 1963
Franchising since: 1970
Total number of units: 152
Number of company-operated units: 14
Total number of units planned, 1995: 212
Number of company-operated units planned, 1995: NA

With 25 years' experience and a network of leading original equipment manufacturers around the world, Mighty distributes quality automotive parts to professional installers. The suppliers ship their products—all stamped with the recognizable Mighty trademark—directly to franchisees, assuring volume purchasing power and eliminating outside distributors, which brings Mighty customers price savings of an average of 15 percent to 20 percent.

Mighty's operation is unique in that it sells exclusively to professional installers, over 1.5 million technicians nationwide at service stations, specialty shops, tire stores, and vehicle fleet groups. Franchisees make weekly sales and service calls on their customers—more than a few Mighty clients have commented, "I can set my watch by my Mighty rep's visit." And they are onsite after product delivery as well, performing such vital extra tasks for their customers as maintaining inventory, updating catalogues, and organizing supply areas. The company believes its success is in large part due to its operators' determining not only what they can *sell* clients but also what they can *do* for them.

The Mighty product line encompasses a vast range of auto parts: spark plugs and ignition products, belts and hoses, brakes and lighting, oil and air filters, as well as chemicals, emission controls, windshield wiper products, shocks and struts, and many, many more. Through Mighty's direct vendor program, delivery is usually made within 5 to 7 days (compared with the industry average of 10 to 14 days). In addition, the company offers its customers a variety of service programs including an instructional video library, toll-free hot lines, and written warranties that feature parts, labor, and even obsolescence guarantees, backed by more than 1,000 authorized warranty centers and another 19,000 locations across the country. Among its innovations, Mighty pioneered the lifetime guarantee on brakes, now an industry standard.

Mighty awards its franchisees an exclusive distribution territory, assuring operators that they will be the only Mighty dealer within that area for the lifetime of the franchising agreement. The franchise also comes with ready-made business, as franchisees are authorized to handle all orders for local outlets of the national and regional chains that are contracted with Mighty.

Franchisees can start up their operation as quickly as 60 days. There's a three-week training period, two weeks at the company's Atlanta headquarters followed by one week onsite in a territory similar to one the franchisee will run. The instruction covers such areas as business planning, product line knowledge, purchase management, accounting, and customer service. Finally, the company works with the franchisee to develop a customized grand opening plan, entailing a targeted advertising and promotion program to introduce the business and develop a client base quickly as well as direct mailing and premium and incentive offers to dealerships.

Ongoing support for franchisees comes from both the home office and regional manager. The Franchise Accounting System supplies extra help during the first year of operation, furnishing detailed monthly financial statements and budget analyses for the new franchisee. Health, life, auto, and liability insurance is made available. Refresher courses, advanced workshops, and regional and national meetings are frequently offered. The company also extends an incentive program, with franchisees and their employees eligible for premiums and prizes. And, most important for improving business performance, regular visits from company professionals provide follow-up training, consultation, and general problem-solving.

Franchisees benefit in another way from Mighty's field presence. Says Eugene, Oregon, distributor Jeff Rose, "The corporate office excels in taking good ideas from the field and polishing them into programs that benefit the entire franchise system."

For further information contact:
   Bill Hargett, Vice President, Franchise Development, 50 Technology Park,
   Norcross, GA 30092, 404-448-3900

Transmission Services

AAMCO Transmissions, Inc.

Initial license fee: $30,000
Royalties: 7%
Advertising royalties: Variable
Minimum cash required: $48,000
Capital required: Approximately $118,000
Financing: None
Length of contract: 15 years

In business since: 1963
Franchising since: 1963
Total number of units: 670
Number of company-operated units: None
Total number of units planned, 1995: NA
Number of company-operated units planned, 1995: None

America's continuing reliance on the automobile as a primary means of transportation sustains one of the nation's largest industries: the auto aftermarket. With millions of automobiles on the road, the market for automotive products and services is enormous. New car prices continue to climb, so car owners want to make sure their cars last. Demand for transmission service should remain strong for years to come.

AAMCO's established reputation and proven methods can help you get a good start in the car repair industry. AAMCO is seeking franchisees throughout the United States and Canada. You can open an AAMCO franchise even without any prior experience in auto mechanics or the auto aftermarket industry. More important, according to the company, is experience in business management. The company will augment your experience by training you in both management and business skills to prepare you to run your own transmission repair shop. Your AAMCO shop should be able to handle just about any vehicle.

New franchisees are required to complete AAMCO's training program in Bala Cynwyd, Pennsylvania. The five-week course will train you in sales, marketing, management, customer relations, production, and other areas essential to the successful operation of an AAMCO center. Throughout the term of your franchise agreement, AAMCO will provide operational assistance by telephone. The Technical Services Department also provides various types of technical assistance and support, as well as ongoing advice on customer relations. Another source of support to franchisees is the new Tech Video Training Library, which provides a series of training videotapes designed, written, and produced specifically for AAMCO franchise centers. It contains tips on training and details ways your mechanics can enhance their skills.

You are free to lease or purchase your site, provided AAMCO approves the location, and you may purchase your equipment, supplies, and inventory from any source that meets AAMCO's specifications. You are, however, prohibited from operating another transmission shop while your contract with AAMCO is in effect. And for two years following termination of the franchise agreement, you cannot operate another transmission shop within a 10-mile radius of your previous AAMCO franchise.

For further information contact:
  AAMCO Transmissions, Inc., Franchise Sales Dept., One Presidential Blvd., Bala Cynwyd, PA 19004, 215-668-2900

Mr. Transmission

Initial license fee: $27,500
Royalties: 7%
Advertising royalties: NA
Minimum cash required: $35,000
Capital required: $110,000
Financing: Company may assist you in obtaining financing through the SBA
Length of contract: 20 years

In business since: 1956
Franchising since: 1978
Total number of units: 123
Number of company-operated units: 2
Total number of units planned, 1995: 482
Number of company-operated units planned, 1995: 1

"To start with, I was a company manager at a company-owned store," says Rodney Randall, whose Mr. Transmission franchise is in Hixson, Tennessee. "I knew it was a great opportunity." Rodney Randall went from employee to entrepreneur in a chain of shops that started over 30 years ago in Nashville with a rebuilt-transmission center called the Automatic Transmission Company.

Mr. Transmission centers usually occupy 2,000 to 4,000 square feet on 7,000- to 10,000-square-foot plots, and house three to eight bays. The company will help you find and develop a site, but you have primary responsibility for these tasks. Among the criteria for site selection are an area's traffic volume, population, and zoning; location of other retail businesses; and local competition.

Training is an essential part of your preparation as a Mr. Transmission franchisee. Your classroom training will cover management techniques, technical procedures, legal forms, customer service, personnel, inventory control, advertising, and cash management. Training places emphasis on the management of your business rather than on installation and repair of transmissions. You do not have to be a mechanic to run one of these franchises, and Mr. Transmission won't teach you how to be one. The manager of your center, who will handle the technical end of your business, will receive one week of specialized training.

Mr. Transmission will help you organize your parts department and install your equipment. Company staff will also help you hire technicians and a manager and schedule your preopening and postopening advertising. A Mr. Transmission representative will remain on the premises during your first week in business, assisting you in applying your training to actual business conditions.

Mr. Transmission emphasizes its postopening support for franchisees. In fact, the home office in Midlothian, Illinois, is available to any franchisees who want to come to visit and talk over their problems. Mr. Transmission will also support you in other ways. From time to time you will get a call from their operations manager to discuss your sales volume, and you will be able to get in touch with the company over its toll-free line. Company field personnel will visit your location periodically. You can get retraining if you need it, and Mr. Transmission offers sales and technical seminars several times a year to update you on new programs and products.

While you do not have to buy from Mr. Transmission's factory, Drive-Train, the company thinks you will probably want to, since through volume purchasing it can save you money on supplies and equipment as well as on transmission parts.

For further information contact:
  Mel Patterson, Director of Marketing, 4444 W. 147th St., Midlothian, IL 60445, 708-389-5922

Multistate Automatic Transmission Company, Inc.

Initial license fee: $7,500
Royalties: 7%
Advertising royalties: Minimum of $100/month
Minimum cash required: $35,000

Capital required: Approximately $88,000
Financing: Available through third-party sources
Length of contract: 20 years

In business since: 1973
Franchising since: 1974
Total number of units: 40
Number of company-operated units: None
Total number of units planned, 1995: 80
Number of company-operated units planned, 1995: None

The evolution of the automobile aftermarket, strangely enough, re-
sembles the development of modern medical practice. At one time
there was the "general practitioner," the mechanic who took care of
your car from headlights to exhaust pipes. But the industry has long
since passed into the age of the specialist. If, for example, your transmission starts to fail, you take it to a transmission repair shop, where
specialists are familiar with each of the transmission's five hundred or
so parts. No longer would you consult an independent all-purpose garage or new-car dealer.

Multistate thinks you should take your transmission to one of its
shops, and it has at least one good argument to offer on its own behalf: "We're Nationwide . . . So Is Our Warranty," the company's slogan goes. An unaffiliated transmission repair shop couldn't offer its
customers that kind of protection out of town. Interstate franchisees
also give one-day service and will tow you in for free if you can't
drive in.

With the average age of cars increasing and the use of automatic
transmissions proliferating, the company estimates that one of eight
cars on the road now needs its services. Automatic transmissions often
need repairs after about two years of driving or 30,000 miles. In fact,
according to the company, some kind of work on the transmission is
usually needed every year. That produces a business that amounts to
almost $2 billion a year for the industry.

Don't let the complexities of automatic transmissions discourage
you. Multistate claims that fewer than 20 percent of its franchisees
have worked with transmissions before taking their training. Mandatory franchisee training includes a week of classroom and a week of
hands-on instruction at the company training site in Michigan. You
pay for your own and your managerial employee's living and traveling
expenses. The training covers advertising, insurance, personnel selection, accounting and, of course, the technical side of the business. The
company encourages its franchisees to pursue fleet service, an aspect
of the business covered in the training. You and your managers may
also take refresher courses from time to time.

The company supports and monitors your operations fairly closely. Company representatives make periodic field visits, and you have to file weekly reports. Multistate dealers get an "Equipment and Supply List" from the company with suggestions for purchase. The franchisor can get you good prices on many items, but the final decision on what and from whom to buy is yours.

For further information contact:
  Mel Patterson, Multistate Automatic Transmission Company, Inc.,
  4444 W. 147th St., Midlothian, IL 60445, 708-389-5922

Tune-Up and Lubrication

Grease Monkey International, Inc.

Initial license fee: $25,000 (in 2 installments)
Royalties: 5%
Advertising royalties: 6.5%
Minimum cash required: $125,000
Capital required: $97,350 to $170,200
Financing: Some offered by suppliers
Length of contract: 15 years

In business since: 1978
Franchising since: 1978
Total number of units: 173
Number of company-operated units: 20
Total number of units planned, 1995: NA
Number of company-operated units planned, 1995: NA

Grease Monkey International, Inc., is not afraid of a light touch. Its house newsletter is called *Monkey Talk*, and the company logo is a grinning simian holding a lube gun. Since it began in 1978, Grease Monkey has grown to become the fourth largest tune-up and lubrication franchise in the nation and the largest 10-minute oil change organization not affiliated with a major oil company.

"We're selling convenience," states Rex Utsler, company president, "where a car owner can drive in, have a complimentary cup of coffee, and drive away 10 minutes later with an oil change, new filters, lube, fluids topped, windows washed, and floors vacuumed." Or, as Harry Blankenship, Grease Monkey's first franchisee, characterizes the operation: "The fast-lube business can be referred to as the fast-food phenomenon of the auto industry."

These days more than half of all car owners still change their own oil. Match that with the fact that for the past 15 years, the number of full-service stations providing lubricating services has dwindled, and you have fertile ground for a business just like Grease Monkey. In 1985 there were about 1,500 quick-lube centers, Grease Monkey included. By the end of 1990, there were between 3,500 and 4,000.

Grease Monkey franchisees come from just about every kind of background, including real estate, civil service, the military, fast food, and sales. Some people even come out of retirement to buy one of these businesses. And they're not all men. In the Denver metropolitan area, for example, 9 of the 33 Grease Monkey units are either run or owned by women.

If you join this group, Grease Monkey will have to approve the site you choose. The company will give you blueprints so your building can meet its specifications. At its Denver training location, Grease Monkey will train you in all aspects of the business in a one- or two-week course, one week of course work and a minimum of one week of hands-on training in a store, depending on how much you need to learn. The course covers accounting, marketing, advertising, business management, and promotion, as well as technical services. Field representatives will provide follow-up help at your business when you open and continuing support as you grow.

For further information contact:
  Roger Auker, Grease Monkey International, Inc., 216 16th St., Suite 1100, Denver, CO 80202, 303-534-1660

Jiffy Lube International, Inc.

Initial license fee: $35,000
Royalties: 5% the first year, 6% thereafter
Advertising royalties: 6%
Minimum cash required: $70,000
Capital required: $158,000 to $164,000
Financing: Limited working-capital loans offered to qualified operators
Length of contract: 20 years

In business since: 1979
Franchising since: 1979
Total number of units: 1,042
Number of company-operated units: 346
Total number of units planned, 1995: 1,450
Number of company-operated units planned, 1995: NA

Jiffy Lube International has developed a business plan designed to provide support, service, guidance, and leadership to those who desire to own and operate a quick-lube business. The pioneer of the quick-lube industry, Jiffy Lube began in 1973 with one service center in

Ogden, Utah. Today, the organization consists of more than 1,000 centers across the United States and plans to continue to grow in the decade to come.

Jiffy Lube centers perform a complete vehicle maintenance service in minutes, with no appointment and at a reasonable price. These services include changing the oil with a major brand; changing the oil filter; checking and filling the transmission; checking the brake, power steering, and window washer fluids; checking the air filter; checking the wiper blades and battery level; checking the tire pressure; washing the windows; and vaccuuming the interior.

Unlike some franchisors, who either choose a site for their franchisee or do most of the work in picking the right location, Jiffy Lube wants you to act as a full partner in the site selection and building process. The company's franchise development department will train you in site selection and then work with you to pick the right place. Jiffy Lube will also train you to do construction bidding and monitoring.

You and your service center manager will work two weeks in an actual center, then receive five and one-half days of management training at a Jiffy Lube training center. A company representative will assist you with preopening work and your grand opening. Ongoing assistance for your business will come in the form of financial and marketing analyses by a Jiffy Lube representative. The representative will evaluate your inventory levels and controls, staffing, fleet account acquisitions, and promotional efforts. Through Jiffy Lube, you will have the opportunity to purchase at a discount the supplies and equipment you will need to run your business.

Jiffy Lube has assisted franchisees with advertising by organizing cooperatives made up of local franchisees. If a cooperative exists in your area, you are required to join, but will receive many benefits from your association and contributions. In addition, the company's national advertising fund supplies the local co-ops with advertising materials.

For further information contact:
Prospect Coordinator, Franchise Development, Jiffy Lube International, Inc., P.O. Box 2967, Houston, TX 77252-2967, 1-800-327-9532

Precision Tune, Inc.

Initial license fee: $25,000
Royalties: 9%
Advertising royalties: 7.5%
Minimum cash required: $70,000

Capital required: $154,000 to $170,000
Financing: None
Length of contract: 10 years

In business since: 1976
Franchising since: 1977
Total number of units: 533
Number of company-operated units: None
Total number of units planned, 1995: 683
Number of company-operated units planned, 1995: None

"Our car service centers have had such obvious advantages as brand-name recognition and superior marketing programs," observes Jim Grey, an areas subfranchisor for Precision Tune, Inc., in upstate New York. An international franchisor of automotive tune-up and diagnostic car-care centers, Precision Tune franchises are in the eastern half of the United States, with concentrations in the upper Midwest, Ohio, and Texas, where the chain opened its first unit. Recently, the company expanded to Canada, Puerto Rico, the Bahamas, Taiwan, and China. Precision Tune uses a subfranchise structure, in which individual franchisors are given support by a regional manager who provides training and ongoing support.

According to the company, its line of business is preferable to other opportunities in the automobile aftermarket because of its low start-up costs, the possibility of fitting its operations into an existing service station, and the minimal staff of three to six it takes to run it. Precision also stresses the repeat-customer aspect of the business, the all-cash basis of the enterprise, and the continued increase in stringent emission control standards that will create further demands for the services it offers.

Most of the company's franchisees have not had previous experience in an automotive business. Their backgrounds range from accounting to sales to medicine to civil service. Many of them end up buying more than one franchise.

The company's required training takes place either at the franchisor's home base in Leesburg, Virginia, or at a subfranchisor's headquarters, if one operates in your area. You absorb the travel-related costs, but the company includes tuition in its franchise package. Precision's training, geared for beginners, includes standards, methods, procedures, and techniques of performing auto tune-ups and managing the business. You can get advanced training in sales, operations, and management in Leesburg and in regional seminars. Precision Tune also offers to its franchisees videotaped instruction on how to run an advertising campaign.

Precision Tune's ongoing support includes field visits to your business by a company representative and weekly technical bulletins to keep you up to date. You will also have access to a film library covering various aspects of management, operations, and the nuts and bolts of doing auto tune-ups. In addition, you can use the company cost-control system, supplemented by consultation on your profit-and-loss performance.

The company will provide you with building plans for your station and review your progress as you build it. You can purchase equipment and supplies from vendors of your own choosing, provided they meet company approval. Precision Tune does, however, maintain a subsidiary from whom you may purchase your inventory: PACManufacturing and Distributing Company.

Optional services you may offer at your station include computerized engine-control-system and carburetor-repair services, for which the company has an advanced training program. Precision Tune will also sell you a portable lift should you decide to do oil change and lubrication.

Precision Tune gives its customers a 12-month or 12,000-mile warranty on parts and labor. To make sure that you do your part to provide the services on which the company bases its warranty and reputation, your customers will get "We Care" cards to fill out, permitting them to evaluate the service you have given them.

For further information contact:
Precision Tune, Inc., New Center Development, 748 Miller Dr. S.E., P.O. Box 5000, Leesburg, VA 22075, 1-800-GET-TUNE (in Virginia, 703-777-9095)

SpeeDee Oil Change & Tune-Up

Initial license fee: $30,000 to $40,000
Royalties: 5% to 6%
Advertising royalties: 8% to 10%
Minimum cash required: $30,000 to $40,000
Capital required: $75,000 to $150,000, excluding real estate
Financing: None
Length of contract: 15 years, with two 5-year renewals

In business since: 1980
Franchising since: 1982
Total number of units: 115
Number of company-operated units: 2
Total number of units planned, 1995: 400
Number of company-operated units planned, 1995: 10

Not much more than a decade ago, automotive companies saw the decline of full-service gas stations, the increase of the number of car owners holding on to their old vehicles, and the lack of consumers' free time as fortuitous signs of a rising demand for speedy auto tune-up shops. They were right, and the quick-lube industry boomed as a result. Very soon, however, the field became pretty crowded, and the overly optimistic ambitions of some companies got them in financial trouble. In this erratic yet still-dynamic environment, SpeeDee Oil Change & Tune-Up has managed steady growth without careless expansion. And with ten-minute lube operations providing almost identical services, it's also managed to outdo the competition in at least one area: SpeeDee centers offer the *nine*-minute oil change.

The marketing skills of Gary Copp, a yellow pages salesperson, nicely complemented car-wash proprietor Kevin Bennett's knowledge of the auto market when the partners opened their first SpeeDee facility in 1980. Within two years, the operation was so successful that the two reincorporated and began building a national franchise system. Their original tune-up center became the prototype for shops now spread across the country.

Using Mobil products, you'll change the motor oil in cars, trucks, and other vehicles, checking and topping off other fluids, too, and replacing bad filters. Customers can also have you tune the engine and clean the fuel-delivery system, helping them prevent costly breakdowns before they happen and improve gas mileage at the same time. In addition, you'll be able to replace spark plugs, check tire pressure, inspect the ignition and emissions control, service the transmission, and vacuum the vehicle. More intricate jobs might take you longer than that nine minutes for a basic lube—but not much longer. Your aim is to finish the work efficiently and inexpensively, leaving your customers satisfied so they'll want to bring you their return business.

SpeeDee uses a subfranchise structure, where a regional "master franchisee" will set you up with an individual operation, providing training and ongoing support, conducting information seminars, and monitoring your shop's performance with a review of your monthly financial statements. The entire SpeeDee network gets together, too, during annual conventions, and the corporate office stays in touch with newsletters and visits from top management.

First, though, you'll receive assistance with site selection for your facility, along with lease negotiation and building design. Because the layout of the shop is instrumental to the efficiency of your service, the company supplies detailed floor plans, specifying pits, rather than lifts, in the bays for faster car movement. Training is held at your regional center, with additional on-the-job instruction and workbooks furnished to guide your technicians through the certification process. For conveniently keeping inventory in stock, you'll be able to obtain all your supplies—at volume discount—from one location, the company's central warehouse.

Outfitting you with TV, radio, and print ads, the company also helps in devising a marketing plan to launch the business and then develop sales programs to tap large accounts, like car dealers, rental agencies, and other fleet owners. You're encouraged as well to participate in SpeeDee promotional campaigns offered through Mobil Oil.

The company's prudent approach to franchising has won the respect of many in the industry. "They have not been eager to sell a franchise just to anyone," according to Larry Northrup, a trade specialist and executive director of the Convenient Automotive Services Institute. "SpeeDee seems to take an especially large interest in making sure than an operation is going to be around in another two or five years. As a consequence," he concludes, "they have grown slower than the other majors, but they seem to have the staying power to last."

For further information contact:
Kevin Bennett, Executive Vice President, SpeeDee Oil Change & Tune-Up, 6660 Riverside Dr., Suite 101, Metairie, LA 70003, 504-454-3783, fax 504-454-3890

Speedy CAR-X Muffler & Brake, Inc.

Initial license fee: $18,500
Royalties: 5%
Advertising royalties: 5% to 10%
Minimum cash required: $80,000 to $90,000
Capital required: $200,000
Financing: Assistance to secure outside financing
Length of contract: 10 years

In business since: 1971
Franchising since: 1973
Total number of units: 138
Number of company-operated units: 53
Total number of units planned, 1995: 175
Number of company-operated units planned, 1995: 60

Speedy CAR-X Muffler & Brake is a chain of automotive specialty shops dealing in undercar services such as exhaust systems, brakes, ride control and front-end repair. As part of the automotive after-market, Speedy CAR-X shops service the growing number of car owners who are holding on to their cars and maintaining them to last longer. They seek individuals with or without experience in the automotive aftermarket who are capable of taking advantage of this opportunity. The company currently offers prime regions in the Midwest to individuals who are willing to work hard and can deal effectively with customers and employees.

The company must approve your location before you can become a Speedy CAR-X franchisee; they will then provide you with a list of contractors who can help you develop your site. Your initial training consists of instruction at the company's Chicago headquarters and company involvement in the opening of your shop. You will learn about auto parts and products, equipment used in servicing cars, and service center management. Speedy CAR-X will supply you with an invaluable operations manual and make sure your shop gets off to a running start.

Throughout your career as a Speedy CAR-X franchisee, the company will be available at all times for telephone consultation. Company representatives will work as troubleshooters on specific business problems you might encounter, and other staff will answer any technical questions that might arise. In addition, the company will conduct refresher training for you whenever they feel it is necessary, so you will be able to keep up to date on every aspect of the automotive service industry. All of the equipment and supplies that you use must meet Speedy CAR-X specifications. Once the company approves your suppliers, you may purchase directly from them with no further supervision by Speedy CAR-X.

If you have previous experience in some capacity in the auto aftermarket, you will be that much better prepared to own your own auto service shop. But Speedy CAR-X does not require that prospective franchisees have any previous technical knowledge. You will learn everything you need to know about the nuts and bolts of auto repair in the Speedy CAR-X training program. The company does, however, stress the importance of management skills in the successful operation of its franchises, so it seeks out franchisees with backgrounds in administration.

For further information contact:
   Bill Olsen, Director Franchise Operations, Speedy CAR-X Muffler & Brake, Inc.,
   8430 W. Bryn Mawr, Suite 400, Chicago, IL 60631, 312-693-1000 or
   1-800-736-6733

Windshield Repair

Novus Windshield Repair

Initial license fee: $2,900
Royalties: 6%
Advertising royalties: 2%
Minimum cash required: $10,000
Capital required: $3,600
Financing: None
Length of contract: 5 years

In business since: 1972
Franchising since: 1985
Total number of units: 625
Number of company-operated units: None
Total number of units planned, 1995: NA
Number of company-operated units planned, 1995: NA

Whether caused by flying debris or everyday driving stress, up to 75 percent of all car and truck windshield damage is repairable. The cost: about one-fifth the expense of replacing the glass. That's why most insurance companies are now waiving deductibles to encourage their policyholders to use the services of operations like Novus. And it's why Novus customers range from private car owners to auto dealers, fleet owners to government agencies . . . customers who have made Novus, according to *Venture* magazine, the fastest growing new franchise in America.

Novus franchisees repair cracks and breaks in vehicle windshields—headlamps, too. In a 30-minute process, pressure from an injector piston forces acrylic resin into the break, which acts as a strong bond that both prevents further cracks and improves the glass's optical clarity. The resin is then cured with an ultraviolet lamp; when complete, the repair—and the break—are virtually invisible.

The company also manufactures and distributes polishes designed to remove nicks and haze from most plastic surfaces. More importantly, Novus has developed the "scratch removal process," what it calls the only system available that actually eliminates scratches caused by faulty wipers from windshields. This extra service gives Novus operators an edge in the market. "Scratch removal helps fight competition. No one else has anything like this," one franchisee reports. Another states, "It's opened doors for my business. I have customers who wouldn't talk to me before who now use both my scratch removal and windshield repair services."

You have your choice of Novus franchise options: a windshield repair operation alone or a business that offers the scratch removal service, too. Either way, your major preparation is an extensive factory training course held at Novus's Minneapolis headquarters, where you will be taught the technical aspects of windshield repair (and also, if you're going that route, scratch removal), as well as business management and sales techniques. You'll learn repair skills by working on actual car and truck windshields, using the same patented Novus equipment you'll be wielding in your day-to-day labor. Starting by fixing simple "bullseye" breaks, you'll progress to star breaks, stress cracks, and other complex and difficult damage. Before the instruction is completed, you'll be adept in the most sophisticated forms of repair and scratch removal skills for handling the bulk of the windshield problems your customers can bring you.

Once you're in business, you'll be able to benefit from Novus's insurance relations program, which develops a coordinated windshield repair policy with leading carriers, and its national accounts program, which signs up major corporate clients, from car manufacturers to trucking companies, whose area affiliates will be using your services. Novus's advertising and promotion strategy, while hardly overlooking the private sector, focuses as well on regional and countrywide prospects that bring business to franchisees across the nation.

Your local Novus sales manager will extend further assistance in building and expanding your client list, and you'll find out about other leads and marketing tactics at the area and national sales conferences. In between, Minneapolis headquarters stays in touch with the monthly newsletter—the company couldn't resist naming it the "Crack Reporter"—which passes on information on new insurance carrier and fleet alliances and technical bulletins that brief you on product updates and new services being developed back at the Novus R&D labs.

For further information contact:
  Robin J. Smith, Vice President, Novus Windshield Repair, 10425 Hampshire
  Ave. S., Minneapolis, MN 55438, 612-944-8000 or 1-800-328-1117

8. *The Business Services Industry*

Contents

Accounting and Financial

Advantage Payroll Services
Checkcare Systems, Inc.
Check Express USA, Inc.
Control-o-fax Systems, Inc.
Creative Asset Management, Inc.
H & R Block, Inc.
National Financial Company
Triple Check Income Tax Services, Inc.

Advertising

All American Sign Shops, Inc.
American Fastsigns
Homes & Land Publishing Corporation
Money Mailer, Inc.
Signs By Tomorrow USA, Inc.
The Signery Corporation

Consulting and Brokerage

LGC & GBS Corporation
Manufacturing Management Associates (MMA)
Professional Dynametric Programs, Inc. (PDP)
Sales Consultants International
Sandler Sales Systems, Inc.

Miscellaneous

EBC Office Centers
Foliage Design Systems (FDS)
HQ Network Systems, Inc.
Independent Lighting Corporation

ProForma, Inc.
Python's Recycling, Inc.
The Office Alternative
Video Data Services

Postal and Shipping

Handle With Care Packaging Store, Inc.
Pack 'n' Mail Mailing Center
Packy the Shipper
Pak Mail Centers of America, Inc.
Shipping Connection, Inc.
UniShippers Association (USA)

Accounting and Financial

Advantage Payroll Services

Initial license fee: $14,500
Royalties: None (company charges wholesale fees for payroll processing
  services)
Advertising royalties: None
Minimum cash required: $14,500
Capital required: $21,000 to $48,000
Financing: $5,000 at 10%; 4 years
Length of contract: 10 years, 10-year option

In business since: 1967
Franchising since: 1983
Total number of units: 32
Number of company-operated units: 1
Total number of units planned, 1995: 75
Number of company-operated units planned, 1995: 1

An Advantage Payroll Services franchise, the company stresses, "is not a 'get-rich-quick' scheme." Nevertheless, it points out, "our better associates do enjoy substantial earnings while at the same time accumulating tremendous amounts of equity in the business."

Geared particularly for small companies—averaging 15 staffers with more than half employing fewer than 10—Advantage handles all payroll and related tax services. Clients range from restaurants to corner stores, doctors' offices to gas stations. Here's how the system works: Each pay period, you contact your clients, enter the relevant information—hours worked, new employee data, personnel status changes—into your computer, and transmit it by modem to the Auburn, Maine, home office. There, the Advantage team of computer and accounting experts processes the data and takes care of the payroll taxes, including the client's state and federal tax deposits, its quarterly and year-end tax reporting, and all IRS correspondence. The finished work is sent back by computer to you for printing and distributing checks and management reports. Guaranteed turnaround period: 24 hours.

Economies of scale mean highly competitive rates for the client—many pay only $10 a week. Advantage gives you total pricing discretion, charging you a flat wholesale fee for its services. At the company's suggested retail price, you'll earn a 55 percent gross profit per client.

With minimal overhead and operating capital, no inventories to carry, and no receivables, the major investment in an Advantage franchise is time and effort, not cash. These energies are primarily spent soliciting clients. While this will admittedly require a great deal of cold calling at first, by your third year, most of your new business should come through the referral network of accountants and banks that you have developed. You can operate your business right from your home, and the work is particularly well-suited to husband-and-wife teams, one going out in the field while the other covers the office.

During a two-week training period in Auburn, you'll learn how to operate the computer that will be your lifeline to the company; training also covers details about wage-and-hours law, employer regulations, and payroll taxes. You'll also work on polishing your sales technique, with the aide of role-playing and recording equipment. After the initial training, you'll receive at least 10 days of additional instruction and support in the field. As you are starting out, advantage staffers or more experienced franchisees will join you on sales calls and help you prepare seminars and presentations for securing business and establishing a network of contacts. And in your first year, you'll earn a bonus for every new client you bring in. Meanwhile, at the home office, the accountants and tax specialists keep abreast of new developments in their area and full-time systems analysts work to maintain and enhance the computer software you use.

Because the technical aspects of the services you offer are handled by the corporate office, you do not need to have a background in either computers or payroll. Nevertheless, while Advantage believes its training is thorough, it doesn't promise the impossible: The company states up front that the training cannot adequately prepare a franchisee with no direct sales experience. Thus, the company requires you to have a history of sales work, ideally involving contact with small businesses and with the emphasis on new account development.

For further information contact:
  David Friedrich, President, Advantage Payroll Services, 800 Center St., Auburn, ME 04210, 1-800-323-9648 (in Maine, 1-800-876-0178), fax 207-786-0490

Checkcare Systems, Inc.

Initial license fee: $20,000 to $40,000
Royalties: 5% of gross profit
Advertising royalties: 2% of membership fees
Minimum cash required: $65,000
Capital required: NA

Financing: NA
Length of contract: 8 years

In business since: 1982
Franchising since: 1985
Total number of units: 35
Number of company-operated units: 1
Total number of units planned, 1995: 65
Number of company-operated units planned, 1995: 1

Personal checks represent some 57 percent of all consumer payments, and 83 percent of consumers use them. Further, customers are more likely to make purchases when there isn't a lot of hassle with check approvals—and tend to spend more, too. Certainly, for the retailer, accepting payments by personal checks can be highly profitable. Except, that is, when bad checks result in large losses.

That's where Checkcare comes in. With franchises throughout the Southeast and plans to expand nationwide, the company offers a check protection and guarantee service for retailers of all types, from supermarkets and restaurants to department stores and medical clinics. Clients can pay an annual fee—based on the anticipated volume of returned checks—and receive reimbursement, within 15 days, for the checks' full face value. A contingency plan is also available, where retailer clients authorize Checkcare to handle all returned checks, receiving the face amount for every successful recovery.

Operating as a Checkcare franchisee in an exclusive territory, you'll also assume responsibility for collecting funds for bounced checks, as well as the bad check fees. Merchants value these services because they eliminate their need to swallow losses from bad checks and to engage in the time-consuming work of tracking down offenders and attempting to collect.

For Checkcare franchisees, however, this is a time-efficient and profitable enterprise. Using the company's advanced data processing and customized software, the nucleus of your operation, you'll be able to collect up to 90 percent of all qualified checks, a 20 percent to 50 percent better collection rate than retailers customarily achieve on their own. You'll give clients weekly reconciled statements of all returned checks. In addition, you'll supply information received from the home office and fellow franchisees and gathered on your own about habitual bad check offenders in the area. You'll even notify a client by phone, when necessary, about potential check risks. At the same time, you'll help your clients maintain customer good will. Checkcare client Bobby Muniz, owner of four Tennessee hair salons, gives one example: "When a longtime, regular customer of ours accidentally wrote a check that was returned, Checkcare made a special effort to handle the situation in a way that made our customer appreciate us even more."

You can run your Checkcare facility as a solo or two-person operation, expanding as business and revenues warrant. The specialized skills you require are taught during training. Beginning with classroom time at company headquarters, the instruction continues with hands-on practice at established franchise operations. The material, as well as Checkcare's ongoing support, centers on two areas: sales and operations.

The company's affiliation with major retail chains helps you create an immediate client base. According to Columbia, South Carolina, franchisee Steven Stafford, "Thanks to Checkcare's affiliations with national accounts, I had solid business from day one." The training, sales manuals, and promotional materials supplied by the company, as well as the regular regional sales meetings, provide additional information and motivation for building your operation. As far as actually running your business, the easy-to-learn software and other Checkcare systems are fully explained during the training and in detailed manuals. In addition, there's a modem link with the home office for computer troubleshooting and other assistance.

One more area in which Checkcare serves both its franchisees and its clients is the company's lobbying effort aimed at strengthening the legal penalties on bad checks. And already, Checkcare can claim its influence helped lead to the increase of return fees to $20 per check in several states.

For further information contact:
  Michael Stalnaker, Vice President, Franchise Division, Checkcare Enterprises, Inc., P.O. Box 9636, Columbus, GA 31908, 404-563-3660

Check Express USA, Inc.

Initial license fee: $24,500
Royalties: 5%
Advertising royalties: None
Minimum cash required: $127,000
Capital required: $111,000
Financing: None
Length of contract: 15 years

In business since: 1982
Franchising since: 1988
Total number of units: 76
Number of company-operated units: 25

Total number of units planned, 1995: 125
Number of company-operated units planned, 1995: 30

Even with the proliferation of electronic banking, check usage is expected to increase well through the next decade. Yet because of the deregulation of financial services during the early 1980s, resulting in more restrictive requirements for opening and maintaining checking accounts and higher service fees, some 25 percent of Americans do not have checking accounts. Numerous account holders without access to 24-hour banking have regular trouble cashing checks as well. Yet, while check-cashing operations are flourishing, there is still no dominant national presence among them.

This huge potential for expansion is a key reason why *Success* magazine recently named Check Express USA one of its top 10 new franchises, the choicest franchise opportunity among all financial service enterprises. Check Express's management believes it's their emphasis on computer operations that brings the competitive advantage. According to executive vice president J. J. Moran, the computerized "Professional Check Cashing System" "gives us and our franchisees a degree of control not available to other check cashers."

Not difficult to learn or operate, this system will allow you, for a competitive fee, to cash almost any kind of check—payroll, government, and personal checks, money orders, insurance drafts, and wire transfers—with little or even no ID required from the customer . . . and with surprisingly little risk. Check Express's rate of losses from bad checks, about 0.2 percent, is actually significantly lower than that of many major banks. Your center will offer other services, too, including money order sales and money transfer opportunities, and you might also choose to offer mail box rentals, photo ID production, and notary services.

The fact that your Check Express store will be open after banking hours and on weekends (typical hours are 8 to 8 Monday–Saturday and 10 to 4 on Sunday), with usually short lines, means that a large portion of your clientele will be bank account holders who prefer the convenience of your services for many of their routine check cashing needs. A recent survey in five major cities, in fact, found that some two-thirds of check cashing center customers did have some kind of bank account. Meanwhile, because you can cash checks without requiring ID, you will also have virtually exclusive access to a large segment of the market that has no other check cashing opportunities. Your typical customer will come to cash his or her paycheck, often buying money orders for rent and utility payments, and will return each week.

Check Express enlists its national demographics firm in assisting you with site selection; other considerations include visibility, parking, and location of competitors. Contrary to popular opinion, a check cashing center need not be located in unsafe, unsavory parts of town, and upscale shopping centers are among the most common locales for a Check Express store. The company also furnishes advice in negotiating lease terms, and must approve any lease agreement before you sign. Floor plans and material and design specifications for the construction of your store (on average, 1,000 to 1,200 square feet) are provided by company architects. Going against the image of check cashing centers as dim and cluttered, whose chief decor motif is cage-like bars, the look of Check Express locations is bright, clean, and streamlined, with well-coordinated color schemes.

New franchisees receive two weeks of training, either at one of the company-owned stores or at Check Express's Tampa headquarters, with additional information given in detailed manuals. Together this material covers instruction in the computer system and such areas as cash management, inventory control, accounting, company policies, and customer and employee relations. You'll receive a grand opening package that includes PR materials for your store's opening. The company supplies prototype media ads, and for those operating in an area with more than one Check Express center, co-op advertising is available as well. Extending ongoing training, company managers make periodic visits for on-site assistance and assessment of your operation and personnel; local field seminars are also held to introduce updated computer systems that are regularly being honed by home-office programmers and at the company-owned stores.

For further information contact:
  Michael Riordon, Director of Franchise Sales, Check Express USA, Inc., 5201 W. Kennedy, Suite 750, Tampa, FL 33609, 813-289-2888 or 1-800-521-8211

Control-o-fax Systems, Inc.

Initial license fee: $14,000
Royalties: None
Advertising royalties: None
Minimum cash required: $3,000
Capital required: $20,000 to $50,000 in working capital to pay for the first
  year's expenses
Financing: Company will finance part of the franchise fee (up to $11,000) with
  a 2-year note
Length of contract: Continuous

In business since: 1969
Franchising since: 1971
Total number of units: 65
Number of company-operated units: None
Total number of units planned, 1995: 80
Number of company-operated units planned, 1995: None

Control-o-fax is a franchised dealership through which you market Control-o-fax office automation systems to health care professionals.

The market for these products has expanded rapidly in recent years. In 1985, there were 15,000 group medical practices in America providing daily patient care. That figure is projected to reach over 30,000 by 1995. Medicare, and the expansion of private insurance plans, have created a glut of paperwork for these doctors.

Control-o-fax has been making products to deal with doctors' administrative problems since 1948. Control-o-fax Computer Systems benefit physicians by accelerating cash flow, streamlining insurance processing, increasing staff productivity, lowering paperwork costs, increasing patient flow, freeing doctors' time to treat patients, preparing management reports, and providing more efficient records control.

Your own cash flow problems are kept to a minimum, you are not required to maintain an inventory, and there are no tedious bookkeeping chores. Control-o-fax takes the responsibility for collecting all accounts receivable and reporting and filing of sales tax.

You will be trained to sell Control-o-fax Computer Systems at the Control-o-fax headquarters in Waterloo, Iowa, and in your market area. Your training begins with a brief period of field training in your territory to get you oriented to the nature of the business. Then you will receive two weeks of formal classroom training in Waterloo. After putting your newly acquired skills to work in your market, you will spend an additional week at corporate headquarters for an advanced seminar.

Control-o-fax regional managers serve as business advisors to franchisees in the field. Managers also help you set up your office and make sales calls. Your regional manager will have responsibility for no more than 25 franchisees and will be available for consultation at any time.

For further information contact:
  Sandy Reicks, Franchise Director, Control-o-fax Systems, Inc., Box 5800, Waterloo, IA 50704, 319-234-4896 or 1-800-553-0011

Creative Asset Management, Inc.

Initial license fee: $12,500 to $17,500
Royalties: $300/month
Advertising royalties: None
Minimum cash required: $14,500 to $19,500
Capital required: $14,500 to $19,500
Financing: Yes
Length of contract: 15 years

In business since: 1982
Franchising since: 1988
Total number of units: 40
Number of company-operated units: None
Total number of units planned, 1995: 200
Number of company-operated units planned, 1995: None

With the heyday of the 1980s financial whirlwind long over, most Americans are searching for safe, sensible, and profitable investment opportunities. Creative Asset Management franchisees show clients how they can embark on a long-term savings and investment plan and use long-term investment strategies to minimize risk. Instead of aiming for the oversaturated upper-class financial planning market, Creative Asset Management targets middle- and upper-middle-class Americans, many of whom have pressing needs to save money for their children's college education or their own retirement.

Creative Asset Management franchisees are trained in the company's exclusive START NOW program, which teaches franchisees how to motivate both themselves and their clients to earn more money by investing for the future. Clients pay Creative Asset Management agents a set fee—usually based on an hourly rate—to help them choose and then transact appropriate investments. No broker's fee is exacted from the money invested, however: The full amount is applied directly to the stock itself.

Although no previous financial experience is required, all franchisees must pass industry and state examinations to become Registered Investment Advisors. Help in passing the exams is provided by the home office. In addition, Creative Asset Management offers its franchisees complete training and ongoing support through newsletters, seminars, and workshops.

For further information contact:
  Christopher Kau, Creative Asset Management, Inc., 120 Wood Ave. S.,
  Suite 300, Iselin, NJ 08830, 1-800-245-0530

H & R Block, Inc.

Initial license fee: Refundable deposit of $600, $800, or $1,200
Royalties: 50% of first $5,000, then 30%, 20% when average of previous 2-year
    volume exceeded
Advertising royalties: None
Minimum cash required: $5,000 to $8,000
Capital required: $5,000 to $8,000
Financing: None
Length of contract: 5 years

In business since: 1955
Franchising since: 1956
Total number of units: 8,955 worldwide
Number of company-operated units: 4,087
Total number of units planned, 1995: NA
Number of company-operated units planned, 1995: NA

Each year in late winter, as sure as death and taxes, the H & R Block commercials begin to appear on television. A comfort to many people who can't or don't want to deal with the rigors of wading through income tax forms, Block has carved a unique niche for itself in the U.S. economy. It prepares about 10 percent of all federal income tax returns filed, each with a written guarantee. In addition, it pledges to be available to answer questions from its customers year-round and to accompany them to an audit, if necessary, to explain how their taxes were calculated. In recent years, Block has expanded its client base by offering electronic filing and refund anticipation loans to both its tax preparation clients and those who prepare their own returns or use another service.

The company runs offices in major population areas and serves smaller communities through its satellite franchising program. If you think such a franchise would do well in your own area, or in a neighboring community, look in the phone book. If you can't find a listing for H & R Block, or if the company seems underrepresented relative to the population of your area, you may have the opportunity to start a good business.

You will need a thorough knowledge of taxes to operate this business. Your tax and management training takes place in the region where you will open your office. You will pay for the travel and lodging expenses related to your training. The company uses a variety of instructional techniques, including videocassettes and audiocassettes and role-playing, in addition to formal classroom instruction. Subjects covered include accounting, marketing, sales, staffing, and management. Your ongoing business will receive support from a district office, and the company will update you with bulletins and other communications about any changes in the tax laws and company procedures. You can receive additional tax training in the summer and fall at many locations in your region.

H & R Block supplies, without charge, everything necessary for you to run your operation, aside from the stationery and office machines usually found in an accounting office. As long as your office appearance meets the company's minimum standards, its specific location is up to you.

For further information contact:
  Field Operations: Franchise Inquiries, H & R Block, Inc., 4410 Main St., Kansas City, MO 64111, 816-753-6900

National Financial Company

Initial license fee: $18,000
Royalties: Fee sharing
Advertising royalties: None
Minimum cash required: $18,000
Capital required: $18,000
Financing: None
Length of contract: 4 years

In business since: 1970
Franchising since: 1970
Total number of units: 609
Number of company-operated units: 1
Total number of units planned, 1995: 900
Number of company-operated units planned, 1995: 1

Finding capital to finance a business venture can be as simple as using a computer dating service. Leonard vander Bie, formerly with the Allstate Mortgage and Investment Company, borrowed the concept of using a computer to match two people who have not been able to find suitable dates and applied it to the search for investment capital. He assembled a data base of potential investors and lenders that people seeking capital may tap for a fee—and an additional commission if they find an investor or lender through his service.

The company's data base contains more than 15,000 sources of capital, with a description of the types of businesses they will consider funding. Investors and lenders include financial and insurance companies, pension funds, leasing companies, brokers, and others. Among the types of funds available are venture capital, accounts receivable, financing, purchase lease backs, mortgages, and start-up capital. Clients might be able to locate some of these sources on their own, but it would take a lot of time and money to track down possible sources and make a presentation to each.

Not only do entrepreneurs get access to possible sources of funding through a National Financial outlet, they also get the services of a financial consultant who will help them prepare a proposal, summarize it for computer matching, and then print and mail the proposal to investors whose interests match theirs.

The company emphasizes that typical clients have unusual investment proposals that have not attracted funding from banks, insurance companies, and other conventional sources. In fact, National Financial will not accept as a client anyone who has not exhausted ordinary sources first. Leonard vander Bie points out that since clients pay both a fee to the company and a commission, if successful, they should not use the service if they can secure funding in ordinary ways. "We are a court of last resort," says vander Bie, "and if a client has a good idea, but is unsophisticated about financial matters, he would be angry if we charged him all these fees and then found he could have gotten the money for less from a more conventional source."

The company is careful to make sure clients realize that, at best, they might get about eight positive responses to their proposal, which only means that an investor or lender wants to hear more and will at least consider it. More often than not, they get no response. But at least this gives the client the satisfaction that they have tried every last possibility. As the company puts it: "Give the capital source a chance to say no."

Getting into this business, if you have "a well-rounded business background" and the money to invest, is as simple as the concept that underlies the enterprise. National Financial Company will train you for three days at your office, which could be in your home. You train hands-on, working with actual clients who need to find lenders or investors. And any additional help you may need at any time is available by phone from National Financial Company.

For further information contact:
  Leonard H. vander Bie, National Financial Company, 7332 Caverna Dr.,
  Hollywood, CA 90068, 213-969-0100

Triple Check Income Tax Services, Inc.

Initial license fee: $1,500 to $3,500 annual fee, paid each year (based on gross
  revenue in current practice)

Royalties: Depends on new income generated from franchise work and
    decreases as volume builds
Advertising royalties: $700/year
Minimum cash required: NA
Capital required: None
Financing: Available
Length of contract: 5 years

In business since: 1941
Franchising since: 1961
Total number of units: 340
Number of company-operated units: None
Total number of units planned, 1995: 500
Number of company-operated units planned, 1995: None

Americans dread the annual ritual of filing income tax returns. More
and more depend upon outside help to do the complicated chore of
tax preparation. For over a half century, Triple Check Income Tax Services, Inc., has been taking care of business for millions of taxpayers.
It is now the second-largest tax preparation franchise in the nation.

What makes Triple Check so profitable—with network-wide sales of
over $85 million in 1991—is its ability to keep busy throughout the
year. Fearing operation costs will outweigh consultation fees between
seasons, most professional preparers close their offices as soon as
April's 1040 roar dwindles to a whisper of taxes gone by. Triple
Check, however, avoids that seasonal trap by providing the year-round
services many savvy taxpayers look for in order to organize their fil-
ings, as well as other forms of financial planning. By gaining the reputation of being a full-year player, Triple Check has "managed to win
confidence and add products," according to the company's president,
David Lieberman.

Financial planners, accountants, and bookkeepers are chief among
Triple Check franchisees. For an annual fee of $1,500 to $3,445 (determined by gross revenue), the franchisee gets the chance to use the
Triple Check name and operating system for five years across a territory that covers an eight- to ten-mile radius. With 340 franchises in
operation now and 160 more projected for 1995, franchisees buy into
an operation with extensive name recognition. And in a field where
clients must trust preparers with their finances, this built-in credibility
is a tremendous asset.

In order to maintain its standing as a high-quality tax preparer, Triple Check requires all franchisees to learn and use standardized operating procedures. Training is somewhat intensive, but it is essential,
consisting of 38 to 96 hours of at-home study. This basic training is
enhanced by mandatory attendance at an annual professional conference and a yearly tax law seminar. Once on the job, franchisees al-

ways have access to Triple Check's tax research department—information can be gotten over the phone.

Triple Check offers a solid opportunity for working within the home. For an annual flat fee of $700, the company lets you in on its elaborate marketing and promotional campaigns, so you won't have to spread the word by yourself. With the demand for financial planning rising, Triple Check's hard-earned reputation has the potential to carry it far into the nineties.

For further information contact:
   David W. Lieberman, 727 S. Main St., Burbank, CA 91506, 213-849-3100 or 1-800-283-1040

Advertising

All American Sign Shops, Inc.

Initial license fee: $10,000
Royalties: 6%
Advertising royalties: 1% (currently waived)
Minimum cash required: $25,000
Capital required: $25,000 plus 6 months' living expenses
Financing: Equipment leasing, $10,000 to $20,000
Length of contract: 10 years

In business since: 1985
Franchising since: 1987
Total number of units: 18
Number of company-operated units: 1
Total number of units planned, 1995: 50 to 70
Number of company-operated units planned, 1995: 1

All American Sign Shops offers its franchisees surprisingly simple entry into the booming "instant sign" business. Neither signmaking experience nor great artistic talent is required—most franchisees, in fact, have little of the former and, probably, vary greatly on the latter. The technical skills of instant signmaking are easily learned, and the details of running a successful signmaking enterprise are within the grasp of any hardworking, entrepreneurial type even without prior business experience.

What's more, the limited overhead means you can open for business without excessive up-front capitalization. Franchisees have a variety of start-up franchise packages from which to choose. You can opt for a basics-only small business initially, expanding as sales increase and you develop an understanding of your particular market, or jump right in with a full-service store—or stores—backed by heavy, aggressive marketing.

With each option, you receive the equipment, training, and ongoing support you need to provide your services and product to your customers. All American's client base is almost exclusively business owners and managers—from virtually every area of commerce. Using computer-cut vinyls, especially well suited for exterior signs, you can produce banners, storefront displays, screen printing, logo reproductions, vehicle, window, and architectural lettering and graphics, and presentation materials in a wide variety of sizes, shapes, colors, and price ranges. The computer equipment allows you to compose and modify the signs easily, accurately, and far more quickly and cheaply than a traditional signpainter can.

A site-selection expert from the home office will work with you in researching potential locations for your operation, and the home office will negotiate the property lease for you, if you wish. Using master blueprints, another company representative helps in the setup of your store or workspace. You can be open for business in 60 to 90 days.

Meanwhile, you'll receive one week of training, covering, most importantly, instruction in sign production and equipment use, as well as bookkeeping, marketing, daily operations, and customer relations. Additional on-site training is available, although experience has shown that most subsequent queries and problems can be handled by telephone. The ongoing support is concrete: research and development to help you keep your equipment and services up to date and on par with the competition, technical assistance, sales analysis, marketing campaigns, and training of the extra employees that many franchisees find themselves needing to hire as their business grows.

For further information contact:
  Mark Richie, President, All American Sign Shops, Inc., 1460-A Diggs Dr., Raleigh, NC 27603, 919-833-9200 or 1-800-966-2700, fax 919-834-5333

American Fastsigns

Initial license fee: $18,500
Royalties: 5.5%
Advertising royalties: 2%
Minimum cash required: $35,000
Capital required: $80,000 to $100,000
Financing: SBA-approved; leasing also available
Length of contract: 20 years

In business since: 1985
Franchising since: 1986
Total number of units: 170
Number of company-operated units: 1
Total number of units planned, 1995: 210
Number of company-operated units planned, 1995: 1

"In other fields I've worked in," remarks suburban Chicago Fastsigns franchisee and former accountant Janet Goldberg, "it was difficult even to see what part of the project was mine. But when you get to hand the customer a good-looking sign you made with your own two hands—that's something to take pride in."

You'll be able to create a beautiful sign with your own two hands, too, with a little help from your computer, a computer that allows you to produce those extremely durable, professional-looking signs in a wide variety of type styles, colors, and materials—and in about 24 hours. The range of sign products is vast, including banners up to 100 yards long, predesigned or specially developed vehicle and architectural graphics, window lettering that clients can either apply themselves or have you apply, and lightweight point-of-purchase materials. You won't be exaggerating when you tell customers, "You can turn any smooth surface, indoors or out, into a working advertisement for your business."

Speed and low cost are what have caused this relatively new industry to grow so rapidly and what make your service attractive to businesses of all sizes. Fastsigns President Gary Salomon elaborates, "Businesses don't have to wait weeks for a print ad to appear. With our high-tech system, they can just place their order one day, and the next day, that sign is there working for them." And it'll be there for a long time, too, guaranteed against fading for five years, with the vinyl graphics lasting indefinitely. Yet, durable as these signs are, many clients use Fastsigns on a regular basis, like retail stores changing their featured promotions or realtors updating property prices and interest rates.

One way to encourage this repeat business is, of course, by locating your store nearby. Fastsigns site-selection consultation emphasizes the importance not only of stores' being visible and accessible, but also of their being surrounded by the specific kinds of businesses that will provide a solid customer base. Your site-selection package features substantial demographic research establishing the parameters for selecting the most advantageous location in your region, followed up by a visit from a company site specialist. You'll also receive assistance in negotiating the lease, if you need it. To build the store, you'll have a complete design package, including a field-tested floor plan, equipment list, and suggested specifications for construction and design. In a typical Fastsigns store, a glass wall separates the lobby, decorated with graphics demonstrating the range of options you offer, from the manufacturing space, allowing customers to observe the signmaking process while the computer area is separated for quiet and privacy.

Fastsigns assumes you know nothing about graphics or computers, not to mention vinyl signmaking. That's taught in the three-week training program for you and one employee, conducted at the Dallas headquarters, which combines classroom instruction and hands-on exercises in a production room mock-up. The material covered includes sign production and installation, accounting, equipment and supplies familiarity, employee training and management, counter and outside sales techniques, and public relations. After you receive the training, an "operations advisor" spends one week at your facility, planning your store opening with you, and continues to provide close guidance throughout your first six months of business by phone and through periodic visits.

To keep you abreast of company goings-on and recent developments in the vinyl sign industry, Fastsigns sponsors an annual meeting and sends out weekly operations bulletins and the unusually informative bimonthly company newsletter, *The Cutting Edge*. One recent issue included a private consultant's savvy advice on handling media calls and a business writer's equally astute advice on dealing with customer complaints, while a photo spread displayed some of the most innovative signs designed over the past months by Fastsign franchisees.

Fastsigns provides an ongoing national advertising campaign along with materials and advice for conducting your own local marketing efforts. Successful media ventures are shared—New Jersey franchisee Jack Schnoll recently had a 30-second TV spot produced for his region that was then reedited into a generic spot and made available to other Fastsign franchisees.

Marketing-oriented individuals like Schnoll are the kind of franchisees Fastsigns says it's seeking. Because the 24-hour retail sign industry is becoming crowded, Fastsigns makes a point of stressing that it relies on its franchisees to help propel the company and keep it well positioned. Beyond the personal and financial qualifications, a strong franchise candidate, the company believes, has had business experience as well as a proven track record of success in past endeavors.

For further information contact:
  Wes Jablonski, Franchise Sales Director, American Fastsigns, Inc., 4951 Airport Parkway, Suite 530, Dallas, TX 75248, 214-702-0171 or 1-800-827-7446

Homes & Land Publishing Corporation

Initial license fee: $20,000 (Homes & Land); $20,000 (Homes & Land Digest);
    $1,500 (Home Guide); $20,000 (Rental Guide)
Royalties: 10.5%
Advertising royalties: None
Minimum cash required: $14,000 to $109,000
Capital required: $14,000 to $109,000
Financing: None
Length of contract: 10 years

In business since: 1973
Franchising since: 1984
Total number of units: 300
Number of company-operated units: 3
Total number of units planned, 1995: 340
Number of company-operated units planned, 1995: 6

In the real estate boom of the 1980s, people found scores of ways to make money from the buying and selling of buildings and land, often by investing "other people's money." The bookstores featured many how-to titles on the subject, and late-night TV ran countless advertisements for audiocassette courses that taught people to become real estate millionaires.

Of course, many people still make a living in this field the old-fashioned way—they earn it by working as real estate agents and brokers. Now, Homes & Land Publishing Corporation provides still another way an ambitious person can make it in real estate—with a little hard work. You can publish one of those real estate magazines given away in banks, supermarkets, restaurants, and other public places. The magazine contains listings from local brokers, with photographs of the houses that are for sale. There are about ten such multiregional magazines currently in circulation, but *Homes & Land Magazine* is the biggest, with local editions in more than 300 locations in 43 states.

Homes & Land Publishing Corporation calls its franchisees associate publishers—a fancy title for real estate advertising salespeople. Your work involves convincing brokers in your community to place their listings in the local edition of *Homes & Land*. Usually, real estate brokers rely on newspaper advertising, on-site signs, referrals, and a multiple listing service to get listings and make sales. The company therefore has to provide its associate publishers with good arguments to use in persuading brokers to place their advertisements in its magazine.

According to the franchisor, people who want to sell their home are more likely to list with a broker who advertises in the magazine because they like to see a picture of their house in an advertisement. The magazine sweetens this appeal with an offer to brokers to photograph houses if they don't have good pictures. People also tend to retain the magazine longer than a newspaper, and there is thus more time for them to react to an advertisement—perhaps having second thoughts about a house they initially passed up.

Franchisees selling advertisements can offer brokers another special service. The magazine lists the locations of its other local editions. A reader thinking of moving to one of these places can call a toll-free number listed in the magazine to get a free copy of the publication in that area. Thus local brokers who advertise can reach a potential buyer in another town. In addition, brokers in the communities from which people have called receive the names of those people. People thinking of moving may have a house to sell, and the broker in their area can use this as a lead for new listings. Homes & Land also offers a unique package of marketing and direct mail services designed to provide real estate brokers with easier means of contacting potential buyers and sellers and a way to create additional advertising materials.

Who qualifies to be a Homes & Land associate publisher? "They are established, participating residents of their communities and bring with them a successful record of growth and productivity in other facets of business," according to company president Douglass Tatum. And they have a "strong desire to be independent." Currently, the prospect for openings is best in the upper Midwest.

Homes & Land falls into the category of home-based franchises, because franchisees collect the material to be published and send it on to company headquarters in Tallahassee, where it is printed. However, some franchisees have gone on to open up separate offices.

Franchisees must go to Tallahassee for their training. You pay for your own transportation, but the company will pick up part of the expense for your lodging. Training lasts a week and includes instruction on photographing houses, as well as sales training and a tour of the company's facilities. Annual sales meetings include follow-up sales training. District sales managers act as liaisons between the company and its associate publishers, providing ongoing support for franchisees.

For further information contact:
  Vice President, Sales, Homes & Land Publishing Corporation, P.O. Box 5018, Tallahassee, FL 32301, 904-574-2111

Money Mailer, Inc.

Initial license fee: $22,000
Royalties: 10%
Advertising royalties: None
Minimum cash required: $5,000
Capital required: $27,000
Financing: Yes
Length of contract: 5 years

In business since: 1979
Franchising since: 1980
Total number of units: 376
Number of company-operated units: 2
Total number of units planned, 1995: 871
Number of company-operated units planned, 1995: 2

Cooperative direct mail is recognized as one of today's best money-saving opportunities for consumers and one of the most reliable ways for businesses to increase their sales. Money Mailer produces cooperative direct mail envelopes chock-full of local, regional, and national advertisements. These well-known red, white, and blue envelopes are sent to 65 million homes across the United States each year. Money Mailer franchise owners arrange for businesses to place their advertisements in the envelopes.

Through cooperative direct mail, businesses can easily participate in coupon offers, brochures, mail orders, and catalogue sales opportunities without the expense of conducting their own direct mail campaign. This form of advertising achieves 100 percent market saturation, and when you consider that according to recent surveys, more than 87 percent of people receiving direct mail want it; 86.5 percent open it; and 72.5 percent use one or more of the coupons, cooperative direct mail is clearly today's advertising medium of choice.

Money Mailer, Inc., has been in business since 1979 and has earned a reputation for quality, value, and leading edge technology in design, production, and distribution of direct mail. Money Mailer has pioneered a variety of programs, including the 6-by-9-inch envelope format, computer design, and, most recently, full-color printing. With nearly 400 franchises in operation, Money Mailer is the number one cooperative direct mail franchisor: *Direct Mail Advertiser* ranked it number one for seven consecutive years; *Success* magazine ranked it 12th out of 100 in its "Gold Franchises for 1991."

With an initial $22,000 license fee, the local franchise owner receives an exclusive territory of approximately 40,000 homes. Because all design and layout services are provided by the regional franchise owner, local franchisees can easily run their businesses from home.

With low receivables, no inventory, and no storefront requirements, sales pros can concentrate on what they do best—selling. Money Mailer provides three weeks of comprehensive training in sales, management, and communications techniques, as well as providing continuing regional training programs and aggressive advertising and promotional campaigns.

For further information contact:
   Money Mailer, Inc., Franchise Sales Department, 14271 Corporate Dr., Garden Grove, CA 92643, 1-800-624-5371 (1-800-MAILER-1)

Signs By Tomorrow USA, Inc.

Initial license fee: $17,500
Royalties: 6%
Advertising royalties: 1%
Minimum cash required: $20,000
Capital required: $60,000 to $80,000
Financing: Available
Length of contract: 10 years

In business since: 1986
Franchising since: 1986
Total number of units: 16
Number of company-operated units: 2
Total number of units planned, 1995: 150
Number of company-operated units planned, 1995: 3

Even though the technology for computer-generated signmaking is highly refined and the demand for the service well proven, there are still a surprisingly small number of "instant sign" shops operating in retail areas. Several companies are scrambling to get a national toehold in this market. And Signs By Tomorrow, offering even same-day service, high quality, a five-year guarantee, and competitive prices, is considered one of those with the highest potential.

SBT franchisees and their staffs use desktop computers to design and cut vinyl to exact specifications. The vinyl—lettering, graphics, and client logos available in a wide variety of sizes and colors—can then be transferred to any smooth surface, be it Plexiglas, wood, metal, banner material, store windows, or vehicle bodies. The results are indoor and outdoor signs and banners for a complete range of businesses, including retailers, realtors, restaurants, auto dealerships, and ad agencies, as well as schools, temples and churches, or any organization or individual sponsoring a special event.

An SBT center, about 1,600 to 1,800 square feet, located in a retail shopping center, functions both as a store, where you'll display your full range of products and services and receive walk-in business, and as a layout facility, where you'll produce all the work itself. A three- to five-person staff is usually sufficient. Normal operating hours are Monday through Friday, from 8:30 to 6:00—since your clients are primarily businesses that are closed themselves on weekends—allowing you to enjoy a more regular work schedule than many other entrepreneurial ventures require.

Managers from SBT will work closely with you to devise short- and long-term strategies and objectives for your facility, using the company's business development systems. Once the franchise agreement is signed, you and the company will create budgets and a formal business plan, which can help you obtain financing if you need it and will later be used for monitoring the progress of your operation. Reviewing market demographics and rent factors with you, an operational advisor will assist in site selection and lease negotiation. Then, using the store design package specifically created for your facility, he or she will oversee the installation of the computer equipment, bought at a significant cost savings through SBT's national purchasing agreements, and help you furnish the store, develop your initial inventory order, and advertise and hire staff prior to your opening. You can have additional support in your daily operations, employing an accounting and billing service that the company will help you select and the payroll service SBT engages at a discount price, or you can choose to handle these details yourself, using the software and forms the company provides. You'll submit quarterly financial statements and have an annual business review meeting with SBT executives to discuss your results for the prior year and set goals for the next 12 months.

The specifics of running a signmaking business are not overlooked. You and your manager will attend a two-week training program at SBT headquarters in the Washington/Baltimore area, designed around the assumption that you're new to the sign industry and have little prior knowledge about computers. The sessions involve both classroom and in-store training, covering such areas as the techniques of computer signmaking and installation, business management, employee training and management, merchandising, counter and outside sales, supplies and materials, and marketing and advertising. For two additional weeks, you and your staff will receive guidance at your store, one week oriented around setting up your facility and teaching your employees how to use the computer equipment, and one week preparing for the actual opening of your store. Your trainer will follow up with weekly visits during your first 90 days in business. And there's further ongoing support in the form of regional workshops, company research and development to help you keep your equipment and methods up to date, and quarterly newsletters.

Marketing assistance begins with a start-up package providing a detailed market analysis for your region and including the name, address, phone number, and contact person for every company in your exclusive territory—usually about 4,000 businesses that are your potential customers. SBT also furnishes you with a three-phase sales and marketing program: a direct mail package featuring an initial mailer, promotional offers, and thank-you cards for new customers; a press kit, supplying news releases for your store's opening; and yellow pages display advertising. And you receive more than the paperwork alone, with a company marketing rep who has extensive direct mail and advertising experience aiding you in implementing these and other programs.

For further information contact:
   Joseph McGuinness, Vice President, Signs By Tomorrow USA, Inc., 6460
   Dobbin Rd., Columbia, MD 21045, 410-992-7192 or 1-800-765-7446, fax
   410-992-7675

The Signery Corporation

Initial license fee: $19,900
Royalties: 6%
Advertising royalties: 2%
Minimum cash required: $19,900
Capital required: $50,000 to $60,000 with leased equipment
Financing: None, but consulting available
Length of contract: 20 years

In business since: 1986
Franchising since: 1986
Total number of units: 35
Number of company-operated units: None
Total number of units planned, 1995: 300+
Number of company-operated units planned, 1995: 1 minimum

With the "instant sign" industry experiencing a level of growth unseen in the business services field since the quick-print boom in the 1960s, there are a variety of attractive franchise options available. The Signery has turned into one of the most successful, a feat confirmed by *Success* magazine, which listed this chiefly Midwest network as one of the top 100 franchises nationwide in any industry. Its achievement is due in large part to finding a special niche in the market, between one-person hand sign painters and multimillion-dollar corporations that design and build huge outdoor displays.

The Signery clientele, on the other hand, is primarily made up of small- to medium-sized businesses. President Rick Gretz says that Signery franchisees are employed by "hot dog stands, churches, and everyone in between." A wide variety of high-quality signs and graphic material can be produced for these customers at a speed unheard of in the days before computers, from architectural signage, advertising and promotion boards, point-of-purchase displays, and vehicle and window lettering to posters, banners, and billboards.

Signery stores usually occupy about 1,200 square feet and are located in heavy-traffic retail shopping centers. Staff size starts small—three persons is the average—but can expand as business does. The company supplies the equipment, the most important being the computerized signmaking machinery, and it can all be leased with a 10 percent down payment. Franchisees also have the option of obtaining much of their own equipment, as long as it meets corporate quality standards and fulfills the required material lists that are updated annually.

While it's the computer-driven signmaking equipment that made the development of instant sign shops possible, Signery franchisees do not need to have prior experience in computers, nor any artistic or even business management background. The company can teach operators what they need to know in the three-week training program conducted at the Naperville, Illinois, headquarters. The course features a combination of classroom and hands-on instruction, not only in operating a Signery shop, but also in layout and creative design, sales, marketing and advertising, bookkeeping, and hiring, supervising, and other management duties.

Signery personnel give start-up assistance right at the franchisees' shops for a minimum of three days. The company works with its operators to develop a grand opening kit, including a direct mail program and other proven promotional techniques. Ongoing marketing support is extended through an ad fund supplying new and creative ideas for advertising in newspapers, radio, and the yellow pages, corporate assistance on media selection, and public relations programs to build community goodwill. Operators also receive periodic visits from area coordinators, fellow Signery franchisees providing field assistance and consultation.

Regional seminars are held frequently to offer continuing education and a forum for the exchange of ideas. And for further feedback, a Franchise Advisory Council, made up of elected franchisees, meets regularly with company officials to voice their concerns and furnish valuable direction and suggestions.

For further information contact:
Franchise Marketing, The Signery Corporation, 1717 N. Naper Blvd., Suite 205, Naperville, IL 60563, 708-955-0700 or 1-800-695-4257

Consulting and Brokerage

LGC & GBS Corporation

Initial license fee: $19,500
Royalties: 7%
Advertising royalties: None
Minimum cash required: 6 to 12 months' living expenses plus $1,000 to $6,000
   in start-up costs, and $5,000 to $9,000 in travel and miscellaneous office
   expenses
Capital required: See minimum cash required
Financing: None
Length of contract: 10 years

In business since: 1962
Franchising since: 1962
Total number of units: 400
Number of company-operated units: None
Total number of units planned, 1995: 575
Number of company-operated units planned, 1995: None

The LGC & GBS market potential is limited only by the number of
professionals and small businesses in a given geographic area. With
more than 20 million small businesses nationwide, the market potential for most LGC & GBS franchises is virtually unlimited.

Every business has the need for LGC & GBS services. For example,
all businesses are required by law to keep records and file tax returns.
Many also need business management, personal financial planning,
and tax planning counseling.

LGC & GBS Corporation, through its franchisees, who are known as
LGC & GBS Business Counselors, offers small businesses and professionals a complete package of services and advice to help them prosper. LGC & GBS Business Counselors provide clients with a variety of
management services, including organization of financial records, tax
planning, and profit development counseling. They may help their clients formulate a business plan, project cash flow, or guide them toward making budget projections. LGC & GBS Business Counselors
help clients with everything from determining goals and priorities to
keeping accurate books.

As an LGC & GBS Business Counselor, you will most likely service
such businesses as owner-operated enterprises and professional offices
with 25 or fewer employees and no more than $1 million in gross
sales. The top ten LGC & GBS client categories, in descending order of
sales volume, are: contractors, auto repair and services, professionals,

retail stores, restaurants, business services, personal services, real estate, printing and publishing, and janitorial and related services.

LGC & GBS Business Counselors often begin by working out of their homes, opening an office only when cash flow permits, so an LGC & GBS franchise requires a relatively small initial investment. Franchisees usually have a college degree. Typically, LGC & GBS Business Counselors have finance, management, or sales experience. They also get along well with people.

Your initial training will be just the start of an intensive, ongoing effort by the company to teach you what you need to know. You will attend a two-week course at the Basic Training Institute at the national office in Columbia, Maryland. Within your first year, you will receive three days of field training from an experienced LGC & GBS Business Counselor. Then you may return to Columbia for advanced training. There are also seminars on tax preparation and business counseling offered frequently throughout the year, so you can continue your professional growth.

Support services from the LGC & GBS national office include the Tax and Business Advisory, which offers advice on incorporation, estate planning, and other issues. The tax preparation division, staffed by specialists in all tax fields, offers several levels of income tax return preparation so you can tailor your services to your clients' needs; it offers a guarantee of accuracy on all returns it prepares. Your clients will also receive *The LGC & GBS Advisor*, the company's tax newsletter for clients. LGC & GBS also provides telemarketing services to GBS Business Counselors. The telemarketers working from the national office set appointments for LGC & GBS Business Counselors with qualified small business owners and professionals.

You can also offer complete record-keeping systems customized to your clients' needs, whether they are more comfortable with a manual system or prefer a computerized system.

LGC & GBS directly serves you with a lending library of materials dealing with various business topics, and specialists whom you can hire by the day to help with particularly difficult problems.

How does all this work in practice? W. Paul Woody has been a franchisee in Oklahoma City since 1972. He counts on the company to help him give tax advice: "I do a lot of research for my small business clients. That is, they will ask me to check into how to handle a particular tax strategy, and I will go to GBS, Inc., for their output. This is very helpful because it allows me to give the correct answers to my clients without having to 'shoot from the hip.'"

W. Paul Woody has already renewed his franchise twice. He says he "could never have earned the kind of income I am generating today if

I had remained with the large company I was employed by when I purchased the franchise. And the independence, along with the excellent earnings potential, has allowed me to spend more time either on vacations or being active with my family."

Bruce Patterson is an LGC & GBS counselor in Burke, Virginia. After retiring as an Army officer, Patterson started a second career with LGC & GBS. He says, "The training I received at the GBS Training Institute, coupled with ongoing professional development programs and support, gave me the tools necessary to build a Business Counseling practice that serves the retail establishments, small manufacturers, and professionals in my community. Most importantly, I am enjoying what I have chosen to do in my second career, and as an independent businessman, I can control workload and thus profits."

For further information contact:
  Franchise Sales, LGC & GBS Corporation, 7134 Columbia Gateway Dr., Columbia, MD 21046, 1-800-638-7940

Manufacturing Management Associates (MMA)

Initial license fee: $5,000 to $50,000
Royalties: 7% to 9%
Advertising royalties: 1% maximum
Minimum cash required: $3,000 initial working capital
Capital required: $14,900 to $79,450
Financing: Some on initial fee
Length of contract: 10 years

In business since: 1982
Franchising since: 1990
Total number of units: 2
Number of company-operated units: 2
Total number of units planned, 1995: 12
Number of company-operated units planned, 1995: 2

Combining 35 years of experience, chairperson Roger E. Dykstra and CEO Alan D. Anderson created MMA to operate in a very specific market niche—management consulting for small to midsize manufacturing and distribution companies. These are businesses that need consulting services but don't find it economically feasible to turn to large consulting firms with their high overhead and unaffordable billing rates. Covering such areas as sales and marketing, service methodologies, systems and technology, human resource management, cost management, and process flow, MMA aims not only to offer the same quality, methodologies, and resources of larger consultants, but to provide specific expertise in the unique concerns and issues facing businesses that earn revenues of $10 million to $150 million and have from 20 to 500 employees.

An MMA franchise is a particularly viable opportunity for individuals with experience either in consulting firms or as an internal consultant, as well as owners of existing consulting firms who want to expand their practice. But MMA's training and support systems are also designed to accommodate those manufacturing executives, sales and marketing professionals, and managers of goods and services who do not have a specific consulting background.

A five-day initial training session at MMA headquarters introduces you to MMA's methodologies and systems, including instruction on computer systems and project management, and tested strategies for approaching decision-makers, writing better proposals, making presentations, bidding on a project, and closing a sale. You'll learn techniques of quickly identifying a prospective client's manufacturing management problems and then assessing the possible solutions, recommending relevant strategies and managing their implementation. You're also informed about MMA's marketing programs, which involve a balance of several approaches—direct mail, seminars, networking, telemarketing, and trade show participation—created and fine-tuned to the circumstances of your market, along with additional co-op advertising potential as the MMA network expands.

Start-up field support, beginning with site selection for the location of your office, is available as well. You're also kept abreast of developments in the manufacturing industry and MMA's new research through continuing education programs, and database and operations manual updates, and your business is monitored through periodic visits from an MMA rep who, beyond basic guidance and troubleshooting, will extend quality assurance reviews.

Beyond general training and ongoing assistance, MMA extends to you concrete support in seeking new clients, making effective proposals, and implementing contracted projects. MMA maintains a regularly updated data base of client leads in your market, companies that it often will have contacted and prescreened for their potential need of your services, providing the basis for your follow-up contact and minimizing your need for "cold calling." You'll also have regular access to MMA's library, an extensive gathering of proposals and game plans for you to benefit from the experience of others who've handled similar projects to the ones you'll be proposing or implementing. Then, there is access to the network of MMA Associates, often nationally known experts in a variety of specialized fields like quality control, warehouse and factory automation, and bar coding. Having these authorities on your team is a major selling point for your services—and helpful for executing your assignments. Finally, you'll be able to work with fellow MMA franchisees, who are available to be brought in on particularly challenging projects—and who will bring you in on large projects of their own. "The central idea of the program," say Dykstra and Anderson, "is the sharing of resources for mutual strength. By creating a system that not only makes such sharing possible, but actually encourages and facilitates it, we have created a dynamic system—a system that can continually develop, evolve, and grow with the knowledge of its members."

MMA offers one franchise in each major metropolitan area. While franchise owners aren't restricted from accepting consulting assignments anywhere they become available, you'll be granted an "area of primary responsibility" in which no other franchise will be awarded.

For further information contact:
  Alan D. Anderson, President, MMA Licensing Corporation, 1301 W. 22nd St., Suite 516, Oak Brook, IL 60521, 708-575-8700, fax 708-574-0309

Professional Dynametric Programs, Inc. (PDP)

Initial license fee: $29,500
Royalties: None ($1,000/year service fee after 6 months)
Advertising royalties: None
Minimum cash required: $15,000
Capital required: $5,000 to $10,000 working capital
Financing: 1-year interest-free notes
Length of contract: 7 years

In business since: 1978
Franchising since: 1980
Total number of units: 30
Number of company-operated units: None
Total number of units planned, 1995: 75
Number of company-operated units planned, 1995: None

Over 1,000 employers looking for a methodical way of evaluating their personnel turn to PDP. Through a system of surveys and computer analysis, PDP provides information its clients can use in hiring and developing their staffs. The data go a lot further than mere statistics: detailed profiles of workers and departments offering insight into such areas as the employees' strengths, weaknesses, motivators, logic abilities, stress and intensity levels, and morale. With this information, clients are able to implement changes that will help them in selecting new personnel—including more effective recruitment and interviewing techniques—as well as in matching people to jobs, building strong teams, and adjusting operations methods. The results can include better hiring decisions; reduced absenteeism, turnover, and dissatisfaction; and easier resolution of conflicts.

Does the PDP system work? Its clients think so, often much to their own surprise. "I never hire a new employee without first analyzing his PDP and discussing it with him," says one client, Toni Stephenson, president of Denver's General Communications, Inc. "This eliminates many potential problems and goes a long way towards establishing a good employer/employee relationship." As you might imagine, PDP has figures to back up its claims of accuracy—"reliability coefficients in the high .80s and .90s," to use statistician lingo. But mindful of the kind of human error and bias that can creep into personnel evaluations, one of PCP's top concerns is that its surveys do not discriminate on the basis of sex, age, race, or religion.

The first instinct might be that it's impossible statistically to quantify the intangible qualities with which these surveys are concerned, or that, in any event, the crunched numbers offer no valuable insight. Quite the contrary, according to satisfied PDP customers. Bill Redding, director of the Knoxville, Tennessee, News Sentinel Company, states, "To me, the greatest use is in providing a vehicle for understanding people. With this understanding has come a better functioning department." And consider the testimonial of one specialist in the field, Bonnie E. Bass, Ed.D., who used the program in case-study work. "The PDP instrument proved to be ideally suited to clarifying differences in work behaviors, motivators, and stressors. The statistics and underlying theories held up under scientific scrutiny." Dr. Bass was so impressed, in fact, that, to paraphrase the entrepreneurial pundit, she bought a franchise.

PDP franchisees sell the company's services to employers and organizations in every field, and then train their clients' chosen executive and management personnel in administering the surveys, evaluating the results, and implementing the programs that the survey outcomes warrant. That involves teaching classes of one to twelve (or more, if the client desires), where you'll explain how to use the sophisticated computer software system, which handles the scoring and survey analysis, and then confer the subtler skill of knowing what to do with that information.

To do this, you will need training yourself. Three and a half days of franchisee instruction are given either at the home office, or if you'll foot the extra expenses, at your facility. The session covers a general introduction to the PDP philosophy, along with the nitty-gritty of software implementation and teaching techniques until you or a staffer can be certified as a trainer for the PDP system.

Each franchisee must either be a trainer or have one working under

him or her at any time. Certification is valid for one year, with recertification classes offered on a regular basis. Because the systems and
information in this field are constantly being updated, keeping abreast
of the developments is crucial. Besides the recertification process,
you'll stay informed through newsletters and annual conventions
where new programs and research findings are presented, as well as
regional seminars for both you and your clients (plus prospects),
where innovative applications of the PDP program are examined,
based on the specific experiences of PDP users worldwide. Furthermore, you and your clients will have regular access to PDP consultants
who'll provide additional applied research and data evaluation.

PDP also supplies sales literature, promotional pieces, and press releases for announcing your services and helping you build your clientele. Your ongoing operation is a low-overhead enterprise, primarily
requiring just standard PC equipment, plus the software and teaching
materials PDP furnishes—no inventory and no expensive real estate or
capital improvements are necessary.

As for helping you determine whether a PDP franchise is the right
choice, the company figures the best way is by having you try the service yourself. Potential franchisees are invited to complete one of the
program surveys, and PDP will prepare your profile. You decide for
yourself: Is it valid? Insightful? Will it be interesting to learn—and
teach—how it's done? Will businesses in your area find such a service
useful? And, the key question: Do you want to be the one to try to
sell them on it?

For further information contact:
  Bruce M. Hubby, President, PDP, Inc., 400 W. Hwy. 24, Suite 201, Box 5289,
  Woodland Park, CO 80866, 719-687-6074, fax 719-687-8588

Sales Consultants International

Initial license fee: $35,000 to $45,000
Royalties: 7%
Advertising royalties: 0.5%
Minimum cash required: $35,000
Capital required: $18,000 to $36,000
Financing: None
Length of contract: 5 to 20 years

In business since: 1957
Franchising since: 1965
Total number of units: 160

Number of company-operated units: 24
Total number of units planned, 1995: 200
Number of company-operated units planned, 1995: 30

"Ours is a very personal business," describes Rhode Island Sales Consultants franchisee Peter Cotton. "Placing people in careers and working with companies to help them find the best people becomes highly intimate. Our organization is the same way."

That's a claim Sales Consultants is proud of, considering that it is the largest organization of its kind, nearly seven times the size of its nearest competitor. But the company manages to keep its focus clear and its services specialized, as expressed explicitly enough in the company's slogan: "Finding and placing sales, sales managers and marketing talent is our only business." A division of Management Recruiters International, itself the world's largest personnel search firm, Sales Consultants concentrates on locating and recruiting sales and marketing professionals for client companies in virtually any industry on an employer-paid contingency basis. Almost every Fortune 1000 firm, as well as hundreds of smaller companies, has used the services of a Management Recruiters division.

The very size of the Sales Consultants network, the first sales search firm to expand nationwide, is one of the key factors that makes your services so attractive to clients. The company's computer data base allows for a vast referral system distributing clients' personnel requirements among every Sales Consultants office, a system expanding to Canada, Europe, Asia, and Australia as the company continues to establish its international operations. This interoffice program also means greater revenues for you. Your shared efforts with fellow franchisees result in shared fees—22 percent of all Sales Consultants revenues, in fact, are attained through the system.

Successful franchisees, in the company's eyes, need talent in sales, communications, and that indefinite constant, "people skills." Some three-quarters were formerly managers with major companies. But potential franchisees need not have specific experience in personnel recruiting. These general skills, along with the specifics of the Sales Consultants operations and computer systems, are taught to you. You'll attend a three-week training session at Cleveland headquarters, followed by three more weeks at your office. The instruction involves a variety of techniques, including extensive use of videotapes and audiotapes, role-playing, and actual hands-on search and placement projects, for which you'll earn a fee. In addition, video training, along with one-on-one instruction, is furnished for your professional staff, as well as the broadcast of live training sessions via satellite. And you'll have the option of joining them in working as a "producing manager," performing account executive duties in addition to your management responsibilities and personally earning additional revenues.

Sales Consultants executives assist you in obtaining any necessary professional licenses, securing suitable office space and negotiating the lease, designing the layout of your office and selecting furniture and equipment, and setting up your filing, bookkeeping, and other operational systems. A national advertising and PR program in popular business and trade publications like *Fortune, Forbes, USA Today*, and the *Wall Street Journal* keeps the Sales Consultants name before the eyes of your prospective clients. Additional company support includes research and development programs, including semiannual updates of computer software; staff attorneys and accountants, there to provide tax and legal advice; regional meetings and workshops; and national conventions, with awards and incentive programs to encourage even greater productivity from you and your staff.

But the final responsibility rests with the franchisee. "We are autonomous," as Peter Cotton puts it, "and have the ability to make decisions regarding the operation of our business as if it was our own." And that, in the company's view, is the greatest incentive of all.

For further information contact:
   Robert Stidham, Director, Franchise Marketing, Management Recruiters International, Inc., 1127 Euclid Ave., Suite 1400, Cleveland, OH 44115-1638, 1-800-875-4000, fax 216-696-3221

Sandler Sales Systems, Inc.

Initial license fee: $25,000
Royalties: $908/month
Advertising royalties: None
Minimum cash required: $25,000
Capital required: NA
Financing: None
Length of contract: 15 years

In business since: 1967
Franchising since: 1983
Total number of units: 65
Number of company-operated units: None
Total number of units planned, 1995: 150
Number of company-operated units planned, 1995: None

"How can you win the Super Bowl," Sandler Sales Systems founder David Sandler asks, "if the opposing team has a copy of your playbook?" Contrary to the common opinion that the basics of salesmanship were settled long ago, Sandler found in his experience that the old rules were "totally out of step with today's realities." Further, he professes, the techniques of other long-established sales training seminars and tape programs are so familiar that "your client knows your strategy the minute you start talking."

Sandler himself didn't enter the sales world until age 36, but almost immediately came to the conclusion that the sales techniques he had been taught "made me feel like a clown." Over the course of five years of trial and error, he developed his own theories of effective salesmanship, and devised his training and motivational program, the "Sandler Selling System," for salespersons and sales managers. For the former, the program's goal is "more sales, more profitable sales, and more enjoyable sales"; for the latter, the aim is "to get your staff to do more, earn more—and love you for it." Drawing attention to the program, provocative sound-bite formulas peppered the seminars, statements like "Selling is a killer sport; if you can't kill, you can't sell" or "If I'm a salesman and there's a prospect and if it boils down to feeding my family or not feeding my family, I'm going to feed my family."

The Sandler System struck a responsive chord, and large numbers of clients wanted more than one-time-only training, leading Sandler to devise "The President's Club," an ongoing program for lifetime members. Sandler's claim is "the more often they come, the greater their rate of success." And Sandler Systems' own success as a company has been considerable, with over 15,000 President's Club members, and franchises in more than 60 cities. The company continues to offer limited or one-time programs, including public workshops, one- and two-day in-house private seminars, and corporate consulting packages, for individuals or companies of more modest means or shorter-term goals.

As a Sandler Systems franchisee, you'll be the one conducting the programs in your area, giving at least 20 hours a month of hands-on sales training to your clients: chairing President's Club meetings, leading seminars and workshops, running eight-week "Breakfast Club" series, and providing one-on-one counseling. The variety of programs you offer means your market will be wide ranging, from individual salespersons to small and medium-size businesses and even major corporations. The one-time seminars and shorter programs provide perhaps your best marketing tool for selling President's Club memberships, ensuring an ongoing relationship with your clients. The company will work with you to develop and expand your client base, furnishing new business through national advertising, lead-generating programs, and 800-line updates, and teaching you how—and where—to look for prospects on your own, through such means as attending trade shows and offering complimentary talks to companies and professional organizations.

Because you'll be providing a training and motivational service, it should be no surprise that the training you yourself will receive is a dominant element of the franchise package. You'll begin with the company's "Quick Start Program," which focuses on your first 90 days as a franchisee, teaching you how to conduct the Sandler System seminars and workshops, how to become familiar with your market, and how to devise an initial business plan. The company advises that you attend two or more "Quick Starts," at least 60 days apart, and the support material supplied at these sessions, including manuals, outlines, scripts, and program curricula, allows you to study and practice further at home. You're also expected to attend as many programs held by neighboring veteran Sandler franchisees as you can. Then, there are monthly franchisee instruction sessions, as well as the three-day "Quarterly Training School" held at the company's Baltimore headquarters. There, you'll be introduced to new Sandler programs with fresh material for you to offer your long-standing clients and attract prospective customers—some of the recent curriculum additions include the seminars "No More Cold Calls," "The Appointment Getter," and "Not For Sales People Only."

Finally, you'll be in touch with the home office on a regular basis, every day during your start-up period, about twice a week thereafter, voicing concerns, receiving advice, getting specific feedback on the pitches and techniques you're using to run your sessions and expand your business. As David Sandler proclaims—as always, armed with one of his trademark formulas for success—"the amount of times you call is in direct proportion to the amount of income you'll generate in the first year."

For further information contact:
  Phil Goodwin, Franchise Director, Sandler Sales Systems, Inc., 10411 Stevenson Rd., Stevenson, MD 21153, 1-800-638-5686 (in Maryland, 410-653-1993), fax 410-358-7858

Miscellaneous

EBC Office Centers

Initial license fee: $25,000
Royalties: 4%
Advertising royalties: 4%
Minimum cash required: $80,000 to $100,000
Capital required: $200,000 total investment

Financing: Financial guidance; recommended suppliers
Length of contract: 10 years, with two 5-year renewals

In business since: 1984
Franchising since: 1988
Total number of units: 22
Number of company-operated units: 20
Total number of units planned, 1995: 68
Number of company-operated units planned, 1995: 30

The largest executive office and shared-service company in the Southeast, with plans to expand nationwide, EBC has managed to avoid the difficulty many in the executive suite industry currently face in attracting sufficient numbers of quality customers. By providing office space and support services, EBC caters specifically to upscale and established client firms rather than the lower end of the market, the more marginal start-up businesses and entrepreneurs who tend to be poorer credit risks and to have higher turnover rates. Some 72 percent of its customers, in fact, are national and regional companies.

EBC centers provide what's known in the industry as "Class A" executive space—an office atmosphere radiating the look and feel of a major corporation. That makes your facility attractive to big firms seeking a territory office as well as to smaller businesses needing to present a "Fortune 500" image. Your tenants sign leases commonly of six months to one year at a time, for either furnished or unfurnished office space. If your market has a heavy concentration of transient businesspersons, offices can also be made available by the week, day, or even hour. And a client requiring a constant presence without regular office use can choose the "company identity option," using your facility as its business address and receiving full-time phone answering and mail services, with office space available purely on an as-needed basis.

In addition to leasing offices, furniture, and telephone equipment, you'll provide a staff who'll offer your clients a complete range of support services—word processing, sending and receiving material by fax or computer modem, photocopying, mass mailing, dictation, record keeping, and desktop publishing. As an extra means of revenue, you can offer these same services to other companies in your building with staff shortages.

Choosing that building is crucial—the prestige of the address, its accessibility, look and upkeep, and the efficiency of building services are among the most important selling points to your clients. A senior-level EBC executive will assist you with site selection and must, in fact, approve your location, afterward participating in the lease negotiation process. The company will then develop with you the layout and design of your center—a combination of individual executive offices, multiperson stations, a reception area, conference room, break room, and office services space—based on its specific configuration and location and the predicted needs of your market.

A training program for new franchisees, conducted by EBC staff supervisors and supported by manuals, is held at the company's Atlanta headquarters, utilizing its specially equipped training center as well as nearby EBC centers in both urban and suburban locations. You'll be taught operating procedures for running your facility, the company's accounting and reporting systems, and marketing techniques. Once your facility is operating, an EBC area representative monitors your progress and furnishes general operations assistance. You'll also be aided in the recruiting, training, and management of your staff, and have the opportunity to attend the company's periodic follow-up seminars covering developments in the industry.

Your EBC operation will be part of the company's regional and national advertising program, both specifically and by inference; however, marketing emphasis should be on your own local efforts, using appropriate print and broadcast media. To help you get started, the company will prepare a grand opening package designed for your market, featuring radio, newspaper, and business publication ads, direct mail materials, and a set of press releases. For additional lead support, the Atlanta executive staff contacts corporations to sell and promote the EBC network, while direct referrals from fellow franchisees can bring you other new clients.

EBC likes its franchisees to have a background in business management and operations, especially those who've owned their own business. Experience in sales, advertising, accounting, engineering, or education is considered helpful, but not necessary.

For further information contact:
  Tom Dye, Director of Franchising, EBC Office Centers, 1080 Holcomb Bridge Rd., Bldg. 100, Suite 310, Roswell, GA 30076, 404-992-1119

Foliage Design Systems (FDS)

Initial license fee: $16,000 to $40,000
Royalties: 4%
Advertising royalties: None
Minimum cash required: $35,000
Capital required: $50,000 to $100,000
Financing: Assistance in obtaining outside financing
Length of contract: 20 years

In business since: 1971
Franchising since: 1980
Total number of units: 42
Number of company-operated units: 2
Total number of units planned, 1995: 60
Number of company-operated units planned, 1995: 2

The greening of America, at least its commercial and residential spaces, is becoming a reality. Foliage is now a key component of interior design, and building managers, architects, decorators, general contractors, and shopping mall developers alike are turning to "interiorscapers" who create and maintain indoor plant arrangements.

The aesthetic and psychological benefits of being among plants have long been championed. But did you know about the business benefits some claim? Happier workers—who'll take fewer sick days; impressed customers—who'll buy more; satisfied tenants—who'll pay higher rents. Add to these the results of a NASA study that found that plants filter out common indoor air pollutants—from cigarette smoke to office and cleaning chemicals—trapped in today's poorly ventilated buildings. With some $750 million in annual revenues, it's no surprise, then, that the interiorscaping business is thriving like, well, a well-watered plant.

This was an industry that barely existed 20 years ago. While the field itself was first developing, two brothers, John and Duke Hagood, founded Foliage Design Systems in a small central Florida town. In the two decades since, as the market expanded, FDS became the first interior landscape franchise and the industry's third largest company.

Now FDS's 200,000 square feet of greenhouses, plus its "test kitchen" units where new species and growing techniques are being tried, are keeping franchisees supplied with the plants that their clients buy, lease, or rent on a short-term basis. Those clients include hotels, banks, restaurants, office buildings, malls, and private residences. One FDS affiliate even furnished the plants used on the sets of nationally syndicated television shows.

The responsibilities of FDS franchisees go well beyond merely providing clients with the greenery. First working closely with them in designing the interiorscape, you'll then install the plants and tend them regularly by watering and feeding, cleaning and trimming, and taking care of insect and disease problems.

To run your operation successfully, you'll need more than just the plants. FDS gives you that start-up and ongoing support. You'll get assistance in obtaining office space and an area where the greenery can be held, grown, and acclimatized. You'll be able to obtain planters, mulch, and other maintenance equipment, all available from the Foliage Supply Company, an FDS subsidiary. You'll benefit from the company's national marketing program, featuring ads in magazines, newspapers, and trade journals; exhibitions at trade shows; and presentations to trade groups and such prospective clients as hotel and restaurant chains, along with local efforts like direct mail campaigns. You'll get tips, leads, and other information to help you improve the management of your office from the monthly franchise newsletter, while your customers will receive the quarterly client newsletter, appropriately titled the *Leaflet*, written by FDS's ad agency and featuring one page per issue specially prepared for your region. And you'll gain from the combined knowledge of your fellow franchisees at annual three-day meetings and from the franchise advisory council, whose elected members meet twice yearly with FDS management to voice franchisee concerns.

But most importantly, you'll have two to three weeks of training in Florida. There, you'll be taught not only the FDS operations systems, but also all about the plants you'll be using: how to identify them, how to choose the right ones for the particular space and climate conditions you'll be encountering, how to care for them, and how to create the kind of foliage designs that have won FDS affiliates a number of industry awards. Detailed guides and manuals provide further information to use in the field, while the home office and other franchisees will help with any questions or problems you have.

FDS offers exclusive territories in which you can operate either single or multiple facilities.

The company also works with silk and dried foliage.

For further information contact:
T. Lisa Harris, Franchise Administrator, Foliage Design Systems Franchise Company, 1553 S.E. Fort King Ave., Ocala, FL 34471, 1-800-933-7351, fax 904-629-0355

HQ Network Systems, Inc.

Initial license fee: Up to $50,000
Royalties: 1.5%
Advertising royalties: None
Minimum cash required: $100,000 to $150,000
Capital required: $359,000 minimum
Financing: None
Length of contract: Perpetual

In business since: 1967
Franchising since: 1977
Total number of units: 80

Number of company-operated units: None
Total number of units planned, 1995: 250
Number of company-operated units planned, 1995: None

Providing office space in prestigious buildings and strategic locations, along with office support services, HQ centers are equipped to meet the needs of growing companies in virtually any sector. As Buffalo, New York, HQ affiliate Paul Snyder proclaims, "We appeal to virtually every market." HQ clients include one-person entrepreneurial firms seeking a single office, small businesses requiring several offices clustered around an administration area, even multinational corporations looking to establish a local branch presence.

HQ was one of the pioneers of the so-called "executive suite" industry, which came of age in the mid 1960s. Businesses have long turned to enterprises like HQ as a low-overhead, cost-efficient way of meeting their workspace and support needs. In addition, relieved from staffing and administrative burdens, they save time as well as money. Even as large numbers of developers enter the field, HQ remains a leader because of its cohesive country-wide network, especially attractive to regional and national client companies that appreciate dealing with a single entity in establishing multiple office locations and meeting ad-hoc needs in cities where they don't have a presence.

Operating an HQ center, the services you'll furnish break down into four specific areas: (1) office space, for full- or part-time use — comfortable offices; well-designed, functional conference rooms; and a pleasant reception area; (2) business services, offered as part of a package or on an as-needed basis, covering areas like secretarial, word processing, and receptionist support; mail handling; phone dictation; photocopying; and travel reservations and ticketing; (3) telecommunications, including fax sending and receiving, electronic and voice mail, telephone answering, and teleconferencing; and (4) corporate discounts, featuring group insurance rates and travel and car leasing markdowns.

Many HQ franchisees turned to the network to expand their already existing executive suite operations, while others were entirely new to the field. In the latter case, the new HQ franchisees are trained by a veteran franchisor in the nearest regional office. Regardless of your experience, the company provides assistance in equipping your facility, initiating and increasing business, keeping up with key industry and network developments, and marketing your services. HQ's purchasing agreements with major suppliers mean you can obtain furniture, equipment, forms, and maintenance services at lower prices, and company layout and decor requirements provide guidelines for establishing the arrangement and look of your facility.

HQ franchisees have access to the company's vast client base of 20,000 business professionals. The company's national sales program, staffed by a team of 90 salespeople, works to sign up additional major accounts, many of which will be requiring your facility's services, and HQ's broad discount program and widely distributed directories provide further strong encouragements for clients to use centers throughout the network.

Besides benefiting from HQ's advertising, marketing, and PR efforts in national and international newspapers, business publications, and airline magazines, to facilitate your own local marketing efforts you'll be able to use the services of the company's in-house ad agency, which will provide you with materials that have been effective for other franchisees or will work with you to design new materials specifically for your market. HQ's support office in San Francisco also dispenses information throughout the network via biweekly mass mailings that detail important business updates, monthly newsletters, semiannual directories, and periodic videotape presentations, while franchisees can gather together and with HQ officials at regional and national meetings and workshops.

For further information contact:
  T. J. Tison, President, HQ Network Systems, Inc., 120 Montgomery St.,
  Suite 1040, San Francisco, CA 94104, 415-781-7811, fax 415-781-8034

Independent Lighting Corporation

Initial license fee: $16,875 to $22,500
Royalties: 7.5%
Advertising royalties: 1%
Minimum cash required: $16,875 to $22,500
Capital required: $22,000 to $52,000
Financing: None
Length of contract: 5 years

In business since: 1983
Franchising since: 1990
Total number of units: 2
Number of company-operated units: None
Total number of units planned, 1995: 45
Number of company-operated units planned, 1995: 15

For commercial, industrial, and institutional businesses occupying thousands of square feet of space, lighting costs make up a sizable chunk of an operations budget, and the amount of time, money, and energy wasted because of inefficient bulbs can be considerable.

That's why factories and warehouses, office buildings and retail stores, restaurants and hotels, hospitals and schools alike have all turned to the replacement products manufactured by Independent Lighting. Backed by a written warranty, each bulb from the Virginia Beach–based company guarantees long service and energy efficiency. "Far better than my expectations," is the appraisal of the Marriott Corporation's Walter Burgdorf, who has introduced Independent products to a number of hotels around the country. "We found we have saved on light bulb replacement, reduced labor costs, and gotten a high return."

Growing by more than 30 percent each year it's been in business, the company has now begun a franchise program to expand its market throughout the Southeast and across the country. In your exclusive territory, you'll be the local representative for Independent Lighting customers, selling them items like the company's 10,000-watt incandescent bulbs, which save up to 80 percent on energy demand, and 9-watt spectrum fluorescent tubes, which burn brighter yet generate less heat than regular 100-watt floodlights.

You'll also be a lighting consultant for your clients, helping them decide how many and what kind of light bulbs should be used for varying situtations and needs. The advice you give will help your customers find more efficient ways to illuminate their establishments. For instance, merely by using 90-watt instead of 100-watt bulbs, an imperceptible difference, a restaurant or other commercial operation open 12 hours a day, seven days a week, saves $3.50 a year per socket. Replacing a 60-watt incandescent light in a 24-hour exit sign with a 9-watt retrofit bulb lessens the electric bill by $35. With a lot of sockets and a lot of exit signs, even these minor alterations can add up to significantly decreased expenses.

But cost savings and energy conservation aren't the only concerns. By suggesting fluorescent tubes to reduce glare in offices or spot lighting to accent merchandise in shops, you'll be involved in creating illumination systems that enhance a comfortable, productive work environment and make commercial spaces more hospitable and retail stores more alluring.

Company staff members will personally teach you and up to two of your employees the technical aspects of the lighting business. Spending at least a week in training, you'll also cover sales methods, financial control, personnel management, and marketing techniques. As soon as you're through with the instruction, you're ready to go to work, taking advantage of the corporate accounts Independent Lighting has established and the leads the home office has generated. You still, however, may be asked to attend refresher courses from time to time to keep abreast of newly developed products and procedures.

Field assistance is extended as well, with an Independent Lighting official dropping by periodically to evaluate the strengths and weaknesses of your operations, answer questions, and help you with sales and marketing. In addition to your contribution to the company-wide advertising and development fund, you'll be expected to devote at least 3 percent of your gross revenues to local promotions.

Conversion franchises are available for those who currently own a business selling and distributing commercial lighting supplies, but candidates seeking a start-up operation are neither required nor expected to have experience in the industry. To make your entry into the field easier, your inventory obligations are low: because the home office handles the shipping of the products you'll sell, you only have to have a small quantity of emergency stock on hand. And while building your Independent Lighting business will certainly take work, you'll keep regular work hours. Most days you'll be able to shut off the lights by five.

For further information contact:
 Chris Carpenter, President, Independent Lighting Corporation, 873 Seahawk Circle, Virginia Beach, VA 23452, 804-468-5448 or 1-800-637-5483

ProForma, Inc.

Initial license fee: $39,500
Royalties: 7%
Advertising royalties: 1%
Minimum cash required: $44,500 to $49,500
Capital required: $42,000 to $48,000
Financing: Available
Length of contract: 10 years

In business since: 1978
Franchising since: 1985
Total number of units: 103
Number of company-operated units: 2
Total number of units planned, 1995: 180
Number of company-operated units planned, 1995: 2

Every company, big or small, needs office supplies. These days, typing paper, filing folders, pencils, and pens make up only part of monthly office orders. Add all the items associated with computers to the traditional list—and you've got a $136 billion industry.

ProForma, Inc. carved out its highly lucrative niche by successfully providing a diverse range of office supplies—from high-tech computer system accessories to the simple but essential customized form—to companies of all sizes. ProForma distinguishes itself from other suppliers by working with its clients to meet their individual needs. This is one company with a "hands-on" reputation, known for sitting down with its customers and teaching them to maximize the products they purchase.

Franchising since 1985, ProForma estimates its present 103 franchises will grow to 180 units by the middle of the decade. From the get-go, the company works toward ensuring the success of each franchisee. Prospective franchise owners spend one day at ProForma headquarters, touring the facility and conversing with executives. Afterward, the company will send you on your way, giving you as much time as you need to decide if ProForma is right for you.

An initial license fee of $39,500 allows you to use the ProForma name and sell its products for 10 years. How do you get businesses to buy these supplies? A required one-week training seminar in Cleveland will teach you the basics of telemarketing, direct mail campaigns, and direct sales. You'll also leave with a strong working knowledge of the company's line of office products.

Selling ProForma products provides a terrific opportunity for those who want to work out of the home, saving you thousands in office rent. Initial contact is made by phone, and sales calls usually require a visit to your customer's site. About $5,000 will get you the equipment you need to set up your den with business telephone line hookups, office equipment, and a software package and modem—a helpful addition, but not always necessary.

ProForma eases you into selling their products by offering you three months' use of a telemarketing service for free. This provides you with a starting supply of potential customers so you don't have to walk into a clientless vacuum. After that, franchisees pay a 1 percent advertising royalty that covers promotional campaigns.

Gross sales for individual franchisees average a healthy $300,000. ProForma's concern for its franchisees breeds this success. An annual convention, regional meetings, and a newly established franchise advisory council sustain dialogue between the company's corporate management and individual franchisees.

For further information contact:
John Campbell, ProForma, Inc., 4705 Van Epps Rd., Cleveland, OH 44131, 216-741-0400 or 1-800-825-1525

Python's Recycling, Inc.

Initial license fee: $15,000
Royalties: None
Advertising royalties: None
Minimum cash required: $65,000
Capital required: $65,000
Financing: None
Length of contract: 3 years

In business since: 1976
Franchising since: 1989
Total number of units: 11
Number of company-operated units: 2
Total number of units planned, 1995: 100
Number of company-operated units planned, 1995: 2

Python's founder, Stuart Hamilton, originally intended for recycling to be merely a sideline when he added an aluminum can redemption center to his St. Cloud, Minnesota, cash-and-carry soft-drink outlet in 1976. But over the following 10 years, the enterprise grew to dominate his business. Seeing where the real money was to be made, Hamilton joined forces with a veteran in the recycling field, added a warehousing expert, and restructured the company to concentrate on building a recycling network in the Midwest. Working with manufacturers that create recycled products, Python's has also begun to make these goods available to franchisees for retailing.

As a Python franchisee, you'll operate a buy-back redemption center of your own, collecting bulk paper, glass, aluminum, and plastic. Meticulously separating and preparing the materials, you'll send the goods to Python's central processing and shipping facility in St. Cloud, receiving top market prices. "The more market-ready the materials," Python's sales and marketing director, Dan Huschke, explains, "the higher price we will pay." Franchisees also have the option of selling the material to a local processor, paying a small royalty to Python's when a service outside the network is used.

In addition to being a collection site, your facility can also operate as a community education center. Like Python's management, you may choose to become involved with developing recycling ordinances in your community. Plus, you'll have the opportunity to carry recycled paper goods for sale, along with products like can crushers, bins, and packaging materials that your customers can use in their recycling efforts.

Most Python's franchisees to date have been private sector haulers, who, according to Huschke, "are recognizing that if they don't get into recycling they will lose business." Others have joined the network to add a recycling venture as an extra service for their established businesses. Even with no background or no complementary enterprise, Python's can provide you with the expertise, materials, and support you'll need to start and build a recycling business. First, Python's will analyze your community, your competition, and your goals to design a collection system to meet your needs. Company managers will help you set up your redemption center, suggesting the proper size and type of facility and assisting with its design and organization. Python's will also furnish you with the necessary equipment, from scales and sorters, to crushers, densifiers, balers, and forklifts, at economic prices, teaching you how to use the machinery for storage, market preparation, and transportation of recyclables. No formal "classroom training" is required. In addition, you'll be able to obtain office equipment and be trained in the company's recommended management and accounting systems.

Python's will guide you in developing marketing strategies, supplying advertising strategies and programs that have proved successful for other franchisees, and furnishing PR and educational materials like Python's "Recycling Video Library." Company representatives will make periodic consultation visits to supplement their regular phone contact. Meanwhile, the home office continues to widen its client base and build its shipping capabilities for transporting materials in large volumes across the country and overseas to obtain top rates. Hibbing, Minnesota, franchisee Steve Jalowski asserts, "Python's market network gives me the security of knowing I'm getting the best possible price for my recyclables."

Until recently, all Python's franchisees have been located in Minnesota; opportunities are now available, however, in other Midwest states as well. As the company's network continues to expand to the point where the St. Cloud processing center is no longer within cost-effective reach of all affiliates, Python's anticipates guiding its franchisees in the organization of cooperative regional processing plants that can ship materials directly to the company's clients.

For further information contact:
  Stuart Hamilton, Python's Recycling, Inc., P.O. Box 6025, St. Cloud, MN 56302, 612-253-9553, fax 612-253-9314

The Office Alternative

Initial license fee: $15,000
Royalties: 5%
Advertising royalties: None

Minimum cash required: $49,000
Capital required: $65,000
Financing: Leasing of equipment can be arranged
Length of contract: 10 years

In business since: 1983
Franchising since: 1986
Total number of units: 25
Number of company-operated units: 1
Total number of units planned, 1995: 100+
Number of company-operated units planned, 1995: 1

Who uses The Office Alternative? New businesses, established small businesses, home-based businesses and out-of-town businesses seeking a local presence, not to mention independent consultants, social and civic clubs, and professional associations—even the Branford, Connecticut, Chamber of Commerce. Any individual or organization, in fact, that requires cost-effective, state-of-the-art business support services beyond the scope of their own facilities can turn to The Business Alternative.

As a Business Alternative franchisee, your "one-stop" professional shop offers the space, equipment, and personnel that clients need to operate their own enterprises. The specific services provided vary from center to center; some options are standard but others will depend on your interests and the needs of your market. These choices enable you to furnish your customers with a complete range of support, including personalized telephone answering, secretarial services, packing and shipping, mail receiving and forwarding, photocopying, electronic money transfer, desktop publishing, printing, and notary and fax service. In addition, you'll have furnished conference rooms, offices, and cubicles available for clients' ad hoc use and temporary rent. Some customers will contract your services and space on a regular, planned basis, while others simply come in from off the street for a particular task or one-time office use. Many opt for The Business Alternative as their *permanent* business alternative—to avoid the much higher costs incurred by renting, equipping, and staffing an office of their own.

To start your business, the company's home office extends site selection (centers are customarily located in strip shopping areas), lease negotiation, construction, design, and decorating consultation. Personalized instruction is given by a team of managers at the franchise headquarters in Toledo, going over in detail all the material in three manuals: the "Start-up Manual," "Training Manual," and "Business and Operations Manual." You'll learn marketing techniques and pricing strategies, as well as such basics as how to use all the office equipment, and you'll regularly put down the manuals for hands-on exercises. Ongoing support and business management assistance includes weekly newsletters, a telephone line for troubleshooting and advice, update materials alerting you to emerging changes in office service technology, and annual meetings. A main focus is on the continued growth of your franchise. As the newsletter, *Office Affairs*, reports, a training session is likely to be punctuated with, "'Take a few minutes and plan out what you want your Center to be doing in one year . . . then two years . . . then three years.' This shocks us into reality and the 'buzz session' really starts humming!"

For further information contact:
  Martha J. Wolff, Vice President, The Office Alternative, One SeaGate,
  Suite 1001, Toledo, OH 43604, 419-247-5400 or 1-800-262-4181

Video Data Services

Initial license fee: $15,950
Royalties: $500/year
Advertising royalties: None
Minimum cash required: $8,000
Capital required: $17,950
Financing: None
Length of contract: 10 years

In business since: 1980
Franchising since: 1981
Total number of units: 236
Number of company-operated units: 2
Total number of units planned, 1995: 400
Number of company-operated units planned, 1995: 2

Video Data provides many of the same services professional photographers sold in the past, replacing still photography with videotaping. Currently, law firms and insurance companies provide the most business for these franchises. Lawyers often need a taped statement from an out-of-town witness. Video Data franchisees can make the tape and then edit out any portions of the testimony a judge would not want the jury to hear. Insurance companies hire franchisees to inventory property. Additionally, many people add a videotape to their will. A tape cannot take the place of a written will, but it can give them the chance to communicate with their survivors after their death.

The company constantly comes up with new ideas for drumming up business, and franchisees share their own ideas on developing new markets through Video Data Services publications. Among new markets recently suggested are corporate seminars, store promotions, body builder shows, and beauty pageants. Weddings provide steady business; some people want the funeral of a loved one taped.

You don't need any experience in the field. Most people begin on a part-time basis, using their home as an office. Many franchisees are retired people seeking a part-time business. Your franchise fee pays for the half-inch industrial-grade VCR tape, camera, color monitor, lights, and editing equipment. You will need an extra VCR to make copies. Because Video Data Services began as a company that sold video equipment and continues in that business, it can provide you with supplementary equipment at bargain prices. The company even makes it possible for you to sell VCRs in your community at prices that undercut even discount stores.

Your franchise will cover a territory with a population of about 100,000. The company has no rules regarding your office or the purchase of supplies. You—and one other person, if you wish—can receive your required training in either Rochester, New York, or San Diego, California. You bear the expense of travel and lodging for the three-day session, which covers all you need to know about the business. Should you need a refresher in this intensive course, the company invites you back for another session. Shirley Porter, a Video Data Services franchisee in Bloomfield Hills, Michigan, took advantage of the offer, and she found it "a real strong point" of the company.

Frequent company newsletters and the annual meeting keep you up to date on the latest technical and business information in the field. Video Data Services will also advise you on specific problems. "The home office has been very supportive," notes Shirley Porter. "They always answer any technical questions that I have." And yet, "they take no active role in managing my company, which is the way I want it."

Video Data Services emphasizes direct mail marketing as a way of bringing in new business. It runs frequent cooperative advertising programs with franchisees, stressing the systematic development of vertical markets, such as legal firms, rather than the scatter approach of going after every type of customer at once.

For further information contact:
  Stuart J. Dizak, Video Data Services, 30 Grove St., Pittsford, NY 14534,
  716-385-4773

Postal and Shipping

Handle With Care Packaging Store, Inc.

Initial license fee: $17,500
Royalties: 5%
Advertising royalties: 1%
Minimum cash required: $25,000
Capital required: $50,000
Financing: Available
Length of contract: Perpetual

In business since: 1980
Franchising since: 1984
Total number of units: 400
Number of company-operated units: None
Total number of units planned, 1995: 1,200
Number of company-operated units planned, 1995: None

Does your customer need to ship the contents of her vintage wine cellar from her Bel Air winter home to the Nantucket summer cottage? Or send a $2.1 million dollar portrait of Michael Jackson to Mom? That is, without breaking a single bottle of Bordeaux or damaging a single brush stroke of the Gloved One's glove? All in a day's work for your Handle With Care Packaging Store.

The company boasts about those two particular parcels, but it's taken care of thousands of others quite *un*like them, too. The emphasis of the Packaging Store services, in fact, is on such unusual, awkward, fragile, and valuable items other shippers are afraid to handle, as well as shipments too large for traditional mail services yet too small for moving companies.

Packaging Store franchisees can prepare and ship items from 1 to 1,000 pounds anywhere in the world to which an established courier or freight service delivers. Often that will involve constructing custom-made crates and using innovative packaging techniques like foam-in-place systems for electronics, furniture, and other delicate articles. The company's national freight accounts bring you discount shipping fees that mean attractive rates for your customers, and the regional warehousing facilities give them storage space and flexibility enough to use Packaging Stores even for their long-distance moving needs.

Unlike many competitors, your Packaging Store concentrates solely on packing and shipping services. The company believes this focus underscores your commitment to and expertise in this specific field, commitment and expertise that impresses and draws small, medium-size, and large businesses alike as clients, along with individual patrons.

Successfully owning and running a Packaging Store requires no specific prior experience; however, you will need both technical and operational instruction. The company provides one week of classroom and in-store training, plus videotapes and manuals, teaching the basics of packaging, ways to build your customer base, and systems for each phase of your facility's management.

Site-selection assistance and construction plans and specifications guide you in setting up your Packaging Store. To help you start on the right foot, an authorized company trainer will join you at your facility during your first days in business to answer questions and handle initial problems. Thereafter, you can get an immediate response by calling the company's 800 number. Regional franchisee meetings are held regularly and there will also be a twice-yearly complete operational review.

The Packaging Store sales staff has developed country-wide commercial accounts, concentrating on larger corporations with a particularly high volume of outgoing and incoming parcels that bring business to franchises throughout the network. Conducting a national advertising program, the company's marketing department also supplies you with materials for coordinating your own local promotional efforts.

Franchisees are granted an exclusive area of operation, and you're encouraged to open other satellite centers within your territory, for no additional franchise fee. The relatively low overhead and start-up costs make this an attractive venture for individuals looking for an economical way to go into business for themselves. That's what Atlanta, Georgia, franchisee Dave Polak did. "Dollar-for-dollar, the Packaging Store is the best deal in franchising," he contends. "We looked at everything from fast food to oil changes and nothing came close for such a small investment."

For further information contact:
   Richard Godwin, Handle With Care Packaging Store, Inc., International Headquarters, 5675 DTC Blvd., Suite 280, Englewood, CO 80111, 303-741-6626 or 1-800-525-6309, fax 303-741-6653

Pack 'n' Mail Mailing Center

Initial license fee: $17,500
Royalties: None

Advertising royalties: None
Minimum cash required: $45,000
Capital required: $50,000 to $60,000
Financing: Available
Length of contract: 10 years

In business since: 1981
Franchising since: 1987
Total number of units: 124
Number of company-operated units: 6
Total number of units planned, 1995: 850
Number of company-operated units planned, 1995: 25

Pack 'n' Mail attributes its success to offering, in the words of CEO Mike Gallagher, "greater convenience, greater flexibility, greater choices than they could ever get from the post office." In addition, Pack 'n' Mail centers extend a combination of other business services, to bring one-stop shopping expedience to its business clients and individual customers.

That means Pack 'n' Mail franchisees are involved in far more than packaging and shipping duties. To be sure, these services remain the core of your operation, as you'll be handling the transportation of any kind of item, be it computer or stereo equipment, glassware or framed pictures, that's legal to send by mail or freight. You'll work with all the major carriers, including the U.S. postal service, overnight delivery companies, and air and motor freight operations, helping your customer determine the most time- and cost-efficient way to send their parcels. Beyond that, however, your Pack 'n' mail center is also a place for customers to purchase stamps, envelopes, boxes, and packing equipment, as well as business supplies and greeting cards, to have presents gift wrapped, to get mail metered, to mail letters, to make copies, to send and receive faxes, to wire money, even to take a passport photo. In addition, you'll furnish mailboxes for rent, offering features that post offices can't: a street address (with the additional option of a suite number) rather than P.O. box number, 24-hour access, the ability to accept packages sent by Federal Express and UPS, call-in mail check services, and telephone mail forwarding. These last two are particular boons for clients on the go, who can find out by phone whether they have any mail before making a possibly unnecessary trip to your store and who can let you know by a simple call where they want their mail to be sent when they're out of town or otherwise occupied.

The franchise fee covers both start-up and ongoing consultation services. They begin with on-site evaluation and assistance in choosing the location of your Pack 'n' Mail center, ideally in a heavy-traffic area near other businesses that can become your client base. The company helps you negotiate your lease and develop your facility, supplying interior store design, installing fixtures, and organizing supplies and inventory. Before you open for business, you'll receive instruction to familiarize you with Pack 'n' Mail's operating, sales, accounting, and marketing systems during a training seminar over a period of at least five days at the company's Lubbock store and training center, followed by a three- to five-day session at your store for you and your staff led by one of the company's traveling managers. The vice president of operations and/or another Pack 'n' Mail executive will make recurrent visits while you're getting on your feet to offer assistance, focusing especially on expanding your business and introducing the new sales and marketing programs that the company develops on a regular basis.

Pack 'n' Mail has established national accounts with major vendors from whom you'll be able to obtain all supplies and inventory at competitive prices. You may, however, use local suppliers instead, as long as the materials meet company quality standards.

There are Pack 'n' Mail centers currently operating in 37 states, and the company plans to continue its rapid expansion nationwide. Most franchisees start with a single facility, which can be operated by a two-person staff plus three to five temporary employees during the peak holiday seasons, and many have opened additional stores after they've become familiar with operations and earned profits sufficient for funding an expansion. Developing agreements are available for qualified franchisees who want to establish an entire marketing area over a negotiated period of time.

For further information contact:
  Mike Gallagher, President and CEO, Pack 'n' Mail Mailing Center,
  5701 Slide Rd., Suite C, Lubbock, TX 79424, 806-797-3400

Packy the Shipper

Initial license fee: $995
Royalties: $0.95/package
Advertising royalties: Co-op; the company matches you at rate of
    $0.05/package shipped.
Minimum cash required: $995 to $1,295
Capital required: $995 to $1,295
Financing: None
Length of contract: Perpetual

In business since: 1976
Franchising since: 1981

Total number of units: 800
Number of company-operated units: None
Total number of units planned, 1995: 2,000
Number of company-operated units planned, 1995: None

The originators of Packy—a subsidiary of PNS, Inc.—spotted a customer need and figured out a way to fill it cheaply and conveniently. The customer who wants to send a gift, or even an occasional business item, has to find an appropriate carton, pack the item, and then locate a parcel shipping office—a time-consuming and inconvenient procedure for many people.

The Packy solution, the installation of a shipping service at locations that people frequent in their everyday activities, offers the customer the option of having a franchisee pack their object for a small fee and arrange to have it shipped by UPS. For the store owner who actually runs the service, Packy offers a small business on the side that generates traffic yet requires little space and relatively little time and attention. According to the company, almost 18 percent of customers who use Packy the Shipper had not previously patronized the store providing the service, and about 44 percent of all customers buy something else while in the store to ship a package.

Packy even handles the onerous paperwork involved in a shipping operation. "Their program takes out all the hassle involved with customer complaints regarding damages and/or tracers," claims Sharon Wassberg, who runs a hardware store in Manitowoc, Wisconsin. "All we need to do is take down the information and pass it on to them; they handle it from there. The customer is always satisfied."

Packy means to spell convenience for its franchisees as well as for its customers. The company audits and pays shipper's bills, insures packages at no expense to the franchisee, absorbs UPS wrong address charges and the charge for a weekly pickup. It also takes care of Interstate Commerce Commission paperwork.

Don't worry about the training, either. The company comes to you at your convenience and takes less than two hours to teach you how to pack and ship. The cartons come from your own inventory—the cartons that your regular store stock came in. "I trained our store manager in half an hour," says Jerry Breen. "I watched him do a few, and that was it."

If a problem should come up, it won't get out of hand because "support is just an 800 number away," notes Jerry Breen. "All questions are always answered, even if it means a visit from a representative who lives 350 miles away."

You purchase sales contracts and shipping labels from the company. Packy also offers an optional scale at a discount.

For further information contact:
  James C. Hill, Vice President, Marketing, PNS, Inc., 409 Main St., Racine, WI
  53403, 414-633-9540

Pak Mail Centers of America, Inc.

Initial license fee: $17,500
Royalties: 5%
Advertising royalties: 2%
Minimum cash required: NA
Capital required: $60,000 to $80,000
Financing: Available
Length of contract: 10 years

In business since: 1983
Franchising since: 1985
Total number of units: 275
Number of company-operated units: 1
Total number of units planned, 1995: 2,000
Number of company-operated units planned, 1995: 1

The company explains the heart of its service succinctly: "Pak Mail
packs anything, ships it anywhere and gets it there on time and in
one piece." But while the statement is simple, the process can be complex. It means mastering a number of methods for packaging often
cumbersome and delicate parcels. It means creating special crates and
containers. And it means appraising the different routes and pricing
scales of every major domestic and international carrier and overnight
service, as well as calculating insurance rates and determining the
most cost- and time-efficient way to handle each shipment. Well, if it
were so easy, why would so many businesses and individual customers need to turn to you?

   They can turn to you—and your Pak Mail center—for more than
just packing and shipping assignments, too. Private mailboxes are
available for rent, with early-morning delivery and round-the-clock
access and providing a more professional mailing address than a P.O.
box number. You'll also offer convenient mail processing and phone
answering services: forwarding, package receiving, and call-in noti-
fication. And while your customers are in the store, they can take advantage of your retail merchandizing program—tailored to their needs
and your display space—getting keys, rubber stamps, business cards,
and photocopies made, having passport photos taken, sending a fax or
telegram, wiring money, and buying packing supplies, postage stamps,
and stationery, all generating, not so incidentally, substantial extra income for you.

At the home office, Pak Mail devises other strategies for expanding your business. The research and development department will help you add new products and services to your store like electronic tax filing, which lets your customers get their refunds within an average of 18 days and can even allow them to obtain a refund anticipation loan. Likewise, the company's sales staff works to sign new national and regional commercial accounts that will bring you a steady income.

Pak Mail's assistance begins right from the point that you are awarded a franchise. Using its demographic "micro market system," the company will aid you in finding a store location that's convenient for the types of offices, businesses, and neighborhoods that have proven in the past to be Pak Mail's best customers. A lease negotiation team will review your rental contracts, and other staffers will supply plans and advice for the construction of your center.

At the National Support Center in Aurora, Colorado, you'll attend a one-week franchise training course. The first topics addressed will be strategic business planning and marketing, followed by the science of packing and shipping. Then, the focus shifts to personnel practices and basic accounting, finishing with lessons on the use of the company's customized computer operations system. Regional training is also offered throughout the year to update you on new information.

A Pak Mail representative will pay a three-day opening visit to your center to develop and review your initial marketing plan. You'll be shown how to use the statistical software the company furnishes to define and target potential customers in your area, and how to direct mailing campaigns and advertising programs to them. Outfitting you with newspaper ads, flyers, coupons, radio and TV commercials, coupons, telemarketing scripts, point-of-purchase materials, and press releases, Pak Mail assists franchisees in forming local advertising associations and administrates a corporate fund for nationwide promotions.

After your business is off the ground, Pak Mail continues to stay in touch through newsletters, bulletins, and the owner hotline. Field staffers will drop by periodically for direct evaluation and troubleshooting sessions, and you'll be invited to attend regular meetings and seminars and the annual franchise convention. Just as importantly, Pak Mail also pays close attention to rival packing and shipping operations and uses computer communications to keep you informed about the activities of your nearby competition.

For further information contact:
   John Simon, Vice President, Licensing, Pak Mail Centers of America, Inc., 3033 S. Parker Rd., Suite 1200, Aurora, CO 80014, 303-752-3500 or 1-800-833-2821, fax 303-755-9721

Shipping Connection, Inc.

Initial license fee: $14,500
Royalties: 5%
Advertising royalties: 2%
Minimum cash required: $28,000
Capital required: $38,000
Financing: Available
Length of contract: 10 years

In business since: 1982
Franchising since: 1987
Total number of units: 20
Number of company-operated units: 2
Total number of units planned, 1995: 100
Number of company-operated units planned, 1995: 2

Betty and Tom Russotti had over 18 years' experience with major package carriers, "doing just about every job in the business, from loading and driving trucks to . . . management," when they founded Shipping Connection. They created their company's niche by serving the general public—people with only a few packages to ship—in ways that the major carriers don't, carriers that have limits and restrictions from which only big businesses can benefit.

New Jersey Shipping Connection franchisee Roger Hummel elaborates, "People don't know how or don't want to wrap their packages and UPS only delivers them. People are willing to pay for that service." Shipping Connection stores specialize in packaging and shipping for both businesses and individual customers. You'll be equipped to handle almost any kind of parcel regardless of size or weight, and customers with packages too heavy to bring to the store can have them picked up at their home or office. You'll pack the item to be shipped in a safe and cost-effective manner, often constructing wood crates and cartons to assure that all parcels arrive at their destination damage-free. Then, acting much like the shipping broker for your clients, you'll arrange for the transportation, choosing with the customer from a wide range of carriers—UPS, as well as Airborne, Federal Express, and other air cargo and motor freight operations.

In addition, Shipping Connection stores offer a complete line of packing and shipping supplies—boxes, crates, tapes, cushioning materials—both as single units and wholesale in large quantities. Fax and gift wrapping services are also available and some locations have mailbox rentals, too.

Running a Shipping Connection store is made easier by the company's custom-designed computer system, which does the job of a cash register, scale, word processing machine, UPS meter, and label maker, and features a program allowing you to determine box size, proper packing material, and labor costs. But operating your store also involves some highly specialized packaging services for fragile or unconventional parcels. That's why a key element of the two-week franchisee training program, at the company-owned store in Littleton, Colorado, is learning the correct way to deal with such items as computer materials, medical equipment, china and glassware, antiques, musical instruments, and artwork. You'll go on to learn how packages are handled by the various carriers so you'll be able to determine the best way to prepare each parcel, and be taught about customs documentation for international shipping. The ins and outs of the computer system are also covered, as well as topics like consumer relations and local marketing.

The company extends assistance in site selection (stores usually occupy about 1,200 square feet and are located in strip shopping centers) and lease negotiation. Shipping Connection provides the specific decor and equipment for your store; the company representative who will join you on site to prepare for your opening will help you put it all together and aid you in obtaining other supplies and materials. He or she will also work to develop your client base by making calls on business prospects in your area, and will drop by for periodic follow-up visits and evaluations.

You'll receive assistance in other aspects of your operation as well. The company supplies franchisees with its own insurance coverage, so you won't have to rely on your carriers' policies for lost or damaged parcels. Discount rates have been negotiated with the major trucking and air express companies, boosting the profit you make on each shipment. And promotional campaigns and other advertising materials are developed by the marketing department for your use.

Individual and area franchises alike are available, and stores have operated profitably in both small towns and large cities. The Russottis make a point of emphasizing that the business—with hours amenable to working mothers—is a particularly good one for women, who make up more than 50 percent of Shipping Connection franchisees.

For further information contact:
Chuck Shrader, Franchise Director, Shipping Connection, Inc.,
7220 W. Jefferson Ave., Suite 305, Denver, CO 80235, 1-800-727-6720

UniShippers Association (USA)

Initial license fee: $7,500 to $75,000, based on population of franchise area
    ($0.03 per person)
Royalties: 4%
Advertising royalties: None
Minimum cash required: $15,000
Capital required: Dependent on size of area
Financing: None
Length of contract: 5 years, with option to renew

In business since: 1987
Franchising since: 1987
Total number of units: 77
Number of company-operated units: 3
Total number of units planned, 1995: 200
Number of company-operated units planned, 1995: None

UniShippers Association (USA), a national third-party shipping contractor that uses the overnight services of Airborne Express, is a new
breed of package transport middleperson. Combining the shipping volume of its over 26,000 clients, mostly small businesses and organizations, USA qualifies for discounted bulk rates and benefits otherwise
available only to the largest multinational firms. And it passes on
those cost and service advantages to its customers while earning its
franchisees tidy profits.

The concept is a simple one: Your clients contact Airborne Express
directly for picking up, transporting, and delivering their parcels. Airborne then sends the invoice to you, and you, in turn, bill your clients. Paying you a markup fee usually averaging $4 to $5 per parcel,
the customer still enjoys shipping rates substantially—up to 40
percent—below regular retail rates.

Things, admittedly, didn't always run so smoothly. Back in the late
1980s, USA had a false start—namely, contracting initially with an
unreliable transport company. But with Airborne, which maintains a
97 percent on-time record, the company has a solid and mutually satisfying relationship. That happy affiliation was a key factor in Norfolk,
Virginia, franchisees Roger and Collet Jubert's decision to join the
USA network. "As managers for Airborne's ground operations in
Florida, where we used to live, we knew of Airborne's reliability and
their commitment to excellent service." And how happy, exactly, is
that affiliation? USA is now Airborne's 10th largest customer, alone
responsible for $600,000 of the carrier's sales per month.

The sheer volume of business between USA and Airborne is enough
to guarantee their relationship for the foreseeable future. New ventures, however, seeking to achieve the same success as USA may not

be so lucky, as USA seems to have carved a nifty niche that competitors are having trouble entering. As industry analysts see it, shippers are increasingly reluctant to work with start-up third-party contractors, extending discounts too small for these operations to be able to make a sufficient profit.

Your responsibilities as a USA franchisee are largely twofold: enrolling new clients—and receiving the $25 enrollment fee in addition to revenues for each parcel they subsequently ship—and servicing existing clients. That usually amounts to contacting between 25 and 50 prospects a day as you get started, through a combination of cold calls and prearranged appointments, and making monthly calls, by phone or in person, on your established accounts. Many USA franchisees have found this to result in a very workable work schedule. Curry and Nancy Vaughan, owners of the Palm Bay, Florida, territory, vouch, "After we build up a customer base and a monthly shipment count, then we simply service those accounts and perform the billing functions which can be done from anywhere in the country. The operation of the franchise was flexible enough to allow us to enjoy life while starting our own business."

Even before your franchise agreement is finalized, USA prepares a market study of your territory for a nonrefundable $1,000 payment that can be credited toward your franchise fee. A USA representative travels to your region, makes sales calls, meets with the local Airborne sales and operations personnel, analyzes the possible competition, and finally determines the viability of a USA franchise there. If your chances for success look good, you'll complete the agreement and soon begin training, spending one week learning sales techniques and billing and collection procedures at the Salt Lake City headquarters, and two to three days at your office, where a USA staffer will lead you through your first invoicing period. If you have any sales representatives working under you, they, too, can be sent to Salt Lake City for instruction, or can simply make use of the training videotapes and audiotapes the company provides.

The home office keeps in touch through monthly newsletters, regular staff visits to your territory, and annual conventions. And USA officials stay busy with perhaps the most crucial aspect of their business—maintaining that happy affiliation with Airborne and handling the yearly rate negotiations to ensure both companies' continued good health.

For further information contact:
  Jodie Erickson, Assistant Director of Franchising, UniShippers Association
  (USA), 4911 S. 900 E., Salt Lake City, UT 84117, 801-262-3300 or
  1-800-999-8721, fax 801-261-4839

9. The Education Industry

Contents

Academic

Day Care

Preschool Activities

Academic

Britannica Learning Centers

Initial license fee: $25,000 to $35,000
Royalties: 8.5%
Advertising royalties: 2%
Minimum cash required: $70,000
Capital required: $40,000
Financing: Up to 80% of $50,000 "start-up kit"
Length of contract: 5 years, with 4 renewals of 5 years each

In business since: 1970
Franchising since: 1985
Total number of units: 86
Number of company-operated units: 80
Total number of units planned, 1995: 400
Number of company-operated units planned, 1995: 80

Parents and teachers are well aware of what can happen when a child
has difficulties with reading or math: His or her attention can dwindle
while hostility toward school—and toward other kids—can grow. And
the unfortunate thing is that many schools today are unable to give
these children the individual attention they need to improve their
skills. So school administrators themselves are frequently recommending that parents seek out supplementary educational programs like
Britannica Learning Centers. In the process, Britannica has become a
hot franchise prospect for those businesspeople with an interest in education . . . and teachers whose entrepreneurial proclivities aren't being satisfied in the traditional classroom.

Britannica Learning Centers are the legacy of Dr. Kenneth Martyn,
a former public school principal. In 1985, the company he founded,
the American Learning Corporation, was acquired by Encyclopedia
Britannica, which expanded the curriculum and brought the prestige
of a highly respected name in education. Now, first graders and high
school seniors alike attend the learning centers, including above-
average and gifted students looking for greater academic challenges
and ways to improve their skills further.

Britannica Learning Centers can handle a wide range of ages and
aptitudes because their emphasis is on individual instruction. Stu-
dent/teacher ratios at the centers average 3:1 and the youngsters are
each given a personal prescription for learning. Students usually spend
three to four hours a week, on weekday evenings and Saturdays, at
the centers, for a program that totals 48 hours of Britannica classroom

time, spread out over four to six months. In that period, according to the company, their reading and math skills will improve, on average, more than one full grade level.

Students start off by taking a two- to three-hour diagnostic test, which you or the teachers you hire will administer one-on-one, that evaluates their skill levels and determines exactly where their problems lie. Preparing a written statement for each student, you'll set their educational goals and map out the strategy for achieving them. The assignments you'll give will be tailored to meet each child's specific needs and learning styles. You'll be using a wide array of specialized teaching materials and equipment, including computers, spending a lot of time working individually with the students, allowing them to proceed at their own pace.

Meanwhile, advanced students who haven't been sufficiently challenged in school are kept busy and absorbed by enrichment materials and projects. Britannica Learning Centers can benefit these kids as much as those with below-average academic skills. "Our son was having difficulty learning to read; now he can read whole books without missing a word," describes one Britannica parent. "My wife and I were so impressed with his improvement that we enrolled our daughter, who was already an excellent reader."

Close parental involvement is a vital factor in the program. Parents will be coming in for monthly conferences with you or your staff, and you'll prepare written status reports for them as well, using results from standardized tests to evaluate their child's progress. At the same time, you'll reward the kids for their daily achievements, giving support and positive reinforcement for even small accomplishments and providing encouragement to boys and girls who are all too familiar with disappointment in the classroom.

To improve study habits and test-taking techniques, you'll also extend special programs for teenagers like SAT and ACT prep classes and a college survival skills course. Plus you'll earn commissions by selling such educational products as Compton's Encyclopedia and the Evelyn Wood Audio Cassette Program.

If you will personally be working as an instructor at the Center, you must be a certified teacher. Franchisees who won't be doing any hands-on teaching themselves should still have expertise in helping children learn and an ability to deal effectively with parents and educators. Business experience is considered helpful but not necessary. You'll learn the necessary operations skills at a 15- to 20-day training course, which covers the Britannica diagnostic testing procedures, instructional and motivational methods, and financial and other administration aspects of running your business.

The company will supply a copy of its Site Location Manual along with telephone assistance for helping you find the right spot for situating your center. Once you've opened, a field consultant will spend one week with you in the first month, while other Britannica staffers will make ongoing visits to answer questions and give advice.

While you can expect that many clients will come through referrals—from teachers and schools familiar with the Britannica network as well as parents—you will be required to make a significant marketing effort, spending 4 percent to 6 percent of your gross income on local advertising and promotion in addition to the royalties you'll pay for the company-wide fund. Britannica will furnish materials, including ad copy, brochures, and ideas for special promotional events, and guide you in implementing a program for expanding your business.

For further information contact:
Douglas Paul, Executive Vice President, American Learning Franchise, Inc.,
310 S. Michigan Ave., 12th floor, Chicago, IL 60604-2485, 312-939-0303 or
1-800-433-7782, fax 312-939-1680

Computertots

Initial license fee: $10,000 to $15,000
Royalties: 6%
Advertising royalties: 1%
Minimum cash required: $15,125 to $27,850
Capital required: $15,125 to $27,850
Financing: None
Length of contract: 10 years

In business since: 1983
Franchising since: 1988
Total number of units: 32
Number of company-operated units: 1
Total number of units planned, 1995: 100+
Number of company-operated units planned, 1995: 1

When it comes to the basics of a child's education, many parents and teachers these days are starting to think that the "three r's" should be joined by a "c"—"c" for computers. The sooner the better, too, as youngsters can be effectively started on a computer literacy program even before they've learned reading, writing, and arithmetic.

Mary Rogers and Karen Marshall, cofounders of Computertots, believe that 3 to 5 years is about the right age to introduce children to computers. That is, as long as it's done right, and that's what Computertots is there for. Using state-of-the-art teaching methodologies,

Computertots classes bring computer education directly to young boys and girls, attempting to help them develop a positive attitude toward the machines and technology that are now an indispensable part of life.

You'd think with all the Nintendo games around it wouldn't be hard to get a kid to like a computer. Not necessarily true, according to Marshall and Rogers, who claim that little girls especially are often turned off by the contraptions when they first confront them in grade school. But with a curriculum designed carefully with accessible equipment and material to capture the attention and interest of a young child, Computertots has an excellent track record of getting its charges intrigued and excited about the technology. "There are so many adults that are just afraid of working with the computer," observes Lake County, Illinois, Computertots franchisee Len King, "but these kids will never be."

Both former teachers with backgrounds in special education, Rogers and Marshall developed the Educational Computer Workshop in a Washington, D.C., suburb in 1983, offering computer tutoring to students with learning difficulties. Five years and several thousand lessons later, they launched the Computertots franchise, modeled after MIT's computer project for young children. Marshall's expertise in the role of computers in education and Rogers's experience as a programmer and software designer are key to the company's success. "By keeping current in children's interests and in educational trends," Rogers says, "we are able to provide our students the most educationally and creatively useful tools in computer technology."

Geared to a general preschool and early grade school audience, Computertots classes are usually limited to five students and held once a week for 30 minutes. Contrary to most assumptions, computer work is hardly a solitary activity. Says Marshall, "You see a great deal of group problem solving—the kids help each other." Franchisees or their team of teachers bring the computers, software, and lesson plans directly to day-care centers, schools, or other places where classes are taught. "Computertots is an attractive benefit to our program. Parents like it and there is little work or concern for the school," according to Debbie Warsing of the Teddy Bear Pre-school. Many facilities agree that the program is an effective marketing tool for them, not to mention inexpensive; it's the parents, not the schools or centers, who pay for the classes, commonly $24 a month.

Familiarizing your students with the basic components of a computer, you make them comfortable with the machine. You'll use special equipment designed just for children—keyboards built for small hands and highly interactive software offering familiar melodies and colorful animation, many programs featuring characters like Peter Rabbit, Snoopy, and Sesame Street regulars. You'll also bring along light pens that let youngsters touch the screen and create images, and the Computertots robot, which can be programmed by the kids to talk and move. In the process of having fun, your students will be learning such skills as how to turn on a computer, insert floppy disks, work a cursor, use command keys and joysticks, and operate an entire computer program, picking up, not so incidentally, a few reading and math skills along the way.

The only prerequisite for your students is that they be toilet trained. For Computertot franchisees, however, there aren't any specific background requirements at all, although preschool or elementary education experience is undeniably helpful. Computertots will provide you with an equipment package, including 23 software programs; an eight-month curriculum; operations manuals; masters for forms, brochures, and flyers; and a list of the additional materials you will need, which the company will assist you in buying. To learn how to use all this, you'll attend five days of training in the D.C. area, where you'll be taught instructional procedures, personnel management, accounting methods, and marketing and PR techniques. You'll also be supplied with a videotape and a teacher training manual for instructing any staff you may hire.

To get you started, the company will provide introductions to possible day-care clients in your territory, and to keep you going, they'll give your operation regular formal reviews for spotting potential difficulties as well as potential opportunities for expanding your program. Ongoing seminars are offered, too, and you'll also have access to the company's resource center, which stocks computer programs, computer education sourcebooks, journals, and other material on early childhood development.

Computertots franchisees are assigned an exclusive development territory. Working mothers themselves, Rogers and Marshall have made this an enterprise well-suited to those like them. "A lot of women out there want to have a business but don't want to work 60 hours a week away from their children. This is a business you can run from the home."

For further information contact:
Karen Marshall, President, Computertots, 10132 Colvin Run Rd., P.O. Box 340, Great Falls, VA 22066, 703-759-2556, fax 703-759-1938

Sylvan Learning Corporation

Initial license fee: $19,500, $25,000, or $35,000
Royalties: 8% and 9%
Advertising royalties: 1.5%
Minimum cash required: $25,000
Capital required: $50,690 to $118,935
Financing: None
Length of contract: 10 years

In business since: 1979
Franchising since: 1980
Total number of units: 478
Number of company-operated units: 23
Total number of units planned, 1995: 600
Number of company-operated units planned, 1995: 4

A steady stream of newspaper articles, magazine stories, and special television reports in recent years have focused on American children's declining scores on standardized academic tests. Many parents, government officials, and education experts are concerned that many American children will fall a step behind in an increasingly competitive society. And because they see public schools as overcrowded places, where even dedicated teachers simply don't have the time to devote to children who need special attention, many parents gladly pay for services that promise improved academic progress for their children. Through Sylvan, you can actually influence the lives of kids in your community by improving their basic educational skills and raising their self-esteem.

Sylvan is a group of neighborhood educational centers, located across the country, offering reading, math, writing, study skills, algebra, college prep/SAT/ACT, beginning reading, and school readiness programs. They provide diagnostic testing to help determine exactly where the child's problem lies, then they design an individual program to meet his or her needs. Positive motivation, friendly encouragement, and an experience of success right from the start make all the difference. The staff of each center consists of a director, a director of education, and part-time certified teachers. With a maximum student-to-faculty ratio of 3:1, Sylvan guarantees individual attention for its students. School-age children generally attend a Sylvan Learning Center for one hour two times a week, between the hours of 3:30 and 8:30 P.M. Tokens, given to students when they master a new level of the curriculum, can be redeemed at a "store" on the premises for toys, games, and other rewards.

Sylvan Learning Centers are located in upscale shopping centers or professional office buildings. The franchise consultant will help determine the ideal location for the business and give you standardized specifications for laying out your operation. Sylvan requires the franchisee to purchase furniture and provides all educational promotional materials.

Sylvan assists you in hiring your full-time staff. There is a two-week training session provided for new franchisees, directors, and directors of education, to learn how to administer the educational programs, manage the basics of the business, and enhance revenue. A franchise consultant, located in each region, will make scheduled visits to help you improve your operation. Regional conferences and an annual meeting provide a forum for further enrichment.

For further information contact:
  Charlotte Bentley, Director of Franchise Sales, Sylvan Learning Corporation,
  9135 Guilford Rd., Columbia, MD 21046, 1-800-284-8214

Tutor Time Learning Centers, Inc.

Initial license fee: $27,500
Royalties: 5%
Advertising royalties: 1%
Minimum cash required: $45,000
Capital required: $75,000 to $125,000
Financing: Up to $106,000
Length of contract: 10 years

In business since: 1980
Franchising since: 1989
Total number of units: 48
Number of company-operated units: 2
Total number of units planned, 1995: 300
Number of company-operated units planned, 1995: 1

Given that NASA chose the company to build a child-care facility for employees of the Kennedy Space Center, it should be no surprise that Tutor Time's approach is unabashedly high-tech. The program has been designed by a group of university professors and honed by a research and development department that continues to explore new educational products, services, and strategies.

At Tutor Time, the day is broken down into 30-minute components, as children rotate through an array of learning modules. They're kept busy in the different classrooms and activity spaces that each Tutor Time facility features—not only a library, music room, art center, and playground (the NASA center's is appropriately equipped with play climb-in space shuttles), but also a computer area, where kids work on early math, reading, and computer literacy programs, and a Tutor Time Village, complete with a mini-pharmacy, schoolhouse, hospital, and other buildings for role-playing. Kids bring home monthly schedules to their parents that outline upcoming activities and theme days. And to encourage thorough involvement, parents are also invited to drop by the centers whenever they want, asked to attend regular conferences with facility supervisors, and treated to periodic "Mom and Pop" nights.

Taking further steps to nurture the health and well-being of its students, Tutor Time employs a clinical physician for ongoing consultation and a licensed speech and language pathologist who screens each attendee at no additional fee. Aptitude tests are administered to kindergarten-aged youngsters to monitor their academic development. And daily meals are provided for a modest charge if parents don't want to pack a bag lunch.

Tutor Time centers are equipped to care for 150 to 200 children, aged 6 weeks to 6 years, and are open year-round. Programs beyond basic school-year day care are available. There are after-school sessions that feature academic tutoring; enrichment classes in such subjects as Spanish, dance, and computers; and organized sports. Extended hours are available for parents who have to bring their children in early or pick them up late, and the company furnishes a drop-off babysitting service, too. There's also Tutor Time's "Summer Schedule," offering a lighter, camplike atmosphere, with programs that include karate, gymnastics, drama productions, and field trips, as well as the inevitable arts and crafts.

While you're establishing your Tutor Time franchise, the home office will be in daily contact, either by phone or computer. Company officials will work closely with you in developing your facility, which will be 6,000 to 10,000 square feet on ¾ to 1½ acres of ground, or in a building with an attached playground space. They'll guide you through the Tutor Time's detailed specifications for educational, safety, and security components—features like one-way mirrors in each classroom for parents to observe their kids unseen, and gates and alarm systems. And they'll assist in screening your prospective employees, from maintenance personnel to teachers, checking references and contacting motor vehicle, criminal, workmen's compensation, and child abuse registries alike to make sure they have clean records.

You'll be required to attend Tutor Time's 90-day training program, an instructional session that the company says is far more comprehensive than that offered by any other child-care franchise. Classes cover Tutor Time business procedures, methods for hiring and training staff, use of the company's computer software, marketing and sales techniques, enrollment and registration systems, and introduction to the materials and lessons you'll be using at your facility.

Your day-to-day operations will be expedited by the Tutor Time computer system, which holds tuition information, financial statements, medical records, attendance lists, and payroll and budget details. And through regular newsletters, the franchise advisory committee keeps you updated on the recent findings and advancements from the company's research and development division.

Tutor Time franchises are located throughout Florida. At present, the company's philosophy is to continue concentrating in that area, opening new centers within a 50-mile radius of current or newly signed locations.

For further information contact:
Ed Secaul, Director of Franchising, Tutor Time Learning Centers, Inc., 4517 N.W. 31st Ave., Fort Lauderdale, FL 33309, 305-730-0332 or 1-800-275-1235

Day Care

Primrose School

Initial license fee: $48,500
Royalties: 7%
Advertising royalties: 1%
Minimum cash required: $100,000
Capital required: $100,000
Financing: Consultation available
Length of contract: 10 years

In business since: 1982
Franchising since: 1988
Total number of units: 14
Number of company-operated units: 3
Total number of units planned, 1995: 200
Number of company-operated units planned, 1995: 3

You think all those stories about ambitious parents-to-be who try to enroll children not even born yet in a choice preschool are exaggerated? Well, that's exactly what some are doing to clinch a good position on Primrose Schools' waiting lists. With publicity like an Atlanta *Constitution* article claiming that "Primrose is to the day-care industry what the Rolls Royce is to automobiles," it's no wonder.

Believing their schools present a superior alternative to the mere glorified babysitting extended at most day-care centers, Primrose aims to provide well-rounded quality education and enrichment activities, supplemented by scrupulous general child care. The Primrose programs attempt to foster healthy growth for children, from infancy to school age, at every level—physically, socially, and academically.

Open from 6:30 A.M. to 6:30 P.M. Monday through Friday, Primrose Schools offer two-, three-, and five-day packages. During the full- or half-day sessions, the children are grouped by age for academic programs: early preschool for 1½- to 2-year-olds, preschool for youngsters aged 2½ to 4, and kindergarten for those who've turned or are about to turn 5. Operating on the theory that children are never too young to start learning, Primrose has designed a class for its littlest charges, too, an infant stimulation program to help babies 6 weeks to 18 months improve their motor and social skills. In addition, there's after-school care for boys and girls up to age 12, and a summer camp session, featuring arts and crafts, water sports, gymnastics, cookouts, and field trips.

The year-round curriculum involves creative arts, music, and physical education, plus Spanish and computer instruction for kindergartners and after-school students. For the convenience of parents, the schools also provide breakfast, lunch, and snacks, transportation, and extra child-care services on an as-needed basis. And mothers and fathers are kept informed and involved by the schools' exhaustive monitoring of their children's progress in daily reports, weekly teacher letters, and twice-yearly complete assessments.

The Primrose management is confident that it has developed a child-care formula that works, and passes on detailed instructions, advice, and support to its franchisees. In a *USA Today* article, one affiliate described President Paul Erwin as "the type of person who dots his i's and crosses his t's when it comes to running businesses." The company starts by making recommendations for the location of your facility, based on demographic information and traffic patterns, and will furnish assistance, if you'd like, in procuring the land, obtaining proper zoning, and meeting other government requirements.

To give your facility the Primrose look, meant to instill professionalism and security along with warmth and homeyness, you'll be supplied with a preliminary set of blueprints and design specifications, including cost estimates. The details are quite precise: topped by a copper rooster weather vane on the roof, the Primrose symbol representing "pride and direction," each school's exterior colors are hunter green and mulberry, accented by brass door handles and kickplates, with complementary wallpaper and braided rugs inside. Every room is equipped with an intercom system used to pipe in music during naps, rest periods, and certain activities, and the colorful playgrounds are divided into separate sections for each age group.

Conducted at both the corporate offices in the Atlanta area and at an operating facility, your training covers the educational, child care, and business aspects of running a Primrose School, including information on prices, payroll services, insurance, licensing, and day-to-day administrative and teaching details. A company official will spend several days at your facility before the start of business to set up the classrooms, instruct personnel, and prepare for your grand opening.

The equipment you'll need, like computers, toys, playground materials, and kitchen appliances, can all be procured from Primrose's suppliers. More importantly, the company will outfit you with a complete curriculum, monthly calendars of events, and specific weekly lesson plans—for each age-group in your school—that are easy to follow and implement.

You'll also receive a grand opening package, ad layouts, and promotional suggestions, as well as marketing ideas to help you maximize your pre-opening enrollment. And don't overlook the value of the car decals, T-shirts, and tote bags with that rooster weather-vane symbol given to Primrose kids and parents, bringing widespread name recognition in your community.

Meeting state licensing requirements is an obvious prerequisite to owning and operating a Primrose School facility in addition to getting approval from the company's franchise committee—based on a review of your application and evaluation rather than any explicit prerequisites. With a background outside the education field himself, Primrose president Paul Erwin is open to signing qualified franchisees from different walks of life.

For further information contact:
   Jo Kirchner, Vice President, Primrose School Franchising Company, 5131
   Roswell Rd., N.E., Marietta, GA 30062, 404-998-8329 or 1-800-745-0728

Wee Watch Private Home Day Care

Initial license fee: $6,000
Royalties: 6% to 8%
Advertising royalties: 2%
Minimum cash required: $15,000
Capital required: $15,000
Financing: None
Length of contract: 25 years

In business since: 1983
Franchising since: 1987
Total number of units: 32
Number of company-operated units: None
Total number of units planned, 1995: 85
Number of company-operated units planned, 1995: None

The premise of Wee Watch is a simple one: that private home day care is the best form of child care available. Children in the Wee Watch program are looked after in the residences of trained care providers, often mothers or fathers of young kids themselves who need or want to work at home.

With no more than five children under their supervision, the care-givers are able to develop a real relationship with their charges and to give them close, individual attention in an intimate setting. The children don't have to do anything according to a group schedule, and they tend to be sick less often, because fewer kids are around to pass on illnesses. The home environment also allows Wee Watch to accept babies as young as 6 weeks—60 percent are 2 years old or younger—making the service particularly attractive to middle-income working parents who can't afford a nanny and who can't use many established day-care centers, which are reluctant to look after children younger than 2½ years.

Jan Fullerton and her husband, Terry, started the Wee Watch network, a Canadian-based operation that they are now planning to expand into the States.

Back in the early 1980s, the couple thought they could earn some extra money by looking after a few neighbor kids while raising their own two small children. But the initial deluge of interest was so overwhelming that within six months the Fullertons began laying the groundwork for a child-care referral service. With funding from the CEO of a multinational home care services operation and his coinvestors, the Wee Watch franchise was on its way. Early affiliates got the same kind of reaction as the Fullertons. Driving down the highway, one franchisee was pulled over by a traffic officer, who stopped her because he noticed the Wee Watch logo on the minivan and wanted information about the program.

As a Wee Watch franchisee, you will be operating a day-care referral agency. That means, essentially, that you will be matching people who'd like to offer day care in their homes with interested parents. You'll be recruiting both the day-care providers in your territory, who'll work as independent contractors, and the families, who will choose among the different home options available and between full- or part-time care.

Wee Watch works closely with you in the hiring of the caregivers. The company checks the references of those who apply, has them undergo a medical examination, and performs a safety and fire inspection of their homes, ascertaining that local regulations and Wee Watch standards are met. Once the caregivers are accepted, the company takes care of training them in areas like nutrition, exercise, first aid, and creative play, and supplies them with all the equipment they'll need, including toys, books, cribs, playpens, highchairs, and strollers.

Because you will be offering a particularly sensitive service, Wee Watch considers your training to be of great importance as well. You'll begin with one week of classes in the Toronto area, involving a combination of instruction, discussion, observation, and hands-on field activity, and covering such topics as general business methods, procedures unique to the Wee Watch network, marketing and PR, and supervision of caregivers. You may also request additional on-the-job training, which will be extended by a fellow franchisee. Field seminars are held regularly for you and the care providers, and you will be kept further up to date with periodic bulletins and operations manual supplements. Along with regular assistance in finding clients for your franchise, Wee Watch will prepare an introductory marketing package for you, featuring ads, brochures, and other promotional materials tailored to your territory.

The home office will work with you to obtain your license to run a day-care agency and will act as a liaison between you and the government on an ongoing basis. Wee Watch officials are also there to answer any questions. And you'll have many—from clarifying government regulations to handling conflicts between providers and parents. The company monitors your business on a weekly basis; if they sense any trouble, they'll contact you immediately. Likewise, you will watch closely over the caregivers under your supervision, and are expected to make an unannounced visit to each one's home at least once a month.

There are no specific prerequisites for becoming a Wee Watch franchisee. You will be required to enroll in a certified early childhood education academic program, however, if you do not already have a degree in the field. While you can run your agency business from your own home, don't think it will be a part-time job. Once the agency is well established, a Wee Watch franchisee is responsible for an average of 60—and as many as 120—children, overseeing a dozen care providers at least. As Terry Fullerton says, this isn't an easy job. "If a provider who looks after three children calls in sick on a Sunday night, you have to find backup providers for those kids before Monday morning." But the work can be highly profitable as well as rewarding.

For further information contact:
   Terry Fullerton, Vice President, Wee Watch Private Home Day Care, 25
   Valleywood Dr., Suite 20, Markham, Ont., Canada L3R 5L9, 416-479-4274

Youthland Academy Daycare Centers

Initial license fee: $27,500
Royalties: 5%
Advertising royalties: $282/month
Minimum cash required: $30,000
Capital required: $100,000
Financing: None
Length of contract: 10 years

In business since: 1982
Franchising since: 1985
Total number of units: 21
Number of company-operated units: 2
Total number of units planned, 1995: 46
Number of company-operated units planned, 1995: None

More babies were born in 1987 in the United States than in any year
since 1964. With an increasing number of mothers in the work force
and an estimated eight million families who require some kind of day-
care arrangements, it's not surprising that child-care franchises are expected to experience unprecedented growth through the nineties. Of
these, Youthland Academy is especially well-poised for continued success, rated by *Entrepreneur* magazine the number-one franchise in the
field for four consecutive years.
    Youthland Academies provide year-round day care, including sum-
mer camp, for children from 6 weeks to 12 years, offering before- and
after-school programs as well as all-day services and furnishing transportation to and from area schools. While the numbers vary from
center to center, a typical Youthland franchise cares for 110 to 130
kids. The curriculum is oriented toward developing their social, emotional, physical, and intellectual needs, and classrooms are designed
and furnished to enhance their experience and provide maximum
safety.
    Being more than "just babysitters" is a point of pride for Youthland,
and it's equally important that parents see that difference. Most of the
facilities are located near a majority of the parents' workplaces, so
mothers and fathers can drop by during the day to join in on the activities. Local ownership is another big advantage to the Youthland
program. The problem with major day-care chains is that they lack
the personal touch. You, however, will be getting to know not only

the kids, but their parents, too, who'll appreciate being able to deal directly with the proprietor of the facility where their children spend so much of their day.

Jan Schmitt, founder and president of Youthland, brought a background in education and motherhood to her business. Working as a junior high school teacher when her first child was born, she was in the position of so many other parents who needed quality day care but couldn't find it. Those operations she did try didn't make it easy for parents to share in the details of their children's day. She felt out of touch and worried, like a lot of parents, that perhaps day care wasn't good for her daughter. Taking matters into her own hands, she studied elementary education, got a job managing a day-care center, and finally opened one of her own in the Cincinnati, Ohio, area, where she put her theories about superior child care into practice. After four successful years in business, she started franchising, using the same formula of close interaction with parents.

Now, Jan Schmitt has a lot of ideas about superior franchise support, too. It begins with assistance in site selection, with the company offering guidance in locating an appropriate facility at a reasonable cost. After you have identified several possibilities, a Youthland representative will evaluate each site in person to help you make the most profitable choice. You may decide to build a separate facility if you wish, but, unlike other child-care businesses, the company recommends a less costly alternative that can be turned into a just-as-effective center. When it comes to equipping the academy, Youthland combines specific suggestions with a flexible attitude, while their supplier contracts will save you money on the materials you'll rent or purchase.

An initial two weeks of instruction is given to franchisees and their staff, as you all work at a full-time Youthland Academy to learn firsthand how the operation really functions. You'll receive ongoing training as well, twice-yearly on-site sessions where new educational programs are introduced.

Youthland will supply a full curriculum each month to let you design and plan your academy's learning activities for the next 30 days. To make sure your business is running smoothly, a Youthland official will come to inspect your facility four times during your first year in business and twice a year thereafter.

The company has no specific prerequisites for its franchisees beyond their being able to meet their home state's qualifications for day-care directors. Most states will require that you have a bachelor's degree (usually in any subject) from an accredited college. The company will help potential franchisees determine if they qualify for certification and will guide you through the often arduous process of obtaining your license.

Youthland grants exclusive territories to its franchisees, while its targeting of companies that seek child-care packages of their own brings other options. You may be able to develop an on-site facility for a corporate employer in a profit-sharing partnership, or find a firm that will share start-up costs in exchange for a specific number of spaces in your academy.

For further information contact:
  Jan Schmitt, President, Youthland Academy Daycare Centers,
  210 University Dr., Suite 402, Coral Springs, FL 33065, 305-779-5148

Preschool Activities

Gymboree

Initial license fee: $9,000 to $19,000
Royalties: 6%
Advertising royalties: 2%
Minimum cash required: $40,000
Capital required: $40,000
Financing: None
Length of contract: 10 years

In business since: 1976
Franchising since: 1980
Total number of units: 320
Number of company-operated units: 5
Total number of units planned, 1995: 400
Number of company-operated units planned, 1995: 5

Fifteen years ago, Joan Barnes invented a product she couldn't find but strongly felt she needed: a developmental center for her two young daughters. "As a young mother," she recalls, "I wanted a positive environment where I could be with other like-minded moms for support, and I wanted my child to be with other kids."

The resulting program involves 45-minute, once-a-week sessions in rented churches, synagogues, and community centers, in which parents join with their children, aged 2 months to 5 years, in a systematic session of play, movement, and song. Special equipment and decorations create a stimulating multicolored environment. Today, about 70,000 kids across the United States and Canada participate in the program.

The Gymboree centers work because they meet a need that most parents share. More and more attention is being focused on the psychomotor and emotional development of children under the age of 5. The time demands of dual-career families and the simultaneous desire of couples not to pass up the experience of parenthood puts a premium on whatever "quality time" parents can spend with their children. Add to that the growing interest in physical fitness and parents' concerns about not pushing young children into competitive atmospheres, and you have Gymboree.

At Gymboree kids as young as 3 months old gather with at least one of their parents in a room chock-full of soft and colorful play equipment, including bouncers, balance beams, and slides. In the middle of the room is a real multicolored parachute. The kids roll, touch, stretch, crawl, and jump, depending on their age. They also chant and sing. The sessions are usually structured around a warm-up exercise period with background music, a directed period of various kinds of movement on the equipment, and a final period of games and singing. Gymboree encourages parents to get right in there with their kids and play.

The point of all this, Barnes says, is "to build a child's self-confidence," while at the same time offering an opportunity for "self-discovery and exploration." Another benefit is an improvement in the children's self-image. Just as important—maybe even more important in terms of marketing—is what the program gives parents. They gain "greater confidence in how to parent and . . . a more positive feeling about their parenting ability and their relationship with their child."

Barnes obviously tapped into what many parents think, because Gymboree has received write-ups in the *Wall Street Journal*, the *New York Times*, the *Atlanta Journal*, *Time*, *Newsweek*, *Ms.*, and many other newspapers and magazines. The *Wall Street Journal* said: "Parents contend the program improves the child's balance, coordination, and social skills." *Newsweek* wrote: "Kids are also encouraged to play independently. As the children climb on diminutive jungle gyms or roll around on huge foam rubber logs, the classroom rings with laughter." *Good Morning America* and other network shows have also featured Gymboree.

Typical Gymboree franchisees are former businesspeople or teachers in their late twenties and early thirties. Several of them became interested in running one or more Gymborees (the company encourages franchisees to operate multiple units) when they entered their own children in the program.

Franchisees participate in a nine-day training period at the company's headquarters in Burlingame, California. There is no extra charge for the instruction, but you have to pay for lodging and some meals. Annual seminars at headquarters and regional training sessions update and reinforce the basic instruction.

If you become a franchisee, the company will give you guidelines for choosing a site, but you make the actual selection. You must purchase a package of program aids and equipment, although some additional material is optional. The company tests all Gymboree programs and equipment at the five company-owned centers before releasing it for use in other units. Gymboree also has a cooperative advertising program that funds national advertising as well as provides franchisees with marketing materials to use locally. Gymboree also has a line of products available for resale at the franchise sites. Especially popular is a line of music cassettes and videos.

Toni Ann Lueddecke, who owns Gymboree of North Central New Jersey, feels that her decision to connect with the company was the right one. She told us she especially likes the combination of company assistance and the freedom to shape her business according to her own ideas. "I bought a franchise in order to have control over my own business," she says. "This is, in actuality, what does happen. I submit quarterly reports, but day-to-day operation is my decision."

Along with being the leader in developmental play programs, Gymboree is also the fastest growing retailer for infants and toddlers. The retail division, which was initiated in 1986, is currently operating 52 stores with a projected 130 outlets by 1994. Each Gymboree store features specially designed activewear and gifts for children. While Gymboree stores are company owned, they are strongly supported by the Gymboree franchise network with cross-promotions.

For further information contact:
  Bob Campbell, Gymboree, 577 Airport Blvd., Suite 400, Burlingame, CA
  94010, 415-579-0600

Kinderdance International, Inc.

Initial license fee: $6,000 to $10,000
Royalties: 15%, declining to 10% with purchase of additional unit
Advertising royalties: 3%
Minimum cash required: $4,000
Capital required: $1,000
Financing: Up to 50% of franchise fee
Length of contract: 10 years

In business since: 1979
Franchising since: 1985
Total number of units: 17

Number of company-operated units: None
Total number of units planned, 1995: 100
Number of company-operated units planned, 1995: None

The most influential child psychologists and educators all agree that a developmental program in movement should be a part of every youngster's education—and more than merely for its own sake. "One of the greatest mistakes of our day," Montessori once wrote, "is to think of movement by itself, as something apart from the higher functions. . . . Mental development must be connected with movement and be dependent on it."

Music and dance, in other words, are great tools for overall learning. What the people at Kinderdance have done is to put the theory into practice, offering programs in music and dance for young children and taking care that classes meant to be good for kids don't interfere with their fun.

Kinderdance is a dance, motor development, and educational program specifically designed for children ages 3 to 5. Boys and girls learn the basics of ballet, tap, acrobatics, and creative dance, while at the same time also building their vocabulary, numbers skills, and knowledge of colors and shapes, not to mention their attention span.

One former Kinderdance instructor, Donna Wear, observed that tap lessons were a particular favorite. "They can't wait to get their tap shoes on. At that age, they like noise. Ballet is a little quiet for them." The point is that a love of movement and music comes naturally to kids, while a love of learning is not always innate. Combine the three and you have a much better chance of getting a preschooler interested in academic material. And with flash cards as important to Kinderdance as leotards, introducing lessons into the sessions is a deceptively easy task: have a 3-year-old practice doing, say, eight toe taps, for example, and see how quickly she learns to count to eight.

The success of the original program led Kinderdance's directors to add three more levels of instruction: Kindertots, sessions geared toward 2-year-olds; Kindergym, a class with special emphasis on basic gymnastics skills; and Kindercombo, a ballet/jazz/tap/modern dance program for children aged 6 to 10.

As a Kinderdance franchisee, you'll be qualified to teach all four programs, offering classes at local nursery schools, day care centers, YMCAs, churches and synagogues, public and private elementary schools, even community centers and military bases, "wherever," as the company puts it, "there are children and an open space." And there certainly are plenty of children. During the 1980s baby boom, the number of preschoolers in the United States increased by 17 percent, a trend expected to last through the 1990s. Bringing your service to the kids—and the facilities—makes it that much more desirable. Parents will appreciate not having to drive their youngsters to yet another class, and the facilities will appreciate having another quality program to help them attract clients.

Your seven days of training to become a Kinderdance franchisee and instructor are very much like an apprenticeship, focusing on giving you hands-on experience with kids in an actual Kinderdance class. In action, you'll be able to see how the lesson plans keep the sessions interesting and how effective behavior management can reinforce a youngster's self-esteem. Discussion periods, video instruction, and one-on-one sessions are also part of the course. "When our franchisees are done with training," Kinderdance vice president Bernard Friedman maintains, "they are more qualified to teach dance for this age group than most dance teachers."

So you can stay on top of the material, you'll keep a complete curriculum and videotapes for each of the Kinderdance levels and programs. A company representative will also work with you as you begin offering classes. There are annual continuing education courses as well, for sharpening your skills, and bimonthly Kindernews Letters to provide updated information.

You'll receive a cassette player and 12 program tapes, along with teaching tools like bean bags, tambourines, numbers, colors, shapes, and, yes, flash cards. An operations manual and business forms are also a part of your franchise package, which even includes dancewear and a gym mat. In addition, the company supplies a step-by-step marketing package, featuring a "Marketing in Your Area" video explaining how to establish a client base, plus brochures, flyers, sample press releases, ad layouts, and direct mail materials.

A background in dance is helpful, but not necessary. Kinderdance considers it more important that you have a high level of energy, to say the least, and enjoy the company of children. This is a franchise opportunity designed especially for women who don't have extensive investment capital but still want to start a viable business. You'll be free to set your own schedule, and can earn extra income by selling customized Kinderdance clothes.

Two different franchise packages are available. The less expensive is a part-time option that entitles you to conduct Kinderdance classes at up to eight locations, but with no limit to the number of children you teach or number of hours you work. The full-time option gives you the opportunity eventually to develop an entire territory and train additional instructors.

For further information contact:
  Bernard Friedman, Vice President, Kinderdance International, Inc., P.O. Box 510881, Melbourne Beach, FL 32951, 407-254-3000 or 1-800-666-1595

Pee Wee Workout

Initial license fee: $1,500
Royalties: 10%
Advertising royalties: None
Minimum cash required: $1,700
Capital required: NA
Financing: None
Length of contract: 5 years

In business since: 1986
Franchising since: 1987
Total number of units: 24
Number of company-operated units: 1
Total number of units planned, 1995: 35
Number of company-operated units planned, 1995: 1

The American Academy of Pediatrics recently reported that only 2 percent of the children who took the Presidential Fitness Test passed. The Presidential Council of Fitness and Sports released studies showing a decline in boys' and girls' physical abilities, endurance, and activity levels. Youngsters today have been found to have significantly higher levels of body fat than kids in the 1960s, and preschoolers are already on their way to setting a lifelong pattern for inactivity and improper nutrition. There's little doubt about it—America's youth is out of shape.

So what's the solution? Baby boot camp? Hardly, says Margaret Carr, developer of the Pee Wee Workout, an exercise program for preschoolers and grade school children. In her 17 years as a certified aerobics trainer, Carr found out what motivates fitness seekers of all ages. Too many adults, let alone children, consider exercise to be more like work than recreation—those endless refrains of "no pain, no gain"—and eating properly to be an unpleasant task. No, Margaret Carr says, you have to make exercising and learning about nutrition enjoyable for kids.

So that's what Pee Wee Workouts aim to do—help children discover that fitness can be fun. Exercise brings them immediate benefits: improved health, a better ability to concentrate and learn, even an increase in self-esteem and confidence. Carr's theory is also that if children start to relish physical activity early on, they'll be more likely to remain active throughout their lives.

Separate curricula have been developed for both preschoolers and kids in elementary school. Franchisees either lead the 30-minute classes themselves or hire trainers, starting with a warm-up, followed by exercises with and without toys and props, done to the accompaniment of sing-along music while the leader explains about heart rate, body parts, and the muscles being worked, and concluding with a cool-down and short anatomy or nutrition lesson.

Sure, there's plenty of stretching and jumping jacks, but the real point is teaching healthy life-styles and respect for the body. New York City franchisee Sherry Ferrante concurs: "The purpose of Pee Wee Workout is not to build muscles as much as to create lifelong fitness patterns. Everything is presented in a fun and positive manner that kids can respond to and enjoy."

You'll be going to where the kids are, offering classes to and at daycare centers, preschools, grade schools, and recreational programs. Oftentimes you'll be filling a necessary niche, as these facilities may lack structured physical fitness programs of their own—even public schools are having to cut back due to funding shortages. What's more, while most sports programs that do exist do a good job to promote skills development and interaction, they do little to encourage aerobic fitness. In addition, you'll be providing a refreshing noncompetitive environment. There are no winners or losers in Pee Wee Workouts; the youngsters receive "Good Work" awards that reward effort, not ability.

You are not required to be a certified aerobics instructor in order to lead a Pee Wee fitness class. Actually, you can start scheduling classes as soon as you've learned the program. Training is furnished through videotapes and guidebooks, allowing you to master the curriculum at your own pace in your home. When you become a Pee Wee franchisee, you'll receive a curriculum package, which includes one instructional video and manual, plus an audiocassette with the music for your classes. You'll be required to purchase two other packages during the first year—both offering new aerobic routines to use in your sessions—and one more in each of the following years that you're a Pee Wee franchisee.

Additionally, you'll be given a nutrition manual and a supplies booklet that furnishes ideas for props, toys, costumes, and puppets to add to your classes. Your start-up package will also include camera-ready copy for stationery and business cards, operations forms, informational pamphlets describing the workout to parents, as well as brochures advertising licensed Pee Wee exercise wear and products. There's an 800 phone line for keeping in touch and getting suggestions and quick solutions to problems, and the company regularly sends along updated nutrition and fitness information.

While it's not required, work in a fitness-related field is considered an excellent background for Pee Wee franchisees. Experience working with kids certainly doesn't hurt, either; the company considers the most important qualification to be what it calls "an ability to relate to children." Child-care center and preschool operators have become Pee Wee franchisees, adding the exercise classes to their own programs. The start-up expense is modest—*Entrepreneur* magazine, in fact, named Pee Wee Workout one of the 25 top low-investment franchises—and the flexible hours make this an especially viable opportunity for those raising children and/or seeking a part-time operation.

For further information contact:
  Margaret Carr, President, Cardiac Carr Co., 34976 Aspenwood Lane, Willoughby, OH 44094, 216-946-7888 or 1-800-356-6261

10. The Employment Industry

Contents

Permanent Placement

AAA Employment

Initial license fee: $10,000
Royalties: Deescalating based on gross income
Advertising royalties: 2%
Minimum cash required: $15,000 to $35,000
Capital required: $15,000 to $35,000
Financing: None
Length of contract: 10 years

In business since: 1957
Franchising since: 1977
Total number of units: 59
Number of company-operated units: 4
Total number of units planned, 1995: 89
Number of company-operated units planned, 1995: 4

Sherridan Revell, owner of an AAA Employment franchise in Roanoke, Virginia, calls the AAA franchise fail-safe: "If any qualified franchisee operates an agency according to the training and policy guides, that person cannot fail. The company's methods have been tested and proven many, many times." One AAA policy, that of applicant-paid placement, under which those placed by the agency generally pay about two weeks' salary to AAA, has made the company popular with employers nationwide. By providing a free service to employers for more than 30 years, AAA has become the largest privately owned employment agency in the United States. AAA agencies place people in all kinds of employment, from professional and executive to domestic help, in both temporary and permanent positions. The company is recruiting new franchisees in every state except Florida, Georgia, Alabama, and Mississippi.

AAA has developed a complete set of policies and procedures for agency owners and offers an optional two- to four-week training program at the home office in St. Petersburg, Florida. Almost all franchisees take advantage of this comprehensive program, in which they receive intensive training in agency operation. Topics covered include bookkeeping, advertising, controls, budget, collections, taxes, payroll, hiring, and all other phases of day-to-day agency operation. The highly recommended sessions are free, except for the cost of travel, lodging, and meals.

In addition to its training program, AAA will provide you with support during every phase of preopening. The company will help you

select a site for your agency, negotiate a lease, obtain the necessary licenses, furnish your office, hire and train employees, and set up procedures for advertising, budgeting, and bookkeeping. During your first
week or two of operation, an experienced agency operator will work
with you at your office. When you feel ready to go it alone, the company will allow you all the freedom you desire to make all of your
own management decisions. And the operations manual will prove to
be an invaluable resource to you as an independent businessperson.

If, like Jane Miller, an AAA franchisee in Pittsburgh, Pennsylvania,
you enjoy owning your own business but "don't have the money to
run it by trial and error," you will benefit from the regular visits that
company field representatives pay to all AAA franchisees. In special
circumstances, your representative will visit you upon request to assist
with unusual problems. You can attend the semiannual seminars for
updates on policy changes, industry information, and improvements in
techniques and procedures, and read the weekly AAA newsletter for
business tips and information on franchise activities.

The training and support that AAA provides franchisees make it
"well worth the royalties paid to the franchise home office to be a
part of this company," in the estimation of Sherridan Revell. As an
AAA owner, you have the independence to make your own business
judgments, your only obligation to the company being the payment of
the royalty. Operating franchisees, however, recommend that you stick
fairly closely to AAA guidelines to increase your chances of success; as
Jane Miller notes, "You own your own business and are paying to use
AAA's business methods. You should be making your own decisions,
but you would be foolish not to follow proven procedures."

For further information contact:
  Joseph Kotow, CEO, AAA Employment Franchise, 4910K Creekside Dr.,
  Clearwater, FL 34620, 813-573-0202

F-O-R-T-U-N-E Franchise Corporation

Initial license fee: $35,000
Royalties: 7%
Advertising royalties: 1%
Minimum cash required: $50,000
Capital required: $50,000 to $70,000
Financing: Up to ⅓ of the franchise fee
Length of contract: 20 years

In business since: 1959
Franchising since: 1973
Total number of units: 65

Number of company-operated units: None
Total number of units planned, 1995: 100
Number of company-operated units planned, 1995: None

People change jobs more often than they used to—sometimes as often as every three years on the middle management and executive levels. Since management jobs command the highest salaries, it stands to reason that placement services will make their greatest profits filling these positions. F-O-R-T-U-N-E confines its activities exclusively to this area. It points out that typical fees for filling these jobs run from $10,000 to $14,000 for a job paying $40,000; and from $15,000 to $19,000 for a job at the $60,000 mark. At these high figures, closing a few placements a month can result in a substantial income.

Because it's not a capital-and-equipment-intensive business, an executive recruitment firm has low start-up costs. And because it is a no-inventory business, monthly operating expenses are minimal. However, you may find you make up for low start-up costs with the extra investment of energy you'll need to accumulate an "inventory" of jobs to offer. That involves a different type of selling: selling corporate executives on why they should use your company, which you will be doing constantly. As Dennis Inzinna, the company's executive vice president, has observed, "Obtaining jobs is a daily effort you cannot afford to neglect."

F-O-R-T-U-N-E feels it has special features to offer both in organization and procedure. The company's placement people are called consultants. Rudy Schott, F-O-R-T-U-N-E's president and CEO, sees them as "experts whose advice is necessary for required solutions." At F-O-R-T-U-N-E, consultants can arrange for placements to be closed through in-house interviewing. In this procedure, the hiring executive comes to the F-O-R-T-U-N-E office and sees several qualified applicants. F-O-R-T-U-N-E feels this facilitates the closing of a greater percentage of placements in an efficient manner. F-O-R-T-U-N-E consultants show corporate executives that it is better for them to travel to the F-O-R-T-U-N-E location and spend half a day interviewing in a setting with no distractions than it is to spend parts of several days doing the same thing less effectively in their own office.

F-O-R-T-U-N-E offices have been opened by a former director of systems engineering for NCR, the director of human resources for Unisys, a vice president of manufacturing at Lenox China, and the deputy executive director of the Greater Detroit Health Center.

If you have a manufacturing, financial, or service-sector background and become a part of the F-O-R-T-U-N-E franchise system, you will receive strong support. You don't need experience in the placement field.

F-O-R-T-U-N-E provides an initial two weeks of training, plus a 90-day start-up procedure. The first two weeks of classes take place at F-O-R-T-U-N-E's New York City headquarters. Instruction includes actual experience in searching out positions and filling them. When you return to your office, the company will advise you on staffing your operation.

Not only does the company help you with site selection for your office, it also assists with the layout and other details, such as phone installation. F-O-R-T-U-N-E also helps you get insurance and qualify for your license.

In your first week of operation, one of F-O-R-T-U-N-E's training managers will remain with you, helping to train you and your people. Even after you're well under way, the New York office will keep close tabs on your progress and you can consult the company on a daily basis if necessary. Joseph A. Genovese, a F-O-R-T-U-N-E franchisee in Boston, says of the franchisor's support program: "I always have access to all of the people in the franchise when I have a special problem. They have never refused a request for help and in many cases have offered help when I didn't think I needed it."

That doesn't necessarily mean that F-O-R-T-U-N-E will cramp your entrepreneurial style. As Genovese puts it: "The company has been very excellent in providing guidelines for the management of my business. Within those guidelines they have become more or less active depending upon my needs and my requests for assistance. I have been very pleased with the arrangement."

For further information contact:
  Michael Meyerson, F-O-R-T-U-N-E Franchise Corporation, 655 Third Ave., Suite 1805, New York, NY 10017, 1-800-886-7839 (in New York, 212-697-4314)

Sanford Rose Associates (SRA)

Initial license fee: $29,500
Royalties: 3% to 8%
Advertising royalties: NA
Minimum cash required: $45,000
Capital required: $45,000 to $60,000
Financing: Available
Length of contract: 7 years

In business since: 1959
Franchising since: 1970
Total number of units: 85
Number of company-operated units: 1
Total number of units planned, 1995: 100
Number of company-operated units planned, 1995: 1

With a network of offices operating from coast to coast, Sanford Rose Associates (SRA) is one of the country's oldest and largest executive recruiting firms, locating management personnel and skilled technicians for corporate clients quickly and confidentially. According to *Success* magazine, which ranked it ninth among the top 100 franchises in any field, it is also one of the best business opportunities for entrepreneurs.

Entrepreneurs, that is, who are carefully screened by the company. Appropriately enough for an operation whose very job is finding the right fit between individuals and career positions, SRA takes this process very seriously. To begin with, SRA wants its franchisees to have a college degree or the equivalent; an advanced degree or what the company terms "some recognition of accomplishment in a specialized field or profession" is also "extremely desirable." You should have significant business or corporate experience in an upper-level position, preferably in a variety of disciplines, functions, and/or sectors, with responsibility for hiring, developing, evaluating, and firing personnel. Willing and able to cultivate an expertise in new businesses, you'll have to be flexible enough to adapt to new situations generated by the constantly changing economy of the nineties. Potential franchisees under serious consideration are required to spend a day, with their spouse if possible, at SRA headquarters in Akron for mutual evaluation.

If you and SRA agree to go into business together, you'll pinpoint a particular industry or work discipline in which to specialize, opting for fields that have the greatest hiring needs, as opposed to those with a high number of unemployed professionals. Unlike employment agencies, you'll be primarily dealing not with those actively in the job market, but with working professionals who are nevertheless interested in having new opportunities brought to their attention. The best candidates, as the industry wisdom goes, aren't in search of a job— they must be sought out.

Selective recruitment is the key. The positions you'll be filling have highly specific criteria; if you haven't carefully targeted truly qualified and interested prospects for the job, you'll be wasting their time, the client's time, and your own time alike. You'll need a thorough understanding of your client's needs and of the particular opening, so thorough that you'll actually be helping the client determine not only the job description, but also the hidden objectives and subtle requirements. The client expects it, and, just as important, so do the candidates, who must have confidence that they can discuss their career goals with you knowledgeably and candidly. As Sanford Rose himself said, "Our first obligation is to the candidate we have recruited. And this will inevitably turn out to be what is best for us as recruiters." Today's candidate, after all, may become tomorrow's hiring executive.

To get to know your clients' needs, you'll visit their facilities, developing a firsthand understanding of their organizational structure, corporate environment, and expectations for employees. Then, benefiting from the recruiting efforts of your fellow franchisees, you'll use SRA's network of referral sources and its data base of already interested prospects to begin to identify candidates for the specific position. You'll brief them on the job and the company and help them prepare for their interview, following up with both them and the client after they've met. If both parties are interested, you'll run a reference check; you'll even help negotiate all aspects of the employment offer and give relocation assistance, when necessary, through SRA's real estate affiliate.

Providing these services to appropriate client firms across the nation, you'll locate management personnel and skilled technicians for both permanent and temporary placement. Many of your assignments will be particularly confidential, and you also may be asked to play a third-party role, again the key being adaptability to your clients' needs. Fees are determined on a contract or contingency basis, or a combination of both.

Franchisees are trained at the Akron corporate offices, with multimedia presentations and an operations manual used to inform you about start-up procedures, recruiting methods, accounting systems, computer applications, and employee training. You also have an open invitation to return to Akron, at no charge, for advanced instruction. Additionally, SRA staff members will visit your office to give guidance in your own environment and help you hire your staff. Along with being in almost daily communication by phone with the home office, you'll be able to attend regional and national workshops and seminars, plus the SRA annual convention. And you'll receive regular memos, bulletins, and newsletters with other updated material.

The company will help with site selection, lease negotiation, and office design, supplying preliminary layouts. Receiving SRA group discounts on supplies, you'll also be guided in choosing and ordering the equipment you'll need for your office. Computers are one vital component, enabling you to have access to SRA's continually revised data base, a vast collection of information about experienced professionals. For the other side of your business, SRA will furnish customer profiles and tender assistance in closing important deals, as well as provide a press kit, ads, sales and direct mail materials, and other promotional items.

For further information contact:
  Douglas R. Eilertson, Executive Vice President, Sanford Rose Associates, 265 S. Main St., Akron, OH 44308, 216-762-6211 or 1-800-759-7673, fax 216-762-7031

Snelling and Snelling, Inc.

Initial license fee: $3,000
Royalties: 7%
Advertising royalties: 0% to 3%
Minimum cash required: $75,000 to $125,000
Capital required: $75,000 to $125,000
Financing: Payroll financing available
Length of contract: Lifetime

In business since: 1951
Franchising since: 1956
Total number of units: 390
Number of company-operated units: None
Total number of units planned, 1995: 800
Number of company-operated units planned, 1995: None

If you buy this franchise, you will become part of the world's largest employment service, one that includes permanent placement and temporary help offices in 47 states, Puerto Rico, the Philippines, and Brazil. Robert and Anne Snelling started the company in Philadelphia in 1951. An innovator in personnel services, Snelling recently introduced the industry's most sophisticated computerized matching system, Silent Search, for job openings and candidates—permanent and temporary.

Snelling is bullish on the future of the employment service business. As more people turn to employment agencies in their search for jobs, especially in the tough 1990s environment, Snelling management sees the outlook for employment services as one of steady growth.

Training for Snelling franchisees takes place at the company's headquarters in Dallas. But training doesn't stop there. An eight-day in-office training is conducted by Snelling area vice presidents, and the company offers ongoing continuing education programs in locations throughout the country. Curtis L. Nabors, owner of a franchise in Morristown, New Jersey, recalls he was impressed with the company's "excellent training." He still feels that way: "Four years later I realize how much it contributed to my success." As a highlight to this program, the company sponsors an annual convention for franchisees and their staff members. Recent convention sites have included Acapulco, New Orleans, and Reno.

The company stresses the importance of employee morale to the success of its operations. Snelling has built an elaborate awards program that recognizes office as well as individual performance.

Snelling advises you over the phone and by mail on how to select an office site, negotiate a lease, and furnish the premises. Its comprehensive supply package includes everything you will need to open your business, from letterhead and business cards right down to pens and pencils. You don't have to order supplies from the company, but it will give you a supply catalogue from which you can buy at a discount if you choose.

Snelling and Snelling stays at the top of the industry through an extensive advertising program. Its advertisements have appeared in *Family Circle, Personnel Journal, HR Magazine, McCall's,* and *Time.* Franchisees usually supplement the company's national campaigns by spending about 5 percent of their revenues on local advertising.

New franchisees have the option of concentrating on one side of the business—permanent placement, temp-to-perm, or temporary help—or all three. Most, however, choose to get a foothold in either permanent or temporary, then gradually add the others in order to offer client companies a full range of personnel services.

For further information contact:
  Franchise Development, Snelling and Snelling, Inc., 12801 N. Central Exp., Suite 700, Dallas, TX 75243, 1-800-766-5556

Temporary Placement

JobMate

Initial license fee: $30,000
Royalties: 0.3%
Advertising royalties: 0.1%
Minimum cash required: $45,000 to $50,000
Capital required: $15,000
Financing: None
Length of contract: 15 years

In business since: 1986
Franchising since: 1989
Total number of units: 12
Number of company-operated units: 1
Total number of units planned, 1995: 100
Number of company-operated units planned, 1995: 5

It was only a matter of time, right? You can rent just about anything these days, why not people, too? JobMate franchisees take over and technically "employ" workers of a company and in turn *lease* the workers back to that same company. JobMate allows the client to operate "business as usual" while providing an economically sound arrangement. Actually, employee leasing was greatly helped along by the 1986 tax reform act, which set much-needed standards for the evolving field. Before that point, regulations were vague and many operations were fly-by-night. Now, the scoundrels have pretty much been run out of business and employee leasing is no longer a questionable or trendy alternative; it's what many consider to be a better way of doing business.

As a JobMate franchisee, you'll be the one handing out the paychecks, handling the payroll, dealing with government personnel regulations, and, perhaps most importantly, providing the medical coverage and other benefits that you'll be able to obtain for a significant discount because of the large number of people you cover. It's an arrangement that can benefit everybody in a small or medium-size company; JobMate's target clients are companies with five to fifty employees. It benefits the employer, who is relieved of the administrative headaches to concentrate on business, saved from paying prohibitively expensive health insurance rates, and freed from the oftentimes troublesome task of having to deal with a union. It benefits the employees, who receive an extensive insurance and pension plan that the company itself couldn't have afforded. A recent survey showed that 80 percent of so-called "leased workers" are happy with the arrangement. Now able to offer superior benefits, companies are better equipped to attract and keep top talent, still another benefit for them.

And you can benefit, too, by entering into a rapidly growing field with great potential. Already there are over 1,000 employee leasing firms, responsible for over two million workers and reporting annual revenues exceeding $1 billion. That won't come close to meeting the demand in the near future, if author and business forecaster John Naisbitt's prediction is correct that by 1995, as many as one in 15 workers in the United States will be leased. Those affiliated with JobMate, the nation's first employee leasing franchise, are particularly well positioned to take advantage of this young industry's expansion.

Once a client signs up for your services, technically its employees are then employed by you. Calculating federal, state, and local tax withholdings, you'll process their paychecks, completing all payroll-associated work with the help of JobMate's easy-to-use computer system, and make out the year-end W-2 forms. You'll take care of unemployment insurance paperwork, workers' compensation insurance and audits, and other official reports and audits. The benefits package you'll provide, what the company calls "the Cafeteria Plan," includes comprehensive major medical coverage, a dental plan, a dependent care assistance package, vision care, life insurance, and cancer and accident policies. You'll also offer JobMate's TLCare Check service, allowing employees to have up to $5,000 a year deducted from their pretax income for child- and elderly-care services.

While you're employing your client's workers, you're also working for the company. Along with handling the administrative "dirty work," you'll use JobMate's proprietary software to generate important management information that clients can use to run their businesses more effectively. And you'll keep the company fully apprised of the expenses it's incurring, following JobMate's commitment to full disclosure. "No hidden costs, no hidden fees," the company promises every customer.

Franchisees receive five days of hands-on training at JobMate's Jackson, Mississippi, headquarters, personally administered by Harold Van Devender, the company's founder. During the session, you'll learn operations and marketing procedures, running a payroll yourself and participating in sales calls. The company will also supply you with the necessary forms for conducting business; however, franchisees are required to buy their own computer system. Beyond that, your equipment needs are surprisingly minimal, and your office requirements can be modest as well. The company, in fact, recommends avoiding an elaborate office set-up, which "could place an extra burden on the time and attention of franchise personnel."

JobMate does run a national and regional marketing program, but it should be supplemented by your own local efforts. Remember that employee leasing is a hot topic in business publications these days—an effective marketing tool in itself. And while employers in your area are reading these articles, it's a particularly ripe time for establishing a highly visible presence.

For further information contact:
  Harold Van Devender, Chairman, JobMate Affiliated Companies, Inc.,
  P.O. Box 959, Ridgeland, MS 39158, 601-856-5010

Norrell Services

Initial license fee: None
Royalties: Variable
Advertising royalties: None
Minimum cash required: $60,000 to $90,000
Capital required: $60,000 to $90,000
Financing: Company will finance temporary employee payroll
Length of contract: 10 or 15 years

In business since: 1961
Franchising since: 1966
Total number of units: 226
Number of company-operated units: 123

Total number of units planned, 1995: NA
Number of company-operated units planned, 1995: NA

Norrell, a nationwide temporary-help service marketing clerical, office automation, and light industrial job personnel to client companies, operates in a growth field. The company's growth figures compare well with the rest of the industry; its revenues have continued to climb steadily.

Norrell's marketing emphasizes that temporary workers can play a permanent role in its clients' personnel plans. Norrell points out that both big and small businesses should consider using temporary help—not just to fill in for absent workers, but to deal with specific situations that arise again and again. Such situations might include any projects in which staffing needs fall outside a business's normal capabilities; peak periods in cyclical operations; and repetitive, unchallenging work for which a company finds it difficult to motivate full-time employees over an extended period of time.

To ensure a good match between Norrell and its franchisees, the franchise application procedure includes several interviews. Your travel expenses are split 50-50 on your first trip to Atlanta. The second or final meeting in Atlanta, at company expense, will serve to familiarize you with the comprehensive support and services provided to the franchisee.

Norrell advertisements, which have appeared in *Business Week*, *Time*, and *Newsweek*, stress the thoroughly trained staff that stands ready to serve client companies. Your initial training will consist of a week at company headquarters in Atlanta, where you will study operations and sales. A self-study course on company operations and field workshops throughout the year supplement the initial training. Your personnel will also receive extensive instruction, including more than 84 hours of classroom work annually.

The company will advise you on site selection and the leasing and equipping of your office. Its preopening team will assist you with recruiting, laying out your office, direct mail marketing, sales calls, and establishing payroll procedures. Field management and the Franchise Service Center will provide a link between you and Norrell. The manager will assist you with hiring and training new staff, developing a business plan, budgeting, and procuring major accounts.

Norrell, and each of its franchisees, promises clients that it will respond to their requests for personnel within 45 minutes of receiving their call. At least twice a year the company will conduct an operations review of your business, and client and employee opinion surveys will give you another measure of your business's performance.

As part of your franchise package, you will receive enough supplies (forms, manuals, training materials, visuals, business stationery and cards, etc.) for three to six months of operations. Your subsequent purchases can come from any vendor whose products meet Norrell specifications.

For further information contact:
  Pat Mashura, Franchise Manager, Norrell Services, 3535 Piedmont Rd. N.E., Atlanta, GA 30305, 1-800-283-4532

Todays Temporary

Initial license fee: None
Royalties: Varies
Advertising royalties: none
Minimum cash required: $48,000 to $125,000
Capital required: Open
Financing: Company finances payroll and accounts receivable
Length of contract: 30 years

In business since: 1982
Franchising since: 1983
Total number of units: 35
Number of company-operated units: 14
Total number of units planned, 1995: 90
Number of company-operated units planned, 1995: 30

If rapid expansion and client contentment are accurate measures of a temporary employment agency network's achievements, then Todays Temporary can be called a success: an *Inc.* magazine ranking as the fastest growing clerical temporary service in the country, a swelling corps of over 14,000 workers, and client satisfaction rates of 98 percent.

Todays Temporary provides corporate clients with personnel for short- and long-term office assignments. Cross-trained in widely used word processing, spreadsheet, data base, and desktop publishing programs, Todays workers are skilled, experienced, clean-cut, and motivated professionals, able to perform clerical, customer service, accounting, and other workplace duties. And by using the agency's "Assist" hot line to get answers to their software questions, they can do their jobs without having to interrupt or bother the client employees around them, a refreshing difference for the temps and regular workers alike.

Todays franchisees work to establish close ongoing relationships with their customers, anticipating, comprehending, and fulfilling all kinds of staffing requirements. "My clients have been frustrated with other companies because nobody had made it their business to understand the needs of the businesses they were staffing," remarks Jacksonville, Florida, affiliate Ric Gwin. "We make it our business to know the company, the products they produce, and how they operate before placing someone."

Part of your services will be to give a quick response—within 45 minutes to be exact—to even last-minute requests for a replacement for an unexpectedly absent worker. You'll also provide appropriate people to fill in for vacationing staffers, or to cover personnel vacancies, and be available to help clients plan a year-long staggered vacation schedule that covers the office for the full 12-month period. And you'll assign a few select employees for a client's one-time projects and work overloads, assembling an entire team, if necessary, complete with a coordinator to oversee the job from start to end, finishing it on time and within the budget. As a guarantee for all these services, the client doesn't have to pay if he or she's not satisfied.

Todays Temporary does not charge its franchisees an initial fee. Instead, payments from your customers go directly to the company, which then pays your temps' wages and then gives you a percentage of your gross billings. With each employee you place, you'll process the time sheets and the home office will send an invoice to the client. Todays then works with you in collecting the payments and processes your payroll, including taxes and fringe benefits, maintaining all records and providing accurate and timely reports and financial statements.

You'll receive assistance in site selection and office design as well as instruction in both sales and operations, supplemented by quarterly follow-up training meetings. Todays helps in the hiring and training of your permanent staff and your crew of temps, who'll also be given its Temporary Employee Handbook, which the company calls the most comprehensive in the field.

Todays will run a credit check on your clients and will supply the forms and much of the software you'll need to run your business (office furnishings, equipment, and other materials, however, are your responsibility). You'll also be outfitted with direct mail pieces and assisted in devising advertising strategies for your area, the company chipping in for up to half the cost of an approved local marketing program. At the same time, the home office will be aggressively seeking new national and regional clients, running such programs as Todays Fairway Invitational, an annual golf tournament for over 100 of the agency's most important existing and potential customers.

Keeping your temps happy and motivated is one other crucial area of support Todays doesn't overlook. Beyond the thorough training and competitive compensation the company offers them, along with your permanent staff, insurance coverage and profit-sharing plans. Then there's "Todays Way Giveaway," an incentive program commended by the National Association of Temporary Services. Temps take the evaluation cards filled out by their client supervisors. Every card with a higher-than-average rating can be entered into a drawing. Todays has awarded over $250,000 in prizes such as cars, trips, and (admittedly a "busman's holiday" reward) computers.

For further information contact:
Kevin Roberts, Franchise Development Manager, Todays Temporary, 18111 Preston Rd., Suite 800, Dallas, TX 75252, 214-380-9380 or 1-800-822-7868

Western Temporary Services, Inc.

Initial license fee: $10,000 to $50,000
Royalties: Variable share of profit based on volume
Advertising royalties: None
Minimum cash required: $10,000 to $25,000
Capital required: $50,000+
Financing: Available to qualified applicants
Length of contract: Indefinite

In business since: 1948
Franchising since: 1958
Total number of units: 325
Number of company-operated units: 220
Total number of units planned, 1995: 500
Number of company-operated units planned, 1995: 320

Western Temporary Services is looking for affiliates who can use Western's ample resources for "back office" support and assistance to maximize sales and service at the local level. This close working relationship, backed by a company with over forty years of expertise in the field, might be just the thing for someone looking to get into the temporary personnel business.

Western may be able to award you a franchise in an area close to your home. The company, which has offices in Australia, New Zealand, the United Kingdom, Norway, Denmark, and Switzerland, has exclusive territories available in many areas of the United States. If you have an approved location in mind, and you otherwise qualify, Western will authorize you to select your location and set up your own "professional" place of business.

You will have to decide which type of temporary help suits you and your market best. Western franchises its Office/Light Industrial, Medical, and Technical divisions separately. You may operate more than one division if the territory is available.

Your training, a two-week program, begins with a week at the company's headquarters in Walnut Creek, California. Here you will study payroll, invoicing, credit, applicant screening, and customer relations. Corporate staff will introduce you to Western's professional sales training program and methods for effective bidding. During the second week, you go to work in an operating Western office. Under the tutelage of an experienced office manager, you will test, interview, evaluate, and place applicants. You will also make sales calls and take job orders.

Back in your own city, a company representative will help you develop a sales strategy tailored to your market and may also go with you as you make your first sales visits to major companies in your area. Western has serviced companies like IBM, Xerox, Rockwell, General Dynamics, Lockheed, and General Electric around the country, and this may stand you in good stead as you solicit accounts in your own territory. The company will assist you in those efforts, and you may also benefit from local business generated by national accounts negotiated by Western.

Western will print and mail grand opening announcements to 500 of your prospective customers at no cost to you; will arrange and pay for your phone installation; and will get you started with an ample shipment of sales, recruiting, and operational supplies. Uniquely, Western even passes up its normal share of the gross profits for the first six months so that you can more easily establish a good cash flow position. Furthermore, Western will provide you with a full library of videocassettes covering a variety of topics, including temporary employee orientation, safety, sales and payroll training, and credit and collection techniques. These are continually updated at Western's expense.

Western will handle most of the accounting for you. The company will pay the temporary employees and take care of payroll taxes, insurance, and workers' compensation. Western will pay you your share of the gross profit every four weeks regardless of when the customers pay Western. That share ranges up to two-thirds of the gross profit depending on your volume. In effect, the company finances the payroll and accounts receivable and you receive weekly reports covering all the activity. There are no monthly "royalties" paid as a percentage of sales.

You need not worry about payroll checks being "lost in the mail" because Western will provide you with an IBM PC, telephone modem, printer, and payroll software. The payroll information is transmitted to and from Western's headquarters overnight, and you can pay the temporary employees the following day. The actual payroll checks come off your printer locally, and Western authorizes you to sign them in its behalf. Many Western offices also use their PCs for computerized training, testing, and scheduling of temporaries.

Western puts a great deal of stock in image promotion. For example, it garners a considerable amount of publicity every year by supplying Santas to such stores as Marshall Fields and Macy's. The company will supply you with press releases for any local promotions you plan, and it may provide further publicity assistance by sending in personalities like Betty Baird, a Western temp and the company's "national typing ambassador." Betty Baird travels around the country demonstrating her 166-words-per-minute typing skill.

On the national level, Western advertises in such periodicals as *The Wall Street Journal*, *Forbes*, *Business Week*, and *Money*, as well as in many trade journals.

For further information contact:
Terry Slocum, Western Temporary Services, Inc., P.O. Box 9280, Walnut Creek, CA 94596, 1-800-USA-TEMP (in California, 1-800-FOR-TEMP)

11. The Food Industry

Contents

Round Table Pizza
Sbarro, Inc.
Shakey's Pizza Restaurant, Inc.

Restaurants

Benihana of Tokyo
Cucos Restaurantes
International House of Pancakes, Inc.
Po Folks, Inc.
Rax Restaurants, Inc.
Village Inn Restaurants

Sandwiches

Arby's, Inc.
Blimpie
Gyro Wrap, Inc.
Schlotzsky's, Inc.
Subway Sandwiches and Salads

Specialty Foods

Frontier Fruit & Nut Company
Gloria Jean's Coffee Beans
Heavenly Ham

Steakhouses

Ponderosa Steakhouses
The Ground Round, Inc.
Western Steer Family Steakhouse

Tacos and Mexican Fast Food

Taco John's International, Inc.
Taco Time International, Inc.

Baked Goods

Dunkin' Donuts of America, Inc.

Initial license fee: $40,000 (production retail outlets); $10,000 (satellites)
Royalties: 4.9% of gross sales
Advertising royalties: 5% or more (depending on other franchisee participation)
Minimum cash required: $175,000, with a net worth of $350,000
Capital required: $400,000 ($200,000 in liquid funds)
Financing: None provided, except for real estate development
Length of contract: 20 years (production retail outlets); 10 years (satellites)

In business since: 1950
Franchising since: 1950
Total number of units: 2,300+
Number of company-operated units: 2
Total number of units planned, 1995: 4,000+
Number of company-operated units planned, 1995: NA

Dunkin' Donuts is the largest franchise chain of coffee and doughnut shops in the world. Ever since the first Dunkin' Donuts shop was opened, the company's mission has been to make the freshest, most delicious coffee and doughnuts, served quickly and courteously, in modern, well-merchandised stores. Recently, Dunkin' Donuts has expanded its menu. Their stores now offer soups and sandwiches and a wide variety of fresh-baked goods, including muffins, bagels, croissants, brownies, and cookies.

Since 1950, when the business began, Dunkin' Donuts sales have increased steadily. In the last five years alone, it has added over 800 new shops. In 1990, Dunkin' Donuts purchased the Mister Donut chain. By 1995, most of the more than 500 Mister Donut franchisees are expected to convert to the Dunkin' Donuts system.

Over 40 percent of all Dunkin' Donuts shops are operated by franchisees who own more than one store. And more than 80 percent of its new shops are being opened by franchisees who choose to develop the real estate themselves in addition to owning the property.

Dunkin' Donuts offers an exclusive development program (exclusivity is limited) to qualified prospective franchisees with enough capital and organizational ability to develop a distribution network of both full-scale production retail outlets and satellites. Dunkin' Donuts, however, reserves the right to tailor the size of your territory, the number and types of retail outlets you can manage, and your development schedule to meet both the requirements of the market and your own particular needs, financial strength, and capabilities.

Dunkin' Donuts encourages you to develop your own real estate properties, including a land purchase or a land, built-to-suit, or mall lease.

You may use your full-scale production retail outlet as a manufacturing facility for a host of unusual and creative satellite stores. Franchisees now sell Dunkin' Donuts products in a variety of settings, including airports, hospitals, colleges, service stations, train and subway stations, and even convenience stores.

Your total cost for the development of real estate, and purchase of equipment and signs (which can be either purchased/financed or leased) and the initial franchise fee to open a full-scale production retail outlet will range from $130,000 to $660,000, depending on the area of the country in which you open your shop and on the type of real estate development for which you opt.

Franchisees attend a six-week program at the Dunkin' Donuts University in Braintree, Massachusetts. Instructors teach you how to produce and market all of the products sold by Dunkin' Donuts. You are shown how to recruit, train, and manage employees, how to use equipment safely, and how to manage inventory. You also receive instruction in basic accounting to assist you in managing your new business.

Dunkin' Donuts currently invests over $35 million annually in advertising and promotion. The company uses a variety of resources, including television, radio, outdoor signs, and print advertisements in every franchise market that contributes to the national advertising fund. The company's advertising team helps you to determine local marketing needs and to coordinate local marketing activities to attract more customers and to find ways to increase shop sales and profitability. Dunkin' Donuts projects that its franchisees will invest over $220 million in advertising and promotion during the next five years.

After your franchise application and your chosen location have been approved by the company, the franchise district manager, supported by the regional operations specialist, will assist you with the start-up tasks necessary to open a new shop.

After you have opened your shop, the franchise district manager will continue to offer support on an ongoing basis. He or she will always be there whenever you decide, and get approval, to open another shop. The regional operations specialist will help you to maintain a superior operation.

Regional distribution centers, owned and operated by Dunkin' Donuts franchisors, help you to manage costs, product availability, and delivery schedules. Cooperation among franchisors in regional buying associations permits cost savings through volume purchase discounts.

The five regional distribution centers are located in the Northeast, Southeast, Mid-Atlantic, Midwest, and Canadian regions.

For further information, call 1-800-543-5400 or contact the office closest to you:
Dunkin' Donuts of America, Inc.
15 Pacella Park Dr., Randolph, MA 02368, 617-986-2200

825 Georges Rd., North Brunswick, NJ 08902, 908-846-1600

Campbell Forum, Suite 650, 801 East Campbell Rd., Richardson, TX 75081, 214-783-8237

Coral Springs Trade Center, 2828 University Dr., Coral Springs, FL 33065, 305-344-5700

1550 Northwest Hwy., Suite 309, Park Ridge, IL 60068, 708-296-1151

In Canada:
3773 Cote Vertu, Suite 350, St. Laurent, Que., Canada H4R 2M3, 514-856-3100

Great Harvest Bread Co.

Initial license fee: $20,000
Royalties: 6%
Advertising royalties: NA
Minimum cash required: $45,000
Capital required: NA
Financing: None
Length of contract: 5 years

In business since: 1976
Franchising since: 1980
Total number of units: 51
Number of company-operated units: 1
Total number of units planned, 1995: 85
Number of company-operated units planned, 1995: 1

The goal of many franchises is to duplicate a prototype system—or store, or product, or service—as closely as possible. The people at Great Harvest don't even try. They've learned, through years of experience at the kneading board, that when it comes to fresh whole-wheat bread, you can't possibly get every loaf to come out the same—true bread aficionados don't want it that way, either. Some breads will rise higher, others will be crunchier. Most are very tasty—when they're made by someone who knows, and cares, about how to do it well— but each is distinctive. Great Harvest will, however, go so far as to say,

"We think that, on a good day, we make the best bread in the world" ... and will help its franchisees have as many of those good days as possible.

Like the bread itself, each Great Harvest bakery doesn't have to be a clone of the others in order to be successful. The system thrives on diversity, operating more as a network of independent bakeries, learning from one another's strengths and weaknesses. No apologies are made for the contrast of new ideas that may surface. The most consistent aspect of the franchise is its commitment to three touchstones: quality, cleanliness, and generosity to customers and employees.

Not that the Great Harvest franchise system is anarchical. Far from it. The home office will share methods honed over 15 years of trial and more-than-occasional error. The foundation of the system is the wheat itself. While you won't be required to obtain it from Great Harvest, the company has a good track record of finding top-quality grain through extensive sampling of wheat lots. Headquartered in Montana, heart of America's proverbial breadbasket, Great Harvest has estimable supplier connections. It won't be the cheapest grain you can purchase, but then, if your customers wanted economy bread, they'd eat store-bought loaves.

You'll function as a mill as well as a bakery, stone-grinding fresh wheat into fresh flour every day. Using Great Harvest recipes, perhaps with some variations of your own—but no preservatives or artificial ingredients—you'll offer an assortment of baked goods. Honey whole wheat loaves, usually weighing more than two pounds each, are favorite choices, but rye and corn flour breads, buns, and muffins are also available—cookies, too, made with dairy butter and fresh walnuts.

Great Harvest won't require you to have a baking background. In fact, the company claims that "none of our franchisees had an ounce of prior bakery experience before opening." That does mean that you'll have to invest considerable time—usually a minimum of five months—to learn the craft and set up your operation. Great Harvest recommends keeping your present job during this period, if possible, so you won't feel financial pressure to open before you, your store, and your equipment are ready.

You'll begin by working at four different Great Harvest bakeries, three days at an establishment that the company will select (one of the more successful ones in the network), and a day each at three other facilities of your choice. To learn the business, you need to knead, and you'll be getting your hands in the dough right away. At the same time, you'll be exposed to several business approaches, store layouts, and daily operations procedures, and begin to get an idea of the systems and methods you'll want to use—and avoid—at your own bakery. Just as important, you'll establish a relationship with these franchisees that you can draw on later, and start picking up the rhythm and language of the business; when someone refers to "bun dividers," you'll know exactly what he or she is talking about.

This combined introduction/trial by fire (or oven) prepares you for the next phase, finding a site for your bakery. Once you've narrowed your choices, a Great Harvest representative will fly out for two days of appraisal. Then, you'll oversee the construction or remodeling of your facility and locate and buy the baking equipment, talking almost daily on the phone with the home office. As soon as the floor is clean and the oven is installed, the company can begin shipping you wheat.

When you are ready to open for business, a couple of Great Harvest staffers—or experienced franchisees—will spend eight days at your bakery training you and your employees. First, they'll tune the mill, show everyone how to grind the flour, and check the other ingredients. Supervising daily bakings, they'll hold meetings with all of you each noon to appraise the day's batch, and teach you accounting, cost control, and equipment maintenance methods while your bakery is actually operating. Toward the end of the instruction period, the trainers will step back and observe your work, ready, though, to answer questions and handle emergencies, concluding by giving you a formal report that will outline areas for improvement.

Working with you as well once you're off and running, the Great Harvest staff, all of whom you'll quickly get to know by name, will continue to make visits, stay in touch by phone, and send along informative and chatty newsletters. And franchisees keep in regular contact with one another, too, sharing advice, marketing strategies, and recipes.

Because it is a small enterprise—and one that prefers to stay small—Great Harvest is able to start only eight new bakeries a year. Even though it may take you time to get the money together, you shouldn't hesitate to contact the company if you are interested in a franchise. "Some of our best bakeries," they say, "were started by people who originally called us years before they signed an agreement, kept the idea in mind, saved their money, and eventually did it." As anyone who's set a loaf aside for rising knows, good things are worth waiting for.

For further information contact:
 Great Harvest Bread Co., 28 S. Montana St., Dillon, MT 59725, 406-683-6842 or 1-800-442-0424

My Favorite Muffin

Initial license fee: $25,000
Royalties: 5%
Advertising royalties: 2%
Minimum cash required: $50,000
Capital required: $130,000 to $200,000
Financing: Assistance in obtaining
Length of contract: 10 years

In business since: 1987
Franchising since: 1988
Total number of units: 27
Number of company-operated units: 1
Total number of units planned, 1995: 235
Number of company-operated units planned, 1995: 5

What would you do if you came up with recipes for over 125 different kinds of muffins? If you're Owen Stern, you decide to open a franchise.

As a man with a craving for muffins—but with a high cholesterol level—Stern had a dilemma. A baker himself, he knew well what actually goes into baked goods—and knew that the muffin's reputation for being a "health food" was highly exaggerated. The butter, milk, and sugar alone boost the fat and calorie content way up even before extra ingredients like chocolate and nuts are added.

So Stern retreated into his kitchen to try to develop a low-fat, low-cholesterol muffin that was still moist and tasty. Using skim milk instead of whole, egg whites without the yolks, and soybean oil in place of butter or shortening, he had his basic recipe. Then, by taking a variety of fruits and vegetables, grains and spices, and putting them together in different combinations, he quickly began creating flavor after flavor. Stern also went ahead and came up with a few dozen more variations using chocolate and nuts. To assuage his guilt, however, he concocted a sugar-free muffin, too, sweetened with apple juice concentrate.

Now, much of Stern's energies are devoted to developing and expanding the My Favorite Muffin franchise program, to the possible detriment of the muffin shop that he and his wife continue to run. "All our franchisees are doing better than we are," admits Ruth Stern.

Customers coming to your store expecting only corn or blueberry muffins may be surprised by such exotic choices as amaretto granola, pineapple macadamia nut, zucchini, Black Forest, and chocolate cheesecake. While you won't be offering all 125-plus selections at once, you will have 20 to 25 flavors available at any given time. Granted, there are some problems. "We've had people come in here almost in tears when they see their favorite flavor is out," Plantation, Florida, franchisee Toby Litt reports. "I tell them to come back in half an hour and we'll have a fresh batch ready."

All that really takes is knowing how to run the food processor and when to fill and empty the tins. Your computerized conveyer-belt oven can be left largely unattended to bake muffins at a rate of 180 an hour while you and your workers concentrate on the customers.

Along with the regular 6-ounce varieties, they can pick up a dozen of your 1½-ounce "mini muffins." You'll have freshly brewed coffee, too, and you may also want to feature an assortment of gourmet "My Favorite Coffee" beans to purchase by the pound. In addition, your customers can order a gift basket like the "muffin breakfast," which includes a selection of jams, jellies, coffees, and teas, and arrange to have it sent anywhere in the country.

Helping you to get started, the company will provide assistance with site selection and lease negotiation, and give direction and advice on your store design and layout. You'll be able to manage with 500 square feet of space for a mall shop and 1,000 square feet if you set up elsewhere. Adding the coffee bean concession, however, will require a larger facility and more extensive leasehold improvement.

You'll learn baking techniques and equipment operation, as well as general administration procedures, during the franchisee training program, and be supplied with purchasing guidelines and recommendations. My Favorite Muffin training personnel will also be available for employee and follow-up instruction as you expand your business.

To support that expansion further, My Favorite Muffin will furnish marketing tools, from ad slicks to coupons, and a variety of promotional ideas. One suggestion is to join your local chamber of commerce, giving 10 percent muffin discounts to your fellow members. Another approach involves the My Favorite Muffin mug, which you'll fill with half-price coffee each time your customer brings it in. Or you can bring the muffins to the customers, offering a delivery service to office buildings. Free samples, incidentally, remain an excellent way to get new business.

Meanwhile Owen Stern, now joined by a team of baked goods specialists, continues to come up with still more new muffin recipes.

For further information contact:
  Ronald Sommers, My Favorite Muffin, 15 Engle St., Suite 302, Englewood, NJ 07631, 201-871-0370 or 1-800-332-2229, fax 201-871-7168

Convenience Stores

Convenient Food Mart, Inc.

Initial license fee: — Regional: Based on population
— Franchisee: $12,000 to $20,000, based on population
Royalties: 4% to 5%
Advertising royalties: None
Minimum cash required: $65,000
Capital required: $80,000
Financing: Some available regionally
Length of contract: 10 years

In business since: 1958
Franchising since: 1958
Total number of units: 504
Number of company-operated units: 40
Total number of units planned, 1995: 20
Number of company-operated units planned, 1995: 5

From apples to aspirin, from milkshakes to motor oil, and from tinfoil to tabloids, you can find almost anything at a Convenient Food Mart store. Founded on the idea that people would patronize "supermarkets in miniature," where they could find whatever they needed—Band-Aids, birthday candles, or bananas—at hours convenient to them, Convenient Food Mart now operates throughout the United States. Located in strip shopping centers and urban storefronts, or established independently as freestanding stores, Convenient Food Marts serve high-traffic areas with a mix of merchandise designed to meet the needs of each specific community. Some offer gasoline, others sell alcoholic beverages, and still others operate full-service delicatessens. But all have in common a dedication to customer service.

The Convenient Food Mart system is actually a network of licensed regional franchisors who sell franchises to individual store owners. Independent businesspeople obtain licenses to operate as regional franchisors and commit to a plan for developing an agreed-upon number of stores in their region within a given time frame. These regional franchisors in turn recruit franchisees and oversee franchisee operations in their region. Convenient Food Mart's strategy of decentralized operations ensures that the particular demographics of each region are more closely taken into account in the operation of stores in that region. At the same time, the company sets forth highly standardized requirements for store image and the methods by which stores are operated, in order to help franchisees repeat the success of Convenient Food Mart stores throughout the United States.

In addition to standardization, Convenient Food Mart strongly believes that the efforts of individual store owners play a vital role in the company's success. The company stresses that "the people in our system are the strength of our enterprise. Our most important assets are our regional licensees and the store owner-operators." The company discourages absentee ownership and part-time management, and makes sure that franchisees receive all of the training and support they need to help make their stores a success.

Starting with site selection and store construction, your regional franchisor will help you meet your goals. The franchisor will research the demographics and traffic patterns of locations you are considering and will provide you with the best possible judgment of the potential of a given site. The ultimate selection is up to you, however, and when you start construction of your new store you must meet time-tested specifications intended to provide your Convenient Food Mart with the friendly, clean, and efficient image maintained by stores throughout the system. The company will provide you with an equipment package chosen specifically for your store and will help with interior design and store layout.

Your step-by-step training covers everything that goes into daily convenience store operation from the time you open your doors in the morning to the time you close them at night. You will learn how to read statements, keep records, maintain your store and equipment, manage employees, and promote your business. Your training continues after your store opening, as merchandising experts pay regular visits to your store to evaluate your operation and offer guidance on inventory, efficiency, and cost controls. You will also be given a manual of operations, which you can use as a daily reference.

Your regional franchisor will help you set up your inventory in a way that will continue to save you time and money throughout your career as a franchisee. The company will help out with advertising on a regional basis and provide you with a bookkeeping system based on the latest accounting technology.

Each day, franchisees complete reports that regional franchisors analyze. From these reports, your regional franchisor will be able to provide you with profit-and-loss statements and other valuable management reports. National franchisor analysts will periodically visit your store and furnish you with an analysis of your operations. Their reports will help you evaluate your product mix and inventory turnover, not to mention aid you in making changes that might lead to higher profits.

For further information contact:
  Convenient Food Mart, Inc., National Executive Offices, 929 N. Plum Grove
  Rd., Schaumburg, IL 60173, 708-995-1100

White Hen Pantry, Inc.

Initial license fee: $20,000
Royalties: 13.5%
Advertising royalties: None
Minimum cash required: $20,000 to $30,000
Capital required: NA
Financing: Available
Length of contract: 10 years

In business since: 1965
Franchising since: 1965
Total number of units: 397
Number of company-operated units: 2
Total number of units planned, 1995: 495
Number of company-operated units planned, 1995: 15

The Midwest and New England are two regions where old-fashioned
values like thrift, hard work, cleanliness, and service are taken seriously. Open a convenience store in these parts of the country and be
prepared to serve customers who expect you to *mean* it by "convenience." That means meeting their food shopping needs quickly—day
or night—with an ample selection of merchandise displayed in an or-
derly fashion and sold at a low price in an immaculate and pleasant
environment.

White Hen Pantries franchisees have been doing this for over a
quarter of a century. Open 24 hours a day and offering national
brands plus local products and private-label items, your store will
carry staples and specialty foods alike, along with fresh-ground coffee,
available by the cup or by the pound, and an assortment of fresh-
baked breads and pastries. In addition, you'll have an extensive produce section and a full-service deli, featuring meats, cheese, salads,
and made-to-order sandwiches and cold-cut trays.

Studying consumer trends and preferences, the White Hen corporate
staff regularly tests new products, screens potential new vendors, and
monitors and modifies its existing programs in response to changing
market forces. You'll receive a list of approved goods and recommended suppliers who the company feels offer the best combination of
quality, cost savings, and service. White Hen also publishes merchandising bulletins, updating you about the wholesale prices you should
expect to pay and the retail prices it suggests you charge, and sends

along window signs and other displays for featured sales. To increase customer awareness and shopping frequency, White Hen's marketing department works with an out-of-house agency developing advertising campaigns, store promotions, and public relations programs. And the home office will lend further assistance if you want to plan additional activities.

Prior to your final acceptance as a franchisee, you, along with any family members who'll be participating in the business, will attend a training program to learn how to operate a White Hen Pantry. (You'll be responsible for training any nonfamily staff members.) Including both classroom and store instruction, the course will cover such subjects as merchandising, staffing, marketing, sanitation, and equipment operation, and teach you methods for attracting and retaining customers, maximizing sales and profits, caring for perishable foods, and controlling pilferage. You'll also be introduced to White Hen's computerized accounting system, which will allow you to track inventory, sales, and expenses; develop a comprehensive business plan; and store payroll and billing information.

While you will pay all operating expenses for your facility, White Hen will lease the property itself, performing exterior repairs when necessary, as well as obtain and install all fixtures and equipment. After the real estate department selects the site, a team of architects and building specialists will supervise the construction and design of your store, creating a compact floor plan and bright, streamlined decor.

White Hen will assign you a store counselor who will be your primary—though not sole—link to corporate headquarters, serving as a day-to-day advisor and problem solver. Through phone contact and periodic visits for on-the-spot management coaching, he or she will explain how to cultivate good customer relations, ensure product quality and freshness, and maintain a neat and clean store. Other White Hen officials will provide ongoing support, too, including members of the accounting department, who will prepare the sales, payroll, and property tax returns for your operation, and personnel representatives, who will help with your business and personal insurance needs.

White Hen currently has stores in five states—Massachusetts, New Hampshire, Illinois, Indiana, and Wisconsin. Although the company does not plan, for the present, to expand outside the Midwest and New England, there are numerous new franchise opportunities available in those regions.

For further information contact:
James O. Williams, Franchising Manager, White Hen Pantry, Inc., 660 Industrial Dr., Elmhurst, IL 60126, 708-833-3100, fax 708-833-0292

Food Delivery

Takeout Taxi

Initial license fee: $20,000
Royalties: 3% to 3.5%
Advertising royalties: 2%
Minimum cash required: $30,000
Capital required: $35,000 to $45,000
Financing: None
Length of contract: 10 years

In business since: 1987
Franchising since: 1991
Total number of units: 6
Number of company-operated units: 2
Total number of units planned, 1995: 150
Number of company-operated units planned, 1995: 10

It's a familiar scene in many American homes. Mom and Dad are too tired to cook dinner—even to herd the family down to a local coffee shop or deli. Besides, one kid wants spaghetti and the other a taco—and everyone's sick of pizza.

With Takeout Taxi, no one has to compromise. Instead, in one call they can arrange to have you bring the food—from several restaurants at the same time—right to their door.

Food delivery options are still limited in a lot of communities around the county. Most dining establishments—pizza parlors and take-out Chinese food joints are the obvious exceptions—just don't find the hassles of organizing and supervising a delivery service worth the benefits. But when your Takeout Taxi store offers to run the operation for them, you'll get quite a few takers.

The concept came from a local service that began in the Herndon, Virginia, area in 1987, representing four neighborhood restaurants at first. That Takeout Taxi was a quick success wasn't surprising to its founder Kevin Abt; the only thing that caught him off guard was the breadth of his customer base. "We figured this business would be driven by two-income households," he remembers—yuppie couples, in other words—but singles and low- and middle-income families, along with office workers ordering lunch in, proved to be even more loyal patrons.

What wasn't a surprise at all was how eager many restaurants were to sign up for the service. "We've become an insurance policy for restaurants," Abt explains, keeping their kitchens busy "on nights when the weather is bad and it's slow inside." And in addition to the extra business, they'll get extra marketing and advertising benefits through your menu distribution and promotional programs. Hotels, meanwhile, have been eager to sign up on the receiving end; budget motels or inns too small to offer their own room service can place your Takeout Taxi menus in each room to give their guests the same at-their-door food delivery—from snacks to complete meals—they'd get at a larger, luxury establishment.

With a wider selection, too, since your service will encompass a broad range of choices and cuisines, including the upscale restaurants that have never been in the delivery business as well as nationally known chains. Through the deal you'll arrange with them, you'll receive a discount—usually around 20 percent to 30 percent—for the food, and then charge your customer the regular price plus a delivery fee, with the difference making up your revenues. When a customer calls with an order, you'll enter it (and the name, address, and phone number) into a computer, and fax the printout to the restaurant. Then, by radio, you'll dispatch a driver to pick up the food, place it in a thermally insulated bag, and deliver it to your hungry patron. The computer is also used to provide the restaurants with a detailed accounting statement, to determine the fastest routes for your drivers, and to print out postcards sent to each day's customers with money-off coupons for their next order.

You'll learn how to operate this custom-designed software, and be instructed in other management, technical, and marketing systems, during a one-week training session, part of the time spent in the classroom and part at a company-run Takeout Taxi store. Then, during a week of on-site assistance in your territory, you'll be taught "The Art of Restaurant Negotiation" by a company representative, who'll show you how to identify likely prospects and help you sign them up for your service. Once you open, a second week of field guidance concentrates on the other side of your business, with assistance in honing your daily operating procedures and identifying the strongest customer base, especially the apartment complexes and office buildings that will bring you a high volume of orders.

Supplied with a launch package, featuring press releases and introductory promotional materials, you'll be furnished on an ongoing basis with ad slicks and direct mailers, plus ideas for using coupons and other incentives, like free meal raffles and birthday discounts, to stimulate first-time customers. Takeout Taxi will also offer advice about ways to get your store in the news, building objective credibility and community awareness of your business. In addition, the company plans to conduct continuing education programs that will include skill improvement workshops on such topics as quality control, sales techniques, and customer service, and schedule regular franchisee meetings to update you on the changes in what is still a new, albeit promising, enterprise.

For further information contact:
  Kevin R. Abt, President, Takeout Taxi Franchising Systems, Inc.,
  1175 Herndon Parkway, Suite 550, Herndon, VA 22070

Fried Chicken

Cajun Joe's Premium Chicken

Initial license fee: $7,500
Royalties: 8%
Advertising royalties: 2.5%
Minimum cash required: $55,000
Capital required: $60,000 to $120,000
Financing: Available
Length of contract: 20 years

In business since: 1985
Franchising since: 1986
Total number of units: 120
Number of company-operated units: 1
Total number of units planned, 1995: 2,500
Number of company-operated units planned, 1995: None

Cajun food may remind people of jovial, heavy-set Louisiana chefs with honeyed accents, but there's no reason anyone should grow fat eating at Cajun Joe's. That's because the menu features options for health- and weight-conscious customers, from roast chicken to grilled chicken sandwiches, and even the fried chicken is healthier than you might expect, with zesty spices and light breading rather than a thick, greasy coating.

The health of the fast-food chicken industry continues to be quite sound. Sound enough that Subway, the nationwide sandwich chain (see listing in this chapter), recently bought a controlling interest in Cajun Joe's, seeing the enterprise as an excellent way for diversifying its franchise program. But although about half of Cajun Joe's current franchisees own a Subway shop as well, the two restaurants remain entirely separate entities, and the companies themselves are autonomous, too. What the partnership has brought to Cajun Joe's, however, is the opportunity for a chain that's only recently begun a rapid expansion to benefit from the experience of an organization that has been down this road before.

Cajun Joe's started off serving fried chicken, strange as it may seem, in a Boston-area hospital. Not surprisingly, it was a tasty alternative to the cafeteria, but when Richard Cromwell and Joe Barrett, Cajun Joe's founders, discovered that they were serving not only patients and visitors but people who were actually *choosing* to dine at a hospital, they realized they were on to something.

As the chain has expanded, the menu has, too. Fried chicken, in spicy and mild varieties, is still the top seller, but now it's served with a wide choice of Cajun and southern-style side orders, like chicken gumbo, black-eyed peas, fried okra, and fresh buttermilk biscuits and corn muffins. Nevertheless, while some new products may be added in the future, Cajun Joe's will remain a pretty specialized operation.

The company will provide you with a list of approved products and suppliers and suggest the prices you should charge. Some items, including the custom-blend spices used in the chicken recipe, must be purchased directly from Cajun Joe's. Benefiting from Subway's buying power, the company will also help you obtain the store equipment you'll need directly from manufacturers at very low prices.

Your local Cajun Joe's representative will assist you in selecting a site for your store, leasing the property for the company, and then subleasing it to you. Because Cajun Joe's is essentially a take-out operation, you'll be looking for a fairly small facility—about 1,000 square feet, requiring only three to five employees to run it—with minimum seating and maximum visibility. The company has store designs for a range of sites and building styles, including strip shopping centers, downtown storefronts, and freestanding buildings; mall food courts are usually considered less desirable locations. The decor will feature a few New Orleans touches—Tiffany lamps, jazz-oriented artwork, and Dixieland music playing in the background—along with such basic fast-food elements as bright, upbeat colors and display areas that keep your food in full view to entice customers.

A two-week training program will be tailored specifically to your business, retail, and food service experience (or lack thereof). In addition, your local Cajun Joe's representative will work with you at your store for at least two days before and several days after opening. Afterward, he or she will continue to stay in touch, visiting your facility regularly to analyze the operation, offer advice on quality control and customer service, and inform you about new products and promotional programs.

Using the services of a national agency, Cajun Joe's conducts chain-wide advertising campaigns and will supply local TV and radio spots, handling media placement for you, if you'd like. Newspaper ads, direct mail materials, and point-of-purchase pieces will also be sent along several times a year. Then there are the personal appearances by "Cajun Joe" himself. In most towns, at least, a guy running around in a chicken costume is certain to draw attention.

For further information contact:
  Franchise Sales Department, Cajun Joe's Development Corporation,
  325 Bic Dr., Milford, CT 06460, 1-800-888-4848, fax 203-876-6688

Kentucky Fried Chicken

Initial license fee: $20,000
Royalties: 4%
Advertising royalties: 4.5%
Minimum cash required: $125,000
Capital required: $350,000
Financing: Available
Length of contract: 20 years

In business since: 1930
Franchising since: 1952
Total number of units: 8,194
Number of company-operated units: 2,223
Total number of units planned, 1995: NA
Number of company-operated units planned, 1995: NA

As company legend has it, Colonel Harland Sanders discovered the Kentucky Fried Chicken secret formula in 1939. The Colonel began to sell franchises in 1952, but business didn't really take off until 1955, when he started to collect his pension from Social Security. Since then the company has changed hands several times, although the Colonel himself stayed on as a goodwill ambassador until his death in 1980, at which time the venerable white-suited gentleman with the goatee earned $225,000 a year to embody the old-fashioned, "finger-lickin'" goodness of the company's main product.

PepsiCo, the most recent owner of Kentucky Fried Chicken, also owns Pizza Hut and Taco Bell. With its purchase of the chain, the company-owned stores switched from Coke to Pepsi, and PepsiCo urged franchisees to do the same.

Kentucky Fried Chicken maintains a uniform appearance for all the restaurants in its chain. Your freestanding store must follow the company's specifications for construction and decoration, and you may have to remodel the premises from time to time, at your expense, in accordance with changes in the chain's look.

Franchisees take their Kentucky Fried Chicken training at the local division level headquarters. The company requires the course for franchisees and recommends it for other key personnel. Subjects covered in the course include sanitation, product preparation, safety, inventory control, equipment maintenance, sales projection, staffing, and accounting. Special in-store training programs are available to train your employees.

Franchisees must make all items on the menu according to specifications in the franchise manual, with supplies purchased from company-approved sources only. The fabled seasonings that enable the company to brag that "we do chicken right," for example, are made only by the Stange Company of Chicago.

When a market area becomes available for franchise, the company may offer it to the nearest franchisee already in business. Franchisees are generally interested in the chance to buy additional units. So, since new franchise areas are limited, if you are interested in becoming a franchisee for the company, you must qualify as a franchisee and then wait for the opportunity to buy an existing franchise.

For further information contact:
  Thomas R. Brule, Franchise Development, Kentucky Fried Chicken,
  P.O. Box 32070, Louisville, KY 40232-2070, 502-456-8904

Hamburgers and Fast Food

A & W Restaurants, Inc.

Initial license fee: $15,000
Royalties: 4%
Advertising royalties: 4%
Minimum cash required: $100,000
Capital required: $450,000
Financing: None
Length of contract: 20 years

In business since: 1919
Franchising since: 1925
Total number of units: 740
Number of company-operated units: 11
Total number of units planned, 1995: 850
Number of company-operated units planned, 1995: 20

Think of A & W, and your brain conjures up a big frosty mug of root beer topped with a rich, creamy head of foam. But A & W offers much more than root beer. The company notes that it has come a long way since it opened its first root beer stand in Lodi, California, back in

1919. A & W has developed a full menu with prices that fall in the middle of the quick service restaurant scale. Although the on-premises mixing of draft A & W root beer, made fresh daily and served in a frosted glass mug, remains A & W's claim to fame, the company also emphasizes the high quality of its food. The A & W menu features hamburgers, cheeseburgers and bacon cheeseburgers, hot dogs, the famous "A & W coney dog," grilled chicken sandwiches, a children's meal package, french fries, onion rings, A & W root beer, A & W root beer floats, and other soft drinks.

With over 70 years of experience in the food service business, A & W is an established restaurant chain with extensive trade recognition, exclusive menu items, and a comprehensive corporate support system. Although A & W operates franchises throughout most of the United States as well as internationally, it is currently concentrating on its Midwestern franchises.

Most of the development and franchising efforts of the company are now directed toward food court and in-line restaurants, but freestanding buildings are also available. If you are interested in opening an A & W restaurant at an unconventional site, or want to convert an existing restaurant facility, the company will consider your request on a case-by-case basis.

For further information contact:
  Franchise Sales Department, A & W Restaurants, Inc., 17197 N. Laurel Park
  Dr., Suite 500, Livonia, MI 48152, 313-462-0029

Hardee's Food Systems, Inc.

Initial license fee: $15,000
Royalties: 3.5% first 5 years; 4% years 6 to 20
Advertising royalties: 5%
Minimum cash required: $500,000 net worth excluding personal residence;
  $150,000 liquid assets
Capital required: $700,000 to $1,700,000, depending upon real estate and
  property ownership costs in the area
Financing: Will assist in securing
Length of contract: 20 years

In business since: 1960
Franchising since: 1962
Total number of units: 2,676
Number of company-operated units: 1,258
Total number of units planned, 1995: NA
Number of company-operated units planned, 1995: NA

With its recent acquisition of Roy Rogers restaurants, Hardee's is now the third largest fast-food/hamburger chain. The company, started by two North Carolina businessmen, absorbed the Sandy's chain in the 1970s and Burger Chef in 1982. In 1981 Hardee's became part of the huge Imasco Limited holding company of Canada, whose other businesses include food products, retailing, and tobacco. Hardee's has expanded steadily, with management maintaining the ratio of franchise locations to company-owned restaurants at three to two.

Hardee's takes pride in its pioneer role in adding a breakfast menu—it is built around "made from scratch" biscuits—to a hamburger chain. Diners who come in later in the day can choose from a menu that has shifted gradually away from a concentration on the simple hamburger. Some of its recent features are the grilled chicken breast sandwich and crispy curls fried potatoes. Hardee's was the first chain to switch to all-vegetable cooking oil, and remains concerned with the nutritional quality of its food. Hardee's plans to introduce Roy Rogers fried chicken in the near future.

Hardee's is one of the few big fast-food chains with substantially untapped territory, according to the franchisor. Currently, the company wants to expand in Colorado, Louisiana, Michigan, New York, Ohio, Pennsylvania, and Texas. However, while Hardee's licenses franchisees who want to run one unit, it prefers multiunit operators. In fact, much of its growth comes from franchisees who already own at least one operation. Two of its biggest franchisees, Boddie-Noell Enterprises, Inc., and SpartanFood Systems, Inc., operate restaurants in more than one state.

Although the company specifies construction materials and designs that franchisees must use in building Hardee's restaurants, you are allowed some self-expression in the appearance of the establishment, especially in the interior. Typically, locations have 165 feet of frontage and are 210 feet deep.

Training consists of a four-week management internship at one of the company's regional learning centers. Franchisees receive hands-on restaurant management experience in the course as well as classroom instruction. An operational supervisor will come to your site 10 days before you open and will stay with you for a period after you begin your business. The company offers advanced training in the form of frequent seminars and workshops on assertiveness training, time management, and other subjects. There may be a nominal tuition charge for some of this training.

Hardee's management stresses the importance of accounting and financial controls in the fast-food business. It offers franchisees help in setting up a computerized accounting system, including point-of-sale terminals to provide up-to-the-minute inventory information. Multi-unit operators can tie these terminals into a central system to provide a comprehensive picture of business at all their locations at any given time.

Hardee's spends about $80 million a year on advertising. Franchisees participate in marketing campaigns through cooperative ads with other regional franchisees and have input into the company's general marketing policy through their representatives on the company's marketing advisory review council. For marketing advice, franchisees can also consult a field marketing executive in one of the six area offices.

Franchisees purchase food from Hardee's distribution company, Fast Food Merchandisers, Inc. This company employs 1,100 people in its nine distribution centers in the East and Midwest. Its trucks travel over 9 million miles a year, delivering more than 38 million pounds of hamburger meat and 17 million pounds of boneless breast of chicken, among other products.

For further information contact:
   Hardee's Franchise Sales Department, 1233 Hardee Blvd., Rocky Mount, NC
   27802, 919-977-8821

Long John Silver's Seafood Shoppes, Inc.

Initial license fee: $12,500
Royalties: 4% of monthly gross sales
Advertising royalties: 5% of monthly gross sales
Minimum cash required: $300,000
Capital required: $700,000
Financing: None
Length of contract: 25 years

In business since: 1969
Franchising since: 1970
Total number of units: 1,455
Number of company-operated units: 992
Total number of units planned, 1995: NA
Number of company-operated units planned, 1995: NA

This fast-food fish chain, with units in 33 states and two other countries, prides itself on changing with the times. In keeping with the recent trend away from fried foods, it has emphasized lighter fare such as salads, baked fish, and chicken. Recently, the company has varied its traditional repertoire of fish, shrimp, and chicken dishes with a new line of lighter, home-style breaded fish fillets, shrimp, and stuffed crab. Other nutritious alternatives are the company's clam chowder and seafood gumbo soups as well as the green vegetables and rice served alongside the baked fish and chicken.

Computers are important in the operation of every restaurant. Computerized time monitors keep tabs on the right cooking time for each dish and also track postcooking holding times. Employees discard as stale anything that overstays its welcome in the holding area.

The elaborate Long John Silver computerized communications system uses sophisticated electronic cash registers. Every night, the system automatically transmits data accumulated at each terminal in every store in the chain to mainframe computers at the Lexington, Kentucky, company headquarters. The company sends marketing and operational information back to store managers over the same lines. Long John Silver's is experimenting with personal computers so that each manager can have more control over his or her store and corporate headquarters can communicate more easily with each of its managers.

There is nothing extraordinary about the site selection and building of Long John Silver's franchise units. You do the work, in keeping with the company's guidelines, with all major details subject to Long John Silver's approval. But there is something special about the required training.

The management training course emphasizes hands-on, one-on-one detailed instruction in the fundamentals of the business. After you take the five-week course, conducted at one of more than 170 accredited training units in the United States, you will be able to manage a meal shift with little supervision. The finishing touches that will make you a well-skilled management candidate are provided by completion of a management skills workshop. Training managers are accredited annually to ensure that they are using current techniques, and each training shop is subject to corporate review at any time.

You will receive some of your instruction at a training shop near your location, and the rest will take place at your own restaurant. The subjects covered will include operational procedures, equipment handling, repair and maintenance, guest service, products, advertising, marketing, and cleaning procedures. Company personnel will assist you with opening preparations and start-up.

You will buy Long John Silver's proprietary items through the company's food distribution system. You may also opt to purchase other food, beverages, paper goods, and equipment through the system.

Currently, the company has franchise openings in almost every market in which it operates. Major opportunities are available in California, the Pacific Northwest, Minnesota, Wisconsin, North Carolina, Delaware, New York, Pennsylvania, and throughout New England.

For further information contact:
  Franchise Department, Long John Silver's Seafood Shoppes, Inc., P.O. Box
  11988, Lexington, KY 40579, 606-263-6372

Wendy's International, Inc.

Initial license fee: $25,000
Royalties: 4%
Advertising royalties: 4%
Minimum cash required: $250,000
Capital required: $50,000 to $1,000,000
Financing: Independent sources
Length of contract: 20 years

In business since: 1969
Franchising since: 1971
Total number of units: 3,423
Number of company-operated units: 978
Total number of units planned, 1995: 3,700
Number of company-operated units planned, 1995: 1,100

The fast-food business slowed a bit in the mid-eighties, and Wendy's,
like the other giants of the industry, experienced lagging sales. In an
effort to generate more revenue, the company targeted the breakfast
trade with a new early-morning menu based on omelets. But the public didn't bite, and the company ended up with egg on its face. To pull
out of this bumpy financial period, Wendy's decided to revamp its top
management. Wendy's chairman and CEO, James W. Near, stated:
"We don't like being number three. So we have a strategic plan in
place, and you'll be hearing from us soon."

Wendy's has since kept up with these increasingly cholesterol-
conscious times by adding a SuperBar and an all-you-can-eat hot and
cold food buffet, which offers fresh fruits and vegetables and ethnic
foods like tacos and pasta. Wendy's also offers baked potatoes and a
breast of chicken sandwich which, according to the company, is
widely acknowledged as the best in the industry.

R. David Thomas, who founded Wendy's Old Fashioned Hamburgers, started with the idea that cooked-to-order hamburgers would
stand out when compared to the prepackaged and reheated food sold
by other chains. Highly publicized taste tests, in which Wendy's has
done well, have borne out his strategy.

Wendy's notes that its broiled burgers have given it a good image
with its nutrition-conscious consumers. The company's most famous
series of commercials highlighted Wendy's quality by comparing its
substantial product to the supposedly skimpy offering of its competi-

tors. The slogan "Where's the beef?" became part of the public lingo and made consumers aware of Wendy's as an alternative to other fast-food chains.

Wendy's will consider applicants for individual franchise ownership, although it had previously favored groups intending to buy the rights to entire areas. But opportunities to buy franchises, according to the company, are "limited," and Wendy's forbids absentee ownership. In fact, franchise owners must live within fifty miles of their restaurant.

If you do buy a Wendy's franchise, you will have an experienced corporate staff ready to guide and assist you. Staff will help you select the right site and provide you with drawings and specifications for your restaurant. Your management team will receive a thorough grounding in the company's operations at the Wendy's Management Institute. Company representatives will visit your Wendy's periodically to assist you with operational details, and the company's advertising department will supplement your efforts to publicize your business locally while continuing to promote the company's image nationally.

For further information contact:
Wendy's International, Inc., P.O. Box 256, Dublin, OH 43017, 614-764-3100

Wienerschnitzel

Initial license fee: $30,000
Royalties: 5%
Advertising royalties: 4%
Minimum cash required: $60,000
Capital required: $180,000
Financing: None
Length of contract: 20 years

In business since: 1961
Franchising since: 1965
Total number of units: 295
Number of company-operated units: 90
Total number of units planned, 1995: NA
Number of company-operated units planned, 1995: NA

Back in 1961, when the first Der Wienerschnitzel opened for business, the menu consisted of hot dogs for 15 cents and soft drinks for a dime. Times have changed. The German article was dropped from the name and the prices, inevitably, have risen. Enclosed dining rooms, at many locations, give customers an alternative to open-patio seating. And the menu is a lot more extensive now, including hamburgers, specialty sandwiches, and a complete breakfast selection featuring fresh-baked buttermilk biscuits.

But some things have remained the same. The prices—though higher—continue to be at the low end of the fast-food scale. Drive-through service, offered at all nonmall locations, endures as one of the restaurant chain's most popular attributes, one that the company is trying to expand further by testing a double-lane system in areas with particularly heavy auto traffic (like southern California). And although many of the newer establishments have a more recently developed, contemporary design, there are still plenty of the familiar brightly-colored A-frame Wienerschnitzel buildings, where customers who were taken as children during their "wonder years" are taking their own kids now.

And in one very important respect, Wienerschnitzel has returned to the original concept that has served the company so well. Wienerschnitzel's decision, in the seventies and early eighties, to downplay its signature hot dogs and become a burger-oriented establishment met with less-than-spectacular results. "Involvement in the burger wars just meant casualties," admitted Wienerschnitzel president Daniel Tass. So a truce was declared, and Wienerschnitzel beat a tactical retreat, retrenching to remain the country's largest privately owned hot dog chain restaurant. To emphasize this homecoming, such as it is, the company changed its marketing strategy entirely, scrapping its "We're not just hot dogs anymore" campaign in favor of the new Wienerschnitzel slogan, "Nobody hot dogs it like we do."

So while you will still offer burgers and the like, your focus will be solidly on hot dogs. To give your customers a wide range of frankfurter options, the company has assembled several variations, including corn dogs, cheese dogs, chili dogs, "big foot" foot-longs, and the "big & beefy," what industry analysts have called "the hot dog world's answer to the quarter pounder." In addition, Wienerschnitzel is exploring the finger food sector with corn dog nuggets.

After the burger debacle, Wienerschnitzel has been careful to ensure that its restaurants feature a consistent menu. Therefore, although you'll have your pick of company-approved vendors from whom to obtain your supplies, you will be permitted to offer only the food and beverage choices that Wienerschnitzel specifies.

A real estate department representative from Galardi Group, the parent company of Wienerschnitzel, will assist you with site selection. Most Wienerschnitzel facilities are freestanding buildings, either close to or within major shopping areas and near other fast-food restaurants, but the company will also consider a mall or storefront location. A dining room setup, what the company calls "concept '86," furnishes indoor seating for up to 60, while the traditional A-frame structure provides patio eating space only. Outfitted with prototype building plans from the development department, you can have them modified by a local architect to suit your special requirements.

While Galardi Group officials guide you through the construction period, you'll also spend the time taking the company's seven-week "basic restaurant operations" training course. It's no gut: the schedule is six days a week, 10 hours a day—not including time for reading and home study—complete with over a dozen written homework assignments and four written exams. You'll spend 14 days in the classroom and the rest of the time at an operating Wienerschnitzel, learning the floor skills necessary to operate all of the production and work stations—and to promote sanitation and preventive maintenance—as well as the management skills required to run the business successfully, including ordering and receiving, inventory and cost controls, and personnel and customer relations.

As your final preparations are concluding, a training team will assemble at your restaurant to instruct your crew and to oversee the opening. You can expect regular troubleshooting visits once you are in business, along with inspections to evaluate the performance of your operation. The Wienerschnitzel franchise consultant and others at the home office will be giving ongoing advice, and the marketing department will provide direction and assistance for implementing local promotional campaigns and taking advantage of the company's franchise-wide programs. In addition, the entire network gets together during national operations seminars.

Wienerschnitzel restaurants are located in California and throughout the Southwest. The Galardi group plans on continuing to concentrate—if not limit—its expansion efforts to that region.

For further information contact:
Alan F. Gallup, Director of Franchise Sales, Galardi Group, Inc., P.O. Box 7460, Newport Beach, CA 92658-7460, 714-752-5800 ext. 610 or 612, fax 714-851-2618

Ice Cream and Yogurt

Baskin-Robbins, USA

Initial license fee: None
Royalties: 0.5%
Advertising royalties: 3%
Minimum cash required: $60,000
Capital required: $135,000 to $180,000

Financing: Company offers some bank financing to qualified candidates
Length of contract: 5 years

In business since: 1945
Franchising since: 1946
Total number of units: 3,456
Number of company-operated units: 28
Total number of units planned, 1995: NA
Number of company-operated units planned, 1995: NA

Everybody loves ice cream: Over one billion gallons of ice cream are produced each year in the United States alone, and the average person consumes about 15 quarts annually. For years Baskin-Robbins has been satisfying the world's ice cream cravings with flavors from vanilla, the all-time favorite, to pralines 'n' cream and peanut butter and chocolate. Dedicated to the notion "We make people happy," the company has developed 636 ice cream flavors so far.

Now the company also offers frozen yogurt, and sugar-free, fat-free, and light frozen desserts. As an innovator, Baskin-Robbins believes it offers the greatest flavor selection and variety of products available in the frozen dessert industry. Consumers in national surveys have repeatedly voted Baskin-Robbins their favorite dessert shop.

Franchising since 1950, Baskin-Robbins offers you the opportunity to become part of a smooth-running international franchise system. The company notes that its tried-and-true methods and its standards of quality service and cleanliness are among the best in the industry. By investing in a Baskin-Robbins franchise, you can benefit from years of experience, not to mention exceptional name recognition. There are still plenty of Baskin-Robbins franchises available across the country. You can choose either new locations that the company has planned and wants to develop, or existing franchises that owners offer for sale. (Owners may sell their stores at any time to buyers approved by the company.)

You must train for three weeks before opening your store. Instructors teach product handling and preparation, employee recruiting, training, management, and customer relations. Your training will take place at the national training center in Glendale, California, and in the corporate training stores, five operating retail outlets in the Glendale-Burbank area. When you complete your training, your district manager will help you open your store and will remain available to advise you about trouble spots and provide a link between you and the home office.

Baskin-Robbins continually researches products and markets in an effort to keep the company in a position of market leadership. With national and regional publicity and advertising, participation in high-exposure activities such as the Tournament of Roses parade, and development of promotions and store decor, the company aggressively pursues a place in the forefront of consumer consciousness. As Jim Earnhardt, President of Baskin-Robbins, USA, puts it, the company's marketing efforts "are all designed to attract customers—to get them to think of us when they think of ice cream." Not to mention frozen yogurt and the company's lighter desserts.

The market and product research division studies the viability of new products and keeps watch over existing products to make sure that they satisfy customers' changing tastes. But the key to Baskin-Robbins's marketing success is its franchisees. Carol Kirby, vice president of marketing, calls on "store owners to play a very vital role in evaluating the results of all our marketing programs. There is no single, one, right marketing plan for Baskin-Robbins or any other retailer. . . . It is critical that we understand what works well and what does not. To do this requires objective, systematic evaluation at the store level." The company regularly solicits franchisee opinion through surveys published in *Scoops*, the company magazine.

Operations managers meet periodically with you and other franchisees in your area to keep you informed about developments in the Baskin-Robbins system. Management workshops will give you the opportunity to learn about consumer-oriented management systems and to share your experiences with other franchisees. Baskin-Robbins staff will help you develop and implement an annual business plan designed specifically for your needs and potential.

Prospective franchisees must meet rigorous standards before they are granted a Baskin-Robbins license. You can purchase a franchise as an investment, but Baskin-Robbins will want to make sure that you have a qualified manager to operate your store. Before approving you as a franchisee, the company will not only review your financial position and business experience, but also seek to learn about you on a more personal level through interviews and maybe even a visit to your home. While this may make some applicants nervous, it helps the company ensure that all of its franchisees are not only qualified, but well suited to operate a Baskin-Robbins franchise. Based on years of experience, the company has concluded that the most important characteristic of successful Baskin-Robbins franchisees is that they like people, especially children. Baskin-Robbins also looks for some other vital traits in applicants: an ability to manage people, a long-range outlook and goals, a true desire to succeed in a small retail business, and a willingness to be actively involved in the franchise.

For further information contact:
Keith Emerson, Director, Franchise Development, International Headquarters,

Baskin-Robbins, USA, 31 Baskin-Robbins Pl., Glendale, CA 91201,
818-956-0031 or 1-800-331-0031

Everything Yogurt and Salad Cafes

Initial license fee: $30,000 (combination rate)
Royalties: 5%
Advertising royalties: 1%
Minimum cash required: $56,000
Capital required: $225,000 to $250,000
Financing: Indirect (will assist)
Length of contract: 10 years

In business since: 1976
Franchising since: 1981
Total number of units: 306
Number of company-operated units: 6
Total number of units planned, 1995: 506
Number of company-operated units planned, 1995: 12

"House Salad—A healthful combination of romaine lettuce, fresh car-
rots, cucumbers, and tomatoes topped with alfalfa sprouts and sea-
soned croutons. EY's Chef Salad—An exciting array of 100% white
chicken meat marinated in our mustard and poppy seed dressing, as-
sorted cheeses, mixed vegetables and romaine lettuce, delicately tossed
for a healthy low calorie lunch." You can find these light, tasty items
on the menu at Everything Yogurt, a fast-food chain of health food
restaurants that was rated among the 10 top franchises for the 1990s
in *Money* magazine's December 1990 issue.

Clearly, there is more than yogurt at these restaurants. But yogurt is
also much in evidence on the menu. Frozen yogurt is Everything
Yogurt's forte, the draw that gave the company its initial success.
Many chains began selling frozen yogurt in the 1970s, but this is one
of the few that survived. The reason, according to the company, is that
yogurt is part—and often the heart—of a full meal at Everything
Yogurt, not just a dessert.

The company tries to appeal to the many people in recent years
who want to eat lighter, healthier food. In additon to yogurt, the
company offers made-from-scratch deli sandwiches served on pita
bread, eight different kinds of salads and several types of soup. Indeed,
the slogan on the menu is "GOOD HEALTH IS EVERYTHING."

While the menu attracts many customers, the appearance of an Everything Yogurt restaurant goes a long way toward selling people on
eating there. Everything Yogurt restaurants generate their ambience by
making fresh fruit and flowers a very visible part of their decor. The

dishes on the menu are displayed and lit to maximize their inherent visual appeal. Richard Nicotra, cofounder of the chain, is frank about the company's methods. "We're in show business, not the food business," he says. "We do everything in front of the customer, and we spend a lot of money on the way the store looks."

Contrary to what you might think, frozen yogurt sales do not decrease in the winter: Most of the franchises are in shopping malls, and, as Nicotra points out, "malls are indoors, they're warm, and they're full of shoppers who like to stop for something to eat."

Should you decide to open an Everything Yogurt store, the company will also give you and your customers an opportunity to go Bananas. Bananas is the sister enterprise—a smaller sister—to Everything Yogurt. These kiosks, which often share a mall location with an Everything Yogurt franchise, feature light snacks, including shakes made from fresh fruit. Here, too, the emphasis is on catching the eye, with large quantities of fresh fruit displayed behind glass.

The franchise fee for a Bananas franchise, $15,000, drops to $5,000 when you buy it together with an Everything Yogurt franchise. Indeed, the company encourages such pairings. The franchises are often located in mall food courts, where there are concentrations of fast-food outlets; so the Everything Yogurt franchisor who "multiplexes" his or her operation by franchising other fast-food chains will be the most successful. As Nicotra says, "Because of the costs in a mall, you get a much better return on investment if you do at least two operations, and three or four makes the return even better because one manager manages all of them."

Currently, the company is concentrating on opening cafes in regional enclosed malls and street locations in major downtown projects and large cities such as New York, Chicago, Philadelphia, and Boston.

Should you purchase an Everything Yogurt franchise, the company will help you set up your business. Company staff will help you pick the site and design and build the store. Training consists of a 75-hour apprenticeship at a company training store. During your training you will be instructed in food display, inventory control, and buying procedures. Follow-up help is available if you need it. The company also gives you advice on how to conduct local promotions.

You are required to buy your food from the company's approved list of suppliers.

For further information contact:
Everything Yogurt and Salad Cafes, Franchise Division, 90 Western Ave., Staten Island, NY 10303-1104, 718-816-7800

Freshens Premium Yogurt

Initial license fee: $20,000
Royalties: 4%
Advertising royalties: 4%
Minimum cash required: $50,000
Capital required: $150,000 to $175,000
Financing: Assistance in obtaining
Length of contract: 10 years

In business since: 1985
Franchising since: 1986
Total number of units: 241
Number of company-operated units: 5
Total number of units planned, 1995: 400
Number of company-operated units planned, 1995: 8

Frozen yogurt, the carry-out dessert that "began as a fad and died out" for a while, according to Anne Papa, spokesperson for the National Restaurant Association, "has reappeared with new strength." One of the reasons why it suffered an initial setback, believes Ed Raymond, Freshens's vice president of marketing, was, frankly, disappointment with the taste. "When frozen yogurt was introduced, it was somewhat tart and the flavors had a heavy aftertaste." But the idea of a low-fat, low-calorie alternative to ice cream was still a sound one, Freshens was certain, so it started working with an internationally renowned food chemist to make the product truly appetizing.

Today, the company claims that the taste and creamy texture of its yogurt measures up to the best premium ice creams. But Freshens backs its claim by pointing to the "Best Frozen Yogurt" citations it has received from local magazines in New York, Atlanta, and other cities across the country. The company also stands by its product with a money-back refund that customers, it says, rarely request.

Made entirely from natural ingredients and containing active yogurt cultures, Freshens comes in three basic varieties: low-fat, containing 80 percent less fat than ice cream; nonfat, with no fat or cholesterol whatsoever; and sugar-free, at only about 17 to 20 calories per fluid ounce. With over 30 flavors, you'll give your customers a choice that goes well beyond the basic chocolate/vanilla/strawberry staples— orange creamsickle and Key lime pie, to name two of the more unique options. You'll also offer them a selection of 26 crumbled toppings, including such exotic concoctions as Scandinavian apple and raspberry currant coconut, as well as fruit and candy mix-ins.

Asking for a fresh-baked gingerbread, chocolate, or vanilla waffle cone does jack up the calorie count, but even ordering a banana split shouldn't cause your customer much guilt. "For people who routinely diet," Atlanta nutritionist Tom McNees agrees, "this can be a fun treat once in awhile." As for other offerings such as hot-fudge sundaes, Mississippi mud pie or chocolate Kahlúa creme cake take-home desserts, well, they might be another matter.

Freshens continues to investigate new product ideas, and has begun to introduce soft pretzels in its larger stores through its "Pretzel Logic" program. The logic of the pretzel option is that it attracts new customers and doesn't eat into, if you will, yogurt sales—indeed, it may improve them, with thirsty patrons grabbing the nearest refreshment they can get. The pretzels, Freshens maintains, are also consistent with the company's health-conscious image, since they actually contain no fat or cholesterol (when the cheese toppings are left off) and are available in saltless varieties for the sodium-conscious consumer.

The Freshens franchise program was designed for people with no background in the food industry. "I certainly didn't have restaurant experience," explains Sue Todd, an Indianapolis franchisee, "so my best protection against failure was to buy a franchise that would give me the support I was lacking. It would have taken me a year to figure out some of the things the franchisor has provided." These include a comprehensive promotional campaign for both your store and your geographic area, with print, broadcast, and point-of-purchase materials developed through the Freshens' local and national advertising funds.

And things like specific guidelines for finding an appropriate site for your store, with a company staffer visiting each location personally when you've narrowed your choices, are also very helpful to new franchisees. You can operate in a mall facility as small as 300 square feet if there are public eating areas, and a kiosk setup is also possible when no available food court space is available. Or you might decide on a freestanding unit offering drive-through service and seating for up to 38.

Whichever choice, the company will provide you with building designs, along with the instructions and materials to create the signature Freshens decor, using tile, mirrors, and plants, plus wall displays with bold product photos. You'll be able to obtain a complete equipment package through the company's subsidiary, Hill Distributing Company, or you can purchase or lease the supplies from approved vendors.

To learn how to run a Freshens shop, you'll attend the company's 10-day training program held at the Atlanta corporate headquarters, which will cover equipment layout and maintenance, product and recipe preparation, personnel policies, accounting, and inventory control, and feature on-the-job training at a company-owned store. After you finish the course, Freshens representatives will work with you to prepare for your store's opening, and an operations specialist will be there to guide you through your first week in business. He or she will also make periodic visits thereafter to address any problems and keep you up-to-date on industry trends, new products, and upcoming advertising and promotion programs.

Freshens franchisees often cite this extensive start-up and ongoing support as a primary reason why they chose the company. The potential for making a good profit would have to be considered a major motivating factor, as well. And there are other, simpler, benefits. "Yogurt shops," Sue Todd remarks, "are really fun to run."

For further information contact:
  Laurie Lanser, Director of Franchise Development, Freshens Premium Yogurt, 2849 Paces Ferry Rd., Suite 750, Atlanta, GA 30339, 404-433-0983, fax 404-431-9081

I Can't Believe It's Yogurt, Ltd.

Initial license fee: $22,500
Royalties: 5%
Advertising royalties: 2%
Minimum cash required: $50,000
Capital required: $200,000 to $250,000
Financing: None
Length of contract: 10 years

In business since: 1977
Franchising since: 1983
Total number of units: 590
Number of company-operated units: 106
Total number of units planned, 1995: 2,000
Number of company-operated units planned, 1995: 108

"I can't believe it's yogurt," Julie and Bill Brice's customers kept telling them back when the brother-and-sister team first began marketing the dessert, when frozen yogurt was a true novelty. That's still probably the highest compliment that could be paid—with too many other brands, after all, it's all too easy to believe it's yogurt. The Brices understood that most consumers choose frozen yogurt because they're looking for a treat that tastes something like ice cream, only without all the fat and calories.

So to create the recipe, they used a very simple approach. "We checked a book out of the library called *How to Make Ice Cream*, and we did it with yogurt," Julie Brice recalls. "We read the book, hired a crew, and that was it." Today, ICBIY makes over 50 flavors of its original frozen yogurt, from French vanilla to almond amaretto, apple pie, and peanut butter fudge, each containing 80 percent less fat and 33 percent more protein than premium ice cream. It also became the first frozen yogurt company to offer both sugar-free and sugar-free nonfat varieties. And, more recently, ICBIY introduced its 10-calorie per ounce "Yoglacé" frozen dairy dessert, available in Belgian chocolate, Swiss vanilla, and Bavarian swirl.

At your ICBIY store, you'll serve the yogurt in cups, waffle cones, and shakes. Your customers can have their choice of fruit, nuts, and candy to add on top, or order a more elaborate concoction like a hot fudge nut sundae or banana split. In addition, you'll feature a selection of gourmet frozen yogurt pies, with a graham cracker or chocolate cookie crust and an assortment of toppings.

ICBIY will help you find a location for your store, outlining selection criteria in the operations manual you'll receive, analyzing statistical data, and visiting proposed sites. But sometimes, admittedly, the franchisees know better. Georgia Evans of Bethel, Connecticut, persuaded ICBIY to let her try opening at a shopping center that the company thought had limited traffic potential. "I told them that my friends wouldn't let me starve," Evans says, and they didn't: The store placed second in system-wide sales during her first year in business, and she was named ICBIY owner of the year.

Furnishing a prototype floor plan or specially drawn blueprints for unusual sites, the company also provides specific construction guidelines for the equipment wall and service counter, as well as other design elements. "You basically want all of the stores to be the same," believes New York City franchisee Stephen Szulhan, but with some flexibility, too.

Dallas is where the franchisee training school, Yogurt U, is located. You'll learn operations and management skills through a combination of classroom and on-site instruction, covering such subjects as equipment operation and maintenance, customer service, accounting, and inventory control. Follow-up training, moreover, is offered at regional meetings and national conventions.

An ICBIY franchise consultant will be on hand during your opening days, to inspect your equipment, brief your employees, and, in conjunction with the marketing department, assist with your initial promotional activities. Throughout the critical first six months of your business, that consultant will remain in close contact, functioning as your direct liaison with the company, and will continue to stay in touch thereafter through phone calls and periodic visits. Performing an annual business evaluation, ICBIY conducts regular store inspections as well, to ensure that all franchisees meet company quality, service, and cleanliness standards.

The marketing department oversees an extensive nationwide advertising program, but will also give you personal guidance in planning and executing local campaigns. To launch ICBIY's new product, Yoglacé, for example, the company sent a media kit to 250 newspapers, magazines, radios, and television stations, at the same time supplying franchisees with ad layouts, flyers, coupons, and detailed bulletins to help them coordinate their own promotional efforts with one another and with the home office. The company also manages public relations programs, including the "I Can't Believe It's Yogurt Believes in You" contest for college entrepreneurs.

To maintain good and close relations with franchisees, too, there is a franchise advisory council, comprised of six elected ICBIY owners and three company executives. "We really wanted a formal way to communicate," explains Julie Brice. "They tell us what's on their mind and we get input and ideas for the company." Yet the committee doesn't merely serve as a forum for discussion and feedback; it also implements programs and policy changes, developing, for instance, an entirely new operations manual . . . and 24 new yogurt flavors. You don't have to be on the council, however, to have a say in the company. Declares Brice, "We treat the franchise owners as our business partners."

For further information contact:
  Jim Smith, National Franchise Sales Manager, I Can't Believe It's Yogurt, Ltd.,
  P.O. Box 809112, Dallas, TX 75380-9112, 214-450-9400 or 1-800-722-5848

International Dairy Queen, Inc.

Initial license fee: $30,000
Royalties: 4%
Advertising royalties: 3% to 5%
Minimum cash required: $95,000
Capital required: $95,000+
Financing: Company will finance ½ the initial license fee over 5 years
Length of contract: No term

In business since: 1940
Franchising since: 1944
Total number of units: 5,207
Number of company-operated units: 5
Total number of units planned, 1995: NA
Number of company-operated units planned, 1995: NA

Dairy Queen, the world's largest dessert franchise, began in 1940 with one store in Joliet, Illinois, selling a soft ice cream product that contained less milk fat than regular ice cream. The ice cream, served with a distinctive curl at the top, came in a cone. The product was a big success, and in 1944 Dairy Queen began to sell franchises, one of the first food companies to do so. The company reorganized into International Dairy Queen in 1962. The current ice cream menu features parfaits, shakes, sundaes, banana splits, frozen yogurt, cakes and logs, and various frozen novelty items, in addition to the cone with the curl that started it all. The Blizzard, an ice cream-and-candy treat introduced in the mid-eighties, has done especially well. One franchisee in Chicago said that the product had boosted his sales by $300 per day.

Also in 1962, some Dairy Queens substantially widened their product mix to include nondessert food. The trend began when a Georgia franchisee added a selection of fast foods to the company's dessert line, thus converting the local Dairy Queen to a restaurant. This Dairy Queen/Brazier store, now one of the forms in which the company sells its franchises, carried items like hot dogs, hamburgers, chili dogs, cheese dogs, fish sandwiches, and french fries. Eventually, even stores that had continued to concentrate on the ice cream trade added some fast-food items. The conversion helped make Dairy Queen a year-round operation, drawing customers even during the winter.

Whether you buy an ice cream–only Dairy Queen or a Dairy Queen/Brazier, you will pay the same fees and require the same amount of land. Your investment in construction and equipment, however, will total at least 50 percent more if you buy a Dairy Queen/Brazier instead of an original Dairy Queen.

Dairy Queen provides guidelines for site selection and the construction of your Dairy Queen store. It will give you plans and specifications for your building and make two on-site inspections during its construction. For an additional fee, Dairy Queen also offers to coordinate construction and equipment installation. The company refers to this service as "optional but highly recommended."

While you're at an advantage if you have had food service experience before buying your Dairy Queen franchise, you don't need it. You will get all the necessary training from the company at its Minneapolis training center. The licensing fee covers instruction for two people; the company charges an additional $600 fee per person for training more of your employees. You pay for traveling expenses related to training. The company's training program includes instruction in product preparation, equipment operation and maintenance, financial management, service etiquette, "suggestive" selling, marketing and merchandising, sanitation procedures, and personnel training.

The company's team of opening experts will oversee the start-up of your business and will offer on-site assistance for your entire first week of operations. Additional help will come from your field representative in the form of frequent consultations on new products, quality/purity evaluation, and employee retraining. National and regional conventions will enable you to compare your experiences with those of other franchisees and also to get a preview of new products and procedures that the company plans to introduce in the coming year.

You must purchase equipment and supplies for your store from the company's list of approved vendors.

For further information contact:
  Franchise Sales Department, International Dairy Queen, Inc., 5701 Green
  Valley Dr., Minneapolis, MN 55437-1089, 612-830-0327 or 1-800-285-8515

Pizza and Italian Fast Food

Domino's Pizza, Inc.

Initial license fee: $1,300 to $3,250 plus $3,000 grand opening deposit for first-
  time franchises
Royalties: 5.5% weekly
Advertising royalties: 4% weekly
Minimum cash required: $30,000 to $60,000
Capital required: $83,000 to $194,000
Financing: Certain lenders have agreed to provide financing to qualified
  franchises
Length of contract: 10 years

In business since: 1960
Franchising since: 1967
Total number of units: 3,549
Number of company-operated units: 1,265
Total number of units planned, 1995: 6,500 to 7,500
Number of company-operated units planned, 1991: 1,000

One of the strongest segments of the food service industry, pizza offers something for everyone. This most versatile of foods can satisfy almost every taste, with variations ranging from thin-crusted New York slices topped with pepperoni to deep-dish Chicago pies with the works, to nouvelle cuisine California creations featuring sun-dried tomatoes and fresh basil. Add to its widespread appeal busy people's growing demand for microwaveable, prepared, and take-out food, and you've got a ready-made market for pizza delivery and carry-out. Domino's Pizza, Inc., specializes in pizza to go, promising their customers that their orders will always be delivered hot within 30 minutes of their call. The company's proven system, its commitment to freshness, and its national advertising campaign have made it the largest pizza delivery chain in the country. Domino's controls 12 percent to 14 percent of the multibillion-dollar pizza business and continues to claim a greater and greater portion of the market.

Prospective Domino's franchisees had to have been managers of another Domino's franchise for at least a year. When you fill that requirement, Domino's will help you select just the right location for your store and will provide guidance in your purchase or lease negotiations. Because any lease for your site must contain certain conditions, Domino's reserves the right to review it before you sign. Once you are ready to develop your site, the company will provide you with equipment, fixtures, furniture, and signs. All food and beverage products, supplies, and materials must meet the company's standards. You can purchase them from Domino's or any other source that can meet the specifications.

Before you open your doors, Domino's requires you to complete its formal three-week training program at headquarters in Ann Arbor, Michigan, and at an existing store location. The program covers the fundamentals of pizza preparation, bookkeeping, sales, and other topics related to the operation of the franchise. Besides store operations, you will learn franchise development (to prepare you to develop your region), commissary operations (if you run your pizza shop in connection with another store), and management. When you graduate and are ready to open for business, Domino's will develop and implement preopening advertising, promotions, and publicity at no cost to you. "A big advantage to the Domino's franchise is that you can capitalize on the exposure the company gives you through its high-quality, high-frequency advertising program," says William Morrow, a Domino's owner in Charlottesville, Virginia. In 1985, the company spent $17.8 million on television advertising, part of its ongoing campaign to carve out a larger portion of the market, and it continues to devote a large part of its promotional budget to the advertisement of its outlets.

An employee of Domino's Pizza for five years before becoming a franchisee, Morrow also says that "the abundance of rapidly improving training materials, the company's orientation to people, and its use of incentive initiatives to encourage development" have been particularly helpful to him as a franchisee. The company's program of ongoing support to franchisees includes operating assistance in hiring and training employees, planning and executing local advertising and promotional programs, controlling inventory, and implementing administrative, accounting, and general operating procedures.

William Morrow is pleased with his Domino's franchise. "Given the smaller amount of money involved in entering the food franchise business, my rate of return has been very high. Running my own franchise has been a profound learning experience. I would recommend franchising to anyone who is willing to work hard and long hours, who is financially stable, and who can maintain a sense of humor."

For further information contact:
  Deborah S. Sargent, National Director of Franchise Services, Domino's Pizza, Inc., Prairie House, Domino's Farms, 30 Frank Lloyd Wright Dr., P.O. Box 997, Ann Arbor, MI 48106-0997, 313-668-6055

Little Caesars

Initial license fee: $20,000
Royalties: 5%
Advertising royalties: 4%
Minimum cash required: $75,000 to $90,000
Capital required: $120,000 to $180,000
Financing: Available
Length of contract: 10 years

In business since: 1959
Franchising since: 1962
Total number of units: 3,300
Number of company-operated units: 924
Total number of units planned, 1995: 7,000
Number of company-operated units planned, 1995: 1,960

Little Caesars is no little franchise. The world's third-biggest pizza chain—and number-one carry-out enterprise—it's continuing to grow still larger. The company's executives don't think they've even come close to saturating the market and have expansion plans to sell hundreds of new franchises in over 25 states.

Not that the company's growth strategy is being left to chance. Quite the contrary, Little Caesars has a painstakingly tuned market development plan based on detailed studies of each area's potential, involving such considerations as demographics, economic conditions, and competition from other local restaurants. Be prepared to move if you want to open a Little Caesars shop badly enough, because the company does have definite locations in mind. While they try to accommodate your preference, they won't promise any specific territory. And be prepared to spend a good chunk of money, too. Start-up costs, as with most food industry franchises, are considerable for even one unit, and the company is looking especially, if not primarily, for candidates who can afford to develop multiple stores.

These may seem like rather elaborate requirements for an innocent, low-priced item like pizza, but it's a system that has served Little

Caesars—and its franchisees—well for three decades now. Remaining successful has, nevertheless, meant making adjustments and improvements along the way—adding drive-through service at many of its stores, for instance, and introducing a "Pizza! Pizza!" two-for-one program—to keep up with the competition as well as the changing tastes and demands of consumers. You'll go to a much greater effort, as another example, than you would have, say, 20 years ago, to inform your health-conscious customers about the nutritional quality of your pizzas—made with no additives and with all-natural ingredients like high-protein gluten flour, grade A cheese, tomatoes custom-grown for Little Caesars, and fresh spices mixed daily at the company's world headquarters and sent straight to you.

More than 90 percent of all Little Caesars stores are carry-out operations exclusively, located in neighborhood shopping centers where customers can pick up their phoned-in orders quickly. You'll serve regular and pan pizza, sold by the slice or by the pie, along with five kinds of sandwiches, garlic and cheese "Crazy Bread," and soft drinks. The other store option is a "Little Caesars Pizza Station," a full restaurant with sit-down service and an expanded menu that includes pasta and an extensive soup and salad bar.

Before you are granted a Little Caesars franchise, you will have to attend a 12-hour evaluation program. And once the franchise agreement is signed, you'll participate in a one-day seminar led by the company's vice president of real estate. Together, you and Little Caesars will pinpoint several possible sites for your store and make a final decision based on the company's analysis of their accessibility, visibility, and traffic patterns. The architecture department will provide you with design, construction, and equipment guidelines. Allowing for diversity based on your particular layout needs and your landlord's demands, Little Caesars facilities have an essentially consistent appearance, with standard features including an open glass exterior that allows a full view inside, and decor that incorporates marketing tools like a four-color full-wall mural of Little Caesars products.

Franchisee training will require you to make a substantial time commitment. But because the eight-week program is divided into three distinct segments—in-store, classroom, and business instruction—you will be able to proceed section by section if you can't complete the entire curriculum all at once. The on-the-job sessions are no mere casual store visits: Instead, you'll really be put to work at the company restaurants, learning how to prepare all of the Little Caesars food selections and becoming involved in each area of operation during day, evening, and weekend shifts alike.

Working in the restaurants, you'll also be able to learn how the promotional campaigns devised by the corporate marketing department are managed on the local level, making it easier for you to run them yourself once you are in business. These programs have been tested in major markets before being introduced throughout the network. When they are ready for implementation, you'll receive comprehensive support from the home office with timetables, instructions, and materials, from award-winning radio and television commercials to newspaper and print ads.

To foster good public relations, and more importantly, to fulfill your civic obligations to the neighborhood that furnishes your livelihood, Little Caesars also encourages meaningful community involvement by its franchisees. That could entail sponsorship of amateur or Little League teams, support of local charities, food contributions for fundraising dinners, or other endeavors of your own choosing. On a national level, the company's efforts focus on feeding the homeless, through such means as "Little Caesars Love Kitchen," a 45-foot restaurant-on-wheels that travels to soup kitchens around the country. Little Caesars wants to show its commitment to social responsibility.

For further information contact:
Gary S. Jensen, Director of Franchise Sales, Little Caesar Enterprises, Inc., Fox Office Centre, 2211 Woodward Ave., Detroit, MI 48201-3400, 313-983-6000, fax 313-983-6494

Mazzio's Pizza

Initial license fee: $20,000
Royalties: 3%
Advertising royalties: 1%
Minimum cash required: $200,000
Capital required: $800,000
Financing: None
Length of contract: 20 years

In business since: 1961
Franchising since: 1968
Total number of units: 246
Number of company-operated units: 109
Total number of units planned, 1995: 251
Number of company-operated units planned, 1995: 5

Approximately one-third of all people who have tried at least two types of ethnic food like Italian the best, according to *Nation's Restaurant News*: "Pasta, pizza et al. are the best-known, most tried, most frequently ordered and most likely-to-be-ordered-again ethnic foods sold in restaurants." Mazzio's Pizza has ridden the tide of popularity, but has also made some innovations to position itself more profitably in an already competitive market.

Mazzio's marketing begins with its menu. To the several varieties of pizza—including deep dish—you might expect in any pizza restaurant, and the familiar assortment of sandwiches and salad bar, Mazzio's adds a Mexican touch, including nachos as an appetizer and a taco pizza. Some Mazzio's stores also serve gelato.

Mazzio's wants to attract wealthy people in the 18- to 34-year-old range with its restaurant design and decor as well as its food. Mazzio's features red brick restaurants surrounded by shrubbery, with striped awnings, plenty of neon, an art deco look, and limited table service. They also offer video games.

You may choose from several restaurant design formats. The most popular one occupies 3,300 square feet, seats 124, and requires a staff of about 40 to 50. Currently available locations include the Southwest, Southeast, Midwest, and West. The company does not select the site or put up your building, but it does offer advice, and it will evaluate and must approve your location and construction.

You and one other employee—presumably your manager—will train at a Mazzio's restaurant near the franchisor's Tulsa, Oklahoma, headquarters. You must absorb all of your expenses except tuition. The course lasts 15 weeks and covers everything involved in running a Mazzio's, including product preparation, customer service, and personnel. A week before your opening, Mazzio's special opening crew will come to your restaurant to train your staff. Company representatives will stay on your premises through your third week of operations to help you get off to a good start. Throughout your term as a Mazzio's franchisee, the company will update your staff's training through field seminars as needed.

The franchisor will show you how to set up a bookkeeping system, and it will help you to keep tabs on your finances so that you can maximize your restaurant's profitability. The company also makes available, as an option, its computer service center. It says that most franchisees pay the "modest cost" to use the center for their record keeping.

Mazzio's does not directly supply food and equipment, but the company does check what you buy from others to make sure it meets its standards.

The franchisor specializes in on-site promotions. A recent program featured punch cards, which restaurants punched every time a patron made a purchase. After a customer had made a minimum dollar amount of purchases from Mazzio's, they became entitled to free merchandise.

The company encourages multiunit ownership by franchisees who have built successful businesses at a single location. Henry Leonard, vice president of Pizza Systems, Inc., which owns several Mazzio's, has enjoyed his experience as a part owner of a multifranchise operation. He especially likes "the autonomy of the situation. Franchisees for the most part are entrepreneurs and want to act independently from a parent company. Without that autonomy, the relationship would be dramatically changed."

Ken's Restaurant Systems, of which Mazzio's is a part, also sells franchises for its Ken's Pizza restaurants and Scooter's Pizza Delivery.

For more information contact:
 Bradford J. Williams, Jr., Ken's Restaurant Systems, Inc., 4441 S. 72nd E. Ave.,
 Tulsa, OK 74145, 918-663-8880

Round Table Pizza

Initial license fee: $25,000
Royalties: 4%
Advertising royalties: 3%
Minimum cash required: $100,000
Capital required: $280,000 to $300,000
Financing: None
Length of contract: 15 years

In business since: 1959
Franchising since: 1962
Total number of units: 565
Number of company-operated units: None
Total number of units planned, 1995: NA
Number of company-operated units planned, 1995: NA

Round Table, the biggest pizza chain in the West, has used the same recipe for its made-fresh-daily sauce for almost 30 years. And why change, when a 1988 survey by Synergy Marketing Associates found that 52 percent of pizza restaurant customers rated Round Table's pizza the best? The closest competitor claimed 13 percent of the vote. The company's freshly-grated, natural mozzarella, provolone, and cheddar cheeses, and the fresh—never freeze-dried or frozen—vegetable toppings and lean freshly-ground sausages may also contribute to Round Table's popularity.

Round Table Pizza's many different meat, vegetable, fruit, and seafood toppings include pepperoni, salami, Italian sausage, ground beef, pastrami, ham, linguica sausage, mushrooms, black olives, tomatoes, pineapple tidbits, anchovies, and shrimp. Specialty pizzas combine large helpings of these toppings in various combinations, with mini-pizzas also available. In addition, the menu features Camelot Calzones, Pizzatato (baked potato with a pizza filling), several kinds of sandwiches, and a salad bar.

Round Table restaurants serve beer and wine in addition to soft drinks.

Round Table will train you at its Los Angeles training center. The course lasts four weeks and includes everything from baking pizza to picking personnel. As part of your training, you will receive hands-on experience at a Round Table restaurant.

The franchisor will help you to select a site, an architect, and contractors, as well as negotiate the lease. The franchisor maintains The Round Table Supply Company as a nonprofit division to supply equipment to franchisees at factory level prices, but you may buy your supplies from any source, with Round Table's approval.

A Round Table field consultant will help you line up local suppliers, hire and train your staff, and set up a bookkeeping system. He or she will also assist you with ongoing support after you open for business. The consultant can provide expertise in many areas, including food and labor costs, inventory, and hiring. The company also provides eight manuals to take you through all phases of operation and marketing, and sponsors periodic regional presentations by experts in such relevant fields as computer software and financial planning.

The franchisor's marketing department will customize a marketing plan for you, possibly including a direct mail campaign. On a wider scale, Round Table promotes the chain through an extensive radio and television advertising program. For the past four years, the company's radio commercials have won the American Advertising Federation's "Best in the West" Sweepstakes for the best radio campaign.

For further information contact:
  Franchise Sales, Round Table Franchise Corporation, 655 Montgomery St., 7th floor, San Francisco, CA 94111, 415-392-7500

Sbarro, Inc.

Initial license fee: $35,000
Royalties: 5%
Advertising royalties: 3%
Minimum cash required: $150,000
Capital required: $199,000 to $644,000
Financing: None
Length of contract: 10 years

In business since: 1977

Franchising since: 1977
Total number of units: 458
Number of company-operated units: 355
Total number of units planned, 1995: 558
Number of company-operated units planned, 1995: NA

Sbarro has created a simple formula for success: Satisfy a gargantuan appetite for Italian food at moderate prices in pleasant cafeteria-style surroundings. Salamis, prosciutto hams, and cheeses hanging from the ceiling evoke an Italian delicatessen motif. Pizza with a variety of toppings is the mainstay of the menu, but Sbarro shops also serve large portions of pasta and other hot and cold Italian entrées, sandwiches and salads, and desserts, like cheesecake made in Brooklyn. Some units sell beer and wine, although these beverages do not generally account for a large share of the revenues. Shopping mall locations predominate in the chain, although Sbarro also operates a few cafe-type operations in city centers. These cafes, with their somewhat upscale ambience but the same moderate prices as those in the malls, have done well.

Sbarro's mall stores range from 1,500 to 3,000 square feet, seat 60 to 120 people, and usually require seven to twenty-six employees, including part-timers. Each restaurant has a manager and two assistant managers, and their hours coincide with the mall's—often 12 hours a day, seven days a week, covering the lunch and dinner periods.

Currently, Sbarro emphasizes multiunit operations for new franchisees. Sbarro will supply you with plans for store layout and specifications for construction and equipment. You may purchase supplies and equipment from any approved supplier, although most franchisees buy from Sbarro at a reduced cost. Your license agreement will include a clause requiring you to refurbish the premises when necessary—probably every five years.

You pay the travel expenses incidental to the 10-week training program, which you or your manager must complete in your area and in Commack, New York. Aside from hands-on experience working in a company restaurant, the training will include background in quality control, personnel management, marketing, and financial management.

A district manager, usually responsible for six to ten restaurants, will assist you in training your employees for three weeks before you open. After that, he or she will continue as your liaison with Sbarro. Should you need it, you can get refresher training at your regional office or at corporate headquarters in Commack.

You can purchase practically all your supplies from any vendor maintaining Sbarro's level of quality. Most franchisees buy from the same distributor as company restaurants because of the price advantages achieved by volume purchasing. The cheesecake, however, must come from Sbarro's Brooklyn facility.

For further information contact:
  Franchise Department, Sbarro, Inc., 763 Larkfield Rd., Commack, NY 11725, 516-864-0200

Shakey's Pizza Restaurant, Inc.

Initial license fee: $25,000
Royalties: 4.5%, 4.3% for 4–9 units, 4% for 10 or more units
Advertising royalties: 2%
Minimum cash required: $150,000
Capital required: $175,000 to $212,000
Financing: None
Length of contract: 20 years

In business since: 1954
Franchising since: 1958
Total number of units: 382
Number of company-operated units: 20
Total number of units planned, 1995: NA
Number of company-operated units planned, 1995: NA

Since that 1954 day in Sacramento, California, when Shakey Johnson opened what he believed to be the world's first "pizza parlor," Shakey's has maintained a brand awareness associated with quality, fun, and family values. Shakey's is an international franchisor with 382 restaurants in 15 countries. Whether you're in Los Angeles, Singapore, or Sydney, you can still find the World's Greatest Pizza, famous fried chicken, and Shakey's Mojo Potatoes. The company tries to make eating at Shakey's a high-quality, fun dining-out experience.

As a franchisee, you can develop single-unit or multiunit stores. You select the site based on the company's specifications. Shakey's provides all blueprints and detail specifications at no additional charge.

The typical shopping center space is 3,500 to 5,000 square feet. Freestanding units require 40,000 to 50,000 square feet of land or a 5,000-square-foot pad.

You will be assured support from Shakey's field operations and marketing staff. A two-week training course at Shakey's University in South San Francisco is offered to all owner-operators and managers. Topics covered include product preparation, operations management, bookkeeping and profit and loss analysis, and marketing. Training is included in the franchise fee, but you must pay for accomodations and travel expenses.

Shakey's professional market division and corporate staff provide ongoing promotions and materials for television, radio, and print advertising. Your 2 percent advertising royalty pays for a variety of point-of-purchase materials, ongoing broadcast and strategic support, and currently, assistance with your local marketing budget. In addition, you are required to spend 2.4 percent of your gross revenues on local marketing programs. Advertising co-ops have been established in multiunit markets. They provide cost-effective media buys and other group discounts and promotions. Advertising co-ops are independent, but receive ongoing support and encouragement from the company.

For further information contact:
Jean Lyles, Franchise Development, Shakey's, Inc., 651 Gateway Blvd., Suite 1200, South San Francisco, CA 94080, 415-873-0640

Restaurants

Benihana of Tokyo

Initial license fee: $50,000
Royalties: 6%
Advertising royalties: 0.5%
Minimum cash required: $550,000
Capital required: Approximately $1,500,000
Financing: No direct financing
Length of contract: 15 years

In business since: 1964
Franchising since: 1970
Total number of units: 52
Number of company-operated units: 39
Total number of units planned, 1995: 60
Number of company-operated units planned, 1995: 45

An evening at Benihana is more than just eating out. From the authentically detailed Japanese country inn decor, to the communal seating around hibachi tables, to the service provided by kimono-clad waitresses, everything about a Benihana steakhouse transports diners to the Far East. But what makes Benihana truly famous is its simple, high quality cuisine, dazzlingly prepared by skilled chefs right before patrons' eyes. Tabletop cooking, Benihana's trademark, makes every meal entertaining as well as delicious, and helps Benihana maintain its reputation as one of the most popular full-service restaurants in the United States.

Headed by the dynamic and energetic Rocky Aoki, Benihana has grown from one restaurant in New York City to a 52-unit, far-ranging chain with over $60 million in sales. Aoki has become famous for his love of risk, which leads him to race offshore powerboats and sail hot-air balloons, among other things. His involvement in such activities serves as one of Benihana's more successful marketing ploys. "Every year," says Aoki, "I try to do something new to promote the name of Benihana." The company also pursues a bigger chunk of America's dining dollar through more traditional but equally aggressive advertising and marketing efforts. Its strategy for expansion includes company-owned units in foreign markets as well as franchises and joint ventures in the United States, focusing in particular on the midwestern states.

You can purchase a Benihana franchise either as an investor or as an owner-operator. Benihana reserves the right to approve your selection of a restaurant, and must approve your building construction or leasehold improvements in writing. Depending on your approach to the management of your restaurant, you and/or your management staff must attend a 12-week training course at a company-owned restaurant. A full-time Benihana employee will train you in restaurant operations, covering such topics as cost controls, staffing, and sanitation.

Essential to your restaurant's success, and a condition of being a franchisee, is that you employ chefs who have qualified as chefs in Japan and completed Benihana's thorough training program in hibachi-table cooking. Benihana offers an intensive eight- to twelve-week training course for chefs, conducted at a company-owned restaurant. You are responsible for chefs' wages and living expenses for this period. To further ensure the success of your franchise, Benihana operations personnel will help you train all other new staff, including your waiters and waitresses.

Throughout the preopening phase and when you open your restaurant, you will receive company assistance, including promotional help from the Benihana public relations staff.

Throughout the life of your franchise, Benihana staff are available for free consultation in all aspects of restaurant operations. Manuals provide guidance in daily operations, and all franchisees receive standard office forms and Benihana recipes. Benihana designates approved sources of equipment and supplies, but will waive this requirement if your alternate suppliers meet the company's approval. Because, as Aoki says, "to franchise a first-class restaurant like this one is not easy," the company conducts seminars for restaurant management at its Miami, Florida, headquarters each year. The workshops cover all areas of concern to unit managers, including bookkeeping, inventory control, menu development, salaries, and benefits.

For further information contact:
  Michael W. Kata, Director of Licensee Operations, Benihana of Tokyo, 8685 N.W. 53rd Terr., Miami, FL 33166, 305-593-0770

Cucos Restaurantes

Initial license fee: $35,000
Royalties: 4%
Advertising royalties: 0.5%
Minimum cash required: $200,000 to $300,000
Capital required: $1,000,000 minimum
Financing: None
Length of contract: 20 years

In business since: 1980
Franchising since: 1983
Total number of units: 35
Number of company-operated units: 12
Total number of units planned, 1995: 58
Number of company-operated units planned, 1995: 24

According to the National Restaurant Association, Mexican food represents one of the fastest-growing segments of the food service industry. As Vincent Liuzza, president of Cucos, puts it, "We've just seen the tip of the iceberg as far as Mexican restaurants are concerned." Now that the eating-out market is dominated by 25- to 40-year-old consumers interested in finger foods and exotic beverages like margaritas, the demand for restaurants serving something other than "continental cuisine" has developed apace. The Cucos concept is to serve the freshest available made-to-order food to diners in the casual atmosphere of a festive watering hole.

Operating from smaller buildings located in areas of limited population, Cucos specializes in Sonoran cuisine, which differs markedly from chili- and pepper-dominated Tex-Mex cuisine. "We're going for a full rich flavor rather than a spicy 'heat,'" explains Vincent Liuzza. "We feel that our menu is acceptable to a lot of people who think they don't like Mexican food." The Cucos menu features appetizers like guacamole, chili con queso, and six types of nachos, and entrées ranging from the house specialty, chimichangas, to vegetarian burritos and fajitas. Pork has recently been replaced by beef, and the restaurant uses nothing but vegetable oil. Many dishes are distinguished by the use of Cucos's special rich brown sauce, which can be altered to taste at the table. Their restaurants attract a lot of bar business, which they encourage by featuring happy hours. Their locations in less populous areas often make Cucos the most prominent eating establishment in town, and the company notes that they attract new patrons because the smaller size of their restaurants makes them appear crowded and successful.

The company has also increased business by adding staff. Liuzza says that while a typical server in the mid-1980s might have had six or seven tables to wait on, now there are only four tables per waiter. "They've got a third more time to serve each table," he says. Favorable recent customer surveys show that its clientele appreciates the difference. A typical Cucos restaurant employs 15 to 20 full-time staff and 25 to 30 part-time employees.

Cucos specializes in conversions of existing chain restaurants or independent operations, which, in combination with the restaurant's modest size of 4,500 to 6,000 square feet, makes for relatively low start-up costs. Because of its emphasis on conversions, Cucos allows for variations in decor. "We wanted our look to be standardized in 'feel' rather than by actual specifications. Our feeling is upbeat southwestern," says Vincent Liuzza. The chain, however, operates restaurants only in the southeastern section of the United States.

The company does offer development agreements to franchisees who want to open only one restaurant, but has previously focused on those franchisees who agree to open multiple units, with fees set at $35,000 for the first restaurant, $30,000 for the second through sixth restaurants, and $25,000 for any other restaurants you develop.

Your restaurant must be operated by a principal operating officer who owns a share in the business and devotes full time to its management. Prior to your first restaurant opening, at least three of your restaurant management personnel must complete the 10-week initial training period in order to become certified Cucos managers. The intensive course covers every aspect of Cucos operations. After you open your first restaurant, you can conduct management training at your location by following company guidelines. After your managers have successfully completed your on-site course, they must attend a two-week certification program at the Cucos training facilities. Training time is, however, subject to change based on the requirements of the Cucos operations department.

Cucos staff will help you to open your unit, providing assistance in everything from construction to advertising. The preopening team will stay at your site throughout the start-up phase to provide ongoing day-to-day help until you feel fully confident of your abilities. Thereafter, you can count on your "System Confidential Manual" and frequent telephone contact with the home office to answer any of your questions. Periodic visits by company staff to inspect your restaurant will help you evaluate your operation.

Since Vincent Liuzza was a Sizzler Steakhouse franchisee long before he founded Cucos, he knows what it's like to be a franchisee and has designed the Cucos program specifically to encourage the entrepreneurial spirit of franchise owners.

For further information contact:
C. B. Walker II, Vice President, Development, Cucos Restaurantes, 3009 25th St., Metairie, LA 70002, 504-835-0306

International House of Pancakes, Inc.

Initial license fee: $50,000
Royalties: 4.5%
Advertising royalties: 3%
Minimum cash required: $50,000 to $60,000
Capital required: Variable
Financing: Available
Length of contract: NA

In business since: 1958
Franchising since: 1960
Total number of units: 490
Number of company-operated units: 61
Total number of units planned, 1995: 525
Number of company-operated units planned, 1995: 48

For over 30 years, International House of Pancakes has made it a little easier for Americans to get up in the morning. The company now directs its advertising toward increasing IHOP's name recognition among those early risers who, later in the day, are more apt to think of McDonald's or Burger King. In an effort to expand its market, IHOP has implemented an aggressive campaign to let diners know that they can find great lunches and dinners at the place where they're used to eating delicious breakfasts. So, while continuing to turn out the pancakes, strawberry waffles, and omelets, the House of Pancakes now has a menu full of lunch and dinner food: hamburgers, London broil, Italian specialties, salads, and seafood. IHOP has extensively promoted this culinary approach with ad lines like: "The only dinners in town that stack up to our pancakes."

International House of Pancakes has recently encountered stiff competition for its breakfast clientele, but its twofold marketing strategy has helped the company to maintain a strong market position. The big fast-food franchises have in the past several years tried to take a bite out of the company's share of the breakfast trade. And pancakes have traditionally finished behind eggs, sausage, and bacon as the favorite main course of Americans who eat out for breakfast: 44 percent prefer eggs, 31 percent prefer bacon and sausage, and 16 percent prefer pancakes. But, by combining promotional activity aimed at increasing demand for pancakes with its pursuit of the wider lunch and dinner market, IHOP remains one of the best-known names in food—and continues to grow.

There are three ways you can become part of International House of Pancakes. You can purchase a company-owned restaurant, in which case your franchise fee ($50,000 initial license fee plus value of building and land) may range as high as about $600,000, depending on the location of the operation. Alternately, you may become an investor for $50,000 and find a site and build your unit to House of Pancakes' specifications. Or else you can convert another restaurant to an International House of Pancakes franchise, remodeling to company specifications. The fee for conversion is also $50,000.

International House of Pancakes will train you at the House of Pancakes nearest you. The course lasts six weeks and covers use of equipment purchasing, floor management, sanitation, advertising, and insurance. Management seminars, given at least once a year, will supplement introductory instruction.

An International House of Pancakes field representative will visit your operation periodically. He or she will supervise and help you to run your business. You can get specific advice at any time from the home office about any problems that arise.

For further information contact:
Anna Ulvan, International House of Pancakes, Inc., 525 N. Brand Blvd., 3rd floor, Glendale, CA 91203, 818-240-6055

Po Folks, Inc.

Initial license fee: $20,000
Royalties: 2.5%
Advertising royalties: $100/store
Minimum cash required: $100,000
Capital required: $650,000 to $900,000
Financing: None
Length of contract: 20 years

In business since: 1975
Franchising since: 1975
Total number of units: 133
Number of company-operated units: 43

Total number of units planned, 1995: NA
Number of company-operated units planned, 1995: NA

While the name of this chain of table-service restaurants evokes a down-home, friendly atmosphere, it does not reflect the profitability of its franchises. Nor does the company treat its franchisees like poor folks. Po Folks is committed to the idea of franchising. Several years ago, Po Folks modified its franchise policy, and this might mean good news for you. The company, which had focused on the sale of whole territories to corporate franchisees, now stresses the individual owner-operator. Po Folks has upgraded its training and support programs in order to more effectively integrate single-unit operators into the growing company.

The decor of Po Folks units gives them a homey look. The menu adds to the country ambience both by the selection of dishes it offers and by its design and humorous text. Seafood dinners, for instance, come with "yore choice of two vegetables, hush puppies an' some good sauce." Greens and "po-taters" complement a variety of chicken and beef dishes. Customers can wash it all down with soft drinks ("belly washers") served in mason jars. If they don't want a whole dinner, they can always have a "samwich." The entire staff wear a uniform of blue jeans.

Po Folks seeks franchisees with some restaurant experience. If you fit the bill, the company will train you at its Nashville corporate offices or at a regional location. In either case, you will absorb the cost of your travel and lodging. Training covers employee management, food preparation and delivery, bookkeeping, public relations, advertising, restaurant maintenance, guest relations, ordering supplies, and sanitation.

Po Folks will help you find the right site for your restaurant and will give you plans for the building design and interior layout, but you must build it yourself. Before you open, a team of employees from the company will come to your restaurant to train your hourly staff in all facets of Po Folks operations. The Po Folks opening team will also remain for a few days after you open for business to make sure all the kinks get ironed out. The company offers ongoing motivational training for your employees and special instruction on new products through on-premises classes, slides, videotapes, and audiocassettes.

A typical Po Folks is a freestanding unit of about 5,500 square feet, which seats 180 to 200 patrons. It employs 100 to 120 hourly workers and four to six managers working two shifts. The company does not maintain a central distribution system for food supplies, so you will purchase your supplies from a list of company-approved sources.

Po Folks, which has previously concentrated its operations in the South, wants to expand to other parts of the country, including the entire states of Connecticut, Massachusetts, Minnesota, and New York.

For further information contact:
  Robert Fayard, Vice President, Franchising, Po Folks, Inc., 311 Plus Park Blvd., Suite 200, Nashville, TN 37217, 615-366-0900

Rax Restaurants, Inc.

Initial license fee: $30,000
Royalties: 4%
Advertising royalties: 4%
Minimum cash required: $125,000
Capital required: NA
Financing: None
Length of contract: 20 years

In business since: 1978
Franchising since: 1978
Total number of units: 363
Number of company-operated units: 105
Total number of units planned, 1995: 450
Number of company-operated units planned, 1995: 115

Rax began as a chain of roast beef restaurants called Jax. Since then, management has adapted its restaurant concept to changing tastes and demographics and developed a new menu and look that has made Rax popular with the "middle market" of the fast-food industry—customers in the 25- to 49-year-old age bracket. Rax customers also include many retired people. In 1991, a *Restaurants and Institutions* poll rated Rax the most popular fast-food sandwich restaurant in America.

The Rax menu features a variety of sandwiches, including roast beef, ham, chicken, and turkey. Customers may also order baked potatoes with a variety of toppings, as well as several kinds of soup. Rax's salad bar offers a large variety of fruits and vegetables, and the restaurants also serve a smaller version of Rax sandwiches for children. The company has added several items to its menu that fit in with the growing demand for foods low in fat and salt. In addition to a salad bar, Rax Restaurants feature low-fat roast beef and turkey and plain baked potatoes served with margarine, all of which meet standards for good nutrition set by the American Heart Association.

Buff-colored stucco on the side and rear walls, decorative tile, and awnings distinguish the exteriors of Rax's custom-built restaurants, while upholstered chairs and carpeted floors create attractive interiors.

The 118-seat, usually freestanding restaurants provide parking for 25 to 55 cars.

Rax seeks experienced food service people to buy its franchises. If you meet the company's requirements, it will assist you with site selection by looking at several of your choices in order to find one acceptable to both you and Rax. You can also consult the company on negotiating land costs or rental and lease terms. Rax requires you to equip your restaurant with items from approved dealers, and in some cases it will specify the machine models that you must purchase. Similarly, you will buy supplies only from company-approved vendors.

Rax will train your management-level employees in a five-week course, for which you will pay only travel-related expenses and employee salaries. The first two weeks of training take place at regional training centers in either Columbus, Ohio, or Pittsburgh, Pennsylvania. There, classroom work is done on supervisory skills, cost controls, quality assurance, sanitation, equipment maintenance, and other subjects. Trainees receive three weeks of on-the-job experience at a Rax unit near their new restaurant. Several days before your opening, the company's training instructors will come to your restaurant to train your other employees and will remain for your first two days of operations.

The Rax market manager will assist you with any problems that arise in your ongoing business and will offer you advice on subjects like marketing, cost control, and updating your business plan. Should you need it, your marketing manager can arrange for supplementary training at your premises. Rax will work with you to determine the level of service appropriate to your operation.

Rax promotes itself through regional television and radio advertising, local newspaper advertisements, and direct mail marketing.

For further information contact:
  Bill Burton, Vice President, Franchising, Rax Restaurants, Inc., 4150 Tuller Rd.,
  Dublin, OH 43017, 614-766-2500

Village Inn Restaurants

Initial license fee: $25,000
Royalties: 4%
Advertising royalties: 2%
Minimum cash required: $100,000
Capital required: $250,000
Financing: None
Length of contract: 15 years

In business since: 1958
Franchising since: 1961
Total number of units: 226
Number of company-operated units: 123
Total number of units planned, 1995: 275
Number of company-operated units planned, 1995: 236

Village Inn family restaurants aim to please with ambience and service as much as with moderate-priced food. Carpeted dining rooms, with their acoustical sound controls, allow for a relaxed dining experience not always possible in family restaurants. When customers order coffee, the waiter or waitress leaves a coffeepot on the table for refills. The menu, which includes all three meals, is so big it requires an index. Aside from pancakes cooked with batter made fresh each morning, the fare includes steak, omelettes, salads, soups, hamburgers, and desserts.

The company sells single-unit franchises for communities of 30,000 to 60,000. Larger populations require the purchase of an area franchise. For $3,000, Village Inn will help you select a location for your restaurant and will provide you with plans and specifications for your unit, which will seat at least 160 people. Should you wish the company to provide extensive architectural, engineering, and construction consulting services, it will do so for an additional fee. But even if you do not require such services, the company still inspects your building's progress and must give its final approval to all construction.

Your general manager and kitchen manager will receive their training at the company's headquarters in Denver, Colorado. The program lasts six to nine weeks and covers restaurant management, service, maintenance, accounting, and quality control. Village Inn's field staff will train your hourly employees a week before you open and will remain at your restaurant during your first week of business to make sure everything runs smoothly. Regional training meetings throughout the year update key employees on company products and techniques.

Vicorp, Village Inn's parent company, has an equipment division, but you do not have to purchase from it. Similarly, you do not have to buy food from any particular company, but what you do purchase must always meet company specifications.

The company has a marketing staff that will prepare advertising and promotional materials for you at your request. Any other marketing materials you use must first receive company approval.

For further information contact:
  Robert Kaltenbach, Vicorp Restaurants, Inc., 400 W. 48th Ave., Denver, CO 80216, 303-296-2121 ext. 230

Sandwiches

Arby's, Inc.

Initial license fee: $37,500 (first franchise); $25,000 (each additional franchise)
Royalties: 3.5% for 2 years; 4% for 18 years
Advertising royalties: 0.7%
Minimum cash required: $100,000
Capital required: $550,000 to $850,000
Financing: Company offers guidance in obtaining financing
Length of contract: 20 years

In business since: 1964
Franchising since: 1965
Total number of units: 2,400+
Number of company-operated units: 251
Total number of units planned, 1995: NA
Number of company-operated units planned, 1995: NA

Take some fresh lean roast beef, slice it thinly onto a toasted roll, maybe top it off with a tomato slice, some lettuce, and a little horseradish, and you've got the quintessential sandwich. Put some french fries and a Jamocha Shake on the side, and you've got Arby's. No other name in the fast-food business is as closely associated with roast beef as Arby's. Consistently ranked among the world's top 10 fast-food franchises, Arby's sells about one-third of all the roast beef sandwiches consumed in American restaurants. Its system-wide sales top $1 billion annually.

Arby's restaurants worldwide offer a variety of roast beef, chicken, and other sandwiches; home fried, curly fried, and french fried potatoes; a salad bar, soft drinks, and Arby's exclusive Jamocha Shake, a thick coffee-chocolate milkshake. The company's menu-development staff continues to develop additions to the menu in response to the dining public's changing tastes and in preparation for Arby's further expansion into new geographic regions.

Reflecting their satisfaction with the Arby's franchise system, a great number of the company's franchisees are multiunit owners. Arby's encourages multiunit ownership by offering second and subsequent restaurants at reduced license rates. You can still find openings in prime markets for multiunit as well as single-unit operations, and you can develop either freestanding, storefront, or mall locations. With the company's national advertising program behind you, developing one or more Arby's units will be a lot easier than trying to break into the roast beef sandwich industry as an independent.

Arby's reserves the right to approve your proposed site and provides counseling and written guidelines to make your search for the right location easier. All restaurants conform to the company's easily recognizable, energy-efficient building design. Following the company's specifications, you purchase equipment and supplies from approved sources: food service equipment, furniture, signs, employee uniforms, etc. You can purchase food and other supplies at significant savings through ARCOP, Inc., a nonprofit purchasing cooperative operated jointly by Arby's and its franchisees. ARCOP members pay a one-time initiation fee of $100 plus quarterly dues of $60 per licensed restaurant.

"We take pride in and emphasize the importance of Arby's training programs," states Jack Ofsharick of Arby's Training Department. "We have put together a group of management training programs that emphasize our commitment to quality products, quality service, and quality management." New licensee training takes place over four weeks at the company's Atlanta headquarters. Designed to develop your management, technical, and business skills to their fullest, the program covers everything from risk management to customer service, and from employee recruitment to equipment maintenance. After completing the classroom portion of your training, you will get hands-on experience at one of the company-operated stores. You and all of your management personnel must complete the training at least three weeks before your restaurant opens, when a field service representative steps in to provide full preopening and postopening assistance.

Each month at corporate headquarters and in major cities across the country, Arby's conducts training and development seminars for restaurant owners and their employees because, as Jack Ofsharick says, "just hiring good employees is not enough. We must help them grow and make them an integral part of the Arby system." You and any of your staff can participate in these seminars at no charge other than your out-of-pocket expenses for travel and lodging. The Specialized Operations Seminar covers the nuts and bolts of restaurant operation and serves as a good refresher for franchisees several years out of initial training. The Impact Supervision Skills course sharpens your supervisory and employee relations capability, while New-Age Thinking gives management personnel a better understanding of motivation, goal setting, and other human dynamics issues. Models for Management explores topics of managerial style and effectiveness. Offered monthly for two to four days, "these programs offer a unique opportunity to hone operational and personal skills that will benefit the individual and the Arby's system," notes Jack Ofsharick.

For further information contact:

James G. Smith or Larry Gustafson, Arby's, Inc., 6917 Collins Ave., P.O. Box
414177, Miami, FL 33141, 1-800-487-2729

Blimpie

Initial license fee: $18,000 for a single unit; area developer, 10 cents per person
   in MSA
Royalties: 6%
Advertising royalties: 3%
Minimum cash required: $40,000 to $70,000
Capital required: $80,000 to $100,000
Financing: Equipment financing available through third party
Length of contract: 20 years

In business since: 1964
Franchising since: 1977
Total number of units: 475
Number of company-operated units: None
Total number of units planned, 1995: 1,000+
Number of company-operated units planned, 1995: None

Looking for a growing franchise with a great product? The product may
turn out to be a sandwich. Whether you call an ample filling between
two pieces of Italian bread a submarine, sub, torpedo, hoagie, wedge,
grinder, poor boy, or hero, Blimpie specializes in it. The company calls
its version, which comes with lettuce, tomatoes, onions, and a special
sauce, "America's Best-Dressed Sandwich." An *Esquire* food writer once
called the company's "Blimpie Best"—a combination of ham, salami,
prosciuttini, cappicola, and cheese—the best fast food he had ever
eaten. He gave it his top rating: four crumpled paper napkins.

   The Blimpie menu, which has seen few changes since the first store
opened in Hoboken, New Jersey, features other cold sandwiches and a
few hot sandwiches. Store personnel use a slicer and a scale to ensure
that each sandwich contains a standard amount of food. The restaurants also serve soup, chili, salads, soft drinks, tea and coffee, and
breakfast. Desserts include cookies, cakes, and pastries.

   Blimpie is the largest franchised chain of sandwich shops in the
country. The food served in this franchise requires no cooking, only
some heating in the microwave for the hot sandwiches, chili, and
soup. This means low overhead and relative simplicity compared to
other food operations.

   Sandwich shops may be the smallest segment of the franchised fast-
food industry but they are growing faster than any other kind of fast-
food business. Their sales increased by over 200 percent in the 1980s.
Blimpie, formerly thought of as a New York operation, now has loca-

tions in many areas of the country, from Atlanta, Georgia, to Boise, Idaho. At the moment, its expansion plans center on New York, New Jersey, Connecticut, Georgia, Tennessee, and Florida.

The company prefers to sell its franchises to people who have already demonstrated managerial proficiency in other businesses or professions. It trains its franchisees at "Blimpie Business Schools" in New York or Atlanta, where they are taught advertising, marketing, and statistical controls. "The company insists you have at least two weeks of in-store training," notes a franchisor. But you may train for as long as you feel it is needed. You can receive advanced training from time to time at your request.

Constructing the freestanding or in-line (that is, in a strip mall or shopping center) building that usually houses a Blimpie, according to the company, is relatively simple. The company will negotiate the lease for your business—typically a store of about 1,200 square feet that seats 50—and then sublease the premises to you. The company will help you plan a successful grand opening, and it will provide you with a list of approved vendors of supplies and equipment. It will also give you a set of business forms that will help you maintain control over cash flow. A Blimpie representative will visit your store periodically to give you advanced management training.

The Blimpie formula is "No Cooking + Limited Menu = Success."

For further information contact:
Dennis Fuller, Director of Franchise Development, 1775 The Exchange, Suite 215, Atlanta, GA 30339, 1-800-447-6256

Gyro Wrap, Inc.

Initial license fee: $25,000
Royalties: 5% (4% first year)
Advertising royalties: 2%
Minimum cash required: $75,000
Capital required: $170,000
Financing: Assistance in obtaining
Length of contract: 15 years

In business since: 1975
Franchising since: 1981
Total number of units: 39
Number of company-operated units: 2
Total number of units planned, 1995: 79
Number of company-operated units planned, 1995: 6

Finding a new food category, as industry analysts will tell you, is a difficult task indeed. Of course, Greek food has been around since before the days of Homer, but as quick-service mall fare, it's still a pretty fresh concept. The image that the cuisine continues to conjure up in the minds of many Americans is of a mom-and-pop establishment.

Gyro Wrap is different. You'll offer a distinctive menu of Greek-inspired hot food, highlighted by the gyro itself, a spiced blend of beef and lamb carved from an upright rotisserie and wrapped in pita bread along with fresh vegetables and yogurt sauce. Variations using strip steak, marinated chicken, and ham and cheese are also available, as are Greek and Mediterranean salads, side dishes like the company's trademark "Kurly-Q fries," with baklava, a sweet honey-and-nut pastry, for dessert.

Since 1989, Gyro Wrap's new management team, chairman Mark Kaplan and president Bob Solomon, have been using their soft-drink marketing and restaurant franchise experience to take the Atlanta-based operation nationwide. Gyro Wrap stores are now located throughout the Southeast, and Kaplan and Solomon are in the process of expanding to other regions of the country, targeting the Mid-Atlantic area in particular. Although it is still a small network, especially by Golden Arches standards, Gyro Wrap already happens to be the nation's largest Greek food chain. That there are no competing enterprises with a national presence is one of the more attractive features of the Gyro Wrap opportunity, in the eyes of its franchisees.

One of the first things Kaplan and Solomon did when they took over the company was to redesign the Gyro Wrap stores, bringing a consistent physical look to the chain and creating a bit of Mediterranean atmosphere through brown and terra-cotta colors and bright tile, with a neon sign thrown in for a contemporary touch. Decor is crucial, the executives believe. "You only have a split second to capture a customer," says Solomon, recognizing the stiff competition at a mall food court. "Once we get them we're confident the quality of the food will bring them back."

Another thing in your favor will be the sheer novelty of your menu. It has certainly intrigued shopping center developers, at least. A restaurant trade journal reported that at a recent industry convention, there was interest in Gyro Wrap from "an unprecedented number of malls," eager to offer their shoppers an alternative to the typical burger/chicken/pizza fare. While the company plans to keep focusing on mall locations, there are a couple of freestanding Gyro Wrap cafes (featuring a broader menu that includes wine and beer) that have been among the network's most successful stores.

Gyro Wrap will either find an appropriate location for you or assess a site that you have in mind, and will pay the legal fees for negotiating the lease. Through national manufacturers and vendors, the company has negotiated contract prices for the food products, equipment, uniforms, and other supplies that you'll require. Although it wants the menu to remain streamlined, Gyro Wrap does selectively experiment with new eating selections, conducting in-store surveys and taste tests at company-run facilities to hone the recipes and measure their popularity before the items are introduced to the franchise.

You'll learn the business, administrative, and marketing systems for running a Gyro Wrap store, as well as food preparation techniques, during a four-week training course that requires no previous experience. After your facility has opened, company managers will pay regular visits, informing you about new programs and helping you smooth out any difficulties in your operation. To provide further guidance for its franchisee, Gyro Wrap has also hired an independent management consulting team, which has advised such national chains as Burger King and Domino's Pizza. The home office does its part, too, sending along a steady stream of advertising materials and furnishing ideas for promotional campaigns.

For further information contact:
  Marvin Young, Franchise Development, Gyro Wrap, Inc., 158 Oak St.,
  Avondale Estates, GA 30002, 404-299-5081, fax 404-292-0081

Schlotzsky's, Inc.

Initial license fee: $15,000
Royalties: 4%
Advertising royalties: 1%
Minimum cash required: $60,000
Capital required: $150,000
Financing: None
Length of contract: 30 years

In business since: 1971
Franchising since: 1977
Total number of units: 235
Number of company-operated units: 21
Total number of units planned, 1995: 420
Number of company-operated units planned, 1995: 55

Hoagies, subs, grinders—they're all essentially the same sandwich; only the name differs depending on the part of the country in which you're eating it. In one American city, however, a sandwich is made that's truly distinctive. The question was: can cheesesteaks sell outside Philadelphia?

Schlotzsky's thought so, and the sandwich store franchise put that theory to the test the hard way by taking cheesesteaks far, far away from the City of Brotherly Love—all the way to the Lone Star State, to be exact, where Schlotzsky's had been a Texas institution for a decade. However, a slight variation to accommodate southwestern tastes seemed appropriate, so the Schlotzsky "Philly" (beef strips, melted mozzarella and cheddar, peppers, onions, and mushrooms) combination is served in the company's signature round sourdough bun, baked fresh daily on the premises.

They may look a little odd to those accustomed to long, skinny sandwich buns, but Schlotzsky's circular sandwiches had been a Texas favorite for years. And once the "Philly" was added to the menu of hot and cold roast beef, turkey, and ham and cheese sandwiches, the Schlotzsky's network expanded well beyond the southwest, accompanied by a new aggressive marketing campaign and store redesign. Now, Schlotzsky's restaurants are located in 26 states, from Virginia to Nevada, and, ironically, customers in many parts of the country can't imagine a cheesesteak without the sharp, zesty taste of sourdough.

The Schlotzsky's menu is a specialized one—no fried foods, for example, saving you labor and equipment costs, and no breakfast items, allowing you to limit your operating hours typically to a reasonable 11 A.M. to 8 P.M. schedule. Along with the sandwiches, though (which come in 4-, 6-, and 8-inch sizes), you'll offer soups, salads, and soda to round out your customers' meals, with self-service counters displaying chips and pretzels, too. And for dessert, they'll be tempted by your fresh-baked chocolate chip cookies, as the sweet smell floats through the restaurant.

A convection oven and double-chain drive broiler for melting cheese and heating sandwiches make up your essential appliances, with the entire food-preparation process taking place in full view of the customers. Ensuring a unified image, all Schlotzsky stores are similarly designed, featuring a contemporary, high-tech look of black and white checkered floors, open kiosks in bright colors, and a lot of neon signs. The company will provide you with the floor plans and layouts and, using its established contacts with developers and real estate brokers across the country, assist in site selection. A strip center or mall food court make suitable locations, or you may want to choose a freestanding building across the street from a high school or college campus.

In a three-week franchisee training program, Schlotzsky officials will guide you through new store development, daily operations, inventory control, baking and sandwich preparation, and employee hiring. And a team of food professionals will be with you at your store during that critical first week in business. After your operation is established, members of the company's franchise service staff will conduct ongoing evaluations and reviews of your store, while the field marketing department will continue developing local strategies for you, including advertising, community-oriented promotions, and sales-building campaigns.

To furnish its franchisees with food products and paper goods, Schlotzsky's has developed contractual relationships with such companies as Pillsbury, Swift, Pepsi-Cola, and Georgia-Pacific Paper. These national accounts will give you the opportunity to purchase supplies at discount rates, so you can keep your prices low. And, of course, customers with an insatiable craving for cheesesteak get to avoid the cost of a plane ticket to Philadelphia, too.

For further information contact:
  Kelly R. Arnold, National Sales Manager, Schlotzsky's, Inc., 200 W. Fourth St., Austin, TX 78701, 512-480-9871 or 1-800-950-8419, fax 512-477-2897

Subway Sandwiches and Salads

Initial license fee: $10,000
Royalties: 8%
Advertising royalties: 2.5%
Minimum cash required: $22,200
Capital required: $44,400 to $72,400
Financing: Equipment leasing program available
Length of contract: 20 years

In business since: 1965
Franchising since: 1975
Total number of units: 6,500
Number of company-operated units: 2
Total number of units planned, 1995: 8,000
Number of company-operated units planned, 1995: None

"I love the business and the people," says Cathy Bauer, who owns a Subway shop in West Lafayette, Indiana. "After 10 years of teaching school and four years of laboratory research, I have finally found a field that gives me satisfaction and enjoyment that more than offsets all the hours of hard work."

Subway has nothing to do with underground transportation, except that one of its founders comes from Brooklyn. And Doctor's Associates, Subway's parent company, has nothing to do with medicine. A 17-year-old premed student and a nuclear physicist started the company in Connecticut with one store. When that store did not do well, they took the least obvious course of action: They opened a second store, and then business began to take off.

All of this may sound like an improbable start for the second-fastest-growing fast-food company in America. But through trial and error, the student, Fred DeLuca, and his partner, Peter Buck, developed a simple operation that has brought satisfaction and enjoyment to many of the company's franchisees. In fact, current franchisees continue to purchase about half of all new Subway franchises sold. New Subway shops open at the rate of about three per day.

A Subway sandwich shop, depending on its sales volume, may require as few as two employees to run it. The menu is simple and requires no cooking. Stores sell 10 varieties of sandwiches and several salads, which use the same ingredients as the sandwiches. The company also encourages franchisees to experiment with sandwiches that have local appeal. For the past two years, many franchisees have baked their own Italian bread on the premises with an easy-to-use oven obtained through the franchisor.

Subway Sandwiches and Salads will advise you on lease negotiations for your store. Although some franchisees locate in freestanding stores, most open in storefronts or strip shopping centers. The stores occupy 300 to 800 square feet and seat as many as 25 people. A distinctive mural featuring photographs of the store's overstuffed sandwiches and scenes from the history of New York City's subway system highlight each unit's decor.

You don't need previous food service experience to own one of these shops. About 80 percent of current franchisees had never worked in the industry before opening their Subway. The company will train you for two weeks in all aspects of its operation at its headquarters in Milford, Connecticut. Classroom study accounts for half of the instruction; hands-on experience in a Subway Sandwiches and Salads shop makes up the other half. You pay for all training-related expenses except for tuition. A field representative will then spend a week with you while you open your business and will be on call whenever you need assistance in your ongoing operation. You can always reach the company via a toll-free number.

The company points out that because of its national contracts, it can save you considerable sums of money if you purchase equipment through Subway. You can, however, buy from any vendor acceptable to Subway. You will purchase your supplies locally, through a distributor approved by the company.

Subway Sandwiches and Salads franchisees control the spending of their advertising funds through an elected council. The company does not place national advertising.

For further information contact:
   Donald Fertman, Director of Franchise Sales, Subway Sandwiches and Salads, 325 Bic Dr., Milford, CT 06460-3059, 1-800-888-4848

Specialty Foods

Frontier Fruit & Nut Company

Initial license fee: $15,000
Royalties: 6%
Advertising royalties: None
Minimum cash required: $23,000
Capital required: $35,000 to $120,000
Financing: None
Length of contract: Coincides with length of lease

In business since: 1977
Franchising since: 1978
Total number of units: 157
Number of company-operated units: 75
Total number of units planned, 1995: NA
Number of company-operated units planned, 1995: NA

Picture your kiosk or fruit and nut store in a regional shopping mall. The decor of your 144- to 200-square-foot establishment relies heavily on wood paneling. Bins of colorful dried fruits, nuts, combination mixtures, candies, and cookies fill its glass cases. Small open wooden barrels, leaning out at an angle from countertops, temptingly display fruits and nuts for maximum customer appeal. Seasonal containers and interesting, everyday glassware and tins are filled with a tempting array of dried fruits, nuts, and candies that are suitable for gift giving in any season.

Frontier stores try to project an image of old-fashioned natural goodness. While the company does not insist that you buy your stock—about $10,000 worth of inventory at any given time—from its supply subsidiary, it will closely examine products from any other vendor you might choose to patronize.

When you buy a franchise, Frontier will do a site survey at its expense to make sure you have the right mall location for your store, given the demographics of the area. It will negotiate the lease for you, and in some locations it will lease the space itself and sublease it to you on terms similar to those in the original lease. If you must build, the company will give you design and construction plans for the store, charging a small fee for the drawings. It will also help you plan your initial inventory.

Frontier trains its franchisees at company headquarters in Norton, Ohio. Your licensing fee covers your tuition, but you will have to pay for transportation, food, and lodging. Your training will consist of three days of classroom work on all aspects of Frontier operations—including merchandising, sales, accounting, and promotion—and a day and a half of hands-on experience at a working store.

Frontier will help you set up your bookkeeping system, with which you must generate periodic updates, including a weekly sales report, for the franchisor. A company representative will attend your grand opening, and Frontier will advise you on dealing with any specific problems that might come up after you begin operations.

For further information contact:
  Raymond J. Karee, Frontier Fruit & Nut Company, 3823 Wadsworth Rd., Norton, OH 44203, 216-825-7835

Gloria Jean's Coffee Beans

Initial license fee: $19,500
Royalties: 6%
Advertising royalties: 1%
Minimum cash required: $155,000 to $215,000
Capital required: $155,000 to $215,000
Financing: Assistance in obtaining
Length of contract: 10 years

In business since: 1979
Franchising since: 1986
Total number of units: 140
Number of company-operated units: 4
Total number of units planned, 1995: 250 to 350
Number of company-operated units planned, 1995: 6

The United States is the largest coffee-consuming country in the world. And American coffee drinkers have shown that they're willing to pay a premium for a better cup. Not that the price is that extreme, when you sit down and figure it out—at least not at Gloria Jean's Coffee Beans. At little more than $7 a pound for many selections, the cost comes out to be less than 12 cents a cup, "the world's most affordable luxury," in the company's opinion.

Gloria Jean's sells only Arabica beans, hand-picked and cultivated in higher altitudes over a longer growing season than those used by most commercial coffee companies, making coffee that has greater body, texture, flavor, and aroma. "There is no comparison between gourmet coffee and regular canned coffee," says Gloria Jean Kvetko, who, with her husband, Ed, founded the company. "It's like trying to compare a fast-food meal with a feast."

With its oak storefront and green and gold interior, your Gloria Jean shop conveys that gourmet image. The focal point is the bean counter, displaying your beans in containers that ensure freshness but still allow their scent to permeate the room. And mingling in will be the smell of the fresh-brewed coffee that you'll offer your customers, allowing them to sample some of your featured flavors.

Gloria Jean's supplies its franchisees with over 150 coffee varieties from around the world, with most shops carrying 64 selections, regular and decaf, medium and dark roast alike. Your customers can special-order a favorite bean that you don't stock, and you'll also prepare custom blends of their choice. In addition, your shop will feature a wide assortment of imported and domestic teas, along with such merchandise as coffee and espresso machines, grinders, mugs and china products, and other coffee and tea accessories, plus gift packages, too.

The company will help you determine your inventory and the right mix of merchandise for your shop. The only item that you're required to buy from them is "Gloria Jean's Special Blend," which every store in the franchise carries; you can get the rest of your beans and supplies through either the company warehouse or approved independent vendors.

You'll also receive guidance in selecting the site for your shop (in some areas, Gloria Jean's has already pinpointed the location). Malls are the most common choices, but other spots may be considered, based on such criteria as vehicular and pedestrian traffic, population density and income, lease costs, and proximity to major residential estate and retail business districts. Leasing the property itself, the company will then sublease it to you, assisting you with store design and construction and helping you select and obtain the fixtures and equipment.

While the setup proceeds, you'll attend Gloria Jean's Coffee 101 class, a 10-day course held at a specially outfitted, fully functional training store in the company's corporate offices that covers topics like purchasing, merchandising, and product knowledge. You'll spend time as well behind the bean counter at a company store to become familiar with the daily operation of a Gloria Jean's shop.

Back at your own store during the first nine days of business, you'll receive close supervision by company personnel, who'll also use the opportunity to train your employees. Thereafter, Gloria Jean's field consultants will visit regularly to introduce new products and sales techniques and help you refine your operation, conducting a performance evaluation and computer analysis to let you know how your shop is doing in relation to other Gloria Jean facilities. The home office staff remains available, too, by phone and fax, and stays in touch with regular newsletters and updates.

They'll also be supervising the company's national advertising campaign and furnishing you with marketing support, which includes brochures and point-of-purchase displays, press releases, ad layouts, and demographic studies to aid you in targeting customers. In addition, they'll show you how to generate publicity for your shop and run promotional programs like Gloria Jean's "frequent sippers" club (drink 25 cups—not all at once—get a free quarter-pound).

Gloria Jean's Coffee Beans are currently operating in 26 states. Coming from many backgrounds, franchisees initially share only an appreciation of fine coffee—but they come to share operation and business tips and ideas for new blends and services. The company considers the character and motivation of potential franchisees to be more important than prior business and retail experience. "Coffee achievers," in other words.

For further information contact:
   James Ludwig, Vice President, Franchise Development, Gloria Jean's Coffee
   Beans Franchising Corp., 1001 Asbury Dr., Buffalo Grove, IL 60089,
   708-808-0580

Heavenly Ham

Initial license fee: $25,000
Royalties: 5%
Advertising royalties: 2%
Minimum cash required: $84,000
Capital required: $136,000
Financing: None
Length of contract: 10 years

In business since: 1984
Franchising since: 1984
Total number of units: 50
Number of company-operated units: None
Total number of units planned, 1995: 150
Number of company-operated units planned, 1995: 1

If there *are* pigs in heaven, a lot of them got there thanks to Heavenly Ham. The company's annual grosses now hover near $9 million, with stores in 20 states.

Hickory-smoked ham will be your specialty, spiral-sliced and glazed with honey and spices, with a selection of mustards, sauces, and seasonings to go with it. In addition, you'll feature meats like smoked turkey and bacon, as well as ham and turkey sandwiches, made with French bread and croissants prepared on the premises. Many franchises have also added items such as ribs, soup, salad, and even freshly baked pies to their menus, and offer cold-cut or sandwich party trays, too.

Heavenly Ham is about as healthy as ham can be, with 2 percent sodium and no added water. Actually, "pork gets a pretty bad rap," maintains Hutch Hodgson, president of Paradise Foods, the company that runs the Heavenly Ham franchise. Hodgson points to industry research that has shown that pork products are, on average, 50 percent leaner than they were 20 years ago. Health food or not, ham remains a popular dish, especially for holidays and parties, and is a popular gift as well, which will keep customers coming to your store. Sandwiches aside, Heavenly Ham doesn't exactly make an impulse snack— not with a typical purchase weighing in at around six to ten pounds. Nevertheless, it's convenience food, too, sold ready to eat, and customers who don't have much time to shop and cook will stop in to pick up half a ham—or try some of your other selections—for a last-minute family dinner.

Once you sign the franchise agreement, your Heavenly Ham store should be ready for business within six to fifteen weeks, with prime grand opening months from January to March, in advance of Easter season, or May through September, to take advantage of the Thanksgiving and Christmas rush. Paradise Foods extends start-up assistance thorough enough even to have impressed the store landlords. "The hands-on approach that you and your staff have taken in the site selection, the negotiation and development of the lease, and the development of a floor plan is quite unusual, in my experience," a New Jersey developer wrote Hutch Hodgson, guidance that he found "to be quite outstanding." Strip centers, Paradise Foods believes, make the best locations—malls are avoided entirely—because of their convenient parking, heavy foot traffic, and competitive rents. A 2,000-square-foot unit should suffice; while you will prepare some of the food selections yourself, the hams and turkeys will arrive at your store fully cooked and presliced, reducing your equipment and space needs.

All orders for hams and other meats will be placed through Paradise Foods, which supervises production and shipping schedules with its suppliers. The company will also inform you about the other products you'll require, providing you with an approved list of vendors from whom you may obtain them.

A three-day training program conducted at Paradise Foods' Atlanta headquarters for franchisees and their operating managers includes a complete course in ham lore, along with instruction on pricing strategies, accounting, inventory control, and customer service. Working with you at your store prior to your launch and through your first days in business, a field service manager will continue to make periodic visits thereafter, monitoring your progress, answering questions, and helping out with marketing. The monthly newsletters and operations manual updates you'll receive will furnish further daily operations advice and information.

To accompany the Heavenly Ham national advertising program, you will be expected to spend aggressively—a minimum of 4 percent of your gross—on local efforts, using the print, radio, television, and direct mail materials the company supplies. Paradise Foods will also show you how to implement effective holiday promotional campaigns and to appeal to the lucrative corporate gift market.

In addition, you'll hear about ideas developed by other franchisees, like Larry and Randee Saffer of Dade County, Florida, who pass out free Heavenly Ham samples to office buildings and churches and at community events. A single visit usually does it. "Once they try the ham," Randee Saffer explains, "they come to us."

For further information contact:
R. H. Hodgson, President, Paradise Foods, Inc., 8800 Roswell Rd., Suite 135, Atlanta, GA 30350, 404-993-2232 or 1-800-899-2228, fax 404-587-3529

Steakhouses

Ponderosa Steakhouses

Initial license fee: $25,000
Royalties: 4%
Advertising royalties: 4%
Minimum cash required: $125,000
Capital required: $1,175,000
Financing: Assistance in finding sources
Length of contract: 20 years

In business since: 1965
Franchising since: 1966
Total number of units: 773
Number of company-operated units: 401
Total number of units planned, 1995: NA
Number of company-operated units planned, 1995: NA

From one steakhouse in Kokomo, Indiana, Ponderosa has grown into an international chain, with units in 33 states and 7 other countries. Most of the company's units are located in the Northeast and Midwest, and in Puerto Rico, Canada, the Virgin Islands, Malaysia,

Singapore, and Taiwan. In 1990, Ponderosa served over 140 million meals. Its menu features broiled steaks, seafood, chicken, sandwiches, and its hearty Grand Buffet. The "No Stopping the Topping Sundae Bar," which allows customers to make their own soft-serve sundaes with several toppings, continues to be popular with customers and profitable for the steakhouses. Some Ponderosa steakhouses offer morning patrons a breakfast buffet that includes eggs, breakfast meats, fruits, and toppings.

Customers order their food in a modified self-service style by helping themselves to the Grand Buffet salad bar, before their main entrées are brought to them by a waiter or waitress. The carpeted restaurants seat over 200, and outdoor parking is available for 80 to 90 cars.

The Ponderosa franchising idea is based upon a strong personal identification between the owners and managers. Ponderosa's experience suggests that the chance that a restaurant will succeed is significantly greater if management and ownership work closely together. Because of this, some equity involvement is encouraged for each steakhouse manager.

Once Ponderosa accepts your application for a franchise, it will give you guidelines, including standard building plans, for choosing a site and erecting a building. Ponderosa's unit development staff will consult with you and your general contractor before construction begins. Equipment may be purchased through any one of a half-dozen approved suppliers. Ponderosa's food purchasing department will help you find a master distributor to provide your steakhouse with food products, dry groceries, dairy products, paper goods, and chemicals. Over 75 percent of the products used in the company's restaurants are purchased on a contract basis, taking advantage of the buying power of a 773-unit chain.

To assure proper operation of your restaurant, you and your management team must complete the company's extensive management training program. Actual in-store training is combined with concentrated coursework to thoroughly familiarize you and your team with all aspects of operating and managing of your restaurant. The initial training is continually reinforced through ongoing training seminars and education programs.

Before you open your steakhouse, a franchising field consultant and a new unit operating team will be on hand to train your staff. The field consultant and marketing manager will establish a marketing strategy for the grand opening. After your restaurant opens, the field consultant will continue to be your liaison with the company by keeping you abreast of the latest developments in steakhouse operations. He or she will also provide ongoing counseling on operation and management. The marketing manager will continue to assist you with marketing your restaurant.

For further information contact:
   Ed Day, Director, Franchise Sales, Division of Metromedia Steakhouses, Inc., P.O. Box 578, Dayton, OH 45401, 1-800-543-9670 (in Ohio, 513-454-2543)

The Ground Round, Inc.

Initial license fee: $30,000
Royalties: 3%
Advertising royalties: 2%
Minimum cash required: $100,000
Capital required: $400,000
Financing: None
Length of contract: 20 years

In business since: 1969
Franchising since: 1970
Total number of units: 200
Number of company-operated units: 155
Total number of units planned, 1995: 250
Number of company-operated units planned, 1995: NA

Do you have your heart set on opening a restaurant in the Northeast or Midwest that will cater to shoppers and businesspeople having lunch—in a shopping center or similar high-traffic area? How about a nice family dinner place that also attracts senior citizens? Or would you rather run a livelier establishment targeted at the late-evening young adult trade? According to Ground Round, if you open one of its establishments, you'll get all three under the same roof for the same price.

Ground Round's management feels it runs the all-purpose restaurant for the densely populated—a market of at least 50,000—average-income area. On the one hand, Ground Rounds give out free popcorn, stage weekly visits from personalities like Bingo the Clown, and cater children's birthday parties. On the other hand, franchisees must get an all-alcohol license. The Ground Round strategy is to keep the food flowing to the table even during hours when many restaurants concentrate on serving drinks.

The menu at Ground Round features charbroiling, steak, hamburger, chicken, and seafood entrées, like shrimp and swordfish with Cajun sauce, at reasonable prices. Mexican and Italian dishes, sandwiches, and salads fill out the menu. All-you-can-eat family days may feature selections like buffalo wings or a fish fry. For those who prefer beverages without alcohol, there are nonalcoholic drinks such as the

"Sourpuss" and the "Unbloody Mary." Ground Round offers distinctive desserts that include New York–style cheesecake (topped with hot fudge, if you wish) and Mexican Apple Delight: "Some apple crisp wrapped in a flour tortilla, deep fried, and topped with powdered sugar and whipped cream."

These 215-seat restaurants are intended to be attractively designed. Ground Round's design and construction department will give you guidelines so that you may achieve the effect that the company has found most appealing. Track lighting, hanging plants, prints, and ceiling canopies all play a part in creating the right atmosphere. While Ground Round will give you a certain amount of leeway to put your imprint on the restaurant's look, the company must approve your decorating plans.

You or your manager will undergo 120 hours of training in all aspects of the business at one of Ground Round's 15 regional training centers. An eight-member team from corporate headquarters will train your staff at your restaurant for two or three weeks. You pay for the lodging and food for these corporate trainers. Once in business, you may want to take advantage of Ground Round's advanced training. Currently, the company offers 20 one- to three-day seminars.

You purchase your food from approved local vendors or from the same source that stocks the company's own restaurants. Some of the products that you sell are preprepared by the company.

Ground Round promotes the company image through national advertising. It also provides you with ideas and material for local campaigns and point-of-sale promotions. You may draw on the company's library of TV, radio, and newspaper ads to supplement your own marketing efforts. And the company has time-tested employee incentive programs.

Robert Bonin, a Ground Round franchisee in Shrewsbury, Massachusetts, enjoys being part of the company. He gives Ground Round high grades, declaring, "The company has given me strong support. Excellent communications and the availability of the franchising department have been particularly helpful."

For further information contact:
Ed Daly, Director of Franchise Development, The Ground Round, Inc., P.O. Box 9078, 35 Braintree Hill Office Park, Braintree, MA 02184-9078, 617-380-3116

Western Steer Family Steakhouse

Initial license fee: $25,000
Royalties: 3%
Advertising royalties: 2%
Minimum cash required: $250,000
Capital required: $250,000 to $350,000
Financing: None
Length of contract: 20 years

In business since: 1975
Franchising since: 1975
Total number of units: 158
Number of company-operated units: 37
Total number of units planned, 1995: NA
Number of company-operated units planned, 1995: NA

These freestanding budget restaurants, concentrated in the South, feature a limited menu but a salad bar that includes hot dishes. Main dishes include steak in a variety of cuts, chicken, and shrimp. Franchisees may also offer their customers two of nine company-approved regional dishes.

Western Steer favors urban locations, preferably near shopping centers and malls, with a substantial representation of people in the middle to upper income brackets. Your lot should be at least 52,500 square feet. The company will help you evaluate possible sites for your restaurant and will provide building plans, specifications, and equipment layout. Company representatives will inspect your unit as you build it.

Western Steer will train your key personnel at one of its own restaurants in Hickory, North Carolina, and at its headquarters in Claremont, North Carolina. Your manager (of whom Western Steer must approve) and assistant manager will each receive 36 days of classroom and hands-on training, and your meat cutter will train for 10 days. You will pay their salaries and cover their living and travel expenses during that time.

Several days before you open for business, a grand opening team will come to your restaurant to train your other employees. The operations supervisor, who heads the training crew, will stay an additional week to help you get your enterprise off to a good start. Thereafter, if conditions warrant, the company will send a representative to help you deal with specific problems. In addition, a Western Steer quality-assurance representative will visit your restaurant every six weeks to make sure that it operates the way it should.

You may purchase the furniture and equipment for your restaurant from the vendor of your choice, although Western Steer has two affiliates, Denver Equipment Company and Howard Furniture Company, that sell these items. The company has an agreement with Institutional Food House, which supplies company-owned restaurants and many franchisees, although the only products you must buy from them are Western Steer proprietary items.

Although your franchise contract calls for an advertising royalty of 2 percent, the company currently collects 0.75 percent and the remaining 1.25 percent is spent locally.

Western Steer continues to focus on multiunit franchises. If your interests lie elsewhere, you should ask about the availability of individual franchises.

For further information contact:
  Western Steer — Mom 'n' Pop's, Inc., P.O. Box 399 WSMP Drive, Claremont, NC 28610, 704-459-7626

Tacos and Mexican Fast Food

Taco John's International, Inc.

Initial license fee: $19,500
Royalties: 4%
Advertising royalties: 2%
Minimum cash required: $21,000
Capital required: $70,000 to $500,000
Financing: None
Length of contract: 20 years

In business since: 1969
Franchising since: 1969
Total number of units: 444
Number of company-operated units: 12
Total number of units planned, 1995: 500
Number of company-operated units planned, 1995: None

John Turner opened the prototype of this chain of Mexican fast-food restaurants in Cheyenne, Wyoming, and called it the Taco House. Jim Woodson and Harold Holmes, the current president and secretary/treasurer of the company, later bought the franchising rights and gave the chain its present name. The first Taco John's restaurants, which consisted of walk-up plywood stands measuring 12 by 30 feet, have given way to 1,400- to 1,600-square-foot units with drive-through service and seating for 30 to 50 customers.

The menu—mandatory in all its restaurants—features standard Mexican food: several varieties of tacos and burritos, tostadas, enchiladas, nachos, and chili. Customers can also order taco burgers. Taco John's does business in 32 states and Canada. The company continues to target the Southeast and the Pacific Northwest for expansion.

The site you choose for your Taco John's, and your building or remodeling plans, must receive company approval. Taco John's International, Inc., will advise you at all stages of this process, and for a fee the company will also do some of the actual work involved in preparing your building for business. You and your manager will take a 15-day training course at "Taco Tech," the company's training facility in Cheyenne. You pay for all travel, lodging, and meals. The training, both classroom and hands-on, covers everything involved in running your business, from taco production to cost control. Managers and other employees who join your business after you open can attend the company's periodic regional seminars.

About five days before your restaurant opens, the company will send a representative to train your crew and to help with last-minute tasks. Ongoing support comes from your franchise services representative, who works with 30 to 40 restaurants. The representative will advise you in various areas of your business, including inventory, cash control, food and labor costs, marketing, and customer service, and will help make sure that you run your restaurant according to company guidelines. You can get in touch with your representative at any time through the company's WATS line.

Taco John's International, Inc., will give you a list of approved equipment suppliers and independent food distributors. These distributors carry the company's proprietary items, and they will call to take your order once a week.

Each year the company will send you eight packages of material, such as banners and posters, for in-store promotions. Your advertising fund money pays for cooperative advertisements with other franchisees in your region, as well as for national advertising. Gary L. Anderson, who owns several Taco John's in South Dakota, feels that the image built by the company over the years has been vital to his success. He says "the public has a very good perceived value" when they think of Taco John's.

For further information contact:
   Taco John's International, Inc., P.O. Box 1589, 808 W. 20th St., Cheyenne, WY 82001, 307-635-0101, fax 307-638-0603

Taco Time International, Inc.

Initial license fee: $18,000
Royalties: 5%
Advertising royalties: 0.5%
Minimum cash required: $110,000
Capital required: $129,000 to $203,000 (exclusive of leasehold improvements
   and land and building costs)
Financing: Some packaging assistance and resource referrals available
Length of contract: 15 years

In business since: 1959
Franchising since: 1961
Total number of units: 289
Number of company-operated units: 18
Total number of units planned, 1995: NA
Number of company-operated units planned, 1995: NA

Taco Time serves Mexican fast food: several varieties of tacos and burritos as well as nachos, enchiladas, tostadas, refritos, and guacamole.
Desserts include cherry and berry empanadas. The company thinks it
features some of the most attractive Mexican fast-food restaurants in
the business. The interior decor of these establishments includes
arched windows, tile, Spanish stucco, and wall hangings. Franchisees
building new units have their choice of including a solarium or a
wood beam trellis atrium. The freestanding restaurants, which occupy
either 1,500 or 1,950 square feet, are designed to encourage high volume sales and a low break-even point. If you choose a shopping mall
location, you will build one of the smaller units.

The company helps you select the site for your restaurant and advises you during the lease negotiation. It will also work with you to
design an attractive and profitable unit. The several restaurant plans
and interior decor packages available will allow you to build a restaurant that reflects your personal taste within the confines of the company's standard "look."

At the company's headquarters in Eugene, Oregon, you will receive
training in how to run your Taco Time restaurant. In the five-week
classroom and hands-on program, you will first learn coworker skills
and then hone your management and administrative abilities. A grand
opening team will assist you with the last-minute preparations at your
restaurant, and the company will offer ongoing supervision and field
support in operations and marketing.

Taco Time will also help you find local suppliers of equipment and
fixtures and will permit you to buy from anyone if they approve the
items first. You may buy your food supplies either from local food dis-

tributors suggested by the company or from company-approved vendors you have located yourself.

The advertising fee may rise to as much as 4 percent. The Taco Time Marketing Council, controlled by franchisee representatives, allocates advertising funds.

For further information contact:
  Jim Thomas, Senior Vice President, Franchise Development, Taco Time International, Inc., P.O. Box 2056, Eugene, OR 97402, 503-687-8222 or 1-800-547-8907

12. The Health and Beauty Industry

Contents

Fitness and Weight Control

Formu-3 International

Initial license fee: $4,900 to $9,800
Royalties: 5%
Advertising royalties: 1%
Minimum cash required: $5,000 to $20,000
Capital required: $25,000 to $40,000
Financing: Available
Length of contract: 10 years

In business since: 1982
Franchising since: 1984
Total number of units: 268
Number of company-operated units: 26
Total number of units planned, 1995: 700
Number of company-operated units planned, 1995: 150

Formu-3's outlook, industry analysts quip, is "weighty." Opportunities in the weight-loss market in general are strong; what seemed to be a fad business in the seventies now is a firmly entrenched service and just keeps on expanding as American waistlines do, with diet programs alone expected to account for $16 billion in annual revenues by 1995. "It's the hottest thing I've seen in 13 years of watching the franchise industry," declares Jerry Wilkerson, president of an executive search firm specializing in the franchise sector.

One of the fastest growing weight-loss programs, building at a pace that rivals (and probably benefits from) McDonald's growth in the 1960s, Formu-3 enjoys system-wide sales approaching $100 million and was recently named *Inc.* magazine's number-14 ranked franchise in any category. Founder and CEO Jeffrey Stone suggests one reason for his company's success: "Sixty percent of all Americans are overweight, but many can't afford to pay the high prices associated with typical weight-loss programs. We've managed to keep our prices low by helping our franchise owners hold the line on overhead and marketing costs."

How low? The company claims its prices are up to 60 percent lower than other nationally advertised programs, making Formu-3 affordable, it says, to 80 percent of the weight-loss market. Actually, the main reason for the modest cost is that there are almost no supplementary expenses. Unlike many rival systems, which require customers to use expensive prepackaged or freeze-dried foods, the Formu-3 system centers around regular grocery store and restaurant food right from the start. Nor are there obligatory supplements, pills, or drugs. Formu-3 does provide "Formu-fast" food products that can accompany the basic meal—soups, puddings, desserts, and beverages—promoting rapid breakdown of fat, but these are only an optional, auxiliary part of the program. Strenuous exercise, another unpleasant companion to many diets, isn't required either, although a walking regimen is encouraged.

The most important aspect of the Formu-3 system, however, is confidential one-on-one counseling, usually held two to three times a week. This isn't just a weigh-in and some motivational pep talk. As counselors, you and your staff supply your clients with nutritionally balanced recipes (many developed by past Formu-3 clients) for relatively high-carbohydrate, moderate-protein, and low-fat meals, and help them plan their weekly menus, composed of a variety of foods to avoid the boredom and tastelessness that scuttles so many diets.

It will take you about 90 days to open your Formu-3 center once your franchise contract is signed. During that time, the company will provide assistance in site selection, laying out and decorating the facility, and hiring a qualified staff. Formu-3 will also teach you and your employees to be professional weight-loss counselors in a five-day basic training course covering the concepts and techniques of the Formu-3 system. Then, you'll attend an additional four-day manager's training course, where you'll learn operations skills and sales, marketing, and motivational techniques. Follow-up instruction and field training takes place at the two or three national meetings annually and during periodic area seminars.

Formu-3's in-house marketing staff devises direct mail promotions and radio and newspaper ads for your use. But word-of-mouth remains an equally powerful marketing tool, and Jeffrey Stone notes that "some franchise owners spend nothing to advertise their business and still show impressive growth."

CEO Stone's strongly held Christian beliefs, he freely acknowledges, underlie his business philosophy, but the Formu-3 centers are not used for religious proselytizing. Charitable concerns, nevertheless, are expressed through the company's "Formu-Love" program, in which each franchise is asked to sponsor a needy child from a foreign country.

For further information contact:
 Walter E. Poston, Vice President of Franchise Development, Formu-3 International, 4790 Douglas Circle, N.W., Canton, OH 44718, 216-499-3334 or 1-800-525-6315

Jazzercise, Inc.

Initial license fee: $650
Royalties: 20%
Advertising royalties: None
Minimum cash required: $360
Capital required: $2,000
Financing: None
Length of contract: 5 years

In business since: 1976
Franchising since: 1983
Total number of units: 4,600
Number of company-operated units: None
Total number of units planned, 1995: 7,500
Number of company-operated units planned, 1995: None

Contrary to what some people may think, Jane Fonda did not invent aerobic exercise. In fact, the contemporary emphasis on exercise that promotes cardiovascular efficiency got its biggest boost from a best-selling book, *Aerobics* (Bantam Books), by Dr. Kenneth C. Cooper. But the healthy sales of Fonda's exercise videotapes do reflect and reinforce the popularity of workouts.

Judi Sheppard Missett has also appeared in several home fitness videos and made a name for herself. But even more familiar than her name is the name of the company she started, Jazzercise, which boasts more than 400,000 students worldwide in its dance fitness classes.

Franchisees hold Jazzercise classes in community centers, YMCAs, churches—wherever they can rent centrally located, relatively inexpensive but large spaces by the hour. The basic equipment consists of a cassette player. Only people in good shape can run this hands-, arms-, shoulders-, legs-, torso-, and feet-on business, learning current dance exercise routines and teaching them. You and your employees must also be enthusiastic and supportive, with the ability to motivate other people.

The company wants only instructors in good physical condition. It requires you to submit with your franchise application a full-body photo of yourself in leotard and tights. And that's not the last test you will have to pass. The two- to three-day regional training workshop required of new franchisees—for which you will absorb travel expenses—also tests your knowledge of physiology (based on non-technical written material sent to you before you begin training) and your ability to do and teach typical Jazzercise routines. In fact, it is an audition.

You must acquire a certificate in cardiopulmonary resuscitation

(CPR) before attending the workshop. About a month before the workshop, the company will send you a training packet, which includes a videotape containing dance routines, a selection of music and choreography, and a physiology manual. The company suggests that you prepare for the workshop by attending Jazzercise classes to get a feel for its system.

The company evaluates you during the first day of the workshop. If you pass, you will complete the seminar, receiving further instruction in teaching and business skills. Should you not pass, Jazzercise will tell you why, and you can apply again in the future. You will also receive a full refund of the franchise fee.

As franchises go, this one has very low start-up costs, and the expenses don't increase much once you begin conducting classes at your own location. You will, of course, need a cassette player, as well as a TV and a VCR. You will use the video equipment to study the tapes you receive from headquarters every two months. Each tape provided by Jazzercise, Inc., is accompanied by written instructions and contains 25 to 30 new routines. You have to purchase the music, and you must confine your teaching to official Jazzercise routines.

Jazzercise gets a lot of publicity, which should pay off in increased enrollments for your classes. Judi Sheppard Missett's guest column on exercise appears in prominent magazines, and the company engages in joint promotions with firms like JCPenney and Revlon.

For further information contact:
  JoAnn Kocyk, Jazzercise, Inc., 2808 Roosevelt St., Carlsbad, CA 92008,
  619-434-2101

Jenny Craig Weight Loss Centres

Initial license fee: $50,000
Royalties: 7%
Advertising royalties: None
Minimum cash required: $150,000
Capital required: $150,000
Financing: None
Length of contract: 20 years

In business since: 1983
Franchising since: 1986
Total number of units: 646
Number of company-operated units: 451
Total number of units planned, 1995: 1,110
Number of company-operated units planned, 1995: 700

When Jenny Craig, born and raised in New Orleans, and her husband, Sid, a Canadian, decided to start their own weight-loss centers after 20 years in the business, they headed for Australia. "People told us we were nuts—they said Australia was the toughest market in the world," Sid remembers, "with 30 paid holidays a year . . . people were hard to motivate." But here was a country without a similar, competing enterprise, a country whose people, even more than those in the United States, tended toward overweight. They soon turned Jenny Craig into a household name in the land down under before the couple returned to the U.S. in 1985 to begin franchising their centers here.

Now operating throughout the country, Jenny Craig Centres offer a program to help clients take off weight and teach them new eating behaviors that help keep it off. The Jenny Craig system involves several components. First, there are calorie-controlled, nutritionally balanced menu plans, based on the client's age, sex, and dietary and taste preferences. To make up those meals, "Jenny's Cuisine" is furnished exclusively to program participants, canned and packaged products that run the gamut from Szechuan Chicken and Rice to Chocolate Mousse, developed by food technologists and approved by physicians and nutritionists. There are life-style classes, teaching clients new ways to think about food, and behavior-education tapes for home use. Finally, there's personal counseling, individual attention, and a supportive, motivating environment provided by franchisees and their staff, all specifically trained how to look for the factors, including the emotional and physiological aspects, contributing to or preventing weight loss.

Whether your clients are trying to combat weight-complicated health problems like cardiovascular disease, diabetes, and hypertension, or simply attempting to look and feel better, you'll use the company's specially devised computer software to establish their personal weight-loss regimen at their initial session, guaranteeing they meet their goals within the predetermined number of weeks or allowing them to stay on the program at no additional cost until they do. Initially, your customers will be eating Jenny's Cuisine almost exclusively, supplemented by fresh fruits, vegetables, and grain and dairy products. At their halfway point, you'll introduce regular meals to their menus, and once they've reached their goal weight, you'll start them on their permanent stabilization program, where you'll teach them lasting ways to stay slim.

It is helpful, the Craigs acknowledge, if you have had experience in the weight-loss business or in a similar service. The company also prefers that its franchisees, along with the necessary financial resources, have a proven record of meeting financial goals and budgets, have a strong commitment to the community, and be willing to commit to close personal supervision of their franchise. If you are accepted as a Jenny Craig franchisee, the company will help you get started by assisting in site selection, including an area evaluation and lease negotiation, construction of your facility, and interior layout and design. There is a six- to eight-week training program at the company's California training center, involving a combination of classroom and on-the-job instruction, which is followed by two to three weeks of further guidance in your franchise territory, where the company will provide personnel to help you hire and train your staff and assist in your center opening. Additionally, there are periodic instruction updates and operational reviews performed by Jenny Craig field representatives.

While the company estimates that some 50 percent of Jenny Craig customers come through individual referrals, it also administers a nationwide marketing effort that supports individual franchises through lead-generating commercials and advertisements, revised regularly. And special promotional material is prepared for your opening to generate awareness of your Jenny Craig Centre and help you create an early client base.

New franchise opportunities are still available in 31 states. While over 90 percent of Jenny Craig employees (and a similar percentage of its customers) are women, men are also encouraged to apply for a franchise.

For further information contact:
 J. Gary Hawk, Vice President, Franchise Development, Jenny Craig Weight Loss Centres, 445 Marine View Ave., #300, Del Mar, CA 92014, 619-259-7000, fax 619-259-2812

Nutri/System Weight Loss Centers

Initial license fee: $13,000+
Royalties: 7%
Advertising royalties: None
Minimum cash required: $100,000
Capital required: $100,000
Financing: None
Length of contract: 10

In business since: 1971
Franchising since: 1972
Total number of units: 1,799
Number of company-operated units: 484
Total number of units planned, 1995: NA
Number of company-operated units planned, 1995: NA

Nutri/System Weight Loss Centers offer the consumer a program that features a multidimensional approach to weight loss and weight control. The Nutri/System program consists of an exclusive meal plan, nutritional counseling, behavior education, an activity plan and maintenance program. Nutri/System Weight Loss Centers offer weight loss without the use of drugs or injections.

Nutri/System provides complete training for franchisees and their staff through on-site instruction, training seminars, and training guides. Operations consultants visit franchise sites to provide follow-up supervision. Continual training and workshops are also provided for diet center personnel, managers, multicenter managers (area, regional, and general managers) and marketing managers.

Weight counselors employed by franchisees use a computer program to analyze clients' life-styles, including age, physical activity, and eating habits, to come up with a weight-loss goal and the length of time it should take to reach that goal. The company guarantees, in writing, that clients will reach their goal. Otherwise they will have full use of the company's services until they reach their goal.

At the heart of the program, of course, is the Nutri/System diet. Clients find it easy to follow—and the company and its franchisees have another source of profits—in the sales of the exclusive line of Nu System Cuisine, available nowhere else. These frozen, freeze-dried, and canned foods are balanced not only for calorie content, but also for carefully controlled levels of saturated fat, cholesterol, and salt.

Your staff will have the skill to devise special diets for clients with particular problems, such as diabetes or hypertension. Weight-loss counselors supplement all diets with suggestions for an exercise program, and some centers have exercise facilities on the premises. Centers also offer classes that help clients change the habits that lead to weight gain. The center encourages clients to continue coming to the center for advice and monitoring for a year after they have achieved their goal, just to make sure they don't backslide.

The company will help you choose a site for your unit and advise you on its construction. And it will provide all the diagnostic and therapeutic equipment you will need.

In addition, Nutri/System provides its franchisees with an accounting system, business forms, and manuals detailing the daily operation of the weight-loss center. The company also supplies radio and television tapes and newspaper ads, as well as promotional items for any kind of local campaign you care to run.

For further information contact:
  Lisa K. Rice, Manager, Franchise Development, Nutri/System Weight Loss

Centers, Inc., 380 Sentry Pky., Blue Bell, PA 19422, 215-940-3000 or
1-800-U-R-NUTRI

Physicians Weight Loss Centers of America, Inc.

Initial license fee: $32,500
Royalties: 10% of weekly gross
Advertising royalties: $250/week
Minimum cash required: $100,000
Capital required: $66,900 to $126,450
Financing: None
Length of contract: 3 years, two 5-year renewal terms

In business since: 1979
Franchising since: 1980
Total number of units: 290
Number of company-operated units: 24
Total number of units planned, 1995: 1,200
Number of company-operated units planned, 1995: 50

The weight-loss industry currently weighs in at $10 billion a year in
the United States. American men average about 10 pounds more than
they did a decade ago; women, about five pounds more. According to
this company, there are over 30 million overweight adults in the
United States, most of them obese.

With its medically supervised diet, behavior modification program,
and aggressive marketing, the management of Physicians Weight Loss
Centers sees its company as well placed to take advantage of this large
market. The key is medical supervision. All centers have a staff physician and a registered or licensed practical nurse, as well as weight-
reduction counselors, two examination rooms, two counseling rooms,
and a laboratory.

To ensure that patients can fit the center's activities into their work
schedules, these weight-loss centers remain open from 9:00 A.M. to
7:30 P.M. The staff puts patients on the "Futra-Loss Diet," a strict regimen, which the company guarantees will enable them to shed three
to seven pounds a week. Physicians Weight Loss Centers says this diet
stimulates the patient's body to burn off excess fat. The company produces the supplementary vitamins and minerals required on this diet,
and it sells them to the patients as part of the plan. To bolster their
efforts to lose weight and keep it off, patients also receive behavior
modification counseling from center employees.

When patients have achieved their dietary goal, they graduate to a
weight-maintenance plan. This provides Physicians Weight Loss Centers and its franchisees with an additional opportunity to profit by

selling the various drinks, shakes, soups, and puddings produced under the company name, in addition to the vitamins and minerals.

Some company franchisees are doctors or nurses, but a medical background is not necessary. When you purchase your franchise you will receive new owner's training at the franchisor's suburban Akron, Ohio, headquarters, where you will have to pick up your own expenses. The week's course will cover the diet program, behavior guidance, marketing and enrolling, as well as the financial and operational systems used at these weight-reduction centers.

The company offers extensive supplementary training. Any members of your staff can receive thorough training in center operations at one of the company's monthly five-day general training seminars in Akron. Physicians Weight Loss Centers also gives semiannual motivational sales seminars, special seminars for managerial-level employees, and a four-day college-level course covering advanced sales techniques. It also has a special set of weekly lesson plans and learning exercises for your behavioral guidance counselors.

Physicians Weight Loss Centers prides itself on the continual assistance it gives franchisees every step of the way, from site selection and layout through help in securing the services of a physician and nurse. The franchisor also conducts frequent consultations to monitor the operational and financial progress of your business.

Should local doctors raise any questions about patients and treatment at your center, you can refer them to the company's national medical director. You can also tap the expertise of the franchisor's corporate legal counsel for problems or questions involving legal matters.

Advertising is a company strong point. Physicians Weight Loss Centers has an in-house ad agency that can create customized materials for any kind of media campaign you wish to run.

For further information contact:
Jeannie Butler, Director of Franchise Development, Physicians Weight Loss Centers of America, Inc., 395 Springside Dr., Akron, OH 44333-2496, 216-666-7952

Hair Care

Accent Hair Salons, Inc.

Initial license fee: $20,000
Royalties: 5%
Advertising royalties: 5%

Minimum cash required: $40,000
Capital required: $135,000
Financing: Available
Length of contract: 10 years

In business since: 1981
Franchising since: 1987
Total number of units: 13
Number of company-operated units: 1
Total number of units planned, 1995: 100
Number of company-operated units planned, 1995: 15

"The large chain operations have completely overlooked black women," points out Accent Hair Salons president and CEO Claude Patmon, a former Green Beret who had 10 years of franchise development experience before founding the company. "We recognized the need and went after it." Accent's services, equipment, and products are geared exclusively to the unique hair salon needs of African-American women, particularly those between the ages of 18 and 34. Focusing on hair care alone and avoiding supplementary undertakings like manicuring and hair removal, Accent salons offer speedy, high-quality, and affordable service to customers, without requiring an appointment. While walk-in service is readily available in the general market, it's still essentially a new concept for salons catering to this segment, and one well suited to the growing numbers of professional black women. But the primary customer draw is the fact that Accent stylists are all licensed cosmetologists who specialize in the area of black hair care.

Franchisees, on the other hand, are business specialists. You should have successful experience in retail or corporate management, and, if your market has potential for more than one salon, you are expected to be willing ultimately to develop a multiunit operation.

Using statistical analysis, a company executive will help you choose a site for your facility in a large upscale urban or suburban mall. Accent salons usually range from 2,000 to 2,800 square feet and are open Monday through Sunday, with 14 to 16 stations for your staff to be able to serve as many as 400 patrons a week.

Before a single hair is cut, however, you'll participate in three weeks of franchisee training, studying operations and service strategies as well as advertising and accounting. Your accredited stylists, meanwhile, each spend a week at the salon learning about the company's hair innovations and about the particular concerns and interests of the typical Accent patron. "We evaluate what our clients will wear and *what they won't wear*," explains Stan Ford, Accent's artistic director. "Most are working people with hectic schedules who require easy-care styles." Stylists receive additional on-the-job training offered regularly to introduce the new styles and styling techniques developed by the company's research and development department, as well as new products and equipment, while you're given guidance on updated salon management procedures and local marketing concepts that complement the company's basic radio-oriented media advertising program.

Accent's success—and its potential—stem from tapping into both an underused talent pool and an underdeveloped market. As the nation's only black-owned franchise, it presents a special opportunity for minority entrepreneurs. And operating in a fragmented industry, dominated by small, independent operators, it offers those franchisees the marketing, support, and security advantages that can come only from a national chain. "I'm sure there are going to be those who are going to come after us and copy our system," CEO Patmon predicts. "I don't care. I want everyone else to play catch-up."

For further information contact:
  Claude Patmon, President and CEO, Accent Hair Salons, Inc., 211 S. Main St., Suite 720, Dayton, OH 45402, 513-461-0394

Cutco Industries, Inc.

Initial license fee: $20,000
Royalties: 6%
Advertising royalties: None
Minimum cash required: $50,000
Capital required: $73,000 to $176,500
Financing: Available to qualified applicants
Length of contract: 15 years, with three 5-year renewable terms at no cost

In business since: 1955
Franchising since: 1967
Total number of units: 650
Number of company-operated units: 50
Total number of units planned, 1995: 300
Number of company-operated units planned, 1995: 25

In the old days—that is, 1955—men got their hair cut in barber shops and women went to beauty parlors. And never the twain did meet. Then Lillian and Karl Stanley put their $10,000 life savings into a beauty parlor in Jericho, New York. "I'm only 10 minutes from the shop," Lillian Stanley remembers thinking at the time, "and I can be home when the children come home from school." But the instant success of the store kept her busier than she had anticipated. Before long, that shop became the basis for the Cut & Curl chain, and the profits poured in.

Meanwhile, Lillian Stanley's children thrived. In fact, her son, Richard, is now the president of the $110 million Cutco Industries, the hair-care empire into which that little shop eventually grew. The Cutco empire is divided into two franchised parts. HairCrafters, to which the remaining Cut & Curl operations were converted, are usually located in shopping centers. The stores concentrate on inexpensive family haircuts—and have done about 100 million to date. Great Expectations Precision Haircutters caters to the fashion-conscious, but its prices are also low. Both chains are decidedly unisex, a policy the company claims to have pioneered.

HairCrafters and Great Expectations were rated number three among hair-care franchisors by *Entrepreneur*. These establishments, which, according to Cutco's president, "have put the last nail in the coffin of barbershops," do not require appointments. Their hexagonal styling booths are designed for an open and airy atmosphere, as well as for privacy. One operation in Phoenix offers the ultimate in convenience for the harried worker with unusual hours: all-night service.

The full-service salons offer what the company would like to think of as a social experience. "We are dealing more with feelings than just the service of haircutting," Stanley says. The background music is upbeat, and one successful slogan the company has employed is "Talk to me."

Whatever else Cutco franchisees may be—and they have included dentists, bankers, and financial analysts—they are usually not professional hairstylists. Cutco doesn't market the franchise as one requiring your technical expertise and full-time presence on the floor. Potential franchisees are encouraged to think big. The company will stress to you that most of their franchisees have ended up buying more than one franchise. Those who have been aboard for more than a decade, according to Cutco, typically own more than eight franchises.

The company helps its franchisees pick a location and set up their business. In fact, if you wish, they will choose the site and build on it for you. Cutco trains you at your store. The instruction covers employee selection and training, advertising and merchandising, marketing, bookkeeping, inventory control, pricing, and accounting. Your stylists receive updated training in the latest cuts and styles at your location at least once a year. Company representatives visit each shop about three times a year. Occasionally that representative is Richard Stanley himself.

While you do not have to buy supplies and equipment from the company, Cutco does make them available. One of the added advantages of the franchise is your ability to sell at retail the company's own brand of hair-care products.

For further information contact:
Don von Liebermann, Cutco Industries, Inc., 125 S. Service Rd., Jericho, NY 11753, 516-334-8400 or 1-800-992-0139

First Choice Haircutters

Initial license fee: $25,000
Royalties: 6%
Advertising royalties: 2%
Minimum cash required: $30,000 to $40,000
Capital required: $80,000
Financing: Assistance provided indirectly
Length of contract: 10 years with one 5-year option

In business since: 1980
Franchising since: 1981
Total number of units: 240
Number of company-operated units: 81
Total number of units planned, 1995: NA
Number of company-operated units planned, 1995: NA

Hair. Over 20 years ago they wrote a musical about it. But some barbers then were going out of business due to people's growing reluctance to part with it. Not anymore.

But haircuts are not what they used to be. Even barbershops catering primarily to men have begun to resemble beauty salons. The prices in those shops also bear a resemblance to salon prices. "Styling" has brought with it a revolution in how Americans approach haircuts.

The founders of First Choice looked at this phenomenon and came up with an interesting idea that would combine the best of recent developments with an economical service that could take care of the whole family's hair-care needs under one roof: an à la carte, no-frills hair salon. It includes free parking at every location, and no appointment is necessary—just like old times. And it's all topped off with a written money-back guarantee that says if you don't like your haircut, you can get a refund or a free recut within one week.

A First Choice franchise is ideal for somebody who already has some managerial or business experience, since the overwhelming number of the company's franchisees do not lay a hand on anybody's head: They hire experienced professionals to do the cutting. Although the company is Canadian and seeks to expand in Quebec and the

Maritime Provinces, it is also expanding the number of franchises it has in the United States, especially in the East and the Midwest.

This franchise is a cash business with almost no inventory. The company claims the business is recession-proof, in part because the demand for its services is based on hair's special characteristics. After all, in how many businesses do you get to deal with a market that, as Cheryl Kostopoulos, First Choice's general manager puts it, "regenerates itself"?

If you decide to invest in a First Choice Haircutters franchise, the company will help you select the right site for your store. Then you learn the ropes at two weeks of training at the company school in Toronto. A First Choice training officer will also train your staff for 10 to 13 days at your place of business. Direct assistance from the company extends to five days beyond your grand opening, and a week's refresher course in Toronto will be available to you after that if you feel you need it. Three-day franchise seminars, offered periodically, also provide brush-up training and franchisor updates.

Ed Furman, who opened his First Choice franchise in Lansdale, Pennsylvania, was pleased with his training, especially the class size of two or three people. He says that his relationship with the franchisor so far has been "excellent. First Choice is very responsive to our needs and questions."

For further information contact:
  George Kostopoulos, First Choice Franchise Services, 6465 Millcreek Dr., Suite 205, Mississauga, Ont., Canada L5N 5R3, 1-800-387-8335

Great Clips, Inc.

Initial license fee: $17,500
Royalties: 6%
Advertising royalties: 5%
Minimum cash required: $30,000
Capital required: $71,000 to $97,400
Financing: None
Length of contract: 10 years

In business since: 1982
Franchising since: 1983
Total number of units: 216
Number of company-operated units: None
Total number of units planned, 1995: 750
Number of company-operated units planned, 1995: None

To indicate its confidence in its operations, Great Clips will send you the names, addresses, and home and business phone numbers of all its franchisees so you can check company claims for yourself.

Great Clips' business is providing no-frills haircuts at a low price. The customer pays only for specific services rendered. For example, Great Clips advertisements suggest that customers shampoo their hair the day they come in for a haircut to avoid the cost of having Great Clips do it for them. Great Clips guarantees the customer a good haircut—and without an appointment. If not satisfied, the customer can have it recut for free or get a refund. With the shop's stylists kept constantly busy cutting hair, profits come from high volume.

The nationally franchised haircutting shop has reached just the right point in franchising development, according to Great Clips. No longer a new and high-risk undertaking, but not too old and over-developed, it could offer a good investment opportunity to somebody who wants to open a business. Great Clips sees great opportunities for carving out a big niche in the hair-care business.

As franchises go, Great Clips has low start-up costs. The company says that most stores achieve profitability inside of four months.

The stores, often located in shopping centers, have a distinctive look, which comes mainly from the colorful canvas sails serving as partitions to create private hairstyling areas. The red and white striped shirts worn by Great Clips hairstylists add another splash of color.

One of the key advantages to operating a Great Clips franchise, the company stresses, is the minimal amount of time you have to spend on the business, even during the opening period. You can even retain your present job while you get under way. Assuming you hire a manager to run things, the business should not demand more than a few hours a week of your time. Over two-thirds of Great Clips franchisees own multiple units, and the average franchisee owns three shops.

Great Clips will train you in your area. Instruction will cover selecting a site and negotiating a lease as well as the basics of advertising, financing, and shop operation. You will purchase your supplies from a list of vendors approved by Great Clips.

Your stylists will get a free four-day training course in the Great Clips method of haircutting, although, of course, you have to pay their salary while they study. After passing a test on what they've learned, stylists receive the company's "Certificate of Competency." They cannot work in your shop without it. Any stylists you hire after your business has started will receive the same training, but at a cost of $75 to you for each one trained.

The Great Clips grand opening promotion, part of your franchise package, includes special coupons with money-off offers on permanents and haircuts. Direct mail advertising, also part of the company's promotional strategy to draw customers to your new store, should also help your fledgling business get off to a good start.

For further information contact:
  Director of Development, Great Clips, Inc., 3800 W. 80th St., Suite 400, Minneapolis, MN 55431, 612-893-9088 or 1-800-999-5959, fax 612-844-3444

Medical Services

Mobility Center, Inc.

Initial license fee: $20,000
Royalties: 5%
Advertising royalties: 1%
Minimum cash required: $70,000
Capital required: $20,000 to $40,000 working capital
Financing: None
Length of contract: 10 years

In business since: 1968
Franchising since: 1984
Total number of units: 10
Number of company-operated units: 3
Total number of units planned, 1995: 36
Number of company-operated units planned, 1995: None

Mobility Center owners take great satisfaction in their conviction that, more than just a local business, they are providing a valued resource for their communities. The franchise, as one Texas affiliate puts it, is "not only a great way to provide our livelihood, but an oppportunity to enhance many people's lives."

Operating a retail and service facility, Mobility Center franchisees are the local representatives for Amigo, a company that manufactures eponymous personal scooter-like motorized vehicles for people with walking limitations and disabilities. These battery-powered three-wheeled carts come with a swivel chair and can reach speeds of 3 to 5 miles per hour, while remaining compact and maneuverable enough to get through doorways and around corners, and versatile enough to be able to run indoors or out. Company founder Allan Thieme invented the Amigo as a labor of love for his wife, who couldn't let multiple sclerosis hinder her in her job of raising six children. Now, some 50,000 people own an Amigo. They may have an amputated limb or be afflicted with arthritis, postpolio, or heart disease, and they may be retired, unemployed, laboring as housewives or househusbands, or be full-time members of the work force. What they all share is a desire to be mobile and independent. "The Amigo," one owner sums up, "has provided me with a happy sense of freedom by opening doors that were previously beyond reach—sports events, theater. . . . Most important, the Amigo has allowed me to do it myself."

At your Mobility Center, you'll stock a complete line of Amigo products, including accessories like baskets, cane holders, and seat lifts, as well as related merchandise from other manufacturers. Rather than having to order by phone or mail, your clients are able to come to your store to see, inspect, and test the Amigos. You'll custom-fit and equip the products for your customers' individual needs and provide maintenance and repair services.

Because it's likely that there are a number of Amigo owners already in your franchise area, you'll start with a built-in customer base of individuals who'll be needing these regular services and who will refer new clients to you. Additional business will come through your and the company's contact with medical professionals, health-care institutes, and government agencies. And your potential market continues to expand: senior citizens, who'll form a large (though by no means exclusive) portion of your clientele, are the fastest growing demographic group in the country.

Amigo representatives will work with you in selecting a site for your Mobility Center. Because of the physical limitations of your customers, location accessibility and convenience are especially strong concerns. The company will furnish, upon request, guidelines for lease negotiation and interior decor. It will also advise you on your initial inventory of both Amigo products and goods from other companies that enhance your stock and services and that you'll be able to get at discounts through Amigo's purchasing agreements.

You and your staff will take a training course in sales and servicing, led by company professionals at the Amigo factory and headquarters. Amigo will provide a plan for your grand opening event and supply personnel to help you on opening day. Procedures manuals will help guide you in day-to-day operations, while newsletters and other publications such as the "Amigo Activator" and the Mobility Center "Center Line" keep you up to date on new products and industry developments. Meanwhile, the company sends its quarterly *Friendly Wheels* magazine to all Amigo owners, keeping them in touch and abreast of the latest merchandise and service offerings available at Mobility Centers, and oversees a national advertising program.

Many who work for the company are Amigo owners themselves. A

Mobility Center franchise, as well, is an attractive opportunity for those whose physical challenges don't limit their entrepreneurial zeal.

For further information, contact:
John Murphy, Franchise Director, Mobility Center, Inc., 6693 Dixie Hwy., Bridgeport, MI 48722, 517-777-6537

Optical

NuVision, Inc.

Initial license fee: $15,000
Royalties: 8.5%
Advertising royalties: 7%
Minimum cash required: $25,000 to $525,000
Capital required: $25,000 to $525,000
Financing: Information available on request
Length of contract: 10 years

In business since: 1950
Franchising since: 1983
Total number of units: 111
Number of company-operated units: 75
Total number of units planned, 1995: NA
Number of company-operated units planned, 1995: NA

Don't think of this business as medically related. True, NuVision and all other eyeglass centers have opticians on the premises to give eye exams and grind lenses. And, of course, they fill prescriptions for eyeglasses from ophthalmologists. But it's a more interesting and lucrative enterprise than just that.

When you buy a NuVision franchise you tap into a fashion industry. People care a great deal about how they look. They don't just want to see better, they want look better. The excitement in this field comes from the contact lenses, designer sunglasses, and the wide variety of frames—some very expensive—that hold the eyeglass lenses. You won't just turn out glasses as a NuVision franchisee. Rather, you will own and operate a business dedicated to selling products that make people look good.

You needn't worry if you lack knowledge about this field. NuVision will show you the ropes. The franchisor will work with you on site selection and development, and you will need the company's go-ahead before you build or remodel. Your training will take place at corporate headquarters in Flint, Michigan, with transportation, lodging, and meals your responsibility. That training will cover all procedures needed to operate a NuVision franchise, including advertising, product buying and handling, personnel management, and record keeping. You will also receive a copy of the company's confidential operations manual.

Every business involves lots of paperwork. Eyeglass centers, with their varied and specialized inventory and customer invoicing, have as much as any, maybe more than most. NuVision recognizes this and takes special steps to help you prepare all the business forms you will need to operate your franchise.

The company will have representatives on the premises to help you clear the opening day hurdles. You can also request follow-up visits. Should you need brushing up afterward, you can take advantage of the franchisor's refresher training courses, offered monthly either at your location or, for more in-depth training, company headquarters. Aside from general management techniques, this advanced instruction covers subjects like cost control and sales training. NuVision also pledges to keep you on top of the changing technical aspects of the optical industry.

Along with the traditional store operation, NuVision also has "One Hour" offices available complete with an in-store lab, giving you the ability to meet the growing patient demand for faster service. NuVision's full service laboratory and distribution system will provide all product and technical services.

For further information contact:
  Joanne Holmquist, NuVision, Inc., P.O. Box 2600, 2284 S. Ballenger, Flint, MI 48501, 313-767-0900

Skin Care

Elizabeth Grady Face First

Initial license fee: $25,000
Royalties: 6%
Advertising royalties: 3%
Minimum cash required: $25,000
Capital required: $90,000

Financing: None
Length of contract: 10 years, with two 5-year options

In business since: 1974
Franchising since: 1981
Total number of units: 26
Number of company-operated units: 14
Total number of units planned, 1995: 45
Number of company-operated units planned, 1995: 5

Elizabeth Grady Face First promotes the achievement and maintenance of healthy skin for men as well as women, young and old alike. At these skin-care centers, the emphasis is on individual consultation and clinical analysis by professionally licensed estheticians. These skin specialists are trained to treat a variety of skin problems without drugs and to administer facials, paraffin face masks, waxes, and cosmetic makeovers. They also devise home care programs for Face First patrons, who can choose from a complete line of Elizabeth Grady products, including cleansers, toners, moisturizers, creams, sunscreens, and cosmetics, developed by dermatologists and chemists and all available, along with other approved merchandise, at the centers.

Concerned with more than just its clients, Face First's policy is to take a leadership position in the industry to see that good business practices are set and maintained. Back in 1978, the company's then-president authored a Massachusetts state bill that became the first skin-care industry control and safeguard legislation in the country.

This concern is shown in its franchise program as well. Your skin-care center must adhere to the company's maintenance and appearance standards inside and out, and your staff will have dress regulations to follow, too. Face First will be involved in finding a location for your center that, whether in a shopping mall, strip center, or freestanding building, will provide the proper professional image, high visibility, and adequate space, usually about 1,000 square feet with area for four service rooms. You'll also receive guidance for the design of your facility, from layout to color scheme, displays to lighting.

Your skin-care consultants must be licensed estheticians and be approved by the company, and need to complete a company training program. You will have to take a training course and study standards of quality, inventory control methods, equipment selection, accounting, cost controls, and marketing techniques. You will gain on-the-job experience both at Face First headquarters and at a company store. Unless you intend to service customers yourself, however, you will not require an esthetician license. You'll also receive the Face First operations manual covering day-to-day business procedures, with regular updates supplied to keep you current on industry trends and new Face First products and services.

A company representative will work with you at your skin-care center for one week during your opening month. Other operations specialists will also visit periodically to consult with you and your staff and furnish suggestions for improving business. This will include assistance in devising advertising and promotion strategies, for which you are expected to devote 2 percent of your gross sales in addition to the franchise advertising royalty. Your own marketing ventures will be complemented by Face First's company-wide program, featuring ads that promote the general Face First products and services and list area Face First Centers, and including a special marketing effort aimed toward the growing men's market.

Face First centers are currently operating throughout New England; many choice markets are still available. Franchisees are assigned exclusive territories and you may designate where you wish to locate as long as you don't infringe on another franchisee's sector. For the present time, however, Face First is offering individual franchises for single locations only.

For further information contact:
   John P. Walsh, President, Elizabeth Grady Face First, Riverwalk Bldg. #9, 360 Merrimack St., Lawrence, MA 01843, 508-975-7115 or 1-800-FACIALS, fax 508-975-7547

13. The Home Construction, Improvement, and Maintenance Industry

Contents

Merry Maids, Inc.
Molly Maid, Inc.
The Maids International, Inc.

Water Conditioning

Culligan International Company
RainSoft Water Conditioning Company

Construction and Home Improvement

ABC Seamless, Inc.

Initial license fee: $12,000
Royalties: Variable
Advertising royalties: 0.5%
Minimum cash required: $25,000
Capital required: $150,000
Financing: Available
Length of contract: Perpetual

In business since: 1973
Franchising since: 1978
Total number of units: 513
Number of company-operated units: 8
Total number of units planned, 1995: 1,000
Number of company-operated units planned, 1995: 8

Providing seamless steel siding for home, garages, and office buildings, ABC Seamless is the largest company in the business. The siding is manufactured right on location, custom cut, shaped and fitted to the structure with no joints or spikes. Finished with vinyl paint, it's also backed with a lifetime warranty.

Seamless siding has distinct advantages for homeowners. Regular siding comes in 12-foot lengths, so for every strip, there are at least two or three seams on each side of a structure, seams collecting dust and moisture that can quickly make the siding look shabby and dirty. Requiring little care to stay shipshape, seamless siding also better protects the building from wind, rain, and other elements, keeping it warmer in the winter and cooler in summer, and saving the owner money on fuel and air-conditioning bills.

ABC Seamless's siding is available in 11 colors—shades like "cinnamon" and "spring green" along with more traditional "colonial white" and "charcoal gray"—and 26 styles. And it's only one item in the company's extensive line of home improvement products. You'll also be able to provide and install seamless gutters and downspouts in steel or aluminum, gable vents, soffits and fascia, window and door trim, even shutters, storm windows, and insulation.

Once you decide to become a franchisee, you'll make a two-day trip to ABC Seamless's offices in Fargo, North Dakota, meeting with the executive staff to verify your territory, develop an initial business plan, determine your goals and objectives, and decide on your equipment needs. The machinery for manufacturing the siding comes right from the company, and you'll be furnished with lists of specifications for the additional approved equipment and tools, along with the names of factory-direct suppliers who'll outfit you at a lower cost.

Siding or construction experience is considered helpful but not necessary; even with no background in the business, you'll be able to learn the process of seamless steel siding manufacture and application. Training takes place in your area, emphasizing on-the-job instruction. You'll concentrate on equipment operation and maintenance and installation procedures, but also cover sales methods, customer relations, and financial management. Recognizing that your first siding job lays the foundation for your business, your trainer will work alongside you through the entire process, making sure that you have mastered each step and will be able to do the work on your own for future assignments. Several follow-up training seminars and franchise meetings are held throughout the year, and you'll be mailed bulletins and updates on new products and strategies from both the company and its suppliers.

ABC Seamless will furnish a marketing plan, with display books, brochures, and sample kits to show prospective customers, information on relevant trade shows in your area, and layouts for print media ads and spots for TV and radio promotion. The company will also provide support for "open house" events at the site of a recent job, one of the most effective—and highly visible—advertisements for your services, demonstrating the advantages of seamless steel siding better than any photo display . . . and far more pleasantly than any hard-sell pitch.

For further information contact:
  Don Barnum, ABC Seamless, Inc., 3001 Fiechtner Dr. S.W., Fargo, ND 58103, 701-293-5952 or 1-800-732-6577, fax 701-293-3107

American Leak Detection, Inc.

Initial license fee: $20,000
Royalties: 8% to 10%
Advertising royalties: None
Minimum cash required: $20,000
Capital required: $20,000
Financing: Available
Length of contract: 10 years

In business since: 1974
Franchising since: 1985
Total number of units: 144
Number of company-operated units: 2

Total number of units planned, 1995: 200
Number of company-operated units planned, 1995: 2

Call yourself a "Leak Buster." Your target: a hole or crack in a pipe system buried deep beneath building foundations, under swimming pools, or within walls. It may be imperceptible, but it's menacing—a hole just ⅛ inch in diameter can leak more than 25,000 gallons of water per week. Using a combination of sonar, sound, and radio technology, you'll start your search, able to detect a leak as much as 18 to 20 feet underground. When you find it, you'll dig right to the leak, eschewing a jackhammer and upsetting no more than a few inches of dirt, plaster, or concrete, a couple of tiles or bricks. And you'll fix the pipe, not with a temporary patch, but with a permanent repair. For these services, customers will pay you from $150 to $700 depending on the size of the job. You'll offer a money-back guarantee, of course, if you can't find the leak, but then again, none of your confederates have ever needed to pay up. Your market: homeowners and apartment managers, pool builders and service people, not to mention grounds personnel at shopping centers, office buildings, utility companies, government facilities and military bases.

American Leak Detection isn't the only company that finds and repairs water and gas leaks. But with pipes located underground—beneath concrete, asphalt, or dirt—or between walls, most repairers have to do a lot of demolishing before they even locate the leak. The process can be quite costly, time-consuming, and disruptive.

A former plumber, American Leak Detection founder Richard B. Rennick spent four years working with the engineers to develop a different kind of leak detection system. Injecting compressed air into a closed piping system, the electronic equipment allows you to listen for the otherwise undetectable sound of the air escaping from the leak or crack, pinpointing its location within inches before you do any digging. No pulling up floors, ripping into walls, or tearing apart yards; you'll usually need to disturb no more than 15 square inches of surface space to make the repair, quickly and inexpensively.

You'll also be able to find and fix cracks in swimming pools, spas, and fountains; track drain, waste, and sewer lines; and locate septic tanks and grease pits. One drawback, according to Pomona, California, franchisee Lee Trimble: "The equipment is so sensitive that even inside a house you can hear the birds chirp."

Good hearing and mechanical aptitude are the essential attributes you should have to be an American Leak Detection franchisee. The actual techniques of leak detection and repair are taught to you during training, along with marketing, accounting, and management procedures. Follow-up instruction is also provided on site once you've started to operate.

The company will be supporting your own marketing efforts with its national advertising program. Additionally, the PR department works at getting local, regional, and national coverage, and articles about the Leak Busters have appeared in trade journals, business magazines, periodicals as diverse as *Family Circle* and *U.S. News & World Report*, and newspapers across the country. You'll be receiving *Newsleak*, the company's bimonthly newsletter, and be invited to its annual four-day convention in Palm Springs, where franchisees interact, share ideas, and learn about new techniques and equipment designed by American Leak Detection's research and development department.

Franchisees are assigned guaranteed exclusive territories. Working from your home, you'll be running a low-overhead operation that keeps you out of doors a large part of the day. A truck will be necessary and the company will offer guidance in its lease or purchase. Then there's diving equipment, which you may be needing if you'll be servicing swimming pools, since searching for hose leaks requires underwater time. At least that's outdoor work, too, and many franchisees find it a refreshing change of pace from the office jobs they held in the past.

For further information contact:
  Richard B. Rennick, President, American Leak Detection, Inc., P.O. Box 1701, Palm Springs, CA 92263, 619-320-9991 or 1-800-755-6697

Archadeck

Initial license fee: $25,000
Royalties: 5% to 8%
Advertising royalties: 1%
Minimum cash required: $50,000
Capital required: $50,000 to $60,000
Financing: None
Length of contract: 10 years

In business since: 1980
Franchising since: 1985
Total number of units: 48
Number of company-operated units: None
Total number of units planned, 1995: 300
Number of company-operated units planned, 1995: None

Archadeck calls it "The Last Great Frontier": the American backyard. And with custom-built wooden patio decks, the company aims to tame it.

Over 75 percent of the 80 million family homes in the United States don't have a deck—but that figure is noticeably decreasing. Trade journals indicate that decks are among the five most popular home additions, and over 1.5 million are being built yearly. "The deck—the front porch's private, more sophisticated, but still fun-loving cousin—has come into its own," reports *USA Today*. "Wood decks are sprouting from the backs and sides of homes coast to coast."

It's easy to understand why. Decks can render an otherwise unsuitable backyard functional and attractive at the same time. The wooden look suits the outdoor atmosphere and follows the growing trend in natural home design. Offering sunshine and a view, holding patio furniture, perhaps a barbecue and a Jacuzzi, too, decks become full-service leisure and entertainment facilities for fresh air–seeking homeowners.

Unlike most home remodeling projects, which require weeks of construction and disruption, decks are simple and fast to build. Decks aren't very expensive additions either, usually costing from $1,500 to $10,000. That means less trouble—for both the home owner and the contractor.

Specializing in the customized design and construction of wooden decks, Archadeck, the nation's largest franchise in the field, can make it still easier. You'll offer simple and elaborate decking possibilities alike, with options like screens, gazebos, built-in seating, cabinets, grills, and even hot tubs. You'll also restore old decks darkened and stained by mold, mildew, and everyday usage, damage that's not only unsightly but sometime dangerous, too, when wood warps and rots. Instead of the traditional toxic acidic solutions usually employed, you'll use detergent and oxidizer, alternatives that are more effective, less expensive—and gentler to the environment. And you'll protect the wood from further water damage by sealing it with a clear finish.

Founded by an architect and a builder, the Archadeck franchise combines professional design and construction techniques with high-powered marketing and sales programs. Your competition will primarily be solo contractors, who may be able to match your prices, but can't equal your name recognition or beat your quality. And the backing of a national company assures your customers of a degree of reliability and stability they just can't expect from an independent operator. One Archadeck customer sums it all up: "They provided ideas which were helpful, a schedule which was adhered to, and a product which has been admired by all who have seen it. Two neighbors who have been in the construction business commented (independently) on the quality of construction."

Using photos, diagrams, and videotapes, you'll meet with

customers—builders, developers, condo associates, and commercial grounds managers as well as homeowners—to hear their ideas and determine their needs and budget. Back at your office, you'll prepare two designs to present them at a second meeting. Once the final design is chosen, you'll send your preliminary sketches to the company's drafting division, which will supply a full construction plan, with complete layouts and specifications. You'll then subcontract Archadeck-trained carpenters, who'll do the actual construction, usually taking no more than two days.

You don't need construction experience yourself; in fact, the company doesn't want you building the decks. The workers you'll use receive specialized technical instruction from Archadeck in the techniques the company has developed for deck installation and quality assurance. That means features like galvanized hardware and solid foundations, with posts set in concrete for proper support, along with procedures that reduce cost and construction time without sacrificing excellence.

Believing that the remodeling and construction industries haven't fostered good management, Archadeck would actually *prefer* that you have no experience in the field whatsoever, instead learning the business and the company's methodology from scratch. Twelve days of instruction combines classroom study, videotape role-playing exercises, and field training, and it covers design, sales, marketing, and business operations. Archadeck will also train any employees you'll hire later on.

You'll receive an administration package with manuals and computer software for handling day-to-day management, and be furnished with the Archadeck advertising file, a collection of direct mail pieces and layouts for newspaper, magazine, billboard, and other print media ads. During your initial training, you'll be advised where, when, and how to use this material, and the company will continue to provide assistance in implementing your marketing program and developing new promotional ideas. Archadeck's sales staff will also be working on your behalf, contacting residential builders and commercial institutions in your area. The company provides ongoing guidance by telephone, fax, and mail, and conducts periodic seminars for you and your staff on such subjects as "New Products" and "Designing for Profit."

You can rent office space, but to keep overhead down, most franchisees prefer to operate their business from their homes. Once you've started spending a large part of the workday around the house, however, don't be a bit surprised, if you don't have a deck already, when one of your first sales is to yourself.

For further information contact:
  Richard Provost, President, U.S. Structures, Inc., 2112 West Laburnum Ave.,
  Suite 109, Richmond, VA 23227, 804-353-6999 or 1-800-722-4668

Bathcrest, Inc.

Initial license fee: $24,500
Royalties: None
Advertising royalties: None
Minimum cash required: $24,500
Capital required: $31,000
Financing: Yes
Length of contract: 1 year, renewable

In business since: 1979
Franchising since: 1985
Total number of units: 174
Number of company-operated units: 1
Total number of units planned, 1995: 230
Number of company-operated units planned, 1995: 1

Resurfacing and refinishing bathroom fixtures is one of the quickest
and least expensive ways for the bathroom—the most remodeled room
in the house, according to the *Wall Street Journal*—to attain a brand-
new look. By far, the most expensive cost of updating the bathroom is
incurred by replacing worn, drab, built-in fixtures (bathtubs, sinks,
and tiles) with new ones, which can cost from $1,500 to $4,000.
Bathcrest, however, has developed products that allow bathrooms to
be refurbished for under $600.

Bathcrest's safe, effective, and economical products have made it one
of the top companies in the $100 billion home-remodeling industry.
Bathcrest is the only company in the industry to manufacture its own
products specifically designed for bathtubs, sinks, and tiles. One of
these products, Glazecoat, shines like porcelain, but is more stain- and
chip-resistant than any other resurfacing product.

A franchisee can expect to spend about $24,500 to $33,500 for
training, equipment, supplies, promotional materials, and a one-year
contract to an exclusive territory with a minimum population of
300,000 residents. Bathcrest also gives free to each franchisee 60
quarts of material that will resurface about 120 bathtubs (when applied in the field at the average cost of $295, a franchisee could earn
up to $35,400 before needing to purchase more material). Although
the franchisee is free to buy all other equipment elsewhere, Bathcrest
requires its franchise owners to purchase its unique resurfacing products from its own facility in Utah.

Now supporting 165 franchises throughout the United States and Canada, Bathcrest provides new franchisees with five days of training in management and marketing, resurfacing techniques, and its other services. No previous plumbing experience is necessary. Ongoing support is provided in the form of monthly newsletters, regular seminars, a toll-free technical support hot line, and marketing and advertising videos. Operations and troubleshooting manuals and videotapes are also provided. Headquarters staff are also readily available to answer questions from the field.

For further information contact:
A. Lloyd Peterson, Bathcrest, Inc., 2425 S. Progress Dr., Salt Lake City, UT 84119, 801-972-1110

B-Dry System, Inc.

Initial license fee: $25,000 to $60,000
Royalties: 6%
Advertising royalties: None
Minimum cash required: $15,000
Capital required: $50,000
Financing: Available
Length of contract: 5 years

In business since: 1958
Franchising since: 1978
Total number of units: 74
Number of company-operated units: 1
Total number of units planned, 1995: 100
Number of company-operated units planned, 1995: 3

Many homeowners think there's not a lot they can do about a damp basement. They're wrong.

Granted, the solution isn't easy, and most contractors provide only a temporary remedy. According to B-Dry System, that's because they're trying to seal the water out, a process doomed to failure, rather that to *control* seepage, the alternative you'll offer. Using a patented waterproofing strategy, you—and your customers—can have confidence in the company's system; all B-Dry franchisees offer an unconditional warranty, guaranteeing against further water leakage for the full life of the structure, regardless of ownership. And articles in *Consumer Reports* and *Popular Science*, as well as the "National Association of Homebuilders' Pilot Study of Basement Water Leakage," attest to the system's success.

The U.S. Census bureau reports that leakage in basements is, by far, the most common home-repair problem. It can be caused by ground conditions or construction defects. Many houses are built on lots with a high water table; when rain or snow saturates the soil, water puts pressure on the basement floor and seeps through cracks or crevices in the cement. Or when "fill dirt" around a house's foundation settles, water-collecting holes can form. Drains can clog; gutters can malfunction. Splices can appear between cellar floors and walls. Whatever the reason, the result for homeowners, especially if they've tried to turn their basement into an extra room, is unpleasant at best, near-disastrous at worst: mildew grows, carpets buckle, tiles curl, floors can even start to cave in and walls begin to crumble. And, of course, household belongings stored down there are ruined.

Over the course of its 30 years in business, B-Dry System has encountered almost every conceivable type of basement leakage problem and has been able to solve most of them. The solution is a pressure relief system around the cellar's interior. With common waterproofing methods like patching floors, sealing cracks, and plastering the outside walls, moisture will be able to get through anyway because the water pressure still isn't abated. The B-Dry system, instead, captures subsurface water that rises from beneath the foundation or comes through the wall, and pumps it out through a pipe. Working inside the basement, you'll first remove a section of the floor near the wall and excavate a trench along the footing. Then, you'll lay a drain channel, drilling holes in the concrete blocks on the bottom of the wall to allow accumulated moisture to flow down the passage and collect in a small reservoir, where it's siphoned out by an electronic pump. The final step is resurfacing the floor.

B-Dry will furnish a list of the equipment and tools you'll need, and let you know about suppliers who carry these materials at preferred prices. At the company's Akron training center, you'll be taught these basement waterproofing procedures, with the aid of one-on-one lessons, written manuals, audiotape and videotape presentations, classroom discussion, and on-the-job instruction. Ongoing field training is also provided regularly, and monthly newsletters keep you further informed about refinements in the system.

Much of your business will come through referrals from former clients. While you won't be using telephone solicitation or other high-pressure tactics to get customers, following B-Dry's policy of letting the company's reputation—and its warranty—speak for itself, you'll learn discriminating sales and marketing methods during your initial training. You'll also receive B-Dry's advertising package, promotional materials honed through three decades of trial and error, from TV and radio spots to newspaper and phone book ad layouts.

The tactic of the company's franchise program is to give you support, but allow you to maintain your independence as well. It's a combination many franchisees appreciate. "I like being in a situation where I have the backing of a national organization, while at the same time having the freedom to make my own decisions," declares Louisville, Kentucky, B-Dry System operator Stephen Rivette. "The response from many satisfied customers has proven that we are on the right track."

For further information contact:
  Joseph Garfinkel, Vice President, B-Dry System, Inc., 1341 Copley Rd., Akron, OH 44320, 1-800-321-0985

California Closet Company, Inc.

Initial license fee: $40,000
Royalties: 5%
Advertising royalties: 5%
Minimum cash required: $150,000 to $200,000
Capital required: $150,000 to $200,000
Financing: None
Length of contract: 10 years

In business since: 1978
Franchising since: 1982
Total number of units: 100
Number of company-operated units: 5
Total number of units planned, 1995: 150
Number of company-operated units planned, 1995: 15

Ever notice how no one ever seems to have enough places to put all the things they own? How most closets are a jumbled attempt to fit too much into too little space?

A pioneer in the growing home services industry that taps America's need for more organized personal time and space, California Closet Company specializes in redesigning the use of existing space in closets, garages, and offices. Trained consultants analyze available space and discuss clients' needs and then design entire systems to increase storage capacity by dramatic proportions. As the era of stay-at-home wives draws to a close and as people become increasingly concerned with maximizing both their work and their leisure time, home services companies like California Closet Company look forward to a period of rapid growth.

As a California Closet franchisee, you will receive two weeks of comprehensive training in closet design, manufacturing, sales, advertising, and management. Training takes place at the company's San Francisco, California, headquarters at no expense to you except for travel and lodging. From site selection to state and local licensing requirements, the company will give you complete preopening support. Operating together, you select the site, plan the interior design of your store, and make equipment purchasing decisions.

High-quality materials and construction and design responsive to clients' needs are essential to the success of your business, so California Closet sets high standards in each area, which you are contractually obliged to meet. The company will maintain close telephone contact with you. Regional managers visit your location whenever necessary to make sure you receive the support you need to operate profitably. Regional meetings, held quarterly, will keep you advised in matters of management, marketing, and manufacturing, and will address various regional topics and concerns. The annual national convention brings all franchisees together with corporate staff to review the past and prepare for the future.

A California Closet franchise should do particularly well in upscale urban areas, or in any region where people tend to hire help rather than do it themselves. Your management and sales skills, flair for design, and knowledge of light carpentry teamed with California Closet Company's experience could result in a formula for success.

For further information contact:
  Megan Hall, California Closet Company, Inc., 1700 Montgomery St., Suite 249, San Francisco, CA 94111, 415-433-9999

Decorating Den Systems, Inc.

Initial license fee: $7,000 to $19,000
Royalties: 7% to 15%
Advertising royalties: 2%
Minimum cash required: $15,900 to $31,900
Capital required: $8,000 to $12,000
Financing: Van and equipment lease available
Length of contract: 10 years

In business since: 1969
Franchising since: 1970
Total number of units: 1,100
Number of company-operated units: None
Total number of units planned, 1995: 2,500
Number of company-operated units planned, 1995: None

"Originally, I wanted to do interior decorating on my own. The problem was, I didn't know suppliers or how to market my own business," remarks Linda Riddiough, a Decorating Den Systems franchisee from Maryland. "Though I am in business for myself, I still have a strong support system backing me in every aspect. This support is a large part of why I am as successful as I am today."

Decorating Den is the only international full-service interior decorator franchise of its kind. Their decorators operate out of the unique "ColorVans" that have become the trademark of Decorating Den Systems. Filled with thousands of samples of drapery, furniture, carpet, wallcovering, and accessories, the ColorVans contain everything you need to work with your clients in their homes. As a decorator, you travel to customers' locations to discuss their needs, plan decorating schemes, and show them samples from which to choose.

Your ColorVan is your Decorating Den office, and with no need to lease or purchase a location, your start-up and overhead costs are minimal. You don't have to maintain an inventory, either, because you only order materials when you need them. Decorating Den has proven to be popular with customers not only because of the in-home service, but because there is no expense to them for the design consultation. All they pay for are the products they purchase.

Decorating Den has developed a system dedicated to the support of its franchisees. "There is support not only at the corporate level, but there are regional directors who provide direction, ongoing training, and support, from the time you become a franchisee, to help ensure a fast start and continued success," says Linda Riddiough. Decorating Den will provide you with one week of intensive training in its classrooms at the corporate headquarters in Bethesda, Maryland. The required courses cover design techniques and principles, business operations, and promotion of your business. And, according to Linda Riddiough, "this one week of intensive training gives the new franchise owner an overview of what being in business for themselves will be like. Intensive corporate training followed by 12 weeks of regional training meant that I had the training and support I needed during those first critical months when starting a new business." An experienced regional coordinator will provide personal assistance as you start to build from this foundation.

Central to the Decorating Den system are the weekly meetings of local decorators. Held in a city no more than two hours from your home, these meetings provide ongoing training as well as "decorating information, sales techniques, and emotional support" that decorators such as Linda Riddiough find helpful. "The group meetings are beneficial because this unique group of interior decorating business owners are not in competition with one another. Each of us has our own geographic area to work within," says Riddiough. "We can discuss common decorating dilemmas, closing sales techniques, as well as share our successes. It makes us feel as though we have a common bond."

Decorating Den provides intensive support and personal assistance in marketing, operations, and customer service by telephone. You can take advantage of this management guidance whenever you feel you need it, no matter how frequently that might be. "Even though there are 1,100 franchise owners worldwide, I always feel I can get help from either my regional director or the corporate staff when I need it," comments Riddiough. Decorating Den conducts periodic seminars, conventions, and runs intermediate and advanced schools. There are 12 intermediate and advanced courses available, held monthly in cities throughout the country. You can attend these classes to sharpen your product knowledge, your management skills, or your sales and marketing techniques, among other things.

There are some nominal materials fees involved in the training programs, but your only significant investments as a Decorating Den franchisee will be in the franchise fee itself and in your ColorVan. Linda Riddiough notes, "If it weren't for franchising, I would have lost a lot of time and money trying to figure out how to run my business. I felt comfortable with Decorating Den's more than 20 years' experience. They have a tested and proven system for success that has worked for me. If I had my own business, I would be just another small business owner. As a franchisee, my company appears in countless articles and advertisements—and that I could never do on my own." And you can save elsewhere as a Decorating Den owner, because franchisees get discounts from approved suppliers, thanks to the company's purchasing power.

"Decorating Den helped me start and build a business. I know it probably sounds too good to be true, but I am truly happy with my choice of a Decorating Den franchise," concludes Linda Riddiough.

For further information contact:
  Decorating Den Systems, Inc., 7910 Woodmont Ave., Suite 200, Bethesda, MD 20814, 301-652-6393 or 1-800-428-1366

Forest Hill Associates

Initial license fee: $25,000 ($35,000 in Virginia)
Royalties: 2% to 5%
Advertising royalties: 1%
Minimum cash required: $25,000 to $35,000
Capital required: $25,000 to $50,000
Financing: None
Length of contract: None

In business since: 1969
Franchising since: 1984
Total number of units: 28
Number of company-operated units: None
Total number of units planned, 1995: 48
Number of company-operated units planned, 1995: None

After more than 20 years in the insurance restoration business, Forest Hill Associates has developed a pretty good understanding of the kinds of problems faced by agents and adjusters in settling property loss claims. At the same time, the company appreciates the concerns of policyholders whose homes or businesses have been damaged by fire, wind, water, or lightning—and who must have repairs done right away.

Don't be surprised, then, if you're called on when the roof has—literally—fallen in and the cold and wet homeowner is complaining to his or her insurance agent hourly. It's a good thing that you'll be able to oblige, offering emergency repair service 24 hours a day, seven days a week, including holidays.

Forest Hill franchisees act as the middle person, working with insurance companies to help their policyholders rebuild their property after minor predicaments and major calamities alike. For the carrier, that means determining the costs of repairing damage that's actually covered by the policy. For the policyholder, it means that repairs are attended to quickly, reliably, and expertly. And it means springing no unpleasant surprises—in price, scope of the work, or completion date—on either party.

Subcontracting the major construction work, you're also equipped to provide basic home improvement services directly to homeowners. Whether it's renovating a kitchen, remodeling a basement, adding a bathroom, or installing a fireplace, you'll plan the project, estimate the costs, hire local professionals, and oversee the job. And, you'll guarantee the work with a one-year warranty.

Running a Forest Hill franchise doesn't require specific experience in the construction or remodeling field, but it does require training. "Our experience over the years," says Robert J. Kasonik, the company's president, "has proven it to be necessary to invest the time and energy in establishing a new dealer." It's a considerable investment, too. First, you'll attend "Technical Training School" at the Charlottesville, Virginia, corporate headquarters for a six-day course, followed by four to six weeks of field instruction, working alongside an experienced franchisee to learn selling, estimating, and production techniques. Travel and lodging are furnished for both sections of the training. Back in your own territory, a Forest Hill staffer will give start-up assistance in setting up your operation, obtaining your necessary licenses, and developing a marketing plan. The representative will also call on local insurance agents to help establish your clientele, and extend technical support while you're completing your first job.

The company supplies computer software that will allow you to figure job costs and estimates, as well as handle payroll and other accounting chores. You're also provided with trade journals, code books, and technical manuals for the construction industry. And you'll receive an initiatory promotional kit, featuring direct mail materials and small-display and yellow pages ad layouts.

Forest Hill's own marketing program targets both insurers and property owners. Along with sending monthly mailings to the major carriers, company personnel make personal visits, conduct seminars, and attend industry conventions. Likewise, newsletters and such free information booklets as "Tips on Surviving a Home Renovation" and "Emergency Tips" are distributed to the private sector. Clever of the company, too, to help these potential customers make the connection between thoughts of remodeling and urgent repairs and the name Forest Hill.

For further information contact:
  Robert J. Kasonik, President, Forest Hill Enterprises, Inc., 2320-B Hunters Way, Charlottesville, VA 22901, 804-971-5641

Four Seasons Greenhouses

Initial license fee: $2,500, $5,000, or $10,000
Royalties: 2.5%
Advertising royalties: None
Minimum cash required: $10,750
Capital required: $10,750 to $90,000
Financing: NA
Length of contract: 10 years

In business since: 1975
Franchising since: 1985
Total number of units: 271
Number of company-operated units: 4
Total number of units planned, 1995: 400
Number of company-operated units planned, 1995: 4

Four Seasons sees big profit potential in the trends reflected in certain U.S. housing statistics, and many entrepreneurs apparently agree, because in its first year of franchising, the company sold 160 units. With more than 40 million homes over 25 years old in the United States, a fertile market exists for the remodeling business. In 1985 alone,

Americans added 1.5 million rooms, 3.6 million kitchens, and 4.1 million bathrooms to their homes. About two-thirds of Four Seasons' business comes from people improving their homes, and the remainder comes from commercial clients and new home construction.

Professionally installed glass enclosures, the main product you will sell as a franchised dealer, include atriums and solarium-type room additions. The company points out that people are sensitive about work done on their homes, and they will go out of their way to find a "name" company to do the work. However, few big names exist in the remodeling business. Since Four Seasons builds name recognition through extensive advertising, owning one of its franchises gives you an advantage over your competition.

Opportunities to sell glass enclosures to commercial customers are expanding as businesses design their premises for a more light and airy look. Some of the big fast-food chains that have added these structures to their restaurants include Arby's, Burger King, McDonald's, and Taco Bell.

You will sell your product from a showroom located on an easily accessible road, preferably near other businesses that sell home building, renovating, and decorating products, such as lumberyards, appliance stores, and carpeting businesses. You will not rely on walk-in trade in this field, so you don't have to pay high shopping center rents for the 600 to 1,200 square feet you will need. In fact, you can convert an old factory building or freestanding house to a Four Seasons center.

In your showroom you will display two models of the company's prefabricated greenhouses. Skilled subcontractors will do most of your installations, usually working on a fixed-fee basis. The company will put you in touch with subcontractors in your area. You will need a general manager and sales manager, if you don't plan to fill those roles yourself, and a construction manager with at least five years of construction experience. Your construction manager will work directly with the subcontractors.

The company trains franchisees at its Holbrook, New York, home office for two weeks. Classroom instruction there covers business management, selling, product knowledge, accounting, and marketing. Then franchisees receive a week of hands-on training at their showrooms, just before their grand opening.

Advertising is a strong point with Four Seasons. The company commits 7.5 percent of its total revenue to advertising, with 5 percent going directly to you and your fellow franchisees for local campaigns. In effect, it runs a cooperative advertising program in which the company's contribution is 100 percent instead of the more typical 50 percent. The remainder of the advertising budget goes for company advertisements in publications like *House Beautiful, House and Garden, Better Homes and Gardens, Home, New Shelter, Metropolitan Home,* and *Popular Science*. The company will also send you the names of anyone from your area who responds to one of its national magazine advertisements so that you can follow up and possibly make a sale.

You do not have to confine your business to the sale of glass enclosures. Four Seasons franchisees often sell related products, such as doors, windows, skylights, ceramic tiles, hot tubs, and spas.

Your protected franchise territory will include about 250,000 people, although for a lesser fee you can buy a minifranchise in a rural area, at a smaller investment, that encompasses a population of about 75,000.

For further information contact:
  Tony Russo, Four Seasons Greenhouses, 5005 Vets Hwy., Holbrook, NY 11741,
  516-563-4000

Kitchen Tune-Up, Inc.

Initial license fee: $9,995
Royalties: 7%
Advertising royalties: NA
Minimum cash required: $11,495 to $11,995
Capital required: $11,495 to $11,995
Financing: NA
Length of contract: 8 years, renewable to 32 years

In business since: 1986
Franchising since: 1989
Total number of units: 123
Number of company-operated units: None
Total number of units planned, 1995: 500
Number of company-operated units planned, 1995: None

"It's nice to be able to look a potential customer in the eye knowing I am offering a service they can really use," South Carolina Kitchen Tune-Up franchisee Ralph Kaner exclaims. That service, restoring wooden cabinet surfaces without sanding, stripping, or varnishing, makes a quick and affordable alternative to kitchen remodeling. Kitchen Tune-Up's nine-step process usually takes only two to four hours to complete—no curing or drying time required—for a price that's commonly under $200.

Using the Kitchen Tune-Up equipment, materials, and methods, you'll remove smoke and grease that permeate kitchen cabinets and damage the wood fiber, apply oils that feed the cabinet surface, touch up nicks and scratches, fix squeaky hinges and hard-to-open drawers, install decorative handles, and buff and wax countertops. But your services are hardly limited to the kitchen. Paneling, staircases, doors, beam ceilings, windowsills, bookcases, and wood furniture of all kinds anywhere in the house can be rejuvenated and revitalized with the Kitchen Tune-Up process. Business establishments, too, are regular Kitchen Tune-Up customers, with many franchisees receiving from one- to two-thirds of their business from commercial accounts, including hotel and restaurant chains, banks, offices, and public buildings.

Moreover, for no extra franchise fee, you can add two additional services to your basic Kitchen Tune-Up operation. You'll be able to offer your customers a full line of custom-measured kitchen cabinet doors, available in a variety of woods, styles, and finishes. And you'll receive training in closet organization to provide consultation and installation of rods, shelving, and drawers for refurbishing closet spaces.

Most Kitchen Tune-Up franchisees work out of their homes, keeping start-up and overhead costs low. The company furnishes you with the tools and equipment you'll require for your work, as well as an initial supply of the oils, polishes, and other wood-treatment products.

Before opening for business, though, you and an employee will attend a one-week training program at Kitchen Tune-Up's Aberdeen, South Dakota, home offices, with meals and lodging expenses covered by the company. Through a combination of roundtable discussions, video presentations, role-playing sessions, and hands-on exercises, you'll learn the Kitchen Tune-Up wood treatment process as well as other aspects of the operation, from employee hiring to sales techniques. Once the formal instruction is complete, you'll have the opportunity to attend regional follow-up training seminars or to return to Aberdeen for a refresher course.

You'll also be assigned an account representative who will help you develop an initial business plan plus marketing strategies for your exclusive territory. Learning how to target home shows, realtors, and local media, and how to make maximum use out of customer referrals, you'll be supplied with advertising materials developed and tested by Kitchen Tune-Up, including mailers, flyers, and telemarketing formats, along with guidelines for running discount and incentive promotional programs.

For further information contact:
  David Haglund, President, Kitchen Tune-Up, Inc., 131 N. Roosevelt St., Aberdeen, SD 57401, 605-225-4049 or 1-800-333-6385, fax 605-225-1371

Mr. Build Handi-Man Services, Inc.

Initial license fee: $26,900
Royalties: 7%
Advertising royalties: 4%
Minimum cash required: $44,900
Capital required: $60,000 to $70,000
Financing: None
Length of contract: 5 years

In business since: 1990
Franchising since: 1990
Total number of units: 34
Number of company-operated units: None
Total number of units planned, 1995: 300
Number of company-operated units planned, 1995: None

Homeowners and businesses alike keep putting off those nagging building repairs. Leaky faucets, stuck doors, broken windows, dirty filters, balky locks, loose railings or stairs, clogged gutters: the chores just accumulate when people have neither the inclination nor the ability to do it themselves and when even having to go to the trouble of hiring a bunch of different repair specialists—plumbers, painters, masons, carpenters, appliance maintenance people—takes too much time. Then there's the problem of finding a professional who'll take on a small job in the first place.

But a single toll-free call to Mr. Build Handi-Man Services can begin the process of getting all this work done. A subsidiary of Mr. Build, a home addition and remodeling network, the company specializes in handling exactly these kinds of modest residential and commercial property repair, maintenance, and renovation tasks. Dispatchers on the 800 line contact the local Mr. Build Handi-Man operation—by beeper or car phone in an emergency. If it's your territory, you'll arrange to meet with the customer, compute an estimate on the project, and gather the workers to undertake it.

You don't need to know contracting yourself; your role, rather, is to manage the job and oversee the actual contractors. Because you're not the specialist, the range of services you'll be able to offer is vast: lighting fixture replacement, appliance installation, small interior and exterior painting jobs, carpentry, electrical, plumbing, roof repair, and masonry work, to mention only some of the possibilities. And when your own maintenance and repair staff is overloaded or doesn't have the expertise to handle a particular project, you can "borrow" workers from other Mr. Build franchisees.

Landlords may ask you to clean up after tenants. Shopkeepers may need you to repave a sidewalk. Home owners may want you to put up a fence in the backyard. Or your customer might simply hand you a whole list of repairs that need attention, which you'll provide, on time, within the budget, and with a one-year guarantee.

Your only restriction is to limit the work to small assignments. Customarily, you won't take projects costing more than $2,000 or taking over two days to complete, referring larger jobs to the Mr. Build parent company. But there's a high profit margin in this kind of work and a broad market, too. Your services are especially attractive to small businesses, who don't employ a regular maintenance staff, elderly homeowners, who can't perform the tasks themselves, and two-income families, who have no time for do-it-themselves house repairs but who *do* have the money to hire someone else. Additionally, many vendors of home improvement goods are employing Mr. Build Handi-Man franchisees to see to the installation and maintenance of their products, furnishing customer leads and advertising for you along the way.

You'll be assigned a protected territory, kept to a manageable size but large enough to provide an extensive client base. The company will help you find and hire skilled workers, who'll be given supplementary technical instruction to amplify their experience. Attending a five-day franchisee training course yourself, at a time and place to be determined, you'll be given a computer software package that allows you to track customers, do quick cost estimates, handle work schedules, and take care of accounting and other administrative duties.

The Mr. Build network conducts a program to generate leads from offices, plants, stores, and other commercial sites. It will also prepare a direct marketing campaign for your first year in business, attracting both business and homeowner customers in your territory. You'll be outfitted with flyers, coupons, direct mail pieces, and ad layouts, while the company continues telemarketing and promotional efforts of its own.

Because you won't have to unlearn bad business practices, Mr. Build actually prefers you have no previous experience in the home repair and maintenance field. The company also encourages you to run your Handi-Man service from home. In addition to individual operations, the company offers an Area Development Agent option. ADAs are responsible for a minimum of 30 individual franchisees in an exclusive development area, receiving commissions on each franchise sold and sharing in the royalties that these Handi-Man businesses generate.

Incidentally, franchisees like Connecticut's Liz Talcot will tell you that the Handi-*Man* and *Mr.* Build labels are not for men only.

For further information contact:
  Mr. Build Handi-Man Services, Inc., 628 Hebron Ave., Glastonbury, CT 06033,
  1-800-242-8453

Perma-Glaze, Inc.

Initial license fee: $27,500
Royalties: None
Advertising royalties: None
Minimum cash required: $27,500
Capital required: $3,000
Financing: Available
Length of contract: 10 years

In business since: 1978
Franchising since: 1981
Total number of units: 162
Number of company-operated units: 1
Total number of units planned, 1995: 325
Number of company-operated units planned, 1995: 1

When a bathtub or sink becomes stained, scratched, or cracked, it just looks plain ugly. Not only that, it's unhygienic, too, with germs and dirt building up on the pitted and porous surface. But there's an alternative to living with the grime and ugliness or replacing the basin, and when you become a Perma-Glaze franchisee, you can be the one to provide it.

Perma-Glaze specializes in the reglazing and restoration of worn or damaged bathroom and kitchen fixtures, as well as tiles, countertops, and appliances, whether they're made of formica, enamel, acrylic, even cultured marble or cast iron. Using the company's exclusive process, you'll create a clean, durable surface, enhanced with rich color. First, the old surface is chemically treated and removed. Then, you'll fill any chips and scratches, finally applying several coats of the Perma-Glaze synthetic porcelain finish. The work almost always takes less than half a day; after 48 hours of curing, the fixture is ready to use again.

Because it's not epoxy-based, the glaze won't yellow over time, a promise backed by a warranty. Your customer is saved the hassle of torn-out plumbing, ripped-up floors, and damaged walls that accompany getting a new sink or tub. And at about 15 percent of the cost of replacement, it's an even more appealing option.

Your refinishing process is available in any color, including neutral and earth tones or bolder pigments, to match other fixtures in the room. Your customer might also want to glaze the interior with one color, using a coordinated accent shade on the exterior, a favored choice for those again-popular antique claw-foot tubs.

Perma-Glaze supplies the basic equipment, tools, and chemicals you'll need, and teaches you how to use them to perform the refinishing procedure in a five-day training session, with lodging, meals, and transportation all provided courtesy of the company. Practicing until you are comfortably proficient with each step of the process, you'll also cover such business administration procedures as pricing and billing, and you'll learn sales techniques for cultivating clients like hotels, condominium complexes, hospitals and other institutions, and apartment complexes, in addition to private homeowners. You'll also have a private session with a Perma-Glaze marketing consultant, who'll go through with you, one by one, the major dailies, weeklies, and "shoppers" in your area, along with the local phone directory and TV listings, to help you develop a cohesive, overall promotion plan.

Perma-Glaze's national advertising program will complement your own efforts at no additional cost, with all inquiries from your territory to the company's well-publicized 800 information number directed to you. You'll also have access to preproduced materials including a TV spot. "Every time it airs, we receive several calls within the next 30 minutes," report San Diego franchisees Ed and Sandy Meyer. Because fixture refinishing is still an unfamiliar service to many, the home office PR staff places numerous articles in widely distributed trade journals and home improvement magazines. They've also arranged with JCPenney and other stores to carry displays promoting the Perma-Glaze process. And you can make other deals on your own, as Albuquerque, New Mexico, franchisees Diane and Jim Deignan have. "We have close to a dozen of the Perma-Glaze retail displays around town—we've placed them in boutiques, hardware stores, and home improvement centers—and established ongoing business relationships with property managers, plumbing contractors, and interior designers, to name a few."

There are Perma-Glaze operations in 31 states and three foreign countries. Franchisees are assigned an exclusive territory. Working either full or part time, you can run your business from your own home, requiring only a phone, worktable, and dry place to store your chemicals. The company also recommends you have a van or truck.

For further information contact:
  Dale Young, President, Perma-Glaze, Inc., 1638 S. Research Loop Rd., Suite 160, Tucson, AZ 85710, 1-800-332-7397

Worldwide Refinishing Systems

Initial license fee: $18,000
Royalties: 5%
Advertising royalties: 2%
Minimum cash required: $15,750
Capital required: $27,100
Financing: None
Length of contract: 10 years

In business since: 1970
Franchising since: 1986
Total number of units: 340
Number of company-operated units: 1
Total number of units planned, 1995: 750
Number of company-operated units planned, 1995: 1

Worldwide's claim that it uses "space-age technology" isn't an exaggeration. The coating involved in the company's bathtub, shower, and countertop refinishing process is the same solution, after all, that was used on the NASA vehicle that traveled on the moon. That substance proved to be the right stuff for our Apollo astronauts, and Worldwide notes that it does the job for homeowners and businesses, too.

According to Worldwide, the National Bureau of Standards has based the criteria for refinishing tubs on the Worldwide system. The EPA and OSHA have both approved the process as well. Worldwide, you see, avoids the lead and isocyanates that many refinishing technicians use, which smell horrendous and often require pumping oxygen in and sending customers out for several hours while the work is being performed.

The Worldwide system can be applied to refrigerators and range tops, kitchen sinks and whirlpools, along with other items made out of porcelain, formica, acrylic, metal, and cultured marble. Fifty-six standard colors, plus custom mixes, are available. About half of your business will come from the industrial and commercial market, providing many opportunities for large projects. Hotel and apartment complex accounts will keep you particularly busy, but you'll also get assignments like fiberglass chairs and booths at fast-food restaurants, restroom wall dividers in dormitories, and elevator panels and decorative surfaces in office buildings.

Essentially, the Worldwide refinishing technique involves a seven-step process: (1) clean the work area; (2) sand or etch the surface to get it ready for the primer; (3) apply the primer coat; (4) apply three finishing coats; (5) clean up; (6) give care instructions to your customer; (7) collect your money. All signs of stains, scratches, cracks, chips, and burns are gone. Backed by a 10-year warranty, the Worldwide finish is bonded, won't absorb water, and is more resistant to acids and nonabrasive cleansers than the original porcelain.

With the option of several exclusive or nonexclusive territory arrangements, you can run either a single-van operation, doing the actual refinishing work yourself, or a multivan franchise, with full-time employees going out on assignments while you concentrate on customer relations and business expansion. Since your only major office requirements are a phone and answering service, a place to coordinate scheduling, and room for storing your inventory, you can operate out of your home, at least until your service grows beyond four vans. You'll be able to obtain the refinishing supplies through the company's distribution center, including new products that have been field tested by the Worldwide's research and development task force, and you can take advantage of the company's van and equipment leasing packages to reduce your initial investment.

During the two-week training school, you'll learn technical and business management skills; like many franchisees, you may decide to return every six months or so for a review and to pick up new ideas and procedures. Employees can also attend, and you'll be receiving materials to conduct additional training programs for your staff back home. Seminars on both national and regional levels are held as well, covering sales, vocational, and even self-improvement topics.

While you're starting out, a Worldwide consultant will be working closely with you to assist in establishing your client base and reaching your initial business goals. Many franchisees find that they get enough work through referrals alone and don't need to maintain a massive advertising program; nevertheless, the company's marketing directors will show you effective ways to use home and garden shows, telemarketing, newspaper ads, and perhaps TV commercials to get new customers.

The fact that this is a cash business generating immediate income is one of the most attractive features to Worldwide franchises. There's a high profit margin, too: a typical bathtub job will net you $285 for about $40 in materials and four to six hours of work. Because replacing the tub can cost from $800 to $2,400, it's a profitable venture for your customers as well. Another advantage is that Worldwide is not a fad enterprise: While there aren't many moon rovers around that need refinishing, as long as bathtubs, showers, countertops, tile, and appliances remain, in rough economic times, there are many businesses and homeowners who prefer resurfacing to replacement. In the company's words, "Those people who evaluate a business strictly on its merits without ego involvement will find [Worldwide] meets the requirements for solid, stable, business growth."

For further information contact:
  Charles H. Wallis, Executive Vice President, Worldwide Refinishing Systems,
  P.O. Box 3146, Waco, TX 76703, 817-756-2282 or 1-800-369-9361

Laundry and Dry Cleaning

Dryclean-U.S.A.

Initial license fee: None
Royalties: $600/month for the first year
Advertising royalties: None
Minimum cash required: $50,000 to $60,000
Capital required: $60,000 to $70,000
Financing: Available
Length of contract: NA

In business since: 1977
Franchising since: 1977
Total number of units: 270
Number of company-operated units: 80
Total number of units planned, 1995: NA
Number of company-operated units planned, 1995: NA

When you drop off your shirts, blouses, and suits for cleaning, you patronize one of the biggest retail businesses in America. The 30,000 dry
cleaning stores in this country employ hundreds of thousands of people. The machines these services use to dry-clean your clothes only
look forbidding and complicated. In fact, they operate much like your
household washing machine, except that they use a solvent instead of
soap and water. And pressing is simply ironing on a larger scale.

All this suggests that you don't need special mechanical skills or
knowledge to succeed in the dry cleaning business. That's the point
that Dryclean-U.S.A. representatives will make when you discuss the
purchase of a franchise with them. They will also emphasize the crucial choice of location in establishing a profitable dry cleaning business. The single most important thing from the customer's point of
view—aside from good service and competitive prices—is convenience. In a "drop-off" business, the store must be near other places
that customers frequent, like supermarkets. Dryclean-U.S.A.'s site selection research, conducted by a full-time expert staff with years of
experience, offers franchisees a distinct advantage over going it alone.

In addition to helping you choose a location and negotiate a lease,
Dryclean-U.S.A. will teach you the dry cleaning business at its Florida
training center. You and your manager will get a thorough grounding
in processing, spotting, pressing, packaging, quality control, customer

service, public relations, and employee training. The company will gear the training, a mix of classroom work and hands-on experience in a store, to your needs and abilities.

You and your manager will get further training at your store before it opens, and the company will arrange for the delivery of your equipment, which it will install and test to make sure it operates smoothly. The franchisor offers a special grand opening package at a nominal charge, and will provide ongoing instruction in new equipment and processes.

You will find Dryclean-U.S.A.'s expertise in promotional activities particularly valuable to you in your new business, since your customers' dry cleaning needs change with the season. You will need to bring your various services—cleaning down comforters before winter comes, for example—to your customer's attention as each season approaches. Throughout the year the company will give you advice on advertising.

Currently available locations include California, Florida, Maryland, New Jersey, Pennsylvania, Virginia, and Washington.

For further information contact:
 Dryclean-U.S.A., 12515 North Kendall Dr., Suite 400, Miami, FL 33186, 305-270-0000

One-Hour Martinizing Inc.

Initial license fee: $20,000
Royalties: 4% of gross monthly sales
Advertising royalties: 0.5% of gross monthly sales
Minimum cash required: $65,000
Capital required: $155,000 to $235,000
Financing: Company will help you find sources of financing
Length of contract: NA

In business since: 1949
Franchising since: 1949
Total number of units: 853
Number of company-operated units: None
Total number of units planned, 1995: 928 per year
Number of company-operated units planned, 1995: NA

Before the late 1940s, this business could not have existed. The biggest selling point of Martinizing dry cleaning stores is that garments, cleaned on the premises, can be ready in as little as an hour. But until the late forties, highly flammable solvents, the only ones available for dry cleaning, could not be used in densely populated areas. Typically, dry cleaners sent the clothes dropped off at their local stores out for processing, and customers could not get them back for as long as 10 days. A substance called perchloroethylene changed that, making possible this very successful business.

Martin, the largest dry cleaning franchisor, stresses the importance of store image in the $2.2-billion-a-year dry cleaning business. Most small independent stores, the company says, look dingy and unappealing to the consumer, creating a golden opportunity for Martin stores, with their bright, airy appearance. The company adds that, with the increasing use of natural fabrics and the rise in the number of two-career families, the demand for dry cleaning services will go up sharply. Martin's quick processing, offering consumers convenience, puts its franchisees in a good position to take advantage of this increase in business. (Some Martin franchises add to their profits by supplementing dry cleaning with shirt laundering and alterations.)

Just as Martin offers consumers convenience, it offers franchisees efficiency. The company, through much experience, has developed a store layout based on a design it calls "Work Flow." Martin systematizes the entire dry cleaning process, from the moment the customer brings in garments to the final delivery of those cleaned garments into the customer's hands, reducing all unnecessary movement. This not only speeds the cleaning process, it reduces the cost. The company says it supplies state-of-the-art dry cleaning equipment, and you can consult the company's experts through a hot line on any problems related to the machines.

You do not need experience in the dry cleaning business to become a franchisee. But you—or at least your manager—will have to take a three-week training program at company headquarters in Cincinnati and at a plant location. The program consists of one week devoted to classroom work and two weeks of in-store experience. Management subjects covered include staffing and personnel management, advertising, marketing, and accounting. Technical skills covered include marking-in and tagging, spotting and cleaning, finishing, assembly, and packing.

The company provides guidance to its franchisees at every stage of the start-up process, beginning with site selection. Through its computer data base, the company will prepare for you a grand opening promotion specifically targeted to the potential customers in your area.

For further information contact:
  Frank Flack, Development Coordinator, Martin Franchises, Inc., 2005 Ross Ave., Cincinnati, OH 45212, 1-800-827-0207 ext. 322

Lawn Care

Lawn Doctor

Initial license fee: $25,500
Royalties: 10%
Advertising royalties: 5% to 10%
Minimum cash required: $15,500
Capital required: $30,500
Financing: Up to $10,000 available — 5 years at 12% interest for qualified
    applicants
Length of contract: 20 years

In business since: 1967
Franchising since: 1969
Total number of units: 290
Number of company-operated units: 1
Total number of units planned, 1995: 500
Number of company-operated units planned, 1995: 4

Picture a million acres of crabgrass and dandelion—enough to break a suburbanite's heart. Lawn Doctor cares for that amount of territory, and the lawns under its treatment no longer have such problems. Lawn Doctor franchisees have a curbside manner that has made the company number one in America in franchised automated lawn care.

"It was one of the least costly ways to get into my own business and get good training," says Robert Dekraft of his experience as a Lawn Doctor franchisee. He started his business in Fairfax, Virginia, because he "could see the growth potential for the future in the lawn-care industry." He adds: "The rewards have been gratifying."

A Lawn Doctor franchise involves no inventory or real estate, so you can focus your attention on attracting customers and giving them good service. That service consists of seeding, weeding, feeding, and spraying lawns with liquid and granular chemical or nonchemical solutions using Lawn Doctor's Turf Tamer, a patented machine that looks something like a lawn mower. With Turf Tamer, you can cover a 12-foot-wide area with one pass and distribute four separate materials simultaneously over at least 1,000 square feet per minute—all evenly and accurately with only an hour of training. The self-propelled machine also saves you a lot of huffing and puffing.

You will get the training you need at the company's training center in East Windsor, New Jersey. In two weeks you will learn all aspects of the Lawn Doctor system, including sales, equipment maintenance, and agronomy. According to Robert Dekraft, the company has a "good training and retraining staff." Periodic local and regional seminars will enable you to get additional training after you start your business. In addition, to help you through your crucial first year of operations, the company will assign you one of its field representatives, who will keep in close touch with you, offering advice and guidance in your new endeavor.

Your franchise package includes hand tools and accessories, the right to lease a Turf Tamer, truck layouts and modifications, a bookkeeping system, and advertising and promotional support. You must lease Lawn Doctor's patented equipment—mainly the Turf Tamer—from them. You can buy or lease all other products and supplies from other companies.

For further information contact:
E. I. Reid, National Franchise Sales Director, Lawn Doctor, 142 Hwy. 34, Matawan, NJ 07747, 1-800-631-5660

Spring-Green Lawn Care Corporation

Initial license fee: $12,900
Royalties: 9% declining to 6%
Advertising royalties: 2%
Minimum cash required: $16,000
Capital required: $13,500 to $30,500
Financing: None
Length of contract: 10 years

In business since: 1977
Franchising since: 1977
Total number of units: 132
Number of company-operated units: 12
Total number of units planned, 1995: 200
Number of company-operated units planned, 1995: 12

Professional lawn and landscape services continue to grow. The increase in the number of two-income families has put leisure time at a premium. In addition, most homeowners realize that beautiful and healthy trees and shrubs and a well-groomed lawn can add to the value of their property. Since more families are spending part of their joint incomes on home maintenance, prospects for home lawn care look promising.

Spring-Green thoroughly prepares you to open and operate your business, which you can run from your home. Robert O'Brien, a Spring-Green franchisee in Morrisville, Pennsylvania, says: "They provided an excellent business plan format with which I easily obtained a business loan from a bank." The company's franchise package contains what you need to begin servicing customers. With the equipment they provide, you can service 20 to 30 lawns a day.

You also receive the benefit of the company's technical expertise. Spring-Green's intensive training will teach the basics of operating a franchise. By the time you arrive at company headquarters in Plainfield, Illinois, for a week of formal instruction, you will have spent a week with a pretraining home-study program. Training in Plainfield consists of classroom instructions; you then receive additional hands-on training at your local franchise. You pay only for your transportation to and from Plainfield.

During your term as a franchisee, "the company provides many training seminars, where new ideas are provided for both franchise owners and employees. This constant use of new ideas and methods keeps us on top of the industry," notes Robert O'Brien. The topics of these seminars range from technical updates to business management, financial planning, marketing, and other such subjects. The company's regional field representative will provide guidance in the ongoing operation of your business.

Spring-Green's accounting system minimizes the amount of time you have to spend on your books. Every week you will receive computer-generated reports on your sales performance and other important items. The company has special computer programs designed to handle the basic operation of your franchise, and will lease you equipment and computers.

The company helps you set up marketing programs tailored specifically for your local market area. Marketing materials, procedures, and ongoing guidance enable you to compete effectively.

For further information contact:
  Spring-Green Lawn Care Corporation, 11927 Spaulding School Dr., Plainfield, IL 60544, 1-800-435-4051

Maid Services

Maid Brigade

Initial license fee: $16,900
Royalties: 7%
Advertising royalties: 2%
Minimum cash required: $32,000
Capital required: $16,000
Financing: Available
Length of contract: 10 years

In business since: 1982
Franchising since: 1982
Total number of units: 218
Number of company-operated units: 5
Total number of units planned, 1995: 450
Number of company-operated units planned, 1995: 5

Recent changes in the American economy have provided fertile ground for the growth of services like housecleaning. Neither adult in the increasing number of two-income families really has the time to clean house. And with their increased income, why should they have to perform this task when they can easily pay others to do it? In addition, young professional singles who work long hours and make good salaries can afford to pay other people to clean their homes.

Maid Brigade franchisees take advantage of this growing market by providing speedy, efficient housecleaning service through a system of three- or four-person cleaning teams. Each team cleans several homes a day, carrying cleaning equipment and supplies with them from house to house. Maid Brigade owner-operators keep numbered keys to their customers' homes in their office, unless customers prefer to leave a key for the cleaning team in a concealed place. Customers pay simply by leaving cash or a check on their kitchen table.

The franchise package from Maid Brigade includes scheduling and administrative software, uniforms, equipment, and supplies for your first team of maids. You also receive 15,000 advertising mailers and pamphlets, stationery supplies, route logs, and customer record forms. In addition, you can bond your employees through Maid Brigade.

Your week of training in the Maid Brigade system will take place in Atlanta. Your license fee covers this instruction, airfare, and accommodations. The training will include field experience with a Maid Brigade team as it cleans customers' homes. Classroom work will cover all aspects of personnel, including interviewing, evaluation, and training. Administrative topics include payroll, scheduling, dealing with complaints, insurance and bonding, vehicles, key control, and the company's scheduling computer software. You also learn about marketing, advertising, promotional mailings, the competition, and pricing.

Maid Brigade prides itself on its support system, which operates through its 10 regional offices. Maid Brigade visits and consults with all franchisees at no cost.

To assist you with your local promotional campaign, Maid Brigade supplies you, where available, with computer-generated market research based on the demographics of your area.

Maid Brigade has no requirements about your place of business—

you can even work out of your home—nor does it require you to buy any products from the company.

For further information contact:
    Don Hay, Maid Brigade, 850 Indian Trail, Atlanta, GA 30247, 1-800-722-MAID

McMaid Inc.

Initial license fee: $10,000 to $30,000
Royalties: 6%
Advertising royalties: 2%
Minimum cash required: $18,400
Capital required: $18,400 to $43,600
Financing: None
Length of contract: 10 years

In business since: 1975
Franchising since: 1985
Total number of units: 15
Number of company-operated units: 4
Total number of units planned, 1995: 100
Number of company-operated units planned, 1995: 10

Contrary to what you may think, the name "McMaid" was never meant to capitalize on the popularity of a certain burger-making establishment. When Christine McLaughlin created the housekeeping agency, she, as many entrepreneurs are wont, named the business after herself: McLaughlin Maids. It was only after customers and staffers became used to truncating the cumbersome title that the management decided to make the shortened McMaid appellation official. The expected legal squabbles with the folks at McDonalds did ensue, but have all been resolved. Commissioners of the U.S. Patent and Trademark Office ruled that McMaid Inc. could continue to use its "Mc" name—as long as the company didn't go into the fast-food business.

McMaid has no intentions to go that route anyway; the company takes its chosen field seriously. "Housekeeping ain't no joke," as Louisa May Alcott wrote in *Little Women*. Today, women and men who find themselves with disposable income—and without time or patience—are happy to leave the work in the hands of professionals like the McMaid team.

The mission of McMaid franchisees is to offer more than merely hired hands with mops, and to avoid the hassles other agencies cause by missing appointments and assigning different maids every visit. You'll supply a uniform—and uniformed—cleaning staff of trained specialists who'll perform personalized service tailored to the specific demands of the customer, reliably and at affordable prices. They'll scour and disinfect bathrooms, wash and iron laundry, polish silver, wax floors, clean refrigerators and ovens—these housekeepers will even do windows (insides only). Bringing along the cleaning equipment and supplies, from vacuums to cleansers, your team executes preassigned tasks thoroughly and efficiently—"not one wasted motion" is the company's canon. Flexibility is another byword: you'll provide four workers for one hour, one worker for four hours, or any other desired combination.

Learning how to hire and train housekeepers who will please your customers and meet your own quality standards is only one part of the franchisee instruction program. You'll spend two weeks being taught the procedures for managing a McMaid operation, with an emphasis on hands-on experience that's cultivated by your joining cleaning teams as they make their daily rounds. Subjects you'll cover in the classroom include scheduling and pricing, sales and marketing, administration methods, customer relations, and key control. The company outfits you with operations manuals with further instructions on handling day-to-day business, and field representatives will drop by periodically to offer personal assistance in your territory. Attending regional and national management seminars, you'll also receive the results of tests conducted regularly by the company's research and development staff on new cleaning products and techniques.

Through McMaid's national manufacturer accounts, you'll be able to obtain the recommended equipment and materials at bulk discounts. The company directs a marketing program, and will supply you with promotional pieces, paying for $5,000 of launch advertising in your territory. You'll also be able to take advantage of McMaid's comprehensive business and medical insurance policies.

Either leasing an office or operating from their homes, successful McMaid franchisees employ several cleaning teams that together serve up to 100 customers daily, and according to Andrew Wright, the company's president, the average sales-per-office rate exceeds that of all other franchised maid services. Currently, there are McMaid operations in New York City, Boston, Chicago, and Minneapolis–St. Paul, but the company will expand to other areas that franchisees wish to develop.

For further information contact:
 John Chesny, National Franchise Sales Manager, McMaid Inc., 10 W. Kinzie, Chicago, IL 60610, 312-321-6250 or 1-800-444-6250, fax 312-321-9716

Merry Maids, Inc.

Initial license fee: $18,500
Royalties: 7%
Advertising royalties: None
Minimum cash required: $18,500
Capital required: $10,000 to $15,000
Financing: Available up to $10,000 franchise fee
Length of contract: 5 years

In business since: 1980
Franchising since: 1980
Total number of units: 500
Number of company-operated units: 1
Total number of units planned, 1995: 870
Number of company-operated units planned, 1995: 1

As more and more women head out of the home for the business world, they leave behind a need for services that complement their new life-styles. This trend has meant rapid growth for Merry Maids, the country's largest maid service franchisor.

Merry Maids offers a systematic approach to training, cleaning, marketing, managing an office, and developing a franchise territory. The company's package includes the industry's most comprehensive training curriculum for new franchise owners; exclusive computer software providing franchisees with an entire information management system; equipment, supplies, and exclusive Merry Maid cleaning products to equip two two-person cleaning teams, and a comprehensive library of professionally produced employee hiring, training, and safety videotapes.

The convenience of Merry Maids' comprehensive systems appealed to Suzanne Young, owner of a Merry Maid franchise in Manhattan Beach, California. She says, "I haven't cleaned in years. Merry Maids trained me to delegate the dirty work, and to sell the same concept to time-starved people. It works. Business just keeps getting better."

Merry Maids trains its new franchise owners at the corporate headquarters in Omaha, Nebraska. The five-day course, taught by instructors experienced in managing a Merry Maids franchise, includes hiring and training of employees, marketing, selling, cleaning, accounting, and scheduling.

The company provides guidelines on site selection, lease arrangements, and furnishing a Merry Maids office. You can consult company personnel about your ongoing business but just as important is the support franchisees receive from their fellow Merry Maids operators. As a Merry Maids franchisee, you're supported by regional coordinators in the field, who also are franchisees, and you can take advantage of the company's buddy system. Established franchisees keep their eyes on new Merry Maids businesses and lend a helping hand to neighboring operations when the need arises.

After the initial week-long training period, Merry Maids stresses support communication with franchisees. There are three regional meetings a year and a national convention in Omaha, where company franchisees can exchange hints, share experiences, and receive further assistance from Merry Maids professionals. The company also uses a computer modem–based weekly bulletin board, newsletters, videotape presentations, and special field workshops to communicate and extend assistance to its franchise owners.

Rich Hobbs, a franchisee in Huntsville, Alabama, says, "Looking back, I should have started sooner. In less than a year, I surpassed some pretty aggressive goals. The training, start-up, and support is rock-solid, just like the Merry Maids people behind it. They really know the business."

For further information contact:
  Bob Burdge, Paul Hogan, or Jon Nelson, Merry Maids, Inc., 11117 Mill Valley Rd., Omaha, NE 68154, 1-800-798-8000 (in Canada, 1-800-345-5535)

Molly Maid, Inc.

Initial license fee: $14,900
Royalties: 3% to 5%
Advertising royalties: Up to 2%
Minimum cash required: $30,000
Capital required: $30,000
Financing: None
Length of contract: 10 years

In business since: 1984
Franchising since: 1984
Total number of units: 300
Number of company-operated units: None
Total number of units planned, 1995: 700
Number of company-operated units planned, 1995: None

This business's time has clearly come. With the United States now largely a nation of two-income families, people have fewer hours to devote to housecleaning. In some families, the wife has the double burden of both bringing in an income and doing the housework. Other families split cleaning chores between husband and wife. Still others, especially professionals with good incomes, hire a maid. People in that last category, and single professionals, provide a potentially huge market for franchised maid services.

As David McKinnon, president of Molly Maid, Inc., puts it: "Today's customer does not have the time, nor the desire, to do a background and reference check on everyone who offers maid service." The franchise connection is especially important for household services. The maid often works while people are away, so they need to be able to trust the person they hire—difficult to do unless they find somebody with ironclad recommendations. A franchised name suggests stability and reliability.

Enter Molly Maid—and possibly you. Molly Maid bought the rights to use the name of a Canadian company that has operated a similar business since 1980. The Molly Maid system rests on two premises: Two people, working systematically, can quickly and efficiently clean a home, and clients will use a service that removes doubt and risk from the hiring of a maid.

Molly Maid franchisees outfit their maids in English-type standard maid's uniforms and give them a company car (with pink-and-blue company logo on the side) to drive to work. The maids bring equipment and supplies to clients' houses. Clients supply only wax (if they wish their floors waxed). The maids work through the house systematically, vacuuming, dusting, and cleaning and sanitizing the kitchen and bathroom. The client also gets peace of mind, with a warranted service and bonded and insured maids.

Franchisees offer several inducements to persuade maids to give up some of their independence to work for the company. Benefits include paid hospitalization and vacations and use of the company car overnight (for the head maid of the team).

The company helps franchisees get off to a good start with a five-day training program at its headquarters in Ann Arbor, Michigan, which covers marketing, accounting, the training and hiring of employees, and the Molly Maid systematic cleaning method. The company also helps you to actually open your business.

Molly Maid maintains a toll-free number to provide franchisee support when needed. A company representative visits you at least two or three times a year, and you also have the opportunity to get support and exchange ideas with other franchisees at annual regional meetings.

A Molly Maid franchise requires little start-up capital and no office space (you operate out of your home), and it offers a considerable degree of independence.

For further information contact:
David McKinnon, President, Molly Maid, Inc., 540 Avis Dr., Ann Arbor, MI 48104, 313-996-1555 or 1-800-289-4600

The Maids International, Inc.

Initial license fee: $17,500
Royalties: 5.5% to 7%
Advertising royalties: 4%
Minimum cash required: $45,000 to $50,000
Capital required: $20,000 to $25,000
Financing: Available
Length of contract: 10 years

In business since: 1979
Franchising since: 1981
Total number of units: 189
Number of company-operated units: None
Total number of units planned, 1995: 600
Number of company-operated units planned, 1995: None

The Maids doesn't just say it wants your business to grow; it gives you the financial incentive to increase your sales volume. In an unusual policy for a franchisor, The Maids will reduce your royalty payments when you pass certain set levels of sales.

The Maids, founded and still directed by prominent commercial cleaning and maintenance services experts, offers its franchisees a total of 175 years of experience. Before they began to sell franchises, the company's founders did professional time-and-motion studies to develop its four-person-team housecleaning system. You will receive the benefits of their specialized knowledge from the day you become a franchisee.

"Among the ranks of The Maids franchisees you'll find both active and retired corporate executives, lawyers, scientists, teachers, and engineers," says company head Daniel J. Bishop. "Most of them are also investors who buy two or three territories, as opposed to mom-and-pop operators who have one fast-food store." In fact, about 70 percent of The Maids franchisees own more than one unit.

The company believes in thoroughly preparing its franchisees for their new careers. A three-week counseling period precedes your formal training at the company's Omaha, Nebraska, headquarters. In Omaha, you and your management staff learn personnel, marketing, promotion, pricing, bookkeeping, and computer operation from The Maids' professional corporate trainers. In addition, you receive videotapes that will help you train your crews, plus instructional tapes on how to handle special projects like carpet, upholstery, oven, and floor cleaning. Further counseling during the three weeks following your training prepares you to open your business. An 800 number provides you with easy access to help at any time.

Marsh and Judy Erskine, franchisees in Calgary, Alberta, Canada, are enthusiastic about their The Maids franchise. "Without question, it's the finest residential cleaning system available today, backed by a strong, innovative corporate family." The Maids' 92-piece supply and equipment package will allow you to put two cleaning teams in the field right away. You have the option of buying supply refills from the company or purchasing them elsewhere. The Maids' vehicle-leasing program also wraps up all your transportation needs in one package. You can lease vans from a dealership in Omaha and have them delivered to you through an affiliated dealer in your community. The cars come with the company logo and your phone number already painted on the side.

The Maids' computerized management system will permit you to spend more time managing and less time keeping records. You can lease or purchase your IBM or compatible computer at a special price, and it comes with customized software that will handle customer and personnel records, scheduling, income and tax reports, and payroll.

The Maids franchise also features one of the most comprehensive insurance packages in the industry. If you choose to purchase it, it will cover liability, crime, and property damage and will include advice from the insurer on loss-control procedures.

The Maids encourages you to do extensive local advertising through its cooperative advertising program. An advertising agency will place your yellow pages display, and The Maids will supply you with promotional items. The company also provides material for you to use in all advertising media, including a recorded jingle for radio spots.

For further information contact:
   The Maids International, Inc., 4820 Dodge St., Omaha, NE 68132,
   1-800-THE-MAID

Water Conditioning

Culligan International Company

Initial license fee: $10,000
Royalties: Varies
Advertising royalties: 1.8% to 4.1%
Minimum cash required: $50,000
Capital required: $100,000
Financing: For resale and rental equipment only
Length of contract: 5 years

In business since: 1936
Franchising since: 1936
Total number of units: 850
Number of company-operated units: 23
Total number of units planned, 1995: 850
Number of company-operated units planned, 1995: 25

Culligan has been in the business of manufacturing, selling, and servicing water-related products and equipment for over 50 years, and has been in the franchising business just as long. While the company has no plans to expand its total number of affiliates, regular turnover and retirement among its hundreds of franchisees means that many opportunities are available across the country.

As a Culligan franchisee, you'll be purchasing products and equipment from the company, leasing or reselling them to residential and business customers, and providing installation and maintenance services. For city and country dwellers alike, Culligan's filter systems substantially reduce impurities, improving the taste of not only water, but also coffee, juice, soups, and sauces, as well as reducing clogging in irons, vaporizers, and humidifiers, and fostering healthier houseplants. The "Aqua Cleer" system produces an average of five to eight gallons of triple-filtered water a day, with optional ice-maker hookups and portable units available as well. In addition, you'll be able to address special predicaments, from cloudy, discolored, or acidic water to sulphur odors and persistent sediment, doing an on-the-spot test— backed, when necessary, by Culligan's lab analysis—to ascertain the problem and determine the right filter for your customer's individual needs.

Installed in basements, utility rooms, garages, or other locations, and serving each tap and faucet in the house, Culligan water softeners remove particles of calcium and magnesium that result in spotty dishes, dingy clothes, dry hair and skin, and clogged pipes, saving homeowners in plumbing repairs and water-heating costs. Along with serving the homeowner market, you'll be able to offer equipment and services specifically designed for commercial and industrial systems.

Culligan will help you set up your business, participating in the site-selection process and training you and your employees. While Culligan looks for franchisee candidates with business acumen, an engineering (or related) degree isn't necessary. The company's one-week "Culligan Dealer Management Seminar" will introduce you to the details of managing a Culligan operation through a combination of lectures, group discussions, team assignments, and case-study analyses. While you won't be required to complete the program prior to opening for business, the company does recommend that you attend the first available session.

Through its technical programs on specific Culligan products and services, ranging from one-day seminars to week-long classes and featuring hands-on application of the material presented, the company ensures that your employees' skills are honed and updated. You and your sales staff are also expected to maintain a current Culligan dealer license, requiring you to pass a renewal exam every two years.

Running national advertising and promotional programs, the company will also supply you with print, radio, and TV materials. Additionally, you'll get advice on strategies for your local and regional efforts, with Culligan sometimes sharing the costs through its co-op fund. A simple, visible ad in your community yellow pages, however, featuring the familiar "Hey, Culligan Man" slogan, is often still the single most effective form of advertising—a time-honored choice that, like the company itself, has outlasted many a flashier gimmick.

For further information contact:
   Alan Jackson, General Manager, Consumer Products Marketing, Culligan
   International Company, One Culligan Pkwy., Northbrook, IL 60062-6209,
   708-205-5800, fax 708-205-6030

RainSoft Water Conditioning Company

Initial license fee: None
Royalties: None
Advertising royalties: None
Minimum cash required: $10,000
Capital required: $20,000 to $50,000
Financing: Some financing available
Length of contract: Open

In business since: 1953
Franchising since: 1963
Total number of units: 220
Number of company-operated units: None
Total number of units planned, 1995: NA
Number of company-operated units planned, 1995: NA

RainSoft runs substantial national advertising for its water purification and softening systems, but it accomplishes some of its most important marketing through the news columns of your daily newspaper and the evening news on television. The company hopes consumers learn from the news that the water they drink is far from pure, and depending on where they live, possibly even harmful. RainSoft advertisements remind people who haven't been paying attention to this disturbing news that the water in some communities contains solvents, hydrocarbons, phosphates, nitrates, pesticides, detergents, metals, cyanide, phenols, and even radioactive material.

Even when it does not contain pollutants, most community systems supply hard water, which often clogs toilet valves, forms scum on porcelain, leaves deposits on pots and pans, damages washing machines and requires you to use excessive amounts of soap to get your laundry clean, and harms water heaters. The company's equipment softens water while it purifies.

RainSoft, the third-largest water treatment company in America, has installed water treatment equipment at Michigan State University, the TWA flight kitchen in St. Louis, the University of Chicago Medical School, and the Dow Chemical Company in Midland, Michigan, as well as in homes.

If you decide to become a franchised RainSoft dealer, the company will train you in all aspects of the business at its headquarters in Elk Grove, Illinois. You'll learn how to sell RainSoft systems to homeowners and commercial establishments. The company will also teach you the fundamentals of water treatment and how to install its equipment, which ranges from under-the-sink units to custom-built systems that can serve an entire village. You can receive additional training through refresher courses given regionally eight times a year.

RainSoft will teach you an effective, dramatic sales method: how to do a simple drinking water analysis in your customers' homes. Seeing the sediment and other impurities in that water will capture your customer's attention. They may also be surprised by the price differential between bottled and treated water. The heavy, bulky bottles of water, whether delivered to the door or lugged home by the consumer, can cost as much as 20 to 25 times more than RainSoft conditioned water.

RainSoft promotes recognition of its brand name through extensive advertising in national magazines like *Reader's Digest, Prevention, Newsweek, People, TV Guide*, and *Better Homes and Gardens*. The company's advertisements have also run on TV programs like *The Price Is Right, Let's Make A Deal*, and *Hollywood Squares*. In addition, RainSoft sponsors the Mrs. America contest, and the winner appears in company advertisements and at promotional events.

RainSoft requires that you, as a dealer, use and sell only its equipment. However, the location of your business is entirely up to you.

For further information contact:
  Dave Cole or Bob Ruhstorfer, RainSoft Water Conditioning Company, 2080 Lunt Ave., Elk Grove Village, IL 60007, 708-437-9400

14. The General Maintenance Industry

Contents

Acoustic Ceiling Cleaning

Ceiling Doctor

Initial license fee: $11,500
Royalties: 8%
Advertising royalties: 2%
Minimum cash required: $17,500
Capital required: $20,000
Financing: None
Length of contract: 50 years

In business since: 1984
Franchising since: 1986
Total number of units: 70
Number of company-operated units: None
Total number of units planned, 1995: 600
Number of company-operated units planned, 1995: 1

Commercial, industrial, and retail businesses have to worry about ceilings that become soiled, stained, and discolored, not to mention coated with bacteria, tobacco residue, and other health hazards. Moreover, most general maintenance firms don't include acoustic ceiling cleaning in their services. Fortunately, companies like Ceiling Doctor are now available to do the cleaning. That will be *your* specialty, using Ceiling Doctor's patented process in stores, offices, factories, and homes to remove the grime while preserving fire-rated surfaces, improving light reflection, and augmenting the acoustic quality of a room—at about one-seventh the cost of replacing the ceiling.

Working during nonbusiness hours so your clients aren't unduly inconvenienced, your team begins by covering the room with plastic sheets and prepping the surface, removing loose dirt with brushes and vacuums. Then, high-pressure equipment is used to spray a fine mist of custom-mixed cleaning solution at 1,000 pounds per square inch, while the metal, t-bars, grills, and air diffusers are hand-wiped. Finally, an invisible, protective film is applied over the entire ceiling immediately after the cleaning treatment, hindering the buildup of dirt in the future.

Along with ceilings, this process can be used on wall acoustic tiling as well as vinyl, cut stone, marble, brick, stucco, concrete, and wood surfaces. Or your clients may simply want the protective coating alone applied to a new wall or ceiling, ensuring that it will need cleaning less often. They won't have to worry about harm to either their employees or the environment, because the chemicals you'll be using are phosphate-free, biodegradable, and nontoxic. As Kaaydah Schatten, Ceiling Doctor's president, puts it, "There's no reason to poison the land, air, and water, just because you want a clean building."

While your employees handle the actual cleaning, you'll be working as the manager and salesperson for your Ceiling Doctor franchise. You'll learn how to run the business during a one-week class, with Ceiling Doctor instructors explaining procedures for hiring and training your personnel and covering day-to-day operating issues through demonstrations and hands-on examples. Assisting you with pricing, job specs, and lead generation, the company extends ongoing support through regional seminars, monthly newsletters, regular update briefs, and yearly three-day national conventions. Furthermore, a field consultant, who'll help you improve marketing efforts and management skills while teaching new cleaning techniques to your staff, will visit at least twice during your first year in business and annually thereafter.

You'll receive van equipment, the cleaning gear and accessories, and chemicals, plus safety supplies and uniforms. Outfitting you with brochures, flyers, and other promotional literature, Ceiling Doctor operates a company-wide marketing program, featuring paid advertisements in business magazines and trade journals, and commissions a PR agency to publicize the company and its franchisees in those same periodicals and on radio and television.

Ceiling Doctor franchisees work from home, if they prefer, and operate in areas with a population of at least 400,000, where there are enough potential clients to make their enterprise profitable. The combination of a large market and a supportive franchise system seems to be an effective one. "The Ceiling Doctor proprietary process works, the equipment is reliable, the training is enough, the promotional support materials are very good, the cost of proprietary products have been reasonable to date," report Ontario, Canada, franchisees Russ Burnham and Rhonda Ray. "As Ceiling Doctors, we have been able to compete very effectively for business in our market area."

For further information contact:
  Rob Forrest, Chairman, Ceiling Doctor, 5151 Beltline Rd., Suite 950, Dallas, TX 75240, 214-702-8046, fax 214-702-9466

Coustic-Glo International, Inc.

Initial license fee: $12,000 to $30,000, depending on territory
Royalties: 5%
Advertising royalties: 1%

Minimum cash required: $12,000
Capital required: $12,000 to $30,000
Financing: None
Length of contract: 10 years

In business since: 1977
Franchising since: 1980
Total number of units: 211
Number of company-operated units: 1
Total number of units planned, 1995: 315
Number of company-operated units planned, 1995: 1

Bruce Weldon, a Coustic-Glo franchise owner in St. Louis Park, Minnesota, is enjoying "all the pleasures of owning my own business." So is Ray Kleman of Chillicothe, Ohio, who says his Coustic-Glo business has allowed him to break into "a market that had not yet been tapped." And Jeff Newby of Studio City, California, says his Coustic-Glo franchise is "growing into a big money-maker. We are developing a solid base of clients with repeat business."

The Coustic-Glo system is a safe, low-cost, effective means of cleaning suspended or sprayed-on acoustic ceilings, which can be provided to businesses and institutions without interfering with their normal schedules. The simple spray-on Coustic-Glo process not only cleans ceilings but improves acoustics, luminescence, and fire retardancy. Approved by the USDA, the FDA, and OSHA as safe and nontoxic, and praised by satisfied customers nationwide, Coustic-Glo's patented products form the basis of what Bruce Weldon calls a "unique service business with enormous income potential. The initial entry fee is low, and the business does not require large sums of money tied up in inventory."

While you maintain your clients' overhead assets, your overhead costs will remain low because you can operate your business from any site, even your home. Your franchise fee covers the cost of a comprehensive start-up package, which includes your equipment, supplies, and the Coustic-Glo products. And you will receive thorough training in how to run your business profitably. "We received very sound training," recalls Jeff Newby. "In addition, our crew was trained by the company. The application training was excellent, and the sales and marketing training was good, although it was probably more useful to franchise owners in smaller markets than ours."

During the initial five-day training, Coustic-Glo emphasizes business plan development and will help you set goals and strategies based on its proven marketing and management techniques. And to make sure you get off to a running start, the company will provide you with ad materials and advice on purchasing advertising space and will issue press releases in your area. Ray Kleman says, "This initial on-the-job training covered all phases of my business and was very useful."

The company's technical advisors and field representatives will pay frequent visits to consult with you and keep you informed about newly developed Coustic-Glo products. Bruce Weldon has found that "the traveling troubleshooter is very helpful, and of course the company is only a phone call away with a toll-free number." Coustic-Glo will help you get in touch with local branches of national clients so you can follow up on those accounts. Its numerous publications will update you on topics of interest, and its national advertising programs will inform potential customers about the services you offer.

"Every seven months there is a sales seminar, and the last one in Las Vegas was very exciting," Jeff Newby relates. Covering sales, applications, and new products, the semiannual seminars supplement the refresher training available at Coustic-Glo's headquarters in Minneapolis, Minnesota. In both initial and ongoing training and support programs, the importance of sales takes center stage. Marketing will be the backbone of your Coustic-Glo business, and Jeff Newby recommends that, "if you can't sell, hire someone who can."

But if you sell your services well, according to Jeff Newby, a Coustic-Glo franchise can prove to be "an excellent investment. We were billing work within one week of training, and we billed three times our initial investment in the first year alone. The profit ratio is exceptionally high throughout the system, and there are several franchisees who are getting very rich." Ray Kleman agrees: "I have done well and feel my opportunity to grow is very good, because I have been prepared to work hard and follow the system." And Bruce Weldon notes, "My business has been successful because of the great relationship I have with the company. I appreciate their knowledge and support, but I'm glad I have the freedom to operate and control my own business."

For further information contact:
  Scott Smith, Coustic-Glo International, Inc., 7111 Ohms Lane, Minneapolis, MN 55439, 612-835-1338 or 1-800-333-8523

Carpet and Upholstery Cleaning

AmeriClean

Initial license fee: $15,000 to $45,000, depending on size of territory
Royalties: 8.5% decreasing to 1%
Advertising royalties: None
Minimum cash required: $5,000
Capital required: $28,000 to $124,000
Financing: Assistance in obtaining loan
Length of contract: 10 years

In business since: 1979
Franchising since: 1981
Total number of units: 85
Number of company-operated units: 1
Total number of units planned, 1995: 100
Number of company-operated units planned, 1995: 3

The carpet and upholstery cleaning industry typically enjoys brisk business in the spring and fall, and can be relatively quiet the rest of the year. Diversification is the only way to ride this seasonal roller coaster to consistently profitable heights and to avoid devastating lows as well.

AmeriClean combines traditional carpet and upholstery cleaning with fire and water restoration services. Recognized nationally for its unique expertise, the company keeps on staff one of only 100 certified restoration specialists currently working in the U.S. Through careful analysis, the Pearson family, founders of AmeriClean, determined that providing these rare but much-needed services would go a long way toward building a future for their fledgling company.

Since 1981, AmeriClean has been charging investors between $15,000 and $45,000 for the right to use the corporate name for 10 years, with a renewal of five years at no extra charge. This franchise fee is contingent upon the population of the exclusive territory secured by the franchisee—ranging anywhere from 30,000 to 500,000. The royalty arrangement starts at 8.5 percent per month, but that figure goes down to 1 percent as volume improves.

Initial investments range from $28,000 to $124,000, depending upon how vast a territory you've taken on. From AmeriClean's perspective, none of this capital should go toward office rental. When you start out, there's really little need for renting office space—a workable area in an empty room at home will do just fine. As you expand, more space might be necessary.

AmeriClean provides operations manuals and instructional videotapes, as well as a one-week classroom and practical instruction course at their offices in Billings, Montana. New franchisees get taken through the start-up process as well, lightening the burden of marketing and sales at the beginning. In addition to this training, AmeriClean requires its franchisees to attend its annual convention. AmeriClean will also help franchisees find the best leases on supplies and equipment. Most franchisees don't mind getting near the dirt at first, taking care of the cleaning themselves. But after a while, profit gives way to privilege, and many hire others to carry out the physical labor, freeing themselves up to focus on management and sales.

Many have found that carpet and upholstery cleaning makes a nice sideline, but the most lucrative business comes from fire and water restoration. These services meet urgent needs and are in demand all year long.

For further information contact:
  Jim Pearson, 6602 S. Frontage Rd., Billings, MT 59101, 406-652-1960 or
  1-800-827-9111

Chem-Dry Carpet Cleaning

Initial license fee: $9,950 (including $3,280 equipment package)
Royalties: $175/month
Minimum cash required: $3,950 down plus working capital
Capital required: $8,950 (includes down payment)
Financing: Company finances, at 0% interest, the license fee after down
  payment; balance is amortized for 60 months
Length of contract: 5 years

In business since: 1977
Franchising since: 1977
Total number of units: 2,008 in U.S.
Number of company-operated units: None
Total number of units planned, 1995: 2,900
Number of company-operated units planned, 1995: None

Gary Sollee of Anaheim Hills, California, decided to buy a Chem-Dry Carpet Cleaning franchise after speaking with friends who operated their own successful Chem-Dry Service, and he's glad he did. "Chem-Dry is the most innovative franchisor in the U.S.," he says. "The main office gives me almost complete freedom in the management of my business, which is how I like it. And the returns on my investment have been phenomenal."

In 1977, Harris Research, Inc., developed and patented the Chem-Dry process, a unique "carbonated" carpet-cleaning system. Chem-

Dry uses a nontoxic effervescent cleaning solution to lift dirt out of carpets without leaving behind dirt-attracting residue or overwetting the carpet. This method, available only to Chem-Dry franchisees, has proved highly successful, and the company continues to improve the process. Franchisees can purchase carpet protectors that retard soiling, fungicides that prevent mold, and a citrus deodorizer, as well as recently developed drapery and upholstery cleaning formulas.

To provide you with a protected market area in which to grow, Harris Research sells only one Chem-Dry franchise per 60,000 population. Though the company has sold out some of its franchise regions, most market areas are still wide open, and the company seeks to expand in all areas of the United States and internationally. Within your territory, you are free to work full- or part-time, to set your own prices, and to develop your market at your own pace: Harris Research sets no quotas.

Your initial fee is virtually the only initial investment you need make because it covers a complete equipment package and enough cleaning solution to yield about $6,000 in gross receipts. The advertising package also included in the fee supplies you with everything you need to promote your business: a taped radio advertisement, brochures, discount certificates, slicks for print ads, letterhead, business cards, vehicle signs, uniforms, and other items that will help you establish a recognized name in your territory.

Conducted at the Harris Research headquarters in Cameron Park, California, or by videotape if you prefer, initial training occurs in two phases. First you will learn how to use the Chem-Dry system and maintain your equipment. According to Gary Sollee, "The Chem-Dry cleaning system is very simple and can be learned quickly." Phase 2 of your training consists of instruction in sales and marketing, employee training, management procedures, and basic accounting. Once you have completed the course in bookkeeping, the company will give you a complete bookkeeping set and a training manual, which has been time-tested to improve your operational efficiency.

Equipped with your advertising materials, bookkeeping set, and three VHS training tapes, as well as the Chem-Dry equipment and chemicals, your only further expense in opening for business will be a vehicle if you do not already have one and any miscellaneous licenses or telephone costs. The equipment fits easily into a small station wagon, so many franchisees use the family car until their profits warrant the purchase of a van exclusively for their Chem-Dry operations.

A monthly newsletter will keep you updated on new ideas and products and will let you know what's going on with other franchisees nationwide. In addition, you will receive new advertising materials developed by the Harris Research marketing department. The company conducts refresher training monthly or whenever you feel you need it, and by special request corporate staff will come to your location to update you or your employees. The annual convention keeps franchisees in touch with one another and corporate officers. And the main office is always available to answer your questions by phone or by mail.

You must use Chem-Dry products, available exclusively from Harris Research, in your business. Your orders for supplies will be turned around quickly—usually within 24 hours—and your line of credit with the company allows you to pay for supplies on a 30-day net basis.

As a Chem-Dry owner, you are truly an independent business in complete control of your franchise. The flat monthly fee means that the more you make, the more you can keep. Chem-Dry's elimination of the percentage-of-gross monthly payment not only allows you to keep a greater share of your profits, but it also answers one of the only complaints many franchisees (of other companies) make: As you become more independent and require less support from the franchisor, it only makes sense that you should have to pay a smaller percentage of your gross. But while the company's costs in maintaining you as a franchisee decrease, your payments to it increase—because your revenues increase. Harris Research has decided that, in the case of its own operations, the percentage-of-gross practice would be unfair. With a Chem-Dry Carpet Cleaning franchise, you truly have your own business. As Gary Sollee puts it, "Other franchises may bleed you dry. But if you have a positive attitude and are willing to work your tail off, Chem-Dry can make you wealthy."

For further information contact:
  Harris Research, Inc., 3330 Cameron Park Dr., Suite 700, Cameron Park, CA 95682, 1-800-243-6379 (1-800-CHEM-DRY)

Color Your Carpet, Inc.

Initial license fee: $15,000
Royalties: 3%
Advertising royalties: None
Minimum cash required: $24,000
Capital required: NA
Financing: Available for additional territories
Length of contract: 5 years

In business since: 1979
Franchising since: 1988
Total number of units: 73
Number of company-operated units: 1
Total number of units planned, 1995: 258
Number of company-operated units planned, 1995: 5

Maybe you found out the hard way how difficult, if not impossible, it is really to get a carpet clean. Those rental machines available at the grocers' don't work so well and the spray-on-and-vacuum foam products are even worse. Many professional cleaning services don't do much better—they have inconsistent methods, using excessive water and temperatures high enough to cause damage, and they lack the proper technical training. Even if the soil and stains disappear, the sun-faded areas remain—cleaning can't do anything about them—and the carpet still lacks that luster you wanted.

This is when many businesses or homeowners just give up and buy new carpeting. Color Your Carpet, however, offers another alternative—a quick, safe, guaranteed dyeing job performed on site that can return a carpet to its original shade or give it an entirely different color—for about 70 percent less than the cost of replacement.

Candy Nelson, property manager of a large apartment complex and a regular Color Your Carpet customer, wasn't, frankly, entirely convinced until she tried the process. "The idea, which seemed farfetched to me initially, now is a clear and logical answer for a normally costly solution." Here's why. Most nylon carpeting manufactured these days is made to last over 20 years, yet many buyers find themselves replacing it when there's still up to 15 years of life left. The carpet isn't worn out; it's only discolored by animal, food, beverage, or bleach stains, and soiled from heavy traffic or mere daily use.

Using the company's exclusive dyeing process, Color Your Carpet franchisees can take care of all these problems. You'll be able to provide any color your customer wants, from an exact match, to a shade near the original, to a completely new tone. And you'll supply the specific service that's right for the carpet, whether its a full dyeing job or a combination cleaning and recoloring, with spot dyeing on stained patches and in faded areas around patio doors, windows, and skylights.

Traveling to homes or commercial establishments, you'll perform the work right on your customers' premises. First, you'll give a free estimate, mix a sample of the hue to be used, and do a color test on a few fibers to make sure the carpet is indeed safely dyeable (about 10 percent of carpeting isn't). All the customer has to do to prepare is vacuum and put away fragile items. After removing the furniture, you or your crew will use a spray gun to apply a fine mist of dye, an exclusive formula that penetrates the original color, with bonding agents that enter the carpet fabric to make it colorfast and stain resistant. The color sets in only 60 seconds; the customer can start walking on the carpet right away while your team is putting back the furniture. A five-year maintenance program is available to rejuvenate the protective coating regularly, while the dye job itself is guaranteed for as long as the customer keeps the carpet.

Color Your Carpet franchisees are initially granted a single designated territory covering a population of about 100,000. Based on your performance, you'll be permitted to purchase up to five additional neighboring regions over a three-year period. To get your business started, the company will train you at a regional Color Your Carpet center, sending you an operations and instruction manual two weeks before the beginning of the session. The classes are limited to four franchisees to ensure individual attention, and cover carpet care and dyeing techniques as well as management and administrative skills.

You'll obtain the equipment and custom-manufactured dyes, which are nontoxic and odorless, from the company, which extends ongoing training and information on updated methods and new products. Color Your Carpet bases its additional support on the amount of assistance—and independence—that the franchisee desires. Because this is a young franchise, the details of the program are still being honed. That does mean some uncertainly, but judging from *Success* magazine's ranking of Color Your Carpet as number two among its top 10 new franchises, it's judged to have potential. It's a dynamic venture, too, according to the franchisees. "We were interested, then fascinated, then hooked," says affiliate Charles R. Kurrle. "Now, we find that we are recommending the franchise to friends and relatives."

For further information contact:
 Carol B. D'Imperio, President, Color Your Carpet, Inc., 24665 Ridgecrest Ave., Orange Park, FL 32065, 1-800-321-6567, fax 904-272-6750

Langenwalter Carpet Dyeing

Initial license fee: $16,500
Royalties: None
Advertising royalties: $125/month
Minimum cash required: $16,500
Capital required: $20,000
Financing: None
Length of contract: 3 years

In business since: 1972
Franchising since: 1981
Total number of units: 120
Number of company-operated units: 2
Total number of units planned, 1995: 500
Number of company-operated units planned, 1995: 2

A simple one-person operation requiring minimal inventory, you can run a Langenwalter Carpet Dyeing service from your home—even as a part-time operation. And yet this business is definitely high-tech, using an exclusive hot liquid dye formula with a special cleaning solution.

Company founder Roy Langenwalter, once an aerospace chemist and engineer, opened a small chemical manufacturing business when he grew tired of working for others and not making enough money. While doing work for maintenance firms and carpet cleaning companies, he developed the formulas that form the basis of Langenwalter Carpet Dyeing.

Langenwalter Carpet Dyeing claims that 75 percent of the carpeting replaced by homeowners and businesses is in good physical shape and would look like new if dyed and cleaned. Until recently, consumers and businesspeople took a chance having their carpets dyed, since dyes provided uneven results. But its process, according to the company, solves that problem, making it possible for franchisees both to clean and dye carpets and upholstery at a given location—all in one afternoon. The operation involves shampooing and coloring the carpet with a floor scrubber, then using a steam extractor to rinse, deodorize, and sanitize.

Your training, in Anaheim, California, will take five days. The comprehensive training covers equipment, color blending, dyeing, cleaning, fabric testing, patching and repairing, stain removal, chemicals, advertising and promotion, sales, and estimating. The company also offers refresher training at its headquarters, and Langenwalter will customize the course if you need to brush up on a particular aspect of the operation. You can consult the company on any problems that come up by calling Langenwalter's toll-free line during business hours.

The comprehensive Langenwalter franchise package includes everything from the equipment and chemicals you will need to start up your business to marketing aids like brochures, flyers, and signs. The package even includes a baseball cap with a company logo imprinted on it. You can buy the company's exclusive dye only from Langenwalter, but you can purchase all other supplies and equipment from the vendor of your choice.

For especially ambitious entrepreneurs, Langenwalter also sells area franchises. These cover a territory with a population of at least three million and can usually support at least 60 franchisees.

For further information contact:
  Roy Langenwalter, Langenwalter Carpet Dyeing, 4410 E. La Palma, Anaheim, CA 92807, 1-800-422-4370

Professional Carpet Systems (PCS)

Initial license fee: $13,500
Royalties: 6%
Advertising royalties: None
Minimum cash required: $8,500
Capital required: $5,000
Financing: Available
Length of contract: 10 years

In business since: 1978
Franchising since: 1981
Total number of units: 496
Number of company-operated units: 5
Total number of units planned, 1995: 900
Number of company-operated units planned, 1995: 5

Offering one service alone won't give you the competitive edge you need to thrive in the carpet care business, insists Professional Carpet Systems (PCS). That's why the company subscribes to what it calls a "total carpet care concept." Putting the concept into practice, you'll perform a multiplicity of assignments for your customers: dyeing, tinting, and mending services; a specialized method for taking care of pet stains; a dry-foam process of upholstery cleaning; a vinyl-repair system that fixes torn, scuffed, or worn floors; and high-pressure steam cleaning that attacks a range of stains caused by substances like oil, ink, mud, shoe polish, rust, food, beverages, along with your general filth.

If you're a typical PCS franchisee, dye jobs for homes, apartments, hotels, and businesses will make up the largest portion of your business. Using refined, company-made hybrid pigments that act on nylon and wool, you'll be able to change altogether the color of an entire carpet, do spot work to restore specific damaged sections, or tint the fabric to revive the original shade, guaranteeing that the color won't streak, track off, or wash away. You'll also mend rips, holes, and burns, using an aging technique for blending in with the surrounding carpet and making the repair invisible.

But a surprisingly large number of your customers will probably be asking for the GOC (for "Guaranteed Odor Control") system, developed in coordination with the University of Georgia's School of Veterinary Medicine, to handle pet stains, which are commonly responsible for 10 percent to 15 percent of all residential carpet replacement. Isolating each particular animal "indiscretion" with an electronic detector, you'll replace the carpet pad, seal the subfloor, and wash both the top and bottom of the carpet before treating it with lime enzymes to remove the acids and ammonia solutions to deodorize and disinfect. These same chemicals can also be used to help return homes to normal after flooding or a fire, eliminating smoke odors and preventing the growth of fungus, mold, and mildew that accompany water damage.

PCS manufactures more than 80 percent of the products you'll be using, and maintains its own laboratory, staffed by a full-time team of chemists. Your franchise fee covers a start-up package of equipment, supplies, and cleansers, plus such marketing materials as brochures and direct mail pieces. Charging no advertising royalties, the company feels that you can make better use of your promotions dollars through local efforts. PCS offers you strategies that have been effective for its other franchisees and ways to develop a successful marketing program for your territory during your initial training. The two-week session, which includes both classroom instruction and hands-on exercises, will focus on teaching you each step of the diverse carpet care services you'll perform, and encompasses record-keeping and business expansion techniques, too.

In addition to sending you follow-up video training modules and the regular franchise newsletter, *Dyegest*, PCS provides ongoing support through regular contact from a field representative and national conventions held twice a year, featuring advanced workshops and the opportunity to get together and trade war stories with your fellow franchisees.

For further information contact:
Investment Counselor, Professional Carpet Systems, 5182 Old Dixie Hwy., Forest Park, GA 30050, 404-362-2300 or 1-800-925-5055

Rug Doctor Pro

Initial license fee: $3,500 minimum
Royalties: 6% on first $10,000; 4% on second $10,000; 3% thereafter
Advertising royalties: 2%
Minimum cash required: $4,000 (in addition to license fee)
Capital required: $4,000 to $15,000 (in addition to license fee)
Financing: Available
Length of contract: 10 years, with two 5-year options

In business since: 1972
Franchising since: 1987
Total number of units: 47
Number of company-operated units: 1
Total number of units planned, 1995: 400
Number of company-operated units planned, 1995: 1

"When I started out in this business, I had a used $150 dry-foam car-pet cleaning machine with no one to look to for guidance or instruction," recalls J. Roger Kent, Rug Doctor's cofounder and CEO. "At that point I determined that there had to be a better method. So I set my sights on designing a better machine." Rug Doctor's cleaning equipment and chemicals have been on the market now for two decades, and the company can claim these days to be the world's largest carpet care firm.

Expanding beyond the manufacture of cleaning tools and products, Kent and his colleagues also developed Rug Doctor Pro, a carpet care service for commercial and residential property owners. It's Kent's "better method" in action, supplying franchisees from the beginning with both the equipment and the guidance that he himself so keenly lacked at first. Using the company's patented materials, you and your employees will be able to do repairs as well as general cleaning on all types of carpeting, fixing burns and split seams and performing emergency water extraction jobs. You'll also work on upholstery—including fabrics like prints, velvet, and velour—and clean drapery, too, without taking down curtains or causing shrinkage. And once the shampooing, deodorizing, disinfecting, and any other special work is completed, you can finish by adding such protective coatings as Scotchgard and Sylgard.

Because convenience is just about as important to Rug Doctor Pro clients as cleanliness, a key selling point of the service is your ability to avoid disrupting the daily life of homeowners or affecting the regular routine or businesses while you do your work. It's an ability many independent carpet cleaners develop only after years in the business, but that you and up to two of your employees will have after attending the week-long training program at the company's Fresno, California, headquarters. Conducted about every 90 days, the sessions feature classroom and hands-on instruction that teach you all the technical aspects of carpet, upholstery, and drapery cleaning and repair, along with administration procedures and marketing strategies. Cost estimating and consumer relations are covered, as well as methods for developing a client base and getting repeat business. Periodic continuing-education seminars are also held, while newsletters and operation manual updates keep you informed about new Rug Doctor products and innovations.

With a truck-mounted unit only one of the options, you'll have a choice among several different equipment and chemical packages that provide you with all the Rug Doctor tools—from vacuums, sprayers, pumps, and hoses, to detergents, shampoos, foams, and defoamers— that you'll need to begin your operation. The start-up checking, book- keeping, and accounting system the company furnishes, meanwhile, helps you with financial management. And for the promotions side of your business, you'll receive different sets of four-color point-of- purchase brochures for residential and for commercial customers, and printed advertising materials also aimed at several market segments, plus professionally produced TV commercials and radio jingles.

Rug Doctor Pro franchisees are granted exclusive territories. You and the company will negotiate the boundaries of the area you'll serve, based on the region's growth potential and your own desires and ambitions. The size of your territory determines the initial fran- chise fee you pay.

For further information contact:
John Mandeville, National Franchise Director, Rug Doctor Pro, 2788 N. Larkin Ave., Fresno, CA 93727, 209-291-5511 or 1-800-678-7844, fax 209-291-9913

Steamatic, Inc.

Initial license fee: $10,000, $14,000, or $17,000, depending on size of territory
Royalties: 8% decreasing to 5% and 4%
Advertising royalties: None
Minimum cash required: $28,000 to $70,700, depending on size of territory
Capital required: NA
Financing: Yes, equipment package of $13,300
Length of contract: 10 years

In business since: 1948
Franchising since: 1967
Total number of units: 246
Number of company-operated units: 10
Total number of units planned, 1995: NA
Number of company-operated units planned, 1995: NA

The Steamatic business is one of the easiest to get into. Your initial li- cense fee will include everything you need to get started—except a van. You can operate your business out of any location, providing you have a telephone answering machine. And you can begin your opera- tion within a month of signing your franchise agreement.

The Steamatic franchise fee covers the equipment and supply package you need to begin cleaning carpets, furniture, drapes, and vehicles for businesses and individuals, including a portable cleaning machine for carpet and furniture and a portable dry cleaning unit for furniture and drapery. You also receive from the company a three-month supply of cleaning chemicals, stationery and business forms, and advertising materials.

Your training and equipment enable you to do general cleaning jobs and restoration work following fires and flooding. On occasion, the company may step in if a big accident or natural disaster in your exclusive franchise territory creates a restoration job you can't handle. If that happens, Steamatic will pay you a referral fee. Conversely, should the company solicit such business in your territory for you, you will pay a referral fee to the company.

Steamatic training takes place at its headquarters in Grand Prairie, Texas, and at training centers in Dallas and Fort Worth. Topics studied include fire and water restoration; carpet, furniture, and drapery cleaning; air-duct cleaning; wood restoration; and deodorizing. Steamatic also instructs you in equipment use and marketing. You pay for transportation and living expenses incidental to your training.

As part of its ongoing support, Steamatic will consult with you by phone on any problems that arise and will provide field assistance if the company's management deems it necessary. The company will also show you how to set up an accounting system, and it will analyze your budget and finances at your request. A company representative will confer with you in person at least once a year.

You buy your own advertising, including your listing in the yellow pages. The company will supply television and radio commercial tapes, but *you* pay a fee to use them. You may also be required to participate in a cooperative advertising program.

Should you wish to expand your business, the company has a leasing program for additional cleaning machines.

For further information contact:
Steamatic, Inc., 1320 S. University Dr., Suite 400, Fort Worth, TX 76107, 214-647-1244

Janitorial and General

Coverall North America, Inc.

Initial license fee: $4,000 to $34,000
Royalties: 10%
Advertising royalties: None
Minimum cash required: $2,000 to $25,000
Capital required: $300 to $1,500
Financing: Available
Length of contract: 10 years, with 10-year renewal

In business since: 1985
Franchising since: 1985
Total number of units: 1,800
Number of company-operated units: 10
Total number of units planned, 1995: 5,000
Number of company-operated units planned, 1995: 10

If you don't have the resources right now to quit your job and jump full-time into running a business of your own, a Coverall franchise may be an attractive alternative. "Since the majority of our franchisees' maintenance work is done at night," explains Alex Roudi, the company's president, "they can start their business and follow a systemic approach to grow to the point where they can give up their regular day job after a while."

Providing janitorial services to professional establishments, you can begin by working part-time. You'll be cleaning and performing routine maintenance for offices and stores covering up to one million square feet, although most of your work will be in more modest facilites, small to medium-size jobs where the profit margins are larger. As part of your franchise agreement with Coverall, you are guaranteed a starting base of customer accounts, the number depending on the extent of the package you purchase—and the initial fee that you pay. Assured a minimum monthly gross, you can expand your business at your own speed by finding and signing additional clients yourself.

Other franchise options are also available from the company. An area franchise, for example, grants you exclusive rights in a specific market. Some "master franchises" are still available, too, allowing you to develop a large territory by selling local Coverall affiliations and financing up to 50 percent of the initial fees.

Whether you're doing the cleaning and maintenance work yourself or managing hands-on fellow franchisees, you'll offer a service that businesses need—during recessions and boom times alike—yet one that's often hard for them to find. In the first place, there just aren't enough janitors available. The U.S. Department of Labor reports that, after cashiers and registered nurses, there is now a greater need for janitors than for any other kind of worker. And too many of the janitorial services around aren't doing a particularly good job. As Coverall's chief operating officer, Ted Elliott, describes, "This is a multibillion dollar industry plagued with unskilled, unmotivated workers. . . . We are selling a service to somebody who's been burned before." Alex Roudi concurs: "Ninety percent of the companies in the field are mom and pop operations without the resources to keep up. The other 10 percent are larger companies with staff problems and heavy turnover."

That, in turn, causes office managers to switch janitorial services repeatedly, meaning most cleaning operators have to deal with the constant headache of an unstable client base. But because of Coverall's stability and quality standards, the company claims, its annual customer turnover rate is kept to about 9 percent, compared with the industry average of 45 percent. Clients are contacted monthly to make sure they are satisfied with the service, and on-site inspections are conducted regularly to keep your workers on their toes. Meanwhile, Coverall uses telemarketing and in-person sales campaigns to continue signing new accounts.

If you'll be running a local or area franchise, you'll receive on-site training from your master franchisee. Covering equipment use and efficient office cleaning methods, particularly carpet, hard floor, and restroom care, the instruction includes business management and marketing techniques as well. Master franchise owners themselves also attend training sessions at Coverall's San Diego headquarters, where they'll develop skills for securing, building, and expanding their network's clientele.

Coverall will outfit you with an initial package of equipment and materials, from mops, brooms, brushes, and vacuums to cleansers and other chemicals, and you can restock your inventory at discount prices through the company's suppliers. Coordinating regional seminars to introduce new office maintenance products and approaches, Coverall will also provide sales pieces and give advice about how to find additional clients on your own. The regional office handles all billing and payment collection for you, extending cash-flow protection; whether or not your customers are delinquent in their payments, you'll still receive your guaranteed monthly income. The company even covers your phone calls and furnishes a backup cleaning crew to handle emergencies or short-term absences.

Yet the essential appeal of a Coverall franchise remains a simple one, in Alex Roudi's view: "We've put owning a business within reach of people who otherwise would be priced out of the market." And judging from Coverall's position as number 32 on *Inc.* magazine's list of the country's 500 fastest-growing private companies, that appeal is considerable.

For further information contact:
  Alex Roudi, President, Coverall North America, Inc., 3111 Camino Del Rio N., San Diego, CA 92108, 1-800-537-3371, fax 619-584-4923

EnviroBate Services

Initial license fee: $25,000
Royalties: 6%
Advertising royalties: None
Minimum cash required: $75,000
Capital required: $90,000
Financing: None
Length of contract: 10 years

In business since: 1988
Franchising since: 1991
Total number of units: 2
Number of company-operated units: 1
Total number of units planned, 1995: 38
Number of company-operated units planned, 1995: 1

The growing concern—even alarm—over the presence of asbestos in residences and workplaces has created a new business niche, and EnviroBate is one of the most respected and reputable in the area of environmental cleanup. Using the most modern equipment yet developed, EnviroBate inspects, detects, evaluates, and removes or encapsulates the asbestos before the substance begins to break down and emit its contaminating fibers. Planning ahead to a time when most asbestos will be eliminated, the company has also recently begun offering lead testing and elimination services to its customers.

This type of service is relatively new, and EnviroBate, though one of the first companies to provide environmental substance control, has been in operation since 1988, and began franchising in 1991. Licensed in 43 states, EnviroBate conforms to the strict federal and state laws governing procedures and policies of dealing with hazardous materials, and has officers with backgrounds in medicine and law as well as business. The company is recognized by both its customers and government agencies such as the EPA and OSHA for its careful technical procedures and proficiency. In addition, EnviroBate's sound corporate structure and plan for a strong support system for franchisees will be an advantage for anyone who decides to purchase an EnviroBate franchise.

The technical nature of the franchise necessitates a thorough training program, which includes required attendance at an EPA-approved training school in addition to its in-house training course in the recognition, testing, danger analysis, and treatment of harmful materials. Training also covers cost evaluation, personnel recruitment, and effective ways to market the business, such as targeting insurance companies.

For further information contact:
  Jeff Anlauf, EnviroBate Services, 500 E. 36th St., Minneapolis, MN 55408, 612-825-6878

Profusion Systems, Inc.

Initial license fee: $20,500
Royalties: 6%
Advertising royalties: None
Minimum cash required: $15,000
Capital required: $15,000
Financing: Available
Length of contract: 10 years

In business since: 1980
Franchising since: 1984
Total number of units: 158
Number of company-operated units: None
Total number of units planned, 1995: 400
Number of company-operated units planned, 1995: 10

"Plastics" was the one word of career advice portentously given to Dustin Hoffman in *The Graduate*. Bill Gabbard took the advice to heart. Juggling a few bank loans, mortgaging his car, and running his charge accounts perilously up to their limits, he funded research by polymer scientists to develop new materials and chemicals for the repair and maintenance of hard plastic products. Once they came up with a polyvinyl chloride compound that was virtually undetectable when used to mend rips, holes, burns, and cracks in leather, vinyl, velour, and numerous other coverings, Gabbard was in business—and out of debt.

If you think that only chairs and sofas can be repaired by Profusion Systems, you're not being nearly imaginative enough. Consider restaurant booths, snowmobile and golf cart seats, auto upholstery and dashboards, even army tank interiors; looking beyond seating, there are also items like suitcases and feed tank lines. Look beyond ground level as well—both above and below, in fact: hot-air balloons and caskets have been repaired by Profusion franchisees, too.

Commercial accounts will make up about four-fifths of your clientele, and you'll be doing most of your work on site. "Basically, we're 90 percent mobile," says Bill Gabbard. As he puts it, "It's a lot easier going to 5,000 banquet chairs than having 5,000 banquet chairs come to you." Be prepared to visit many different venues; Profusion franchisees have been hired by airlines and airports, sports arenas and bowling alleys, restaurant and hotel chains, car lots and transit systems. The company's regular customers include the Disney theme parks and the U.S. military. One Profusion affiliate in San Diego has two Navy bases and a few marinas as clients, while a Denver franchisee services both police stations and prisons.

Generally, each individual repair takes only 5 to 15 minutes. Starting by cleaning the surface, you'll use infrared light beams or a high-powered hot-air gun to melt several layers of the patented compound and fuse them to the material. You'll set the texture and grain with a mold of the original fabric and apply dye to the repair after matching the color with a computer. The extent of the damage doesn't matter.

"We can repair an area 20 feet long or one the size of a pinhole," according to Gabbard. And because the process is based on fusing methods rather than applying adhesives or bonds, the repair is permanent, guaranteed by a lifetime warranty. The compound has a tensile strength of 951 pounds per square inch, more than two times that of original vinyl or Naugahyde.

To learn the technical aspects of Profusion Systems, you'll spend nine days training at the company's Denver headquarters. Your employees can also attend the instruction at no additional cost, but even if they'll be doing all the hands-on repair work, you'll still be expected to master the procedure details yourself, while you'll also receive guidance in management, accounting, public relations, and business planning. The company provides an additional four days of field supervision in your territory, which includes assistance in negotiating your initial client contracts, and informs you of research and development advances from the home office and the laboratory through monthly newsletters, annual conventions, and occasional videotapes demonstrating new technical applications.

Teaching you how to generate business is an important aspect of both the initial training and the company's ongoing support. You'll receive brochures, flyers, and other promotional materials, and have national and regional Profusion clients in your territory as customers from the start. But there are two special challenges in the marketing of your service: the fact that, as the company's motto proclaims, "your best work is never noticed," and the common misconception that your service is, in the words of Bill Gabbard, "one of those TV-commercial type of things." Profusion will show you effective ways to substantiate the quality, versatility, and cost-efficiency of your work through demonstrations and other specialized sales calls.

No specific experience is required to own a Profusion Systems franchise. While leather and plastic repair may have the image of a male-dominated field, *Entrepreneurial Woman* actually highlighted the company as "among the best opportunities for women in franchising today." Over a dozen women are sole owners of a Profusion Systems franchise, along with numerous others who are partners in a family-run operation. True, some clients may not be used to seeing women working in this field. But as Wisconsin-based Gayle Smith found, "When people see the job I do, they're so impressed, the fact that I'm a woman doesn't matter anymore."

For further information contact:
   David Lowe, Director of Franchising, Profusion Systems, Inc., 2851 S. Parker Rd., Suite 650, Aurora, CO 80014, 303-337-1949 or 1-800-777-3873, fax 303-337-0790

ServiceMaster

Initial license fee: $8,400 to $19,400
Royalties: 4% to 10%
Advertising royalties: 0.25% to 1%
Minimum cash required: $5,500 to $9,800
Capital required: $5,000 to $10,000
Financing: Company finances up to ⅔ of the cost of the total franchise package
Length of contract: 5 years

In business since: 1948
Franchising since: 1952
Total number of units: 4,285
Number of company-operated units: None
Total number of units planned, 1995: 225
Number of company-operated units planned, 1995: NA

ServiceMaster franchisees provide carpet and upholstery cleaning, window cleaning, cleaning after accidents and disasters, and general contract cleaning to homes, businesses, and institutions. The company's business statistics reflect its excellent standing in the cleaning industry: The company passed the $2 billion mark in revenues in 1991, and *Fortune* declared it first in return-on-equity among all industrial service companies in 1989. Yet, at the same time, it is one of the less expensive businesses to buy—and one for which you need no previous experience. *Entrepreneur* has ranked it number one among low-investment franchises.

The company sells four basic franchises. The on-location service specializes in cleaning and maintaining carpets, upholstery, floors, and walls. You will also be serving homeowners, building managers, and insurance adjusters by restoring property damaged by fire, smoke, or water. ServiceMaster's carpet and upholstery franchise focuses on professionally cleaning carpets and upholstery in homes and businesses. The company's commercial contract cleaning operation targets institutions, offering them regular janitorial services. Last but not least, the company's small-business cleaning service focuses on meeting the cleaning needs of businesses that occupy less than 5,000 square feet.

ServiceMaster offers a three-tiered training program. You will first receive a package of home-study manuals and audiovisual aids that explain and illustrate methods of running and building your business. Then, one of the company's local distributors will give you on-the-job training that includes an introduction to making sales calls.

At the company's headquarters in Downers Grove, Illinois, company experts will teach you the basics of sales, marketing, operational procedures, and business management during the five-day Academy of Service.

When you're ready to begin your own ServiceMaster business, a company representative will spend two days in your hometown showing you how to set up a simple bookkeeping system and develop a marketing strategy. The company's field manager will keep close tabs on you during your first year, monitoring your progress and arranging for training in any areas in which you need additional work. And the company continually runs seminars, workshops, and conferences to update you on new methods and materials that you can use in your business.

Your franchise package includes everything you need to start your business, including stationery, initial chemical supplies, and even a company blazer. You must buy refills of the proprietary cleaning chemicals that you use in your business from your local ServiceMaster distributor.

ServiceMaster advertises the services of their franchisees nationally. It will provide you with prepared advertisements for your own advertising in the print and electronic media. ServiceMaster sponsors cooperative yellow pages advertising, and will help you to place those ads.

For further information contact:
   ServiceMaster Residential/Commercial Services, L.P., 855 Ridge Lake Blvd.,
   Memphis, TN 38120, 1-800-338-6833

Servpro Industries, Inc.

Initial license fee: $17,800
Royalties: 7% to 10%
Advertising royalties: 0% to 3%
Minimum cash required: $15,000
Capital required: $15,000 to $20,000
Financing: Company will finance up to 50% of your investment
Length of contract: 5 years

In business since: 1967
Franchising since: 1969
Total number of units: 832
Number of company-operated units: None
Total number of units planned, 1995: 1,100
Number of company-operated units planned, 1995: None

Servpro aims to offer customers one-stop shopping for most of their
housecleaning needs, so its franchise licenses authorize Servpro operators to sell a wide range of services—carpet, furniture, and drapery
cleaning; fire and flood restoration; janitorial and maid services;
acoustic ceiling cleaning; deodorization; and carpet dyeing—using the
company's name. Franchisees purchase supplies and equipment from
Servpro, unless the company has specifically authorized another
vendor.

Kathy Stone, a Richardson, Texas, franchisee for the past 14 years,
remembers how she decided on a Servpro franchise. She wanted to
get into the cleaning business, but didn't want to get bogged down in
technical details. "We have known others who have done it on their
own," she says. "A great deal of their time and effort is spent in researching chemicals, literature, etc. Servpro provides most of this and
leaves us free to do what we do best."

Through extensive training, Servpro will prepare you to perform
and supervise a variety of cleaning services. Your classroom instruction will involve 10 days of work at the company's national training
center in Rancho Cordova, California. The course covers office procedures and filing systems, telephone sales, invoicing, accounting, cash
flow, employee recruiting and training, advertising, and public
relations.

Back home, you will work with a nearby established Servpro franchisee for two weeks—during which you will draw a salary—and will

receive an on-the-job introduction to the Servpro system. A company representative will then spend two days helping you set up your Servpro business, accompanying you on your first sales calls. The representative will make sure that your facilities reflect Servpro standards, but the company does not require franchisees to rent any particular type of store or office. That representative will also assist you as your franchise grows, helping you with advice on specific problems that may arise. For Kathy Stone, access to such advice was "critical," especially once she got started.

Kathy Stone finds the company's ongoing training, offered at various meetings throughout the year, a great help. "Management and financial information are particularly helpful after you have been in business awhile. Sales and motivation training are also provided," she notes. The company sponsors four franchisee meetings a year in local areas, two regional conferences, and an eight-day national convention at a resort area. Servpro will refund 10 percent of your royalties each year as a "convention allowance" if all your payments to the company have been timely.

For further information contact:
  Richard Isaacson, Servpro Industries, Inc., 575 Airport Blvd., Gallatin, TN 37066, 1-800-826-9586

Sparkle Wash International

Initial license fee: $8,250 minimum
Royalties: 5%
Advertising royalties: None
Minimum cash required: $15,000
Capital required: $20,000
Financing: Available
Length of contract: 5 years, with two 5-year options

In business since: 1965
Franchising since: 1967
Total number of units: 180
Number of company-operated units: 1
Total number of units planned, 1995: 100
Number of company-operated units planned, 1995: 1

The key to Sparkle Wash's self-contained mobile "power" cleaning system is its versatility. There's no shortage, to say the least, of the types of clients you'll be able to accommodate or of the variety of structures, vehicles, machinery, and other miscellaneous dirty items you'll be able to service.

You'll clean truck fleets and railroad cars, decks and pools, exteriors of houses and commercial buildings. Contracts may involve not just boats, but entire marinas; not just heavy industrial equipment, but whole factories. "No job too big" is a Sparkle Wash motto, and operators who have cleaned airports, stadiums, bridges, and tunnels have lived up to that claim. So did a team of Ohio franchisees who toiled overtime for months after a refinery accident sent oil splashing over a three-mile-wide residential area, covering hundreds of homes, stores, and offices with grime.

"No job too unusual" could be another company claim. A cemetery might hire you to clean crypts (exteriors only). Or you may be asked to wash graffiti off statues, war memorials, or other landmarks. Wisconsin Sparkle Wash affiliate Paul Hinz has regular work cleaning dairy barns. "The farmers are ecstatic the first time they see the job Sparkle Wash does on their barn. . . . Every one of them says they'll never do it again themselves." Small wonder.

The diesel-powered cleaning equipment features high-pressure pumps that can spray 4 to 10 gallons of water and cleaning agent a minute. That allows you to do more than merely wash dirt away. You'll be able to degrease vehicles and machinery and prep them for maintenance and painting. Mildew, fungus, film, and oxidation can all be removed from aluminum, vinyl, or steel house siding. You can strip paint, too, and brick, sandstone, concrete, and other masonry are no problem either, because unlike sandblasting, the Sparkle Wash process doesn't damage the surface or mortar joints. Wood restoration is becoming one more profitable service for franchisees like Bonnie Toner of New Hartford, New York. "We've had marvelous success with our process. Different chemicals are needed for removing different types of stains. We do three test sections and let the customers select the result they prefer."

The company provides a complete Sparkle Wash mobile unit, a customized Ford or GMC truck containing all cleaning equipment and biodegradable products, field-tested for environmental safety as well as quality. You'll also receive a spare-parts package, operations forms and manuals, and a uniform kit. Training is conducted in two phases: five days of technical instruction at the Sparkle Wash factory, where you'll learn how to operate and perform maintenance on the pump system and to determine the correct cleaning agents and methods to use, followed by three days of sales and start-up guidance in your territory.

With the list of the national accounts and potential new clients in your area that the company supplies, you'll implement a targeted marketing program and other special sales strategies, backed by brochures, flyers, coupons, and direct mail pieces, along with general media advertising. Sparkle Wash operators are also often able to get local press coverage for particularly ambitious or offbeat jobs. Your promotional efforts should be ongoing, the company recommends, yet many franchisees don't find it all that necessary. "We do very little advertising," admits a Maryland franchisee, a former teacher. "The system virtually sells itself once a customer sees a demonstration. And we get a lot of calls from people wanting our services because they were recommended by someone else."

Sending out newsletters and information bulletins, the company conducts regional clinics and international meetings, too. You'll have access, in fact, to the entire Sparkle Wash network. "If I require expertise beyond my own, guidance, support, direction, research, development, or any combination of these," Bonnie Toner declares, "I always have Sparkle Wash headquarters and my fellow franchisees to consult."

Granted an exclusive territory, you'll be running your business from home, and you can choose to operate part-time while continuing your previous career. But, as that Maryland franchisee found, those plans might change. Originally, her husband planned to run his Sparkle Wash franchise alone. "After only a month, the business grew so fast that Gary came to me and said that he wanted to quit teaching and work full-time with Sparkle Wash right away," she remembers.

The happy ending? "With Gary's full-time attention, the business grew even faster and soon we added our second mobile unit."

For further information contact:
Wallace J. Nido, President, Sparkle Wash International, 26851 Richmond Rd., Cleveland, OH 44146, 216-464-4212 or 1-800-321-0770, fax 216-464-8869

Triad Equipment Maintenance Systems, Inc.

Initial license fee: $10,000
Royalties: 3% to 5%
Advertising royalties: 1%
Minimum cash required: $24,000 to $74,600
Capital required: $24,000 to $74,600
Financing: None
Length of contract: 5 years, with three 5-year extensions

In business since: 1949
Franchising since: 1990
Total number of units: 9
Number of company-operated units: None
Total number of units planned, 1995: 60
Number of company-operated units planned, 1995: None

One of the ironies of the cleaning supplies business is that equipment repair rooms are notoriously messy. The disarray extends beyond the mere clutter of tools and scrap metal scattered about, the gloom and darkness, the grease stains that spatter the walls and floors. There's also run-down and inadequate machinery, erratic pricing systems, and poorly trained, poorly paid mechanics that don't even know how to do the repairs. Many distributors of janitorial products wind up viewing their equipment maintenance departments as a necessary liability.

Triad offers a program to turn these money-losing divisions into highly profitable service centers, so much so that individuals previously unaffiliated with a distribution business can buy a franchise to start a successful business from scratch exclusively devoted to cleaning equipment repair and maintenance. Others do have an established retail or wholesale supply business and choose the conversion franchise option to add Triad's system to their operation, enhancing their sales efforts by satisfying existing customers with better, more cost-efficient repairs and attracting new ones who need equipment repair today . . . and supplies tomorrow.

Emphasizing preventive maintenance as much as spot repairs, the Triad program enables you to sustain a client base that brings regular assignments and guaranteed revenues. It was developed through the actual experience of Aalen Aides, Inc., a prominent Midwestern sanitary supplies distributor that turned its admittedly inefficient repair room, highly unprofitable despite significant annual billings, into a thriving service center, through trial and error and considerable cost. Phil Consolino, a key player in the restructuring, figured that others in the industry were having the same problems and making the same mistakes because they were starting with the same misconceptions. "A repair business is as different from distribution as contract cleaning is. It requires different systems of accounting, sales, and compensation for employees." Documenting the system he and his colleagues successfully developed for Aalen Aides, Consolino began giving seminars at trade meetings and then turned to offering a formal franchise package.

With that package, you'll have management systems for controlling costs, calculating bills, and determining parts inventories that are appropriate for your particular market. You'll take advantage of Triad's broad network of suppliers to obtain these materials at good prices, while the company's IBM-compatible software package allows conversion franchisees to consolidate the financial planning and records for the sales and the repair wings of their business. And you'll also have an efficient structure for employee recruitment, hiring, training, and compensation, to maintain a staff of skilled technicians who are also adept at sales.

Most importantly, you'll be working with the patented tools invented by Triad engineers and exclusively available to franchisees; devices like the Tri-analyzer, a diagnostic apparatus that measures the performance of janitorial machinery and pinpoints equipment problems; the Tri-lift, which assists your technicians in raising and supporting the equipment while it's being repaired; the Tri-hoist, which lifts batteries out of equipment being serviced; and other new contraptions regularly being created.

You'll receive specialized instruction at the company's Michigan headquarters, consisting of three separate programs in general management, technical training, and mechanical training. And before you open your service center, a Triad representative will spend a minimum of five days there training your staff. The company conducts refresher training courses and seminars as well.

You'll be expected to spend 1 percent of your gross revenues on local advertising, in addition to the amount you contribute to Triad's corporate fund. For that contribution, you'll be supplied with direct-mail materials, brochures, ad copy and layouts, and other communications pieces; receive guidance on effective promotions strategies; and benefit from the company's system-wide marketing and lead-generation campaigns.

For further information contact:
Craig L. Rockwell, Director of Franchise Sales, Triad Equipment Maintenance Systems, Inc., 3300 E. Michigan Ave., P.O. Box 1108, Jackson, MI 49204, 517-788-7423 or 1-800-468-7423

Wash on Wheels, Inc. (WOW)

Initial license fee: $3,500 ($7,900 for Marine Clean)
Royalties: $80/month
Advertising royalties: None
Minimum cash required: $6,500 to $9,000
Capital required: $37,500 to $58,290
Financing: GMAC available
Length of contract: 5 years

In business since: 1966
Franchising since: 1987
Total number of units: 144

Number of company-operated units: None
Total number of units planned, 1995: NA
Number of company-operated units planned, 1995: NA

Wash on Wheels' founder and president George Louser got into his business rather by accident. After efforts to build a car wash were dampened by zoning regulations, the entrepreneur outfitted a trailer with a pressure-cleaning system and took his service directly to his customers. He quickly discovered that "mobile anything has a bright future," and by adding several different pieces of equipment and using a selection of chemicals and products, Wash on Wheels units could take care of a lot more than just cars. Now, franchisees handle an enormous range of outdoor and indoor cleaning needs for home-owners and businesses alike.

You may choose among several cleaning packages to provide either a specialized or comprehensive service. The high-pressure WOW exterior system allows you to clean buildings, roofs, walkways, parking lots, motor vehicles, industrial equipment, signs, and swimming pools, using water softeners to prevent spotting and high temperatures to sanitize more effectively. With the company's "Indoor Clean" service, you'll be able to rid ceilings and walls of stains, dust, grime, tobacco tars, and black carbon diffuser buildup without disrupting your clients' normal schedules, while the "HyDry Carpet Clean" gear is a spray mist dirt extraction method for carpeting, upholstery, and drapery, a low-moisture process that avoids harsh chemicals and oversaturation of sensitive materials. And if you have a yen to work around boats, the company's new "Marine Clean" package is also now available. In a typical four- to six-hour assignment at a yacht club, marina, boat yard, or individual vessel, you'll perform such jobs as washing decks, cleaning and degreasing the engine room, vacuuming and shampooing the carpeting and upholstery inside to remove the mildew and spills that plague life on the sea, and even use sandblasting guns and water-spraying equipment to strip barnacles from boats in dry dock.

You can commence your Wash on Wheels operation by offering any one of these services, expanding to others as your cash flow and experience increases, or you can start with a complete franchise package. Because of the breadth of work they handle, full-service WOW franchisees avoid slow seasons and can do several jobs for each customer during a single call, providing comprehensive all-in-one exterior and interior maintenance. Don Kesler of Athens, Georgia, takes care of 40 schools, washing kitchens, playground equipment, carpeting, classroom and gym floors, and removing gum and graffiti. Cincinnati franchisee Sandy Hafer is equally busy doing clean-ups of newly constructed houses and buildings, clean-outs for apartment complex managers after tenants vacate, and weekly all-purpose cleaning for several restaurant chains.

Outfitted with the equipment you purchase from the company, your Wash on Wheels mobile unit will be custom-built at the company's factory. You'll learn how the machinery and chemical products are used to perform the full range of cleaning tasks during two weeks of training, covering the management and administrative aspects of running your operation, too. Spending the days in the classroom and several evenings with Wash on Wheels crews doing jobs in the area, you'll be taught by a team of nine professionals, including a CPA, a chemist, a home economist, and a marketing expert. After you've been in business for 45 days, you'll return to the Orlando area for a brush-up session. The company keeps you further informed through newsletters, regional meetings, and national conventions.

Wash on Wheels devises a 30-day business development plan to get each franchisee started. The home office will run a telemarketing campaign to reach potential commercial accounts in your territory, while you implement company-developed direct mail programs, make calls on prospects using the sales portfolios with which you're supplied, and place predesigned yellow pages and other print ads. For each of your first three months in business, Wash on Wheels sends along a follow-up kit with tapes and other support tools that offer additional technical, sales, and marketing guidance.

Wash on Wheels fashioned its training and ongoing support systems with the understanding that many of its franchisees have little or no cleaning service experience. And the variety of equipment packages makes opportunities available to those with limited capital. "WOW works with people on financial assistance," says George Louser. "When we decide that the individuals are right for us and we're right for them, we find we can get things done together. There are not many obstacles that we can't overcome."

For further information contact:
 WOW Inc. of Orlando, 5401 S. Bryant Ave., Sanford, FL 32773, 407-321-4010
 or 1-800-345-1969, fax 407-321-3409

15. The Printing and Photographic Industry

Contents

Photographic Services

Ident-A-Kid Services of America

Initial license fee: $12,500
Royalties: None
Advertising royalties: None
Minimum cash required: $12,500
Capital required: $12,500
Financing: None
Length of contract: Perpetual

In business since: 1986
Franchising since: 1987
Total number of units: 190
Number of company-operated units: 1
Total number of units planned, 1995: 230
Number of company-operated units planned, 1995: 1

Perhaps nothing is more frightening to parents than the thought that their child may become one of the 1.8 million children who are reported separated from their parents each year. Many of these children turn up safe and sound, but the need to be prepared is underscored by the fact that the number of children who run away or are kidnapped rises every year. In fact, Ident-A-Kid's founder and president, Robert King, started the company when a friend of his lost a child in a shopping mall and was unable to describe her own child to authorities because near-hysteria had rendered her speechless.

An Ident-A-Kid franchisee offers parents a laminated card featuring a photograph of their child along with all the child's vital statistics, at a relatively inexpensive price (approximately $5 for one card; $8 for two; $10 for three). Should a child become separated from his or her parents, the card will prove a valuable source of information to police, the media, and anyone else involved in the search.

With the inital license fee of $12,500, the franchisee obtains the right to market the ID service to schools, day-care centers, churches, and community centers. The required equipment, engraved with the Ident-A-Kid trademark and logo from headquarters, including portable photographic, fingerprinting, and laminating equipment; backdrops; and a computer system and software, are all included in the price of the license fee. A two-day training session, during which franchisees learn how to use the photographic equipment and how to market Ident-A-Kid service, is also provided.

For further information contact:
  Robert King, Ident-A-Kid Services of America, 2810 Scherer Dr.,
  St. Petersburg, FL 33716, 813-577-4646

One-Hour Moto Photo, Inc.

Initial license fee: $35,000
Royalties: 6%
Advertising royalties: 0.5%
Minimum cash required: $40,000
Capital required: $116,200
Financing: Assistance in obtaining
Length of contract: 10 years

In business since: 1981
Franchising since: 1982
Total number of units: 340
Number of company-operated units: 71
Total number of units planned, 1995: 600
Number of company-operated units planned, 1995: 100

The development of the U.S. film-processing industry bodes well for
Moto Photo. The industry's sales have increased annually for the past
20 years, and it currently does $5 billion a year in business. Forty per
cent of that already goes to laboratories that produce prints virtually
while you wait, and analysts think the almost-instant processing segment of the business will increase. Moto Photo is the largest franchisor in this field.

Moto Photo has received smash reviews in the business and trade
press. The *National OTC Stock Journal* wrote: "The very nature of Moto
Photo's operations suggests a long and healthy life in the photo-
processing industry." According to *Photo Weekly*, "Moto Photo has
never been a play-it-by-ear operation. It was carefully conceived,
every detail planned, and all of it executed with great skill and intelligence." And *Processing Week* points approvingly to the company's
"top-notch advertising program, including TV and radio
commercials."

About 90 percent of the company's franchisees have no background
in photofinishing. They have been homemakers, government employees, accountants, and retail store managers. A few who already
owned a photofinishing operation decided to convert to Moto Photo
because of the franchisor's advertising program and the discounts
available through its volume purchasing of paper, film, and supplies.

The company assists franchisees with site selection, store design, construction, and equipment installation. Since both the industry and the franchisor are relatively young, franchisees have a wider latitude in choosing locations than they would in a more mature business, such as fast-food franchising with a major company.

Training at Moto Photo corporate headquarters in Dayton, Ohio, lasts four weeks. As part of its store-opening assistance, a Moto Photo representative will work at your side during your first week in business. Thereafter a company representative will visit your store quarterly to give you any business assistance you might need. The company customizes an advertising and marketing plan for each franchise and requires that you spend 6 percent of your gross sales on local advertising.

For further information contact:
  Paul Pieschel, Vice President, Franchise Development, One-Hour Moto Photo, Inc., 4444 Lake Center Dr., Dayton, OH 45426, 1-800-733-6686

The Sports Section, Inc.

Initial license fee: $14,500 to $29,500
Royalties: None
Advertising royalties: None
Minimum cash required: $14,500
Capital required: Sufficient to cover 1 month's living expenses
Financing: Available
Length of contract: 2 to 5 years

In business since: 1983
Franchising since: 1984
Total number of units: 51
Number of company-operated units: 2
Total number of units planned, 1995: 175
Number of company-operated units planned, 1995: 2

"It still amazes me that I can make more in some months than I used to make in a year," proclaims Nashua, New Hampshire, Sports Section franchisee Bill Thorp. "All this is happening in a lousy New England economy, but people keep buying pictures."

His experience isn't uncommon: recessions don't usually keep many parents from being willing to spend $10 or so for some nice, professional photographs of their kids. Which means there are plenty of youth sports groups, from Little Leagues to Pee Wee football, hockey, and soccer organizations, that will be glad to contract you to take team and individual pictures that the Sports Section home office makes into a wide line of products. Nursery schools and child-care centers, too, are target locations, where you can provide a slightly different selection of merchandise.

You'll have pennants, buttons, key chains, posters, statuettes and trophies, and other collectibles to offer, incorporating both posed and action shots, along with a basic set of wallet-sized to 8-by-11 photos. Parents who chewed a lot of Topps bubble gum in their youth especially go for the "MVP" player cards that come complete with a picture of their child on the front, and his or her stats printed on the back.

Surprisingly, no photographic experience is required to run the operation. "When I consider that I knew little about sports and even less about photography, I'm rather amazed that I actually took the plunge," admits Mickie Cooles, an Arlington, Texas, franchisee. "As I begin my sixth year, my business is growing. I have one full-time salesperson/photographer working with me now and several part-times. As usual, we have booked more kids than we can shoot before we'll have our spring season wrapped up. These kinds of problems I can live with."

Working out of your home, you'll shoot on location, sending the film into Sports Section headquarters for processing and developing at wholesale prices. "The lab has worked hard and done a wonderful job for us on both quality and delivery," Mickie Cooles reports. "The few problems we have encountered have been taken care of quickly and efficiently."

Even before you pay your initial franchise fee, a company representative will come to you to give sales and marketing training, plus photographic instruction, at the same time determining the viability of your territory. Once you've made the final decision to join The Sports Section, the company will supply camera equipment, both outdoor and indoor gear depending on the franchising package you choose, as well as an operations manual, starter kit, photo presentation book, and all necessary administrative and customer order forms. The home office keeps in touch by phone and with a monthly newsletter. For more substantial updates and follow-up instruction, semiannual photography and sales seminars are conducted at Atlanta headquarters. "It's a lot of information, but I really enjoy meeting with all the other franchisees and exchanging ideas," says Bill Thorp. "The social aspects aren't bad either."

That's not an unimportant consideration to The Sports Section's managers, who believe enjoying your job is key to your and the company's success alike. "You don't have to clean houses or carpets or make food or wear a tie," they explain. "You don't have to watchdog any disgruntled or bored employees. There are other franchises that you can make money with, but as long as you're going to be making money, shouldn't you have fun doing it?"

For further information contact:
   Nancy Wood, Franchise Director, The Sports Section, Inc., 3120 Medlock
   Bridge Rd., Bldg. A, Norcross, GA 30071, 404-416-6604 or 1-800-321-9127

Quick-Printing and Related Services

AlphaGraphics Printshops of the Future

Initial license fee: $49,900
Royalties: 8% decreasing to 3%
Advertising royalties: 2% after first year
Minimum cash required: $75,000
Capital required: $300,000
Financing: Approximately 70%
Length of contract: 20 years

In business since: 1970
Franchising since: 1980
Total number of units: 325
Number of company-operated units: 10
Total number of units planned, 1995: 500
Number of company-operated units planned, 1995: 25

When AlphaGraphics officials call themselves a global electronic printing and graphics network, they're not exaggerating. In 1989, the first quick-print shop opened in the Soviet Union—an AlphaGraphics franchise.

Money magazine, for one, thinks those possibilities are excellent, naming AlphaGraphics one of the top 10 franchises for the 1990s. Actually positioned somewhere between a quick copy business and a commercial printer, AlphaGraphics Printshops offer many services to stand out in a crowded market. The company, for example, was the first to implement a laser typesetting system. You'll also provide high-speed duplication, offset printing in multiple colors, and extensive desktop publishing capabilities, including computer-generated artwork, charts, graphics, and color slide production. Adding a glitzy touch to business cards, stationery, or invitations, embossing and foil stamping are available, not to mention custom self-stick notes and printed Rolodex address cards.

Your customers won't even have to leave their offices, sending their orders, text, and specifications by fax. You and your staff can furnish graphics design expertise. "Customers don't need to bring in a camera-ready original, just a camera-ready idea. We create the original." Or, taking advantage of the self-service opportunities you extend, they can work on your easy-to-use equipment to create and print documents themselves.

Another important service is the AlphaLink computer communications network directly connecting your shop with other Alpha-Graphics franchises around the world. Well beyond the capabilities of fax service, it allows a full package of material to be transferred instantly to an out-of-state or foreign location, reproduced with the same quality and in the same professional format as the original. That means a client can send a document to Moscow, for instance, in seconds and have it printed and distributed there within hours.

AlphaGraphics favors franchise candidates with corporate management experience. While some existing print shop operators have converted their businesses into an AlphaGraphics franchise, you don't need to have a background in the field. You'll receive a total of ten weeks of training during your first year in business, including three to four in class and at an existing facility before you open your shop, as well as a package of audio-, video-, and computer-based instruction tools to train your staff. And AlphaGraphics' "sweat equity" program will help you attract talented, ambitious employees who work toward the goal of owning their own Printshop in the future.

The company assists with site selection. Its staff compares markets, evaluates the potential competition, helps you to arrange an equitable lease, and gives you guidelines for the construction and high-tech decor of your facility. You'll be set up with equipment like a high-speed electronic copier, a press, and a graphics camera, and receive a computerized point-of-sale system, with custom software for generating price quotes, producing work orders, printing invoices, and maintaining financial data. With regional managers and field personnel visiting periodically to assist your growth and the home-office staff available by phone to answer questions, AlphaGraphics also provides monthly, quick-turnaround accounting services so you'll have up-to-date and accurate information about the shape of your business.

Printed advertising and sales materials will be sent to you to use in your shop, in local print media, and in direct mailings. Taking advantage of the network's "ad share" system, where franchisers make their own successful promotional pieces available for one another's use, you'll also benefit from the company's automated catalogue mailing program, which markets AlphaGraphics' products and services to selected potential customers.

Along with following corporate procedures, you're requested to extend one additional courtesy: adhering to the company's environmental policy. AlphaGraphics asks its franchisees to integrate ecologic considerations into their business planning and decision making, important considerations indeed for operations that use a lot of trees. Appropriately, the policy suggests that you make maximum use of recycled paper (while maintaining quality standards and cost effectiveness), supply your customers with conservation information to encourage them to implement measures of their own, and offer them financial incentives to cut down on waste. In today's environmentally conscious world, it's a message that AlphaGraphics patrons are taking to heart.

For further information contact:
Helen Franklin, Director of Franchise Sales, AlphaGraphics Printshops of the Future, 3760 N. Commerce Dr., Tucson, AZ 85705, 602-293-9200 or 1-800-528-4885, fax 602-887-2850

ALU, Inc.

Initial license fee: $4,795
Royalties: $1/job for client acquired by company .
Advertising royalties: None
Minimum cash required: $4,795
Capital required: $4,975
Financing: Available
Length of contract: none

In business since: 1987
Franchising since: 1988
Total number of units: 150
Number of company-operated units: 5
Total number of units planned, 1995: 200
Number of company-operated units planned, 1995: 15

Countless repair services swear they fix products "better than new." ALU is one of the few that can actually live up to that claim: The laser printer cartridges that you'll refill print at least 25 percent to 30 percent longer than new ones.

This is a relatively new industry, made possible by the development of the personal copier in the early eighties, followed a few years later by the laser printer. Today, over 100 companies worldwide—Apple, HP, and the original manufacturer, Canon, to name a few—market these machines, most of which use disposable toner cartridges that cost between $65 and $135 and that usually need to be replaced after every 2,000 to 3,000 copies. Anyone who's used these printers knows what happens when the toner runs out: smudged print, light print, *no* print.

ALU (which stands for Alpha Laser Unlimited) developed a method for "recharging" the cartridges, as it were, refilling them with toner at less than half the cost to the customer of a replacement. The work is fully guaranteed, and 3 percent of the money may be donated to a nonprofit organization in the customer's name, if the customer desires. And, ALU has profited from the environmentally safe aspect of its business. The State of Michigan, for example, now requires that cartridges be refilled rather than thrown away.

Your clients will either mail you the cartridge or have you pick it up for a small surcharge. Testing first to make sure the cartridge can be refilled—about 7 percent can't be, because of damage or age—you'll add toner. Because you've put in up to 20 percent more toner than the original manufacturer did, the cartridge will indeed last longer and print better than a new one.

With cartridge sales for these machines topping 9 million annually—each owner going through an average of seven to eleven per year—your business potential is substantial. And don't forget that the same cartridges are used in many of the top-selling fax machines, another booming segment of your market. To expand your services further, ALU will train you, for an additional $1,300, to perform preventive maintenance and basic repair of laser printers and copiers. You might consider retailing new and used machines, and their support equipment, to your customers as well.

To learn the mechanics of refilling toner cartridges, you'll attend a five-day instruction session in Dallas. You have the option of bringing a second person along, and, while you'll have to pay for your own airfare, ALU provides the accommodations at the hotel where the training will be held. In small classes averaging one instructor for every two to three students, you'll also be taught how to set up your business and establish working relationships with computer dealerships and printer and copier salespeople. If you've signed up for the extra training, you'll learn how to fix laser printers and copiers over an additional two days—a sufficient amount of time to master the details of machinery whose complexities lie in their design and manufacture rather than in their repair.

ALU will extend ongoing consultation and send out information updates on new technological developments in this rapidly evolving industry. The company also supplies you with the necessary tools and

60 bottles of toner, replacement wicks, magnetic and plastic separator tabs, and antistatic mailing bags. You'll be able to purchase additional toner and material factory-direct at lower prices.

Depending on the franchise's location, business is conducted either by mail or by pick-up. And location of refill centers vary according to need. ALU representatives help you to determine the best space for your business.

To help you develop your client base, ALU will furnish 1,000 names and addresses of laser printer and copier owners in your region, and the company's marketers will work to acquire regular accounts for you. Administering a co-op advertising program, ALU focuses on print ads in computer magazines, trade publications, and national periodicals like *USA Today*, the *Wall Street Journal*, and *Barron's*.

In return, the only royalties you'll be required to pay are $1 for each cartridge you process, and only when it's for a client that ALU acquired. But that's a two-way street, and you could wind up making money from the deal. For if you negotiate a national or corporate account yourself, well, then, your fellow ALU affiliates will be sending *you* the dollar.

For further information contact:
  Robert McNabb, President, ALU, Inc., 1438 Crescent, Suite 208, Carrollton, TX 75006, 1-800-752-7370

Insty-Prints, Inc.

Initial license fee: $24,500
Royalties: 4.5%
Advertising royalties: 2%
Minimum cash required: $30,000
Capital required: $30,000
Financing: Available through third parties
Length of contract: 15 years

In business since: 1965
Franchising since: 1967
Total number of units: 300
Number of company-operated units: 1
Total number of units planned, 1995: NA
Number of company-operated units planned, 1995: NA

Think of all the printed forms you see in one day. At work, there are letterhead stationery and business cards, standard business forms, and special forms for specialized business needs. Depending upon where you work, you might also encounter stacks of résumés. And when you get home, there's the wedding invitation that came in the mail and the thank-you card from a friend for the condolence card you sent.

Print circumscribes modern life, much of it the kind of printing that small shops do in a short period of time. Did it ever occur to you that somebody makes a good living doing all that work? And that you could be that somebody? The quick-print industry has enough business to supply a good living to thousands of people. According to Insty-Prints, only about 25 percent of quick-printing work is currently being done by franchise shops. That, as the company sees it, leaves a lot of business that can be lured away from the independents by the brand-name recognition that can be built by national advertising and the purchasing clout that can be created by buying in volume.

Insty-Prints wants you to know that you can easily enter this field if you have the necessary finances. You do not need to know printing. Someone else can manage your store—or stores—someone whom the company will help you find and train if you wish. It only takes two to run an Insty-Prints store, and your franchise package includes free training for both.

If you do run things yourself, you may be delighted to know that this franchise keeps normal business hours. So you can have your cake and eat it, too—at a normal dinner hour, with your family. Husband-and-wife teams, in fact, operate many Insty-Prints shops. One such family was formed when an Insty-Prints franchisee married one of his customers and brought her into the business.

The franchisor will supervise your site selection and building or remodeling work. A clean, efficient look is part of the company image, and your store has to reflect this. To make sure that it does, Insty-Prints will help you set up a layout that facilitates efficient work traffic.

You will learn good business management in your two weeks of training at Insty-Prints' Minneapolis headquarters as well as the nuts and bolts of running the machines you will use in your shop. A week of on-site training at your printing center will lead up to your opening day. After opening, you can get help through the company WATS line at any time.

Although you can ultimately run your store through a manager, the company insists that for the first few weeks you get your hands dirty and run it yourself. Insty-Prints wants you to get a feel for the way your business works. It wants you to know what you're doing, even if you finally pay somebody else to do it for you.

Of your initial investment, $87,000 goes toward fixtures, equipment, and signage, and $5,000 goes for inventory. After that, you can choose your own sources for supplies, although the company emphasizes that you can reduce your costs by buying through its national accounts.

For further information contact:
Francis E. O'Neil, Insty-Prints, Inc., 1010 S. Seventh St., Suite 450, Minneapolis, MN 55415, 612-337-9800

PIP Printing

Initial license fee: $40,000
Royalties: 6% to 8%
Advertising royalties: 1%
Minimum cash required: $77,000 plus living expenses
Capital required: $201,000 to $211,000
Financing: Available
Length of contract: 20 years

In business since: 1965
Franchising since: 1968
Total number of units: 1,129
Number of company-operated units: 3
Total number of units planned, 1995: NA
Number of company-operated units planned, 1995: None

PIP didn't exactly decide to quit while it was ahead. Instead, the company that virtually founded the retail instant printing industry has shifted its focus away from that now-crowded field.

"Enough of the 1990s," as franchise consultant Patrick J. Boroian advises. "Anyone shopping for a franchise right now should be thinking in terms of the year 2000."

The PIP strategy is to go after the lucrative $15 billion-a-year business printing market. Gone is the old red, white, and blue decor used when PIP centers catered primarily to individual customers, replaced by a stylish, streamlined, corporate-oriented logo and visual identity that the company spent over $10 million to create. "The image issue is very important," according to vice president of marketing Doug Reiter. "It could mean the survival of your business."

But PIP has made more than surface changes, upgrading its equipment and services to encompass the huge range of printing services required by businesses. And those professional clients are more sophisticated and demanding than they were even just a few years ago, insisting on quality paper, multiple colors, sleek, eye-catching designs, and wanting all their printing needs handled in one place with the same speedy service available at quick-print shops. With machinery like color and forms presses, high-speed duplicators, and desktop publishing equipment, and backed by a reliable team of vendors, you'll be able to produce such materials as bound presentations and catalogues, posters and menus, business forms and stationery, and two-sided, full-color brochures in enormous amounts or quantities as low as 1,000, usually for little more than half the price that commercial printers charge. In addition, you'll help your clients select ink color and paper, devise the layout and design for their pieces, and determine ways to meet deadlines and budget conditions.

Structuring its franchise support services to benefit new and veteran PIP center owners alike, the company both eases the growing pains of a recently opened shop and aids in centralizing an expanding multiple-store operation. As a new franchisee, you'll receive guidance and assistance in site selection from a PIP regional manager, while the company's legal department will review your lease. The printing operations staffs will develop an equipment package for you, customized for the particular printing needs of the businesses in your territory; prepare a store layout and floor plan that positions fixtures, printers, and counters for good work flow; and supervise the installation of the machinery.

While the finishing touches are being put on your store, you'll attend a two-week training program at the company's Agoura Hills, California, headquarters. Taught by a team of printing, finance, and marketing experts, you'll be instructed in graphic arts, business and personnel management, sales methods, and customer service, spending a large part of your time in the printing lab to become familiar with the technology and techniques you'll be using. PIP furnishes ongoing training as well; you and your key staff members will choose from a wide selection of workshops regularly held across the country, featuring audience participation and covering such topics as advanced printing and graphics, employee recruiting, and telemarketing.

To help franchisees stay abreast of the constant technological advances they'll need to make, PIP employs a full-time research staff that attends trade shows, meets with vendors, and culls information from industry data bases. The department studies, evaluates, and makes recommendations on new equipment and processes, along with suggesting pricing strategies for your expanded services, presenting its reports in the company's newsletter, bimonthly *PIPline* magazine, and special bulletins.

Because effective marketing is sometimes as crucial to success in the printing industry as research and development, PIP's strategy is to maintain consistent, highly visible advertising, including award-winning television commercials. Benefiting from a national campaign that, according to research, has brought PIP the greatest brand awareness of any retail printer in the country and that positions you as a one-stop source for business printing, you'll use the radio spots, newspaper and print ads, point-of-purchase displays, brochures, and posters that PIP supplies for your local efforts. The company also assists by helping you form regional advertising cooperatives with other franchisees and coordinating a direct mail program that will reach hundreds of potential customers within three weeks of your opening. And through PIP's national preferred accounts program, you can add large, established businesses to your client base.

Your PIP field support representative will offer further aid in developing your clientele, dropping by regularly to gauge your center's overall performance and advise you on ways to strengthen your business (you can also request special visits to get help on a specific problem or opportunity). In turn, the company gets feedback from the franchisees through a 10-person owner advisory committee and the biennial PIP conclaves.

Most PIP franchisees had no printing background when they started their business; the qualifications are of a more intangible variety. To evaluate your prospects, the company's senior executives will ask you to meet with them in California, reimbursing your expenses (if you join the franchise) by the time you open your PIP center. That vote of confidence does, however, need to be matched by your own initiative. "Don't be afraid to work," suggests Tom Fulner, who owns 15 PIP centers in Nashville and Indianapolis. "If customers are satisfied in the service and products you offer, your business is going to grow. It's no great secret."

For further information contact:
  Teresa Guerin, Business Development, PIP Printing, 27001 Agoura Rd., P.O. Box 3007, Agoura Hills, CA 91376, 818-880-3800 or 1-800-292-4747

PrintMasters

Initial license fee: $18,500
Royalties: 4% first year, 6% thereafter
Advertising royalties: 2%
Minimum cash required: $39,500
Capital required: $40,000
Financing: Available
Length of contract: 20 years

In business since: 1976
Franchising since: 1976
Total number of units: 116
Number of company-operated units: None

Total number of units planned, 1995: 800
Number of company-operated units planned, 1995: None

Emphasizing profitability above volume, PrintMasters' management understands that it takes time for a business to get off the ground. So it has its franchisees begin with modest operations, expanding as their business warrants. You won't be required to obtain a lot of equipment for which you won't have much use right away, or be burdened with a heavy initial overhead. Even your franchise royalties are kept to a minimum as you're starting out.

Nevertheless, from your opening day, you'll be able to provide a broad range of printing services for your clients—small businesses, law firms, medical and professional offices, and manufacturing companies. You'll handle short-run one-color jobs and multipage, multicolor projects alike, producing letterheads, envelopes, business cards, flyers, forms, and other materials that businesses need in their daily operations. Photocopying, collating, stapling, binding, and folding are other basic tasks you'll perform. And your layout and design, desktop publishing, and fax capabilities will be further draws for customers.

PrintMasters' "quick start" program helps its franchisees get their businesses going quickly—without rushing any of the necessary steps. Company officers will perform a marketing study for your region and help with site selection. Most PrintMaster shops can be started with about 1,000 square feet of space, but you'll want to have additional room available for future growth. Analyzing possible locations, PrintMasters will participate in negotiating the lease and assist you in obtaining the necessary licenses and permits.

Training is another area, PrintMasters believes, in which time is well worth spending. You'll receive four weeks of instruction, in fact, two at the company's Torrance, California, training center and two in your own shop. During this month, you'll be methodically taken through the whole PrintMasters service process, from initial contact with a customer, to obtaining camera-ready artwork, through production and final delivery. And, of course, you'll be taught the technical skills to operate and maintain all equipment—including the computer system you'll use for inventory control, business forecasts, and sales and customer analysis—as well as day-to-day management methods and marketing techniques.

Helping you hire and train your staff and initiate your bookkeeping and accounting systems, the on-site PrintMasters instructor will also install and calibrate your equipment. The company's group purchasing power means you'll be supplied with advanced printing machinery and business computer software, along with cabinetry, shelving, and fixtures, at discount prices.

Field personnel make regular visits to your shop, offering guidance and performing equipment and operation evaluations, while the home office remains reachable by phone. Long Beach, California, franchisee Rachel Vincent reports, "When I need something, there is no waiting around for help, instead of 'tomorrow' or even days, which I hear is common with other franchises. I get help most times within two hours." And you'll be able to meet corporate staff and fellow franchisees at reularly scheduled gatherings.

Marketing support begins with a custom-designed grand opening advertising campaign, a "total sales promotion package" that takes advantage of direct mail and local print media. Managing a country-wide program, PrintMasters will continue to furnish ad copy and art-work for you as well, and its sales network will be signing national and regional clients, many of whom may be operating in your territory.

About 75 percent of PrintMaster franchisees have middle-management business experience, which the company considers the best qualification for the job. That's not, however, a requirement, nor is a background in the printing industry. PrintMaster shops are cus-tomarily a three-person operation: one to work the counter, taking orders and dealing with the customers; one to operate the machines; and one to manage the store and be the marketing person. While some franchisees hire managers and employees, many find this setup highly suitable for a family business.

You're free to establish whatever operating hours seem best for your location. An 8 A.M. to 6 P.M., five-day-a-week schedule will normally suffice, but you should expect longer work days early on while you're starting out.

For further information contact:
  Stephan Metz, National Sales Director, PrintMasters, 370 S. Crenshaw Blvd., Suite E-100, Torrance, CA 90503, 213-328-0303 or 1-800-221-8945, fax 213-533-4836

Quik Print

Initial license fee: $15,000
Royalties: 5%
Advertising royalties: None
Minimum cash required: $109,000
Capital required: $50,000

Financing: Available
Length of contract: 25 years

In business since: 1963
Franchising since: 1966
Total number of units: 210
Number of company-operated units: 78
Total number of units planned, 1995: NA
Number of company-operated units planned, 1995: NA

Quik Print does not require franchisees to have a background in the printing field and they need no technical expertise. In fact, Quik Print likens its presses to office machines—even though they turn out everything from forms, letterhead, and envelopes to bulletins, catalogues, and price sheets. Store owners create plates for their presses with a push-button camera, use a paper drill no more complicated than a drill press, work with an easy-to-use paper cutter, and fold paper with a machine that works with the turn of a screw—all this in a store that occupies 800 square feet.

Finding the location for your Quik Print franchise is also easy. Quik Print will select the site for your business (a downtown or suburban area with a dense population) in consultation with you, and it will examine the lease, give you a floor plan, check the building codes, arrange for utility service, and put you in touch with suppliers.

Your franchise package will also include all the cabinetry, office and printing equipment, supplies, and inventory you need to start your business. While you can buy your supplies from whomever you wish (as long as they meet Quik Print's standards), the company will offer you the opportunity to take advantage of its national contracts.

Quik Print franchisees train for four weeks at company headquarters in Wichita, Kansas, where the company picks up all expenses, including your round-trip airfare. There you will study bookkeeping, personnel, marketing, and advertising.

Two weeks before you open your Quik Print business, a company representative will come to your store and train you in the operation of your equipment. After you start your business, Quik Print will monitor you through daily reports and generate periodic analyses from them that will give you an overview of your ongoing performance. Your bookkeeping, done according to Quik Print's system, which you will implement using the daily work ledger, invoices, and statement forms the company provides, should take no more than 20 minutes of your time each day. To minimize your financial burdens during the start-up period, Quik Print will not collect a royalty the first 90 days you are in business.

Quik Print will set up and conduct a direct mail campaign during the first few weeks of your business without any additional expense to you, and it will give you the mailing list to use in the future. In addition, the company will give you advice on how to customize an advertising campaign to your market and will also provide advertising copy at your request.

For further information contact:
Johnny Tarrant, Senior Vice President, Quik Print, 3445 N. Web Rd., Wichita, KS 67226, 316-636-5666

Sir Speedy Printing Centers of America, Inc.

Initial license fee: $17,500
Royalties: 4% first year, 6% thereafter
Advertising royalties: 1% first year, 2% thereafter
Minimum cash required: $50,000
Capital required: $175,000
Financing: $125,000
Length of contract: 20 years

In business since: 1968
Franchising since: 1968
Total number of units: 875
Number of company-operated units: None
Total number of units planned, 1995: 1,000
Number of company-operated units planned, 1995: None

At the end of 1989, Sir Speedy became the first quick-printing system to reach $300 million in sales. This was the second consecutive year Sir Speedy franchisees led the industry.

Things were very different in 1981 when company president and CEO Don Lowe took the helm. At that time, the franchisor was emerging from Chapter XI reorganization, system-wide sales were $50 million, and many of the company's franchisees couldn't pay their royalties.

Currently, average sales for the company's top 25 printing centers run well over $1 million. And Sir Speedy's more than 800 franchisees continue to outsell all other quick printers by a sizable margin.

Your Sir Speedy printing store will have the capacity to turn out a variety of material, including credit forms, catalogue sheets, employment applications, legal briefs, purchase orders, maps and charts, form letters, menus, contracts, and scratch pads.

Sir Speedy prides itself on its ability to originate and improve the appearance of customer material. Much of this work is done through electronic publishing technology, which includes graphic design, layout, and typography. The company also has the largest installed computer base in the industry.

Since 1989, Sir Speedy has been able to offer fast, economical creation and reproduction of color text and graphics on paper, 35-mm slides, or overhead transparencies.

In 1987, the company introduced Fastfax, the world's largest public facsimile network. Besides the ability to send and receive documents worldwide, Fastfax helps franchisees expedite orders with customers who have their own fax machines.

Sir Speedy chooses the right spot for your quick-print store—typically occupying 1,000 to 1,500 square feet—and helps with the lease negotiations. Your franchise package contains all the supplies you need to begin your business, from a roller desensitizer to box wax, which you can reorder from the company or other approved sources. You can get discounts of up to 40 percent off retail prices by ordering through Sir Speedy.

The company pays for the training of two people, including their transportation and lodging (but not their food), at its training center in Laguna Hills, California. The two-week course consists of units on equipment operation, business management, marketing, and sales. You can also send additional people to the company school in California, but you will pay for all expenses incidental to their training except tuition.

Sir Speedy also offers "graduate training." At your option, you can spend an additional week learning the company's system at one of the Sir Speedy stores. This will give you hands-on experience in counter sales, pricing, and paper recognition.

A company representative will help you hire your employees in the two-week period before you open, and he or she will assist you in establishing a work routine that will keep your shop functioning smoothly. You can call the company expediter toll free to discuss any problems that arise once you begin operations.

For further information contact:
   Sir Speedy Printing Centers, 23131 Verdugo Dr., Laguna Hills, CA 92653,
   1-800-854-3321

The Ink Well of America, Inc.

Initial license fee: $29,500
Royalties: 4% first year, 6% thereafter
Advertising royalties: 2.5%
Minimum cash required: $40,000

Capital required: $144,600 to $190,200
Financing: Lease programs and SBA loans available
Length of contract: 25 years

In business since: 1972
Franchising since: 1981
Total number of units: 65
Number of company-operated units: 1
Total number of units planned, 1995: 300
Number of company-operated units planned, 1995: 1

It seems like practically yesterday that businesses started putting the carbon paper away for good, turning to the marvels of personal copiers and quick-print shops. For a while the mere instant gratification was satisfying enough. But speed alone doesn't cut it any longer and gone already are the days where black ink on white paper sufficed. Now, businesses want multicolored printed products and color copies, electronic publishing, and electronically transmitted documents. And they still want it done right away.

According to The Ink Well's chairman and CEO George Domsic, too many print shops aren't evolving to meet these new customer demands. "The real problem with the old-line quick printing operations is that the sophistication of the management system really wasn't there," he explains. "Many of them learned most of what they know in the first year or so of operation and are still doing the same things 15 or 20 years later." Although Ink Well centers have been in business for a couple of decades themselves, the company keeps updating its systems to provide advanced capabilities, higher quality, and more service.

Along with basic printing and duplicating, you'll be able to do jobs once manageable only by far more elaborate and expensive facilities. That means lower costs and greater convenience for your clients, mainly small and medium-size companies who can avoid parceling their work out to several different shops and have all their printing needs met at one location. Those needs are ongoing, too, and if you treat your customers right, The Ink Well's theory is, they will come back. To encourage repeat business, you'll keep their artwork on file for reorders, and act as a dependable printing consultant, helping them choose among the wide variety of options available. And to emphasize your professionalism, the customer-service section of your Ink Well center—partitioned from the work area—features an office look with carpeting and modular cabinetry.

The company helps you set up the facility, starting by either selecting a site for you or evaluating the location you have chosen, analyzing local demographics, competition, and market potential. Strip-shopping malls, business parks, and downtown office areas with proximity to a minimum of 800 to 1,000 businesses tend to make the best choices. Then, The Ink Well gives construction and design guidance, and assists you in obtaining equipment and supplies. There's no standard package: The layout and the machinery you'll use will be determined by the work your particular market demands. Taking equipment placement, storage needs, work flow patterns, and traffic into account, and seeking to economize on interior space requirements, The Ink Well develops a custom facility configuration with you.

You'll obtain your equipment—tested and evaluated by the company's technical staff—from leading manufacturers at prices significantly lower than retail. The company, meanwhile, will provide you with an initial inventory of supplies like papers, ink, film, and chemicals that you'll require to begin operations. And by projecting printing demand and specialty needs based on experiences in similar markets, it makes sure you won't be saddled with unnecessary stock.

With a combination of classroom sessions and work at an established Ink Well shop, the franchisee training aims to make you adept in print sales and production, and to help you become a highly profitable business manager as well. You'll spend two weeks at the Columbus, Ohio, training center, where you're guided through each phase of The Ink Well operation, with special emphasis on offset printing, shop administration, marketing techniques, and accounting procedures. You'll also have two more weeks of instruction at your facility prior to and following your opening.

To publicize your new shop, the Ink Well will send press releases to local media and announcements to your personal mailing list. You'll also be outfitted with marketing and promotional materials on an ongoing basis, an assortment of newspaper and magazine ads, radio spots, and direct mail and point-of-purchase pieces.

The Ink Well recognizes that it can't extend sufficient direct support to the nationwide network of franchises from corporate headquarters alone, so regional offices have also been established. The staff in Columbus still stays in touch, and keeps you informed with news bulletins about the new products, profit-making ideas, administrative hints, and organizational developments. But your regional manager will serve as your closest link to the company, handling your questions and problems, conducting regular area seminars, offering advice on expanding your operation, and conducting regular sales and operations reviews to help you identify how to reduce costs, beef up service, and refine buying and selling procedures.

The Ink Well seeks franchisees with a professional business background; specific sales or management experience is considered a strong plus. A full-time commitment to your Ink Well shop is expected. Even though your state-of-the-art computerized equipment can speed the most complex printing and duplicating jobs, be warned that there are no shortcuts for the hard work you'll have to perform. It's work, however, that you may find very rewarding.

For further information contact:
  Ronald Strahler, 540 Officecenter Pl., Suite 250, Gahanna, OH 43230, 614-337-9937 or 1-800-235-2221

16. *The Real Estate Industry*

Contents

Property Inspection

AMBIC Building Inspection Consultants, Inc.

Initial license fee: $16,500
Royalties: 6%
Advertising royalties: 3%
Minimum cash required: $25,000 to $35,000
Capital required: NA
Financing: Consultation only
Length of contract: 10 years

In business since: 1987
Franchising since: 1988
Total number of units: 10
Number of company-operated units: None
Total number of units planned, 1995: 30
Number of company-operated units planned, 1995: None

All but nonexistent 20 years ago, the home inspection industry has penetrated the real estate business to such a degree that companies like AMBIC can honestly claim, "We're changing the way America buys houses." For many in the market today for a new home, a professional inspection of property is a vital part of the purchase process, the inspector now joining brokers, attorneys, and mortgage bankers as a key consultant in the decision making.

Choosing a home, after all, involves not just a huge financial investment, but also the family's safety. With asbestos, radon, and other health hazards all too common in American houses, yet not always easily detectable, prospective buyers recognize that skipping a thorough, professional inspection before signing the deed for their "dream house" can result in a nightmare.

Your AMBIC inspection will usually cost well under 1 percent of the home's purchase price. But it provides your customers with invaluable information—often assuring them that their decision to buy is a sound one, but perhaps alerting them to a structural, wiring, or safety problem that may cause them to reconsider. Scheduling most inspections within one to two days, you'll follow the American Society of Home Inspectors' standards of practice, evaluating the roof, ceilings, walls, floors, windows, and doors, looking for deficiencies in the heating and cooling systems, the electrical and plumbing systems, the foundation and the basement, the insulation and the exterior siding. Unlike most inspectors, you'll urge your clients to accompany you as you scrutinize the property, addressing their questions and concerns on the spot and offering safety and preventive repair suggestions.

Less than 48 hours later, you'll furnish a comprehensive report covering more than 750 inspection points and including a summary of key points, along with maintenance and energy-saving tips. You'll also give your customers a checklist for performing their own preclosing inspection, and be available thereafter for free telephone consultation as long as they own the property.

With an exclusive territory, you can run your AMBIC franchise from your home, or the company will work with you to determine a suitable location. Approximately 30 days prior to the anticipated opening of your business, you'll attend a week of classroom instruction at AMBIC's headquarters, staffed by licensed and certified building inspectors, engineers, pest control operators, and radon testing specialists, each with 15 to 20 years of experience in the home inspection industry. Using videotapes, slides, and various other visual aids, you'll learn office procedures and phone communication skills in addition to inspection theory, and receive advice on such administrative concerns as staffing and equipment purchase. Then you'll spend one to two weeks in the field observing home inspection techniques and actually performing supervised jobs including septic and well tests, radon evaluations, and termite inspection.

At the conclusion of your classroom and field instruction, AMBIC's marketing staff will visit your franchise territory to assist you in devising and implementing an initial marketing campaign to establish your business in the local real estate market. Thereafter, you'll be supplied with custom-designed advertising materials and given outlines for proven and cost-effective promotional programs.

AMBIC's franchise package includes a computer software package designed for producing your inspection reports, with software updates available online at no additional cost. You'll also be signed as a member of an exclusive national corporate relocation and referral network, a helpful source for new business prospects. To ensure that you maintain your technical proficiency and knowledge of industry developments, the company conducts seminars and refresher programs. Furthermore, AMBIC's field representatives will visit periodically for further consultation, while the company's troubleshooting network is reachable by phone.

For further information contact:
W. David Goldstein, Vice President, AMBIC Building Inspection Consultants, Inc., 1200 Rte. 130, Robbinsville, NJ 08691, 609-448-1500 or 1-800-882-6242

AmeriSpec, Inc.

Initial license fee: $18,900
Royalties: 7% of gross monthly sales
Advertising royalties: 3% of gross monthly sales
Minimum cash required: $20,000 to $30,000
Capital required: $20,000 to $40,000
Financing: Available
Length of contract: 10 years

In business since: 1987
Franchising since: 1988
Total number of units: 94
Number of company-operated units: None
Total number of units planned, 1995: 350
Number of company-operated units planned, 1995: None

The recent growth in the property inspection service industry attests to the prevalence of careful spending attitudes—inspection is a way to investigate a large and important investment: a home. In addition, some states have enacted and many states are considering full seller-disclosure laws, which will be an advantage to a franchisee already set up to perform a valuable service to individual buyers and sellers, real estate agencies, attorneys, banks, and insurance companies. Ameri-Spec's service, a two-hour on-site review of a property, provides information on heating, plumbing, and electrical systems, and special environmental testing (such as water and radon) upon request.

Though based in California, the first state to legally require full seller-disclosure, AmeriSpec's 94 franchises currently in operation are located throughout the United States, and the company sponsors a national advertising campaign. The company plans to continue its rapid expansion, and projects that 350 AmeriSpec franchises will be in business by 1995.

AmeriSpec recruits franchisees from a sales or managerial background and trains them in a two-week training course in technical, sales, and management skills. Classes also stress professionalism and credibility, since a successful home inspection business depends upon the franchisee's ability to establish a positive and reliable local image. The company supplies franchisees with promotional material for customers. Many of AmeriSpec's franchisees are couple teams, and though most begin operating the business from home, the company recommends that the business expand eventually into commercial office space.

For further information contact:
  Director of Franchising, AmeriSpec, Inc., 1855 W. Kattella Ave., Suite 330, Orange, CA 92667, 714-744-8360 or 1-800-426-2270

HouseMaster of America, Inc.

Initial license fee: $17,000 to $35,000
Royalties: 7.5%
Advertising royalties: 2.5%
Minimum cash required: $27,000
Capital required: $10,000 to $15,000
Financing: Guidance provided
Length of contract: 5 years

In business since: 1971
Franchising since: 1979
Total number of units: 132
Number of company-operated units: None
Total number of units planned, 1995: 177
Number of company-operated units planned, 1995: None

Marge Rodell needed a change. "I was working for a large corporation, and I wanted to start my own business—something I was directly responsible for," she says. The business she decided on? A HouseMaster of America franchise in New Fairfield, Connecticut. This house inspection service caters to the needs of home buyers who want to know ahead of time if there are flaws in what will easily be the biggest purchase they will ever make. Currently, the company seeks franchisees who want to own a branch in the Midwest, Northwest, and Canada. The initial fee varies with the number of owner-occupied homes in the area.

The company points out that franchisees have not yet oversaturated this field. HouseMaster management feels confident that house inspection is just coming into its own. If you buy this franchise, you will operate a cash business, which simplifies accounts receivable; and you will conduct business over the phone rather than in a walk-in office, so site selection is not critical. You will even work reasonable hours: Home inspections must take place during daylight hours.

What exactly will your staff of engineers check for during a house inspection? Each inspection checks the central heating and cooling system of a house; its interior plumbing and electrical systems; the structural soundness of the siding and roof and whether water leaks through the roof; the structural soundness of the basement, walls, floors, and ceiling; and the large kitchen appliances. Some franchisees also offer other services, like inspection for termites and wood borers, evaluation of well and septic systems, checking of docks and bulkheads, and swimming pool inspections.

HouseMaster offers warranties to home buyers. To their franchisees, HouseMaster offers pay-as-you-go errors-and-omissions insurance. As a local franchisee, you can sell to client home buyers an optional one-year warranty on the roof and structural and mechanical elements of the house.

HouseMaster pays for all your training-related expenses. You will spend a week at their Bound Brook, New Jersey, headquarters for technical instruction in the classroom and field and then a day in an active office for operations training. Then you spend two days in the field for sales training.

The training schedule allows you to spend extra time on anything you feel you need to concentrate on. Marge Rodell appreciates that she "was able to spend any amount of time I needed to at the home office." And she also remembers the help she received after her formal training. She says the yearly operational meeting "is very informative," as are "the updates on the technical and operations part of the business." "Most important" she notes, HouseMaster personnel "were always available by phone."

Marge Rodell cautions all potential franchisees that they "must be totally dedicated to making their business work because that can get one through the first couple of years when the work is high and the profits are low." But she doesn't mind the hard work. In fact, she says, "I love it!"

For further information contact:
Linda Sigman, HouseMaster of America, Inc., 421 W. Union Ave., Bound Brook, NJ 08805, 1-800-526-3939

National Property Inspections, Inc.

Initial license fee: $17,000
Royalties: 8%
Advertising royalties: None
Minimum cash required: $13,000
Capital required: $22,000 to $24,000
Financing: Available
Length of contract: 10 years

In business since: 1987
Franchising since: 1987
Total number of units: 49
Number of company-operated units: None
Total number of units planned, 1995: 150 to 200
Number of company-operated units planned, 1995: None

"Most people today can't even change a light switch," National Property Inspections President Roland Bates points out, "and they don't have the time to really take a good look at what they're buying." Realtors and contractors aren't usually any more qualified to evaluate the condition of the property. Commercial and residential property owners and buyers and real estate professionals alike have come to recognize that the job requires special expertise — expertise that, with National Property Inspection's training and ongoing support, you'll be able to provide.

Over 50 percent of all houses sold each year are now inspected by a professional before purchase. The FHA, in fact, has indicated that it's going to start requiring an inspection on all its transactions. But your business isn't limited to the private home market — National Property Inspections franchisees have also been hired to scrutinize apartments, office buildings, condominiums, and shopping centers. Your clients can include institutions, realtors, and current property owners as well as prospective buyers.

A home inspection usually averages about $200. You'll be examining the integrity of the structure's foundation, roof, plumbing, wiring, and heating and cooling systems, and looking for insect damage. Furthermore, you'll address such environmental concerns as radon, lead paint, formaldehyde, and drinking water quality. Upon completion of the inspection, you'll deliver a comprehensive yet concise report either in writing or on computer disk.

According to Roland Bates, "A number of the franchisees are engineers or ex-contractors, but an extensive background in the construction industry is not necessary." During a five-day classroom and field training course at the company's Omaha headquarters, you'll receive instruction on the scientific methodology developed to perform property inspections and an overview of every phase of property construction, along with comprehensive guidance in setting and running your operation on a day-to-day basis. "Every instructor is an expert in their respective fields," Bates says, "and they have each built a successful business from scratch. Not only can they teach franchisees how to do inspections but they can also relate to the franchisees on how to build a business."

In addition, your training will cover marketing and sales strategies, and a marketing representative will be available to spend two days with you in your exclusive territory as you are starting out. National Property Inspections will supply a complete promotions package, including press releases and field-tested literature and advertising materials. Meanwhile, the home office will work to solicit national, regional, and local accounts on your behalf.

National Property Inspections will furnish you with the tools you'll need to perform your inspections, plus a set of accounting records and business stationery. And you'll be kept up to date on innovations and developments in the industry by regular contact from the Omaha staff and through the company's monthly newsletter and annual franchise meeting.

For further information contact:
  Roland Bates, National Property Inspections, Inc., 236 S. 108th Ave., Suite 3, Omaha, NE 68154, 402-333-9807 or 1-800-333-9807

Sales

Better Homes and Gardens Real Estate Service

Initial license fee: $9,900 to $39,900
Royalties: 0.6% to 4.6%
Advertising royalties: 1.25% to 2.2%
Minimum cash required: NA
Capital required: NA
Financing: Deferred payment plan on 50% of conversion
Length of contract: 4 years

In business since: 1902
Franchising since: 1978
Total number of units: 1,400
Number of company-operated units: None
Total number of units planned, 1995: 1,900
Number of company-operated units planned, 1995: None

Larry Landry's real estate agency was in a familiar predicament. "We were young upstarts competing against old-line companies." Joining the Better Homes and Gardens network, the Springfield, Massachusetts, franchisee claims, "granted instant credibility for us."

Established and relatively new brokerages alike have profited from their association with BH&G. According to Allen Sabbag, president of the national network, the real estate service is "a logical extension of the 65-year tradition of service to American families and their homes provided by *Better Homes and Gardens* magazine." But BH&G offers more than a powerful imprimatur. From a core group of successful realty firms, the franchise has grown to become of the nation's top real estate networks, with over 1,400 offices and 25,000 sales associates in all 50 states.

Not that all comers are accepted into the franchise. "One of most important philosophies," explains Joel Riggs of Nashville, owner of one of the founding BH&G firms, "is the way we select companies, then provide a positive environment for them to increase their management capabilities and grow with the system. It is much more productive than the scattershot approach of signing up anyone who is willing."

If your agency joins BH&G, you'll be able to take advantage of an array of management tools to support your business. You'll gain—or improve—office automation through the network's computer support system, helping you to create a series of concise reports concerning sales activities, listing inventory and commissions, and to determine your firm's profitability and market share. BH&G's business-generating services will be available to you, including nontraditional but lucrative enterprises such as managing the sale of foreclosed properties for financial institutions. And you'll benefit from the presence and experience of your fellow BH&G firms. Larry Landry has found one of the greatest benefits as a franchisee is "being able to sit down with other brokers—large and small—throughout the country and find out how and what they've done and be able to pick and choose what we feel would work for our organization."

BH&G offers a variety of optional programs in which you can participate—programs like the Home Buying System, which helps agents identify and satisfy the needs of home buyers through the use of a needs analysis form, a property evaluation card, and a mortgage kit to speed the loan application process. There's also the Home Merchandising System, with home repair and fix-up books to assist owners in preparing their property for market and increasing its market value. One of BH&G's newer support features is its 40-hour Advantage Training Program. Using a combination of live training and video and print materials, the course combines basic training for staffers who are new to the real estate business with material for you and your more experienced agents to hone your skills in such areas as prospecting, listing, and selling. There are other levels of training available, as well as ongoing seminars, focused on specific aspects of real estate sales.

BH&G will furnish you with promotional materials like the *Home Front Consumer* newsletter for your clients, with articles and full-color photos from *Better Homes and Gardens* magazine, along with a regular supply of the publication "Your Guide to Homes," which you can use as both a newspaper supplement and a direct mail piece. You'll also profit from the networks' cooperative advertising campaigns, highlighted by commercials that run in more than 87 percent of the nation's TV markets on all three networks plus cable stations, and also featuring camera-ready pieces to use for local marketing. In addition, BH&G's in-house agency will assist with your media planning and buying and will write and design custom ads and brochures to fit the needs of your territory, charging you only for production and printing costs.

For further information contact:
  Scott Hale, National Marketing Director, Better Homes and Gardens Real
  Estate Service, 2000 Grand Ave., Des Moines, IA 50312, 515-284-2711 or
  1-800-274-7653, fax 515-284-3801

RE/MAX International, Inc.

Initial license fee: $15,000 to $25,000
Royalties: Varies regionally
Advertising royalties: Varies regionally $50 to $150/month
Minimum cash required: $5,000 to $50,000
Capital required: $10,000 to $50,000
Financing: Financing of franchise fee available in some regions
Length of contract: 5 years

In business since: 1973
Franchising since: 1976
Total number of units: 1,761
Number of company-operated units: None
Total number of units planned, 1995: 2,800
Number of company-operated units planned, 1995: None

When RE/MAX appeared on the real estate scene in 1973, industry experts said the new company's maximum compensation plan would never work. By the end of the 1980s, the RE/MAX International franchise organization was preparing to become the number-one real estate network in North America. The company is based on the principle that the key to solving the basic problems of any business is to bring out the best in the best people you can hire. The people who feel like winners act like winners, become winners, and they attract other winners to the company.

That managerial belief became the RE/MAX high commission concept, an innovative alternative to the traditional commission split practice. Under the RE/MAX concept, sales associates retain the highest possible percentage of commissions earned in exchange for paying management fees and sharing in the monthly office overhead. The name, "RE/MAX," stands for "real estate maximums."

The company founders knew, though, that top producers want more than just a high commission. They also want traditional services and benefits. Programs were developed, including RE/MAX's international relocation and asset management services, and an international referral network. The company reorganized as well, adding or expanding communications, advertising, public relations, and a corporate legal department. Approved suppliers, quality control, and a system-wide computerized network have provided advanced training courses and seminars along with an annual international convention, focusing on awards, recognition, and continued education. All of these improvements were designed to contribute to the professional success of associates throughout the RE/MAX system.

RE/MAX sales associates throughout the system average 24 transactions annually. RE/MAX is the second-largest residential real estate franchise organization in the United States and is the very largest in Canada.

You will make a fair profit from each agent, rather than depending on half of the commissions of just a few good ones, and you will have a predictable income. You will also spend much of your time as a RE/MAX broker recruiting the best agents, instead of retraining mediocre performers in the basics of the profession.

Franchisee Betty D. Hegner, president of RE/MAX of Northern Illinois, Inc., suggests that you think about the implications of the RE/MAX arrangement before you leap at this opportunity: "Will your ego suffer if your salespeople outdistance you?" she asks. "In many companies the owner or manager is the top producer and makes all the decisions. The role of the manager in a 100 percent company is that of leader, advisor, motivator, and organizer. Are you ready to share decision making and planning with your salespeople?" And she adds: "Are you prepared to give up your share of your salespeople's commissions?"

The RE/MAX system also affects the kind of office you will have. To make the system work, you may have to spend a little more to attract the best agents. This will probably mean providing at least semiprivate offices for each agent.

RE/MAX will give you five intense days of training in its system at its Denver, Colorado, headquarters. You pay for your travel expenses. Ongoing assistance and refresher training is available through audiocassettes and videocassettes, and you can obtain additional in-person training both in Denver and at your location. You can also consult company professionals on specific problems.

In addition to real estate, many RE/MAX franchisees sell corporate relocation and asset management services as well as insurance.

For further information contact:
  Bob Harple, Marketing Director, RE/MAX International, Inc., P.O. Box 3907, Englewood, CO 80155-3907, 303-770-5531 or 1-800-525-7452

17. The Retailing Industry

Contents

Video

Video Update, Inc.
West Coast Video

Clothing and Footwear

Gingiss International, Inc.

Initial license fee: $15,000
Royalties: 6% first 2 years, then 10%
Advertising royalties: 3%
Minimum cash required: $60,000
Capital required: $120,000 to $160,000
Financing: Available
Length of contract: 10 years

In business since: 1936
Franchising since: 1968
Total number of units: 242
Number of company-operated units: 28
Total number of units planned, 1995: 325
Number of company-operated units planned, 1995: 35

Since the 1980s, wedding parties have been dominated by the formal wear favored by most generations. Gingiss, the largest retailers and renters of men's formal wear in the country, with sales about 500 percent higher than their nearest competitors, has benefited greatly from this tradition.

Seemingly impervious to economic hard times, this business even did well in the recession of 1982, when tuxedo rental volume rose by 8 percent. The company, founded during the Depression, began its period of greatest expansion in 1968, just when inflation began to shake the economy.

Weddings provide the bulk—75 percent—but not all of Gingiss's business. Prom goers are also going formal—"On prom night, she should love your body, not your mind," as one Gingiss advertisement boldly put it. And executives buy or rent tuxedos for an increasing number of social functions.

Politicians and luminaries from the world of sports and entertainment account for some of the company's 600,000 yearly customers. Gingiss franchisees have seen the likes of Robert Altman, Muhammad Ali, Spike Lee, Ed McMahon, Bob Hope, and the NCAA All-Star Baskeball Team come through their doors.

Gingiss franchisees fit no particular profile, but they include even former Gingiss executives who felt they knew a good thing when they saw it. Multistore owners run more than a third of the company's franchised operations. The Pacer family operates seven Atlanta stores, with several more in the planning stages. This team of husband, wife, sister-in-law, children, grandma and grandpa share the work of running its mini-empire.

In a Gingiss franchise, the franchisor makes many of the decisions, at least initially. For example, the company will choose your location after careful research. That may even mean lining up a spot in a shopping center still under construction. The company takes responsibility for design and construction. Gingiss will give you a ready-to-go retail store, a turnkey operation stocked with about 260 suits.

To learn how to run this operation, you will spend one week getting some hands-on experience in a Chicago company store. Another week of classroom instruction supplements that, covering topics like merchandising, sales promotion, finance, hiring, personnel training, and advertising. A company representative will also spend the days before and after your opening at your store. Thereafter, your store will get frequent visits from your regional advisor.

Gingiss has the preeminent name in the formal wear business, and they mean to keep it. The company "road tests" new models of formal wear before authorizing them for your stock. That could mean dry-cleaning tuxedos 20 times in a row to make sure they can stand the stress of repeated wear and cleaning.

The company also keeps up its good name by keeping it constantly before the public. Advertising plays a big part in the Gingiss operation. Since the bride often makes the decisions about the formal wear for men at her wedding, company advertisements appear in *Modern Bride* and *Bride's*, as well as in numerous other bridal-related publications. Gingiss continues to expand in all areas of the country, as well as in Toronto and Quebec.

For further information contact:
  John Heiser, Gingiss International, Inc., 180 N. LaSalle St., Suite 1111, Chicago, IL 60601, 1-800-621-7125

Heel/Sew Quik, Inc.

Initial license fee: $15,500 to $17,500
Royalties: 4%
Advertising royalties: 2%
Minimum cash required: $20,000
Capital required: $35,000 to $110,000
Financing: Assistance in obtaining
Length of contract: Varies, depending on location

In business since: 1984
Franchising since: 1985
Total number of units: 325

Number of company-operated units: 5
Total number of units planned, 1995: 3,000
Number of company-operated units planned, 1995: 3

Raymond Margiano is a great believer in using space efficiently. So once the Heel/Sew Quik CEO saw that his shoe-repair franchise program had been successfully launched, he started thinking about complementary services that franchisees might also offer in their shops. Now, you can either concentrate entirely on footwear, or opt for a combined Heel/Sew Quik center, taking on simple clothing alteration jobs such as hemming and stitching on buttons as well. Like other affiliates, you might consider adding monogramming capabilities to that, too, maybe even with some key-cutting and knife-sharpening work on the side.

It's a bit surprising, perhaps, that cobblers have been going out of business just as demand for their services has increased. Yet, from a high point of 43,000 repair shops during World War II, there are now only about 16,000 left. Still, the average American owns at least four pairs of shoes, and with the price of new footwear ever increasing, research has shown that a majority of consumers would gladly use a shoe repair service—if only, that is, they could find a store nearby and the work didn't take days to get done.

Unlike the repair shops of yesteryear, tucked in out-of-the-way downtown nooks and crannies, your Heel/Sew Quik center will be conveniently located right in a neighborhood mall. When the franchise was beginning, Margiano admits it wasn't easy to interest mall owners in leasing space and getting them past the impression that shoe repair stores weren't sufficiently upscale. "It took me a year to convince them," he remembers; he changed their minds by showing them the high-tech equipment and fashionable decor of his prototype stores. Now, Margiano claims, mall developers are eagerly soliciting him and his franchisees.

Most of your service can be conducted on a while-you-wait basis, with your customers taking a seat on a counterside stool and enjoying a comfortable and clean environment that will remind them more of a soda fountain or bar—depending on their proclivities—than a cobbler shop. Usually, they won't be sitting long. "We fix heels on women's shoes in two minutes," Margiano says, "and heels on men's shoes in four to five minutes." It's the high-speed equipment manufactured in England and Italy—countries where the arts of cobbling and mending have never gone out of fashion—that will allow you to do the work so fast, devices like pneumatic hammers, state-of-the-art stitchers, and computerized monogram units, along with such materials as quick-drying, odorless glue.

Even for a combined Heel/Sew Quick facility, you probably won't be needing a store larger than 800 square feet—the biggest shop in the franchise measures somewhere around 1,600. After they've assisted in site evaluation and selection, company staff members work with you to develop the layout of your store and install and test the equipment. Decorated in gray and burgundy, accompanied by brass accents and, often, wall-to-wall carpeting, the shop is designed not only for efficiency and customer appeal, but also to create an atmosphere conducive to impulse buying, with shoelaces, polish, and other small merchandise attractively displayed along the walls. The company's central warehouse program gives you the opportunity to obtain these products, as well as private-label Heel/Sew Quik items, at a 10 percent to 20 percent discount.

At one of the company's training centers, you'll attend an instructional program lasting two to three weeks, the length determined by the type of franchise you buy. In addition to studying sales analysis and inventory management, you'll also be taught the techniques of shoe repair and basic clothing alteration using the Heel/Sew Quik tools. Practicing on items donated by—then returned to—Goodwill, the Salvation Army, or other agencies, you will also be asked to offer free services to homeless organizations once you're in business.

Nearly 90 percent of that business will come from repeat customers, but the Heel/Sew Quik organization manages an aggressive marketing effort, informing consumers that cobblers are alive and well and have advanced technologically to greet the 21st century. You'll receive layouts for local advertising to accompany the company's national campaign, and be guided in the planning of seasonal promotions. And by attending Heel/Sew Quik–sponsored trade shows and seminars, you'll learn about new trends, buying programs, retailing methods, and technical procedures.

For further information contact:
  Ray Margiano, President, Heel/Sew Quik, Inc., 1720 Cumberland Point Dr., Suite 17, Mariett, GA 30067, 404-951-9440, fax 404-933-8268

Sox Appeal

Initial license fee: $20,000
Royalties: 5%
Advertising royalties: 1%
Minimum cash required: $50,000
Capital required: $100,000 to $170,000
Financing: None
Length of contract: 10 years

In business since: 1984
Franchising since: 1986
Total number of units: 25
Number of company-operated units: 1
Total number of units planned, 1995: 80
Number of company-operated units planned, 1995: None

Everybody needs socks—which is reassuring when you're in the business of selling them. And since the days of darning seem to be long gone, old pairs are being replaced more often. Even more significantly, over the past two decades or so socks and hosiery have emerged as genuine fashion statements. Crew socks, "nude" hose, and the black/brown/blue business suit accessories alone won't suffice anymore. Men, women, and children alike want a greater selection than what they can find, if they can find them at all, secluded along the back walls of department stores, shoe sections, and sporting goods shops.

That's why specialty sock stores are now appearing in almost every major shopping mall. The first of these operations to franchise nationwide, Sox Appeal has established a solid foothold, as it were, in this rapidly expanding market. Sox Appeal locations carry over 2,000 colors and styles, traditional and novelty selections in a variety of fabrics for formal and informal wear, work and recreation.

The fitness boom has helped create entirely new categories of specialized athletic socks, and advances in manufacturing technology have allowed top designers to do some pretty creative things with these fashion accessories. Almost every major label, from Calvin Klein and Ralph Lauren to old standbys like Hanes, now offers a line of socks or hosiery, and you'll be stocking a great many of them.

Browsing at first, then succumbing to impulse purchases, most of your customers will go away with more than one pair; on average, they'll spend about $15 per visit and may even pick up such big-ticket items as a $140 lace body stocking. The trendy merchandise, flaunting dynamic colors and patterns, will fuel your business. Some of your bestselling products combine novelty with utility, like the "Pair and a Spare," a set of three matching socks for when one inevitably becomes MIA in the wash. Gift packages like "Six Feet of Socks," where customers select three different pairs for a friend or relative, are popular, too. And don't underestimate the men's market—it makes up as much as 40 percent of the total business at many Sox Appeal stores.

Before you become a Sox Appeal franchisee, you'll need to travel to the company's headquarters in Minnesota to meet with corporate officers (expenses for that trip will be refunded if you are accepted). You'll also have to find an acceptable location for your store, a 700-

square-foot space in a fashion mall, downtown shopping center, or up-scale tourist area, with the company's sales staff or its real estate representatives assisting you in the site selection and reviewing your lease. Back in Minnesota, you'll attend a training class for franchisees, learning how to set up the store and operate the business, how to take advantage of a sock fad and how to tell when that fad has run its course, and in general becoming educated about the literally thousands of sock options available. Doing a lot of the legwork to find the inventory for your store, buyers at the home office keep in touch with designers, attend trade shows, and make regular visits to wholesale and retail marts. They also engage manufacturers to produce a customized Sox Appeal line of products, providing the styles your customers want at lower prices than most designer labels.

Sox Appeal's national marketing program includes advertising in major fashion and general interest magazines, and the company supplies promotional material as well for your store and for local publications. The gift market is targeted in particular. December obviously warrants a special campaign, highlighted by seasonal merchandise, including Christmas stockings equipped with a computer chip that plays "Jingle Bells," but other holidays ("Give Mom some socks to go with her great genes," goes one Mother's Day ad) aren't overlooked either.

No specific experience is required to own a Sox Appeal franchise. A good fashion sense and enthusiasm for the product are certainly helpful, as Gibson Carothers, the company's founder and co-owner, notes. "People always check out what kinds of socks I'm wearing." Luckily, with 150 pairs in his wardrobe, Carothers happens to be one of his own best customers.

For further information contact:
Jack Abelson or Bill Travis, Vice President of Franchise Development, Sox Appeal Franchising, Inc., 6321 Bury Dr., Suite 1, Eden Prairie, MN 55346, 612-937-6162, fax 612-934-5665

Computers and Software

MicroAge Computer Centers, Inc.

Initial license fee: None
Royalties: 3% to 8% (product marketing royalty)
Advertising royalties: None

Minimum cash required: Conversion of existing business with $200,000+
  most desirable
Capital required: Conversion of existing business with $200,000+
  most desirable
Financing: Flooring, bank financing, and net terms available
Length of contract: 10 years

In business since: 1976
Franchising since: 1980
Total number of units: 311
Number of company-operated units: 6
Total number of units planned, 1995: NA
Number of company-operated units planned, 1995: NA

By the standards of the personal computer industry, 1976, the year
MicroAge Computer Centers started, was close to the beginning of
time. It predates the beginning of Apple Computer by two years. Demonstrating astute management, this now large chain of resellers also
outlived the many computer stores that failed in the great shakeout of
the mid-1980s.

MicroAge management believes computer businesses that survived
the mid-decade winnowing-out remain good investments because
they've proven their mettle in a tough business environment. And
they see bright prospects for selling personal computers in the future.

Jeff McKeever, CEO, and Alan Hald, vice chairman of the board,
founded the company and still head its management team. They give
MicroAge leadership that has solid business roots. McKeever served as
vice president of First Interstate Bank of Arizona. Hald, a Harvard
MBA, was named one of the industry's top executives by *Computer Re-
seller News.*

MicroAge would like its franchisees to have a strong business background. If you want to run a MicroAge Computer Center, you should
be able to manage people, and you should have a knack for sales, a
good grounding in the basics of accounting, and preferably some experience with personal computers. Use of the MicroAge brand name is
not granted to all franchisees, however—only to those with outstanding support and service records. All other franchisees keep their existing company names.

Your MicroAge regional account manager will serve as your direct
connection to the company once you start your business. He or she
will help you recruit and train your staff and will advise you on advertising, finance, and distribution. Training is available for technical,
sales, sales management, general business operation, and strategic
planning, and is held at corporate headquarters and in major metropolitan areas. The company's management, viewing the sale of complete computer systems designed to meet client companies' needs as

vital to MicroAge's business, maintains a special staff to assist you with marketing in this area.

The company prepares you to anticipate and provide for your customers' changing needs by constantly updating your knowledge of the industry. MicroAge personnel will conduct seminars in your store and courses at regional stores and company headquarters.

For further information contact:
Paul Krall, MicroAge Computer Centers, Inc., 2308 S. 55th St., Tempe, AZ 85282-1824, 602-968-3168

Hardware and General Merchandise

K & N Mobile Distribution Systems

Initial license fee: $23,500
Royalties: 13%
Advertising royalties: 1%
Minimum cash required: $35,000
Capital required: $80,000 to $120,000
Financing: Assistance available
Length of contract: 5 years

In business since: 1972
Franchising since: 1987
Total number of units: 36
Number of company-operated units: 17
Total number of units planned, 1995: 95
Number of company-operated units planned, 1995: 35

Electrical components like battery terminals, connectors, cables, and wires may be small, but when they malfunction, an entire assembly line can shut down. From manufacturers to repair centers, businesses need these products to keep their machinery working, to service customers, and to make the products they sell. With operations slowed to a crawl, companies have to get replacement parts right away. But a catalogue order can take weeks to receive, and trips to a local hardware store are almost as inconvenient. What's more, even if either mail order or hardware stores have the right part in the first place, you can bet they'll charge a premium price for it.

So when you pull up in your K & N van, a mobile warehouse carrying over 2,700 electrical products, you'll be a welcome sight. "Our sales representatives tell me time and time again that customers on board the van are like kids in a candy store," claims Jerry L. Nelson, the company's founder and president. "Often, what was going to be a one- or two-item sale turns into a delivery of several hundred components." It's not difficult to see why they appreciate the service. Busy purchasing agents don't have to pore over heavy catalogues, studying hazy photos or vague drawings and hoping that they're choosing the right items. All the actual merchandise you'll sell is there on display and in stock, including many specialized components that are hard to come by even from parts distributors.

Your van functions as an office as well as showroom. Using the on-board computer system, you'll produce accurate invoices on the spot and be able to monitor your inventory, reordering supplies automatically from K & N's central warehouse by computer modem. You'll also have portable dictating equipment to take down orders, eliminating errors caused by hastily scribbled notes. And being on the road doesn't mean you'll be out of touch, thanks to the cellular phone you'll use to arrange appointments and communicate with the home office. With the benefit of all this equipment, according to Greg Beam, who runs a K & N operation in Corpus Christi, Texas, "I spend a minimum amount of time on administrative duties, giving me more time with customers."

While clients can contact you directly to set up an emergency visit, most of your business will be conducted during regularly scheduled meetings with repeat customers—factories and hospitals, contracting firms and truck stops, and a host of other establishments. On average, you'll call on each customer about every two to four weeks. Fort Worth franchisee Bill Manning reports that frequently "we go in and do their stocking for them." Maintaining strong pricing relationships with electrical parts manufacturers, K & N will help you determine a product line of in-demand items—avoiding antiquated components that businesses are no longer ordering—that is customized to the specific mix of industries in your territory.

All new K & N franchisees receive initial training that lasts 15 to 20 days, structured to impart product knowledge, sales skills, and business management techniques. Periodic refresher courses are also offered. Within your first two months in business, a company operations specialist will work with you in your territory for at least three days, and other K & N representatives will pay follow-up visits from time to time thereafter. Guiding you both in the field and by phone from the company headquarters, for example, they'll furnish advice on conducting local promotional campaigns and using the materials produced through the franchise advertising and development program.

K & N currently has franchisees operating in 13 states, primarily in the South and Midwest; some affiliates, however, are located outside of that core region and the company is continuing to expand nation-wide. In addition to an individual franchise, you have the option to apply for a multi-unit development package, purchasing two or more territories in a given area for reduced start-up fees.

For further information contact:
  Curtis Nelson, Vice President, K & N Electric Franchising, Inc., 4909 Rondo Dr., Fort Worth, TX 76106, 817-626-2885 or 1-800-433-2170

Home Furnishings

Deck the Walls

Initial license fee: $35,000
Royalties: 6%
Advertising royalties: 2%
Minimum cash required: $60,000
Capital required: $165,000 to $210,000
Financing: Assistance available
Length of contract: NA

In business since: 1979
Franchising since: 1979
Total number of units: 198
Number of company-operated units: 2
Total number of units planned, 1995: 250
Number of company-operated units planned, 1995: 5

Americans like to hang things on their walls, and in recent years they've broadened their choice of style and subject matter for these home decorations. Gone are the days when a painting or print on your neighbor's wall was predictable — Currier and Ives, a Norman Rockwell, or a simple landscape. Now people hang everything from abstract art to photographs to posters advertising long-gone museum exhibits.

Why are Americans now willing to part with their hard-earned cash for wall decorations that might not have made it past the front door in times past? The three biggest reasons are: more education, constant exposure to art of all kinds through the media, and a desire for the status that can be gained by showing off good taste. Even advertising, with its emphasis on graphics, acts as an educator of the senses, making us tolerant of a whole range of images. And there is the increasing tendency to view what we display as making a statement about ourselves. In an age that values self-expression, any business that can appeal to such feelings taps something powerful.

The management of Deck the Walls spotted the profit potential in this social trend. The company's product mix includes 800 to 1,000 types of frame moldings as well as posters and prints featuring 1,100 different images.

You can get into this timely business through the Deck the Walls franchisee training program, conducted at corporate headquarters in Houston, Texas. Subjects covered in the course of instruction include custom framing techniques, merchandising, selling, purchasing, inventory control, bookkeeping, promotion, and employee management. Hands-on experience at a corporate store will give you a taste of the "real thing" before you ever open the doors of your own store for business.

Deck the Walls will research and assist with the selection of a site for your store as well as negotiation on the lease and construction or remodeling. The company will also give you an approved list of vendors, from whom you will be able to buy at advantageous prices.

Don't worry about choosing all those pictures for your inventory. The company helps you choose your initial stock. It also helps you train your employees. And it will stick with you to lend its expertise right through your first weeks of operation. Deck the Walls offers periodic retraining and publishes monthly merchandising guides to update your "education." Regional franchise directors are also available for consultation on a regular basis.

According to John G. Tipple, who runs a Deck the Walls unit in a shopping mall in Austin, Texas, a franchise from this company "requires close follow-up and hard work." But he likes the mix of company support and the freedom to run his own store and make many of his own decisions. And, Tipple says: "It has been an excellent investment."

For further information contact:
Ann Nance or Ginger Walton, Deck the Walls, 16825 Northchase, Suite 910, Houston, TX 77060, 1-800-543-3325 or 1-800-443-3325

Floor Coverings International (FCI)

Initial license fee: $9,700
Royalties: 5%
Advertising royalties: 2%
Minimum cash required: $9,700
Capital required: $1,500 to $3,000

Financing: None
Length of contract: 10 years

In business since: 1985
Franchising since: 1986
Total number of units: 205
Number of company-operated units: None
Total number of units planned, 1995: 995
Number of company-operated units planned, 1995: None

Several economists and consumer focus groups forecast that home shopping will account for half of consumer purchases by the year 2000. Floor Coverings International (FCI) president Joe Lansford picked up on this trend. "The retail world is changing as buying patterns change," he says. "The future is coming—we can ignore it, or profit from it."

Lansford had already been profiting from his Professional Carpet Systems carpet care network (see listing under "General Maintenance," page 342). Thinking that floor covering was a particularly well-suited product for home sales, he launched FCI as well, which has recently been ranked as one of the 25 fastest-growing franchises by *Entrepreneur* magazine.

Part of the reason the company has been such a popular franchise opportunity is that it's a fairly simple operation to run. You don't need an office, showroom, equipment, or inventory. Instead, you or your sales rep will take your van, stocked with over 1,700 samples of name-brand carpets in a wide variety of styles, colors, textures, and fibers—plus other floor coverings like vinyl and ceramic tile—to your customers. Seeing how the carpet looks in their home's natural light, they'll be able to coordinate their selection to the upholstery, drapery, and decor, and can even create a custom-designed area rug. That's far more convenient for them than dragging samples home from a carpet store, only to find over and over again that what looked good in a showroom doesn't necessarily look good in a living room.

After you take thorough measurements of the floor space, ensuring that no excess yardage is bought, you'll place your customer's order with the manufacturer and arrange to have the mill deliver it to an FCI-approved professional installer. The carpeting or floor covering is usually in place within three to five days of the purchase. By dealing directly with the maker and by eliminating overhead costs of warehouse and retail store space, you'll be able to pass on savings as high as 20 percent to 40 percent of the regular retail price. And because you won't be carrying any inventory yourself, you can instantly update the styles and colors you'll offer as fashions and trends change.

Although you'll also do business with professional establishments, most of your sales will be to homeowners. "Commercial customers tie up a lot of money in receivables," Joe Lansford points out. "Residential customers pay COD and that frees up ready money for franchisees."

You'll begin preparing to become an FCI franchisee with a home-study course, followed by one week as a student at the company's "Carpet College" in Atlanta. Along with instruction in sales, marketing, operating procedures, and customer relations, you'll be given a background on the history of carpeting, its manufacture, and installation, which FCI considers essential knowledge for retailing the product. Carpet College's curriculum is taught through a combination of classroom sessions, videotape modules, and measurement, layout, and design exercises. While you're going through the training, the company will set up accounts for you with the major mills and carpet distributors, who'll automatically extend you a line of credit, and get a Chevrolet Astro "carpet van" ready to take with you. When new franchisees depart Carpet College, Joe Lansford says, "they can sell carpet on their way home."

By the weekend after you return to your territory, your first newspaper ad will be set to run and a direct mail campaign will begin soon after. FCI extends another two weeks of field training, which focuses on preparing for your grand opening and developing a marketing program. You'll learn effective ways of using the print, radio, and television ads, brochures, door hangers, and yard signs that the company provides. Your van itself is a rolling advertisement—and a rolling FM radio station, too. Equipped with an FCC-approved transmitter, you'll be able to broadcast a continuous commercial, changed every two weeks, within a three-block radius.

Experience in the carpet business is not required (neither is a broadcasting background). Carpet College, in fact, is geared to those who have little prior knowledge about the industry, and ongoing support that includes a toll-free help line, monthly newsletters, regional workshops, and annual conventions helps you stay abreast of unfolding changes. What is necessary, however, is an ability to monitor sales and operations, create a sound business development program, maintain a customer-oriented service approach, and implement an organizational structure that encourages growth.

For further information contact:
  Investment Counselor, Floor Coverings International, 5182 Old Dixie Hwy., Forest Park, GA 30050, 404-361-5047 or 1-800-955-4324, fax 404-366-4606

Mr. Miniblind

Initial license fee: $28,000
Royalties: 5%
Advertising royalties: 5%
Minimum cash required: $40,000
Capital required: $28,000
Financing: None
Length of contract: 5 years

In business since: 1986
Franchising since: 1988
Total number of units: 130
Number of company-operated units: 1
Total number of units planned, 1995: 800
Number of company-operated units planned, 1995: 2

A pioneer in the at-home shopping service, Mr. Miniblind has been offering customers the convenience and ease of deciding on a window treatment in their homes since 1986. Clients choose from a wide assortment of micro blinds, wood blinds, vertical blinds, pleated shades, and shutters, then Mr. Miniblind custom-makes the orders and returns to install them free of charge. The at-home service is very attractive to customers who want to avoid the hassles involved in shopping for window dressings.

Home decorating is a $6 billion industry, and Mr. Miniblind, with its record of service and quality products, national advertising campaign, and years of successful franchising, is a well-established company.

At the 2½-week training program at corporate headquarters in Orange County, California, franchisees receive complete instruction on the products, installation, sales, and marketing of their Mr. Miniblind business. Once the business is set up, the company provides franchisees with substantial support, including a national advertising campaign, a research and development department, and a variety of promotional and management programs. Mr. Miniblind franchisees are required to buy a Chevy Astrovan or GMC Cargovan, and a car phone is strongly recommended. The samples and training are covered in the licensing fee. The actual products, however, are purchased by the franchisee directly from the brand-name manufacturer. Because Mr. Miniblind is a recognized and reputable franchise, the manufacturer sells its product to franchisees at a discounted rate. Savings are then passed on to the customer—but the franchisee still makes a considerable profit.

Mr. Miniblind franchisees have included police officers, CPAs, carpenters, and mortgage brokers. The company also attracts mom-and-pop operations who prefer the support of a company-based franchise. With its minimal equipment requirements and low overhead, Mr. Miniblind is a smart choice for mobile entrepreneurs.

For further information contact:
  Mark Huckins or Christina Huckins, Mr. Miniblind, 20341 Irvine Ave., Suite 1, Santa Ana, CA 92707, 714-979-9221 or 1-800-877-7712

Naked Furniture, Inc.

Initial license fee: $19,500
Royalties: 3.75%
Advertising royalties: 1%
Minimum cash required: $48,000 to $82,000
Capital required: $143,000 to $245,000
Financing: Assistance in obtaining outside financing
Length of contract: 10 years

In business since: 1972
Franchising since: 1976
Total number of units: 44
Number of company-operated units: None
Total number of units planned, 1995: 75 to 90
Number of company-operated units planned, 1995: 1

It's a provocative name, all right. Marketing studies, in fact, have revealed that the "Naked Furniture" label is the company's most effective lure in drawing customers into the stores.

The importance of that shouldn't be underestimated, because there are, after all, a lot of establishments competing for the attention—and the business—of furniture-seeking shoppers. But a clever name alone isn't enough to make a retail operation successful, so Naked Furniture has worked hard to provide an attractive alternative for consumers seeking superior home furnishings at affordable prices.

All furniture retailers, of course, swear that their goods are made from the finest materials and put together with the most meticulous skill and care. At Naked Furniture, though, your customers can judge for themselves the quality and durability of the merchandise, because the pieces aren't slathered with shiny glaze that could disguise a cheap piece of workmanship underneath. Instead, the all-natural wood furniture you'll feature is displayed and sold unfinished, or rather, ready to be finished. If the buyer doesn't want to do the work, you'll perform a custom varnish, stain, or spray job right in your shop, matching any color and using the line of products made exclusively for Naked Furniture.

Franchisees benefit from the extensive retail and home furnishings industry experience of Naked Furniture's corporate staff. Staying on top of the prevailing trends, knowing which manufacturers are reliable, and determining whether the merchandise is of sufficiently high caliber, the company has assembled a comprehensive, regularly revised inventory of popular and salable furniture for you to offer in your store. You may also be able, depending on your location, to take advantage of the company's centralized, computer-linked warehousing system, giving you access to an even wider assortment of merchandise and letting you devote more of your store space to display and less to storage. As the Naked Furniture network expands, the warehouse program has been growing as well, so that every franchisee will soon be able to participate.

The company will supply marketing and demographic information it has gathered to aid in your site selection, and then acquaint you with franchisees' past leasing experiences to help you negotiate favorable terms on the property and decide on the kinds of physical improvements that ought to be made. Before you open, you'll receive training from retail professionals, who will supplement general lessons about the furniture business with statistics, anecdotes, and exercises. Assuming you have little prior experience in the industry, they'll cover topics including product selection, showroom display, and finishing techniques, along with office procedures, sales and customer service skills, and employee relations. You will also be given an extensive operations manual to take back with you to your store, but since a handbook can't answer every question that arises in the actual running of a large retail center, you'll be able to get personal assistance and support by telephone and during field visits by Naked Furniture representatives.

The company will provide you with a complete advertising program and ongoing marketing guidance, too. Newspaper ad slicks and radio scripts, with the option of fully produced commercials, are sent along regularly, and you'll also be outfitted with retail support materials like point-of-purchase pieces and promotional items such as T-shirts and tote bags. And to coordinate your efforts, you'll get a yearly calendar filled with suggestions for seasonal campaigns. Naked Furniture won't let a Presidents' Day holiday go by without reminding you of the sale possibilities.

For further information contact:
  Director of Franchising, Naked Furniture, Inc., P.O. Box F, Clarks Summit, PA
  18411, 717-587-7800 or 1-800-352-2522, fax 717-586-8587

Wallpapers To Go

Initial license fee: $40,000
Royalties: 8% (less rebates and first year credits)
Advertising royalties: 1%
Minimum cash required: $50,000
Capital required: $146,000 to $156,000
Financing: Assistance available
Length of contract: 10 years, plus two 5-year intervals

In business since: 1968
Franchising since: 1968
Total number of units: 115
Number of company-operated units: 21
Total number of units planned, 1995: 200
Number of company-operated units planned, 1995: 50

Hanging wallpaper has gotten an unfair reputation for being a difficult procedure. Now, homeowners recognize that doing it themselves doesn't have to mean crisscrossed stripes, paste caking their hair for weeks, or lumps and bubbles that give a wall surface the texture of stucco.

Indeed, wallpapering has become one of the most popular categories of home improvement, and industry analysts report that specialty stores are the overwhelming choice for consumers ready to take on the task. With the kind of selection, service, convenience, and value you'll provide at your Wallpapers To Go center, it's not hard to see why. You'll stock over 750 patterns—in a vast array of current styles, colors, and trends—that your customers can take home with them right away, and have thousands of other choices available by special order. In addition, you'll sell custom-colored trim paints, window fashions from shades to drapes, coordinating fabrics for bedding and pillows, and other decorative accessories. And your store will display evocative room settings and other presentations to show how all these elements can be stylishly coordinated. It's an attention-getting feature, even if it doesn't always spur the kind of attention you'd like. Gary Gabso, owner of two Wallpapers To Go centers in Florida, once tried hanging a suit in his store window, backed by a no-nonsense pattern, to demonstrate that wallpaper works effectively in a business setting. "The next day, a gentleman came in," Gabso reports, "and asked how much the suit was."

Along with the wallpaper and accessories, you'll stock a complete line of the tools and supplies your customers will need for doing the installation, plus instructional videos and free checklists and brochures. But they'll require fewer materials than they might expect, since many of the rolls you'll offer come with prepasted backs, limiting the trouble and mess of a hanging job. To explain the proper procedures, a number of franchisees hold regular demonstrations at their stores, and you can provide professional installation services, too.

Understanding the difficulty of making the right wallpaper selection, you'll let your customers take home entire sample rolls, rather than just a couple of tiny swatches, so they can better determine which patterns work in their chosen room. And you'll honor the Wallpapers To Go "you gotta love it" policy guaranteeing customer satisfaction—even for rolls they've already put up. If your customers are happy, there's a high potential for repeat business, because "home improvement purchases," as Tom McMahon, the company's visual presentation director, points out, "frequently aren't complete on the first visit."

The Wallpapers To Go franchising system was designed for those with no previous experience in the wallcover industry. Furnishing you with site selection guidelines and market research, the company supplies layout plans for your store and conducts field evaluations of the construction. The distribution division will keep you in stock with popular merchandise, delivered to your center wrapped, priced, and ready to put on the shelves. Taking advantage of the purchasing power of Wallpapers To Go and its preferred accounts with major manufacturers and distributors, you'll be able to offer these name-brand and private-label products at competitive prices that still generate a sizable profit.

To learn effective retailing methods and installation techniques, and to prepare you for daily operations, you'll receive both classroom and in-store training in the Houston area, where the Wallpapers To Go headquarters are located. The company will help you plan and coordinate a grand opening event for your store and continue to extend support through phone communication, newsletters, product seminars, installation clinics, and franchisee conventions. Pooling the resources of Wallpapers To Go store owners nationwide, the corporate advertising fund exists in part to finance national marketing campaigns, but most of the money is spent producing promotional materials for you to use in your local market.

That's in keeping with the company's policy of not letting its guidance and backing interfere with your independence as a retailer. It doesn't mean, however, that there won't be anyone to answer to. "I still have a boss," maintains franchisee Nina Zettinger, who owns two Wallpapers To Go stores in southern California, "and that's the customer."

For further information contact:
Deborah Steinberg, Vice President, Franchise Development, Wallpapers To Go, P.O. Box 4586, Houston, TX 77210, 713-874-3608 or 1-800-843-7094

Weekend Furniture, Inc.

Initial license fee: $15,000
Royalties: 5%
Advertising royalties: 1%
Minimum cash required: $89,500 to $145,500
Capital required: $89,500 to $145,500
Financing: None
Length of contract: 10 years

In business since: 1981
Franchising since: 1990
Total number of units: 4
Number of company-operated units: 4
Total number of units planned, 1995: 50
Number of company-operated units planned, 1995: 4

Weekend Furniture is geared to individuals living in small towns and looking to supplement their income or even develop a business to fill free hours. Running a retail operation generally poses two problems: (1) you're afraid there aren't enough potential customers around to support a store; and (2) you don't think you'll have enough time to devote to it anyway.

The Kriff family, owners of several full-service discount retail furniture centers in upstate New York, had been trying to figure out a way to enter the small-town market for years. It's not that residents of those communities wouldn't welcome having such a store nearby, their other alternatives being to travel far for bargains—and get charged extra fees for long-distance delivery—or to pay full retail prices at a local department store. But a big discount center can't really thrive outside of an urban area—unless, that is, the operation is scaled down. Raising prices or cutting back service would only defeat the purpose. That's when the Kriffs came up with the concept of Furniture Weekend (as the stores themselves are called), a store that's open three days a week, from Friday to Sunday, the time when most consumers prefer to do their furniture shopping anyway. Reducing labor and utility costs, overhead is minimized and even with lesser volume, merchandise can still be offered at low prices that are competitive with the largest, high-volume big-city emporiums.

After eight years of trying out different store locations, inventory and accounting systems, and merchandising techniques, the Kriffs have begun to sell both start-up and conversion franchise packages. Your Furniture Weekend center will be a no-frills store with a functional warehouse look, the furniture neatly displayed in rows. Although you won't have an in-house delivery service, you can make arrangements for your customers; most, however, will simply take their purchases with them. You'll maintain a selective inventory of the type of name-brand merchandise that consumers buy most often: living room, bedroom, and dining room sets; sleeper sofas; chairs and recliners; lamps; and kitchen tables. The items you'll stock come from manufacturers that the company has screened and approved and with which it has negotiated favorable prices.

A Furniture Weekend center can be run by a two-person team, making it a practical enterprise for couples who want to go into business together. And while there is some work to do when the weekend is over—bookkeeping and receiving and setting up new inventory, for example—the demands on your time are limited.

You will, however, have to invest a week to attend franchise training. Getting on-the-job instruction at a company-run store, you'll learn the techniques of furniture sales—how to guide prospective customers to the merchandise that meets their needs and how to close the deal—along with effective ways to display furniture and post the (higher) prices of your competitors. You'll also cover management practices, marketing procedures, purchasing principles, and inventory selection.

Offering assistance in site selection, the company will help you determine the right size and layout for your facility, showing you how to make maximum use of the space, and will participate in your rent negotiations and leasehold improvement decisions. You'll be supplied with step-by-step instructions for a grand opening celebration that will get the attention of local media and prospective customers, and a Weekend Furniture representative will lend a hand at your facility for a minimum of six days during your first month in business, guiding you through initial sales and aiding in the generation of direct mail campaigns and other promotional programs. After your launch is completed, staff members will continue to provide field assistance, while you can also call the home office with any problems, rather than wait for the next visit.

For further information contact:
  Larry Kriff, President, Weekend Furniture, Inc., 21 W. Main St., Malone, NY 12953, 518-483-1328 (in New York, 1-800-562-1606)

Window Works International, Inc.

Initial license fee: $22,500
Royalties: 4%
Advertising royalties: 1%
Minimum cash required: $10,000 to $30,000
Capital required: $36,500
Financing: None
Length of contract: 5 years

In business since: 1978
Franchising since: 1978
Total number of units: 70
Number of company-operated units: None
Total number of units planned, 1995: 300
Number of company-operated units planned, 1995: None

It is pleasing, to be sure, to have a room with a view, but even when windows look out only onto a brick wall, they can be made appealing to the eye. Your Window Works store will provide the custom interior window treatments to do that, combining style with function, and throwing in affordability, too. The options only begin with drapery; you'll also offer pleated shades, shutters, vertical blinds, cornices, and other accessories that make a window of any size and shape the highlight of the room's decor—whether the choice is a layered, country look for a dining room, a sophisticated, metropolitan look for a den, or a colorful, whimsical look for a child's bedroom.

Between new buildings being constructed and homes being redecorated, the market for your merchandise and services is large. While the majority of your sales will be to homeowners, you'll also be able to accommodate a large commercial sector—establishments like schools, apartment complexes, hotels and restaurants, and private offices—facilities where low maintenance, energy efficiency, and light control are considerations equally as important as style. For these thrift-conscious customers, you'll offer advice on the practical pluses and minuses of various window dressing possibilities.

Functioning as a showroom, your Window Works store will feature samples and displays of a complete range of window treatments. But it's your shop-at-home services, ensuring that your customers make the right choice for their decor and lighting needs, that will produce most of your sales. With the prearranged samples you've brought along, you'll review the selections with them, take measurements, and provide an estimate. When the final choice is made, your customer will give you a deposit, paying the balance after installation. You'll place the order with the manufacturer, who will have the merchandise delivered to your store within one to three weeks. Sending employees to do the installing, you'll guarantee that the curtains, blinds, shades, or shutters will fit precisely and function accurately, or they will be replaced to your customer's satisfaction.

Through Window Works' buying clout, you'll get substantial vendor discounts. You can easily update your sample books and store displays to stay on the cutting edge of fashion trends, since you won't actually have any inventory in stock. That means you won't need much storage room, either, so your Window Works center can fit in about 1,500 square feet of space, keeping overhead down and meaning that no large capital investment is required. The company will assist you with site selection and lease negotiation, and guide you in setting up your showroom, without requiring any rigid layout or design.

After you finish a home-study course, you'll go to Window Works headquarters in Wisconsin for two weeks of classroom, in-store, and in-field training. Having a thorough understanding of the products you'll be selling and the financial systems you'll be using, however, is only the beginning of the knowledge the company feels you'll need to acquire to run your operation properly. That's why your instruction will also address the more intangible aspects of a total business philosophy, areas such as customer relations, time management, employee motivation, service attitudes, public-perception, and self-perception. On the more concrete side, you will be taught how to complete a "Profit Plan" at the beginning of each year, projecting monthly sales, marketing activities, earnings, and expenses to provide yourself with a comparison base for the actual progress of your business.

Although Window Works maintains that word-of-mouth recommendations from satisfied customers is the company's most effective advertising, it runs a comprehensive marketing program, using a combination of high- and low-profile strategies with procedures designed to increase awareness of the company and network-wide sales. The home office extends step-by-step assistance with your most concerted promotional effort, the launch for your Window Works center, supplying a preopening checklist, timetable, and advertising pieces. Once you're in business, you'll continue to receive printed materials, from four-color brochures and mailers to newspaper glossies and yellow pages ads, along with radio jingles and other new marketing tools that the company continues to develop.

Normal Window Works store hours are 9 A.M. to 5 P.M., Monday through Friday, and 10 A.M. to 3 P.M. on Saturdays. A typical operation consists of three to five people; you (working as the chief salesperson), a store manager, a full-time installer, and additional sales staff as needed.

For further information contact:
  Window Works International, Inc., 6321 Bury Dr., Suite 2, Eden Prairie, MN
  55346-1739, 612-937-2004 or 1-800-326-2659, fax 612-934-5665

Rental Stores

Nation-Wide General Rental Centers, Inc.

Initial license fee: None
Royalties: None
Advertising royalties: None
Minimum cash required: $45,000
Capital required: Working capital, $10,000; packages from $50,000 to $140,000
Financing: Company offers 100% financing for inventory you buy after initial
    purchase of rental goods
Length of contract: 3 years

In business since: 1976
Franchising since: 1976
Total number of units: 210
Number of company-operated units: None
Total number of units planned, 1995: NA
Number of company-operated units planned, 1995: None

Nation-Wide has built its business on a simple idea. Many people occasionally need tools and equipment of various kinds for specific jobs. It doesn't pay for them to buy, so renting without having to worry about maintenance does make sense. A business that could meet the needs of such do-it-yourselfers—contractors, party givers, convalescents, and campers—all from one location could turn a healthy profit. Customers who rent for one occasion or task would see the wide variety of tools and equipment available and might return in the future when their rental needs changed.

Nation-Wide distributors run just such businesses; they have something in stock for just about everybody. Their inventory includes reversible drills, sod cutters, toboggans, wheelchairs, folding cots, torque wrenches, party tents, staple guns, dollies, paving breakers, wallpaper steamers, typewriters, pipe threaders, sanders, sleeping bags, and cement mixers. They also rent Santa Claus suits.

As a Nation-Wide distributor, you can choose what kinds of equipment to rent in your business. The company ensures that you won't have to take a loss on unprofitable stock by offering a buy-back guarantee: Nation-Wide will take back for full credit any equipment that does not produce income in the first year.

If a Nation-Wide franchise appeals to you, you will need a building with at least 2,000 square feet inside and 15,000 square feet of securely fenced area outside. Some Nation-Wide centers occupy buildings as big as 7,000 square feet. You will need good traffic flow in the area and parking for six to ten cars.

Nation-Wide will train you to run an equipment rental center at its Columbia, South Carolina, rental center. Your five-day training course will cover equipment maintenance, the company's computerized accounting system, advertising and promotion, rental rates, insurance, and inventory control. Your accounting system will generate an itemized inventory report detailing monthly rental income per item, in addition to a balance sheet and income and cash flow statements.

Your Nation-Wide business preparation package, the cost of which varies according to franchise location and other differentials, includes your licensing fee, a grand opening pennant, decals, 10,000 flyers, 10,000 rental contracts, and stationery. Nation-Wide supplements your local promotions with national advertising.

For further information contact:
  Ike Goodvin, Nation-Wide General Rental Centers, Inc., 1805-C Hembree Rd., Alpharetta, GA 30201, 404-664-7765 or 1-800-227-1643, fax 404-664-0052

Taylor Rental Corporation

Initial license fee: $20,000
Royalties: 2.75%/year up to $200,000 gross sales; 2.5% from $200,000 to
   $500,000; 2% over $500,000
Advertising royalties: None
Minimum cash required: $90,000
Capital required: $267,000
Financing: Assistance in obtaining bank financing
Length of contract: 10 years; renewal every 5 years thereafter

In business since: 1949
Franchising since: 1962
Total number of units: 312
Number of company-operated units: 80
Total number of units planned, 1995: NA
Number of company-operated units planned, 1995: NA

Taylor Rental, the largest general rental chain in America, is a subsidiary of The Stanley Works, a manufacturer of building tools for professionals and do-it-yourselfers. Taylor franchisees rent out champagne fountains, cement mixers, popcorn machines, jackhammers, baby cribs, carpet cleaners, typewriters, pitchers and serving platters, wheelbarrows, lanterns—and just about everything else. Offering a broad line of rental merchandise has the advantage of partially insulating Taylor stores from recessions, since they draw customers from every walk of life.

When you buy a franchise, Taylor's staff will help you select a site for your rental center and will advise you on construction if you decide not to rent an already existing building. Your facility will occupy at least 5,000 square feet indoors and include a fenced outdoor area of approximately 1,500 square feet. A bigger building can compensate if you can't find a store with outside space. You also need parking space for at least six cars.

You will train to run your rental store at one of Taylor's company-owned centers. The program lasts two weeks and covers personnel, advertising, customer relations, cash control, financial systems, inventory management, loss prevention, and the operation and maintenance of equipment. You can have future employees trained by the company for a minimal charge. Once in business, you will receive informal ongoing training from your regional director.

The company will work with you to determine the right product mix for your location. If you buy at least 60 percent of your inventory from Taylor, it will send a representative to your store to help you assemble and display your stock. Similarly, if you purchase your display fixtures from the company, Taylor will provide the information needed for installation, which should assist your local contractor.

The company offers several optional computer programs to help franchisees manage their businesses. Since 1980, TOPIC, the first general rental industry computer system, has been in use within the company. This system allows you to track your inventory and handle your accounting. Other available software enables you to communicate your rental sales data to company headquarters and receive from the company an analysis of your inventory utilization. Through the company you can also buy liability insurance for your business.

Taylor has a co-op advertising program, through which it refunds to you 25 percent of your advertising expenditures up to 1 percent of your gross revenue. Its advertising department will also help you place your yellow pages advertisements and will provide you with direct mail and other types of promotional materials.

For further information contact:
  Taylor Rental Corporation, 1000 Stanley Dr., P.O. Box 8000, New Britain, CT 06050, 203-229-9100

Specialty Retailing

Docktor Pet Centers

Initial license fee: $20,000
Royalties: 4.5%
Advertising royalties: 0.5%
Minimum cash required: $75,000
Capital required: $200,500 to $260,000 (new stores); some existing stores
    available, priced above and below the cost of new stores
Financing: Provides outside sources
Length of contract: 10 years

In business since: 1967
Franchising since: 1967
Total number of units: 246
Number of company-operated units: 17
Total number of units planned, 1995: NA
Number of company-operated units planned, 1995: NA

If you go into this business, it should be for love of animals as much
as for love of running your own store, since you will spend your days
surrounded by dogs, cats, fish, birds, and other kinds of household
pets. Working on the theory that pet stores sell not only animals but
love, Docktor Pet Centers encourage potential purchasers to handle
animals in the store.

Of course, any pet store is more than fur and fins. There are also
combs, cages, flea collars, and food. The Docktor Pet Center merchandising system will make it possible for you to sell more than 2,000
items, over 800 made by the company itself. Supplies and accessories
make up a good part of the business of Docktor Pet Centers, the
largest chain of shopping center–based pet department stores in the
country. Individual franchisees must buy their pets from a breeder or
broker who appears on the Docktor Pet Center certified list. The qualifications for certification are high—for starters, the breeder or broker
must be USDA-licensed, and Docktor Pet Centers researches each candidate thoroughly.

If you love animals but worry that you don't know a cockatiel from
a cockatoo and have real familiarity only with cats and dogs (your
store will sell 40 breeds), you'll feel reassured once you realize that
Docktor Pet Center store owners range from former automobile industry executives to salespeople to teachers. The company's three-week
training course, given in Wilmington, Massachusetts, will teach you
every facet of the business, from management to animal care. Through

your regional consultant and regional seminars, Docktor Pet Centers will continue its assistance and instruction once you open for business.

Docktor Pet Centers will work with you on site selection for your pet store, negotiate the lease, and assign a representative to monitor the success of your store.

For further information contact:
Docktor Pet Holdings Ltd., 355 Middlesex Ave., Wilmington, MA 01887, 1-800-765-4PET

Ecology House

Initial license fee: $20,000
Royalties: 5%
Advertising royalties: NA
Minimum cash required: NA
Capital required: $123,000 to $211,500
Financing: None
Length of contract: 10 years

In business since: 1983
Franchising since: 1987
Total number of units: 6
Number of company-operated units: 1
Total number of units planned, 1995: NA
Number of company-operated units planned, 1995: NA

"Gifts of Environmental Consciousness" is the focus of Ecology House, assuredly a retail store for the nineties. "We combine the goal of producing an honest profit with actively creating a better life on earth," the company proclaims, selling products explicitly not derived from animals, goods whose proceeds support environmental efforts, and items that educate consumers about ecology.

That doesn't mean that Ecology House stores have a dry, science fair–like atmosphere. Founded by an artist/physical therapist and a former construction worker who helped Greenpeace develop its first retail outlet, the stores feature clever displays and eclectic merchandise. Within the company's carefully defined parameters are an abundance of gift selections, many depicting wildlife themes. Whales and seals are favorites, but an entire menagerie of animals will be represented at your store in the vivid art prints, sculptures, jewelry, and clothing items you'll have for sale. You'll also carry mugs and glassware, wind chimes and New Age music recordings, toys and games, books and magazines, cards and stationery, as well as cosmetics and household cleansers that are guaranteed not to have been tested on animals. In addition, you'll offer such conservation products as water-saving devices, solar-powered goods, and rechargeable batteries. And while Ecology House doesn't represent any particular group, free literature and information is provided at the stores for a variety of environmental and animal rights organizations.

According to Ecology House's cofounder Will Anderson, "we wanted products that would express our value system." The same goes for its franchisees. You are required to be a vegetarian ("a major component of the Ecology House philosophy is a belief that what we eat has the single most important impact on the environment") and expected to donate a meaningful portion of your annual revenues to nonprofit organizations. Beyond your good intentions and social consciousness, you should also have at least two years of retail experience and basic computer skills.

Providing advice on site location and store layout, Ecology House offers two weeks of hands-on training at an established franchise, start-up assistance, and ongoing guidance and support tailored to your needs. An operations manual and point-of-sale computer software are also part of the franchise package. Because you won't be able to rely on conventional vendors, the regularly updated computerized list of trade sources you'll receive is vital. The company has screened its merchandise suppliers to ensure that they uphold ethical standards and that their goods and manufacturing and testing procedures meet Ecology House's exacting cruelty-free and environmentally conscious criteria.

In business since 1983 and with stores currently operating in Colorado, Hawaii, Maine, and Oregon, Ecology House has shown that supportive, ecologically minded communities needed for the success of this kind of venture can be found across the country. Consequently, there are promising franchising opportunities available in many regions, with the size and exclusivity of your territory open to negotiation.

For further information contact:
  Will Anderson, Vice President, Ecology House Franchise, Inc., P.O. Box 40428, Portland, OR 97240, 503-223-1842

Fastframe USA, Inc.

Initial license fee: $25,000
Royalties: 7.5%
Advertising royalties: 3%
Minimum cash required: $35,000 to $50,000

Capital required: $110,000 to $150,000
Financing: Available
Length of contract: 10 years, with two 10-year options

In business since: 1983
Franchising since: 1987
Total number of units: 181
Number of company-operated units: 4
Total number of units planned, 1995: 1,000
Number of company-operated units planned, 1995: 10

Don't think there are never emergencies in the picture-framing business. Artist Alexandra Jacobs once needed to have 36 of her paintings framed as soon as possible for a gallery showing; a Fastframe store got the entire job done in 12 hours.

Just how fast is Fastframe? Fifteen minutes is all you'll need for most of your assignments. Here's what makes Fastframe so fast: a large inventory of materials—not only samples, but hundreds of moldings and mats actually in stock that can be used right there for some 95 percent of your orders; a simple, efficient pricing system; exclusive state-of-the art equipment; and a streamlined assembly method where frames are fastened invisibly from behind.

Of course, last-minute art openings aren't exactly everyday occurrences, but for that matter there's more to your Fastframe store than speedy service—reasonable prices and high-quality work, to name two other features. Besides artists and nonpainting, nondrawing homeowners, your customers will include interior decorators and architects, hotels and restaurants, galleries, and museums. You'll offer a wide range of framing options for oil paintings, watercolors, lithographs, photographs, diplomas, tapestries, and quilts, with shadow boxes also available for three-dimensional pieces like metals, military uniforms, and musical instruments. Complicated framing jobs such as these will take extra time to complete, but even custom work can be done far more quickly than the week or longer that many other shops require.

You'll learn the techniques for instant and specialty picture framing, along with general operations procedures, during initial franchisee instruction sessions that are held at Fastframe's Newbury Park, California, training center. The company follows up with biweekly phone calls, monthly newsletters, and regular store visits, as well as with regional meetings, national conventions, and merchandising materials that are circulated as new products and systems are introduced.

Founded in Great Britain, Fastframe now has locations on four continents, making it one of the largest worldwide chains in the industry and producing a global network of suppliers and distributors whose wares you'll be able to obtain at volume discounts. The company's entry into the American market has been successful, according to *Entrepreneur* magazine, which recently named Fastframe the top franchise in the retail business.

Whether in Australia or America, each store site is selected with care. You'll receive assistance, including demographic data that are thoroughly scrutinized by the company's real estate personnel, in choosing a high-visibility location, usually at a mini mall or strip center in an affluent neighborhood. Producing floor plans and detailed layouts, the operations department will supervise the construction. A management team will arrive shortly before your store is ready to open to help you organize your inventory and decorate the retail area, where you'll display paintings, prints, and limited-edition artwork for sale to generate additional income. Meanwhile, the home office will aid in planning a full schedule of advertising and promotional activities to launch your business.

Marketing support and guidance from the company is ongoing, although many Fastframe store owners come up with their own strategies, too. Torrance, California, franchisee Frank Bellinghiere, for one, hired a professional magician as his general manager and has him perform sleight-of-hand tricks for customers while pitching the store's goods and services. Telling them, "Money goes further when you spend it at Fastframe," he sends a crumpled ten-spot floating above the sales counter.

For further information contact:
   John Scott, President and CEO, Franchise Marketing, Fastframe USA, Inc.,
   30495 Canwood, Suite 100, Agoura Hills, CA 91301, 818-707-1166 or
   1-800-521-3726, fax 818-707-0164

Flowerama of America, Inc.

Initial license fee: $17,500
Royalties: 5% to 6%
Advertising royalties: None
Minimum cash required: $25,000
Capital required: $50,000 to $90,000
Financing: None
Length of contract: 10 years

In business since: 1967
Franchising since: 1972
Total number of units: 98

Number of company-operated units: 15
Total number of units planned, 1995: NA
Number of company-operated units planned, 1992: 18

Somewhere between luxuries and necessities lie the things that brighten our lives. Much of the thriving home-decoration business is based on people's desire to make attractive things part of their daily life-style. Flowers used to be a luxury; now growing numbers of Americans, especially those between the ages of 25 and 45, are thinking of them as an integral part of good living, something they buy as a matter of course.

For most people, flowers used to be reserved for special occasions— birthdays and anniversaries, for example. Now, flowers are as likely as a bottle of wine to be the gift you bring when invited to a friend's house for dinner. And many people buy fresh-cut flowers for their homes as a regular practice—simply because flowers bring with them a sense of graciousness at a reasonable price.

So it is not only people with high incomes that the florist business caters to now—it is just about everybody. That's why you shouldn't be surprised to learn that Flowerama confines its operations to regional enclosed shopping centers, where its stores operate alongside those selling shoes, records, housewares, and the thousands of other things people buy regularly.

Flowerama units, whether 1,000-square-foot in-line shops or 3,000-square-foot freestanding stores, aim to attract a wide public and sell flowers at popular prices. Flowerama wants people to get into the flower-buying habit. And the company wants to do this throughout the country, although they do not offer franchises on the West Coast.

You'll be kept busy selling fresh-cut flowers, floral arrangements, plants, and related accessories. Flowerama also makes up special orders for social functions, and most franchises participate in sending and receiving service orders. Flowerama will give you a considerable amount of help to get started. Not only does Flowerama take charge of selecting a site and negotiating your lease, but the company itself signs the main lease agreement and then subleases the location to you at no profit to itself.

The company will teach you the ins and outs of the retail flower business at its Waterloo, Iowa, headquarters. The nine-day training seminar covers everything you will need to know about floral design as well as store operational procedures and accounting. You will also receive on-the-job training at a Flowerama store.

Flowerama will have somebody on hand to help you open your store, and a company representative will drop in several times each year. You can get further training at Waterloo by taking the seminars it offers about five times during the year. Blooming plants, hard goods, packaging, professional signs, and how to create successful promotions are subjects likely to be covered.

Flowerama assures potential franchisees that help is never more than a telephone call away. Greg Heid, who with his wife, Pat, operates the Flowerama franchise at the University Square Mall in Tampa, Florida, tells us that they are more than satisfied with that aspect of their franchising experience. "The company provides us with any help we ask for," he says, "whether it be legal, accounting, or merchandising techniques."

You do not have to buy your equipment and inventory from Flowerama, although franchisees generally opt for the convenience of purchasing from the company.

For further information contact:
  Chuck Nygren, Flowerama of America, Inc., 3165 W. Airline Hwy., Waterloo, IA 50703, 319-291-6004

Paper Warehouse

Initial license fee: $19,000
Royalties: 3%
Advertising royalties: maximum 1%
Minimum cash required: $50,000
Capital required: $100,000
Financing: Assistance in obtaining
Length of contract: 10 years

In business since: 1983
Franchising since: 1987
Total number of units: 44
Number of company-operated units: 32
Total number of units planned, 1995: 100
Number of company-operated units planned, 1995: 65

A Paper Warehouse isn't exactly a *no*-frills retail center—"low"-frills is more like it. At your store, the merchandise will be functionally displayed on basic metal shelving or kept in boxes stacked on the floor, with hand-lettered signs guiding customers to their selections and listing the prices. Credit cards are not accepted—you'll operate entirely on a cash-and-carry basis, functioning as a one-stop source for home, office, and entertainment-related paper (and plastic) goods. But the range of products that you'll be selling, some of them recycled products, is vast indeed: bath and facial tissue, napkins and paper towels, plates, cups, and eating utensils, gift wrap and streamers, packing and mailing materials, along with other related supplies such as staples, paper clips, and file folders. And of course there's the paper itself—legal note pads and spiral notebooks, and computer, typing, graphic, and copy paper available in reams and reams.

The warehouse environment not only allows you to keep overhead and daily operation costs down, it also reinforces your store's image as a no-nonsense discount retail center that stocks a large inventory of products. The stock is in large quantities, too, with still-greater price reductions offered for bulk purchases.

Because you'll furnish volume that isn't often available at conventional stationery, party-supply, or gift stores, much of your business will come from commercial and professional establishments like small businesses, caterers, schools, and churches, in addition to regular retail customers.

The efficient, space-saving displays will allow your Paper Warehouse to fit in a relatively small—2,800- to 3,000-square-foot—location. From the company's experience, the best locales are inexpensive retail warehouse districts, small strip centers, or freestanding sites adjacent to high traffic shopping zones. Providing assistance with site selection and guidance in negotiating the lease, if you'd like, Paper Warehouse will also supply designs and store plans, including a fixture layout and a merchandising plan to make it easier for you to follow the company's warehouse concept.

A four-day sales and operations training session will be held for you at the company's Minneapolis corporate office. Helping you coordinate your inventory, Paper Warehouse will guide you through your initial orders. In addition, company staff members will spend a week at your facility prior to opening to assist you with general store setup, recruiting and training employees, and developing a launch PR and advertising campaign. In between visits from Paper Warehouse field representatives, you'll continue to receive communications about new products and trends in the paper trade once you are in business. You'll also get to attend semiannual merchandising and operational planning meetings back in Minneapolis.

Because you'll stock such a wide assortment of products, there should be no particularly slow sales stretches during the year. The company has identified 10 major holiday or seasonal selling periods, however, when business should be particularly active—and will show you how to plan ahead for them with augmented inventory orders and marketing and promotions programs. One way you *won't* be taking advantage, though, is by carrying greeting cards. They're simply contrary to your image as a no-nonsense supplier of bulk goods at near-wholesale prices. Your Paper Warehouse will never be confused with a cutesy boutique, and that's exactly, the company believes, what will help you carve a successful niche.

For further information contact:
   Yale Dolginow, Director of Franchising, Paper Warehouse, 7120 Shady Oak Rd., Eden Prairie, MN 55344, 612-829-5467, fax 612-829-0247

Petland, Inc.

Initial license fee: $25,000
Royalties: 4½%
Advertising royalties: None
Minimum cash required: $50,000
Capital required: $125,000 to $250,000
Financing: Company will assist with business plan and local proposal
Length of contract: 20 years

In business since: 1967
Franchising since: 1967
Total number of units: Approximately 137
Number of company-operated units: 1
Total number of units planned, 1995: 191
Number of company-operated units planned, 1995: 1

To get an idea of the potential market for pets, pick up a copy of your local white pages and point to any listing at random. The odds are better than even that at least one pet lives at that number. A 1980s pet census found that Americans own close to 250 million tropical fish, 48 million dogs, 27.2 million cats, and 25.2 million birds. Since 1990, the number of cats owned by Americans has even surpassed the number of dogs. People have to buy many of these animals somewhere, and all pets need food and supplies—continually.

Petland wants to put you in the business of providing people with animal companionship and the supplies they need to keep their pets healthy and happy. This franchisor usually provides its franchisees with a turnkey operation: Petland will locate a site, build your store, install the prefabricated fixtures, and stock it with animals and accessories. In many cases, franchisees sublease their stores from Petland when the company has found and set up their store for them. If you sublease your premises, you will receive the same terms that Petland gets from the landlord. Petland stores range in size from regional mall or strip center stores of 2,500 to 4,500 square feet to "super" stores that occupy as much as 8,000 square feet. Sometimes franchisees can select their own site and build their own store to Petland's specifications.

You can operate one of these franchises even if you don't have animal expertise. The company will teach you everything you need to know, from how to work with a veterinarian to how to tame a bird by thinking like one. Petland has one-week classroom training at its headquarters in Chillicothe, Ohio. In addition to animal care, the company's instruction will cover store management, personnel, accessories, inventory, merchandising, bookkeeping, and community relations.

Several days before you open for business, Petland's merchandising team will come to work at your side while you stock your store and get it ready for your grand opening. Company representatives will stay with you for up to 10 days after you open, guiding you through the new experience of operating your own pet store.

Not only can you call Petland for advice on specific problems, it will call you regularly with advice and encouragement and to review your monthly financial statement. This close attention generally enables the company to spot any trouble before it becomes a big problem. You will also receive regular visits from a Petland representative, who will follow a 1,000-point checklist to inspect your store and make sure that everything is up to company standards.

You have your choice of buying dry supplies from the Petland distribution network or from company-approved local suppliers. Individual franchisees decide for themselves what breeders and brokers to buy their pets from, and Petland strongly recommends purchasing from credible distributors. Petland ships by truck from its 18,000-square-foot warehouse in Chillicothe, Ohio, or it can drop ship directly from the manufacturer to you, in which case you receive the same discounts that you get when you buy directly from the franchisor. Even if you choose to buy from local sources, your supplier will have to match the low prices available to you through Petland. You can also purchase a line of private-label Petland supplies.

Each year when you begin to think about purchasing your Christmas inventory, Petland's distribution network sponsors an annual fall trade show at which manufacturers and distributors show animals as well as new products. There you can further your education in the business and also get together with your fellow franchisees to exchange information.

Petland runs several seasonal and year-round promotions through its franchisees. The company also provides giveaway calendars and sponsors contests and fish and bird clubs with membership cards and publications.

The best opportunities to open a Petland franchise are in the Sun-belt states of California, Florida, and Texas, and in Colorado, Illinois,

Content

Wisconsin, Michigan, Pennsylvania, Ohio, Illinois, North Carolina, Virginia, and Maryland. Petland also has two franchises in France and two in Japan.

For further information contact:
  J. Whitman, Franchise Sales Coordinator, Petland, Inc., 195 N. Hickory St., Chillicothe, OH 45601-5606, 1-800-221-5935 (in Ohio: 1-800-221-3479)

The Pro Image, Inc.

Initial license fee: $16,500
Royalties: 4%
Advertising royalties: None
Minimum cash required: $95,000 to $189,500
Capital required: $125,000
Financing: None
Length of contract: 10 years

In business since: 1985
Franchising since: 1985
Total number of units: 200
Number of company-operated units: 2
Total number of units planned, 1995: 400
Number of company-operated units planned, 1995: 5

You've seen them when the TV camera pans up to the stands between innings or during halftime. They can only be described as sports fanatics, decked out head to toe in full regalia, from the fright wig—in team colors—down to the matching socks, with a pennant in one hand, a beer mug in the other, and a boom box between the legs plastered with stickers. Then there are the saner fans, who just like to wear a sweatshirt or cap emblazoned with their favorite team's insignia. It's not enough for many sports enthusiasts merely to root, root, root for the home team; at the game or watching it on TV, on the streets or even on the job, they have to wear their passions on their sleeves, so to speak. And having a Pro Image shop at their neighborhood mall gives them a convenient alternative to trekking out to the stadium for sportswear, souvenirs, and gifts, where the items are brazenly overpriced and available only on game days, and where those who aren't home-team fans are out of luck anyway.

The licensed merchandise that you'll carry salutes not just the local teams, but professional and collegiate organizations alike from across the country. Each team's official emblem adorns a wide array of products—T-shirts, sweatshirts, tank tops, sweatbands, caps, pennants, buttons, and glassware, to name just a few. Hopeful parents can dress their future slugger or linebacker in an infant-sized uniform, and can pick up a replica team jersey or jacket for themselves. And with the posters, wastepaper baskets, bulletin boards, bedding, and other home furnishings available, your customers will practically be able to decorate an entire room. All the major sports are represented—baseball, football, basketball, hockey, soccer, even the more esoteric games that might enjoy popularity in your area.

To help you fill orders and obtain hard-to-get items, the Pro Image runs a huge warehouse and distribution operation through its subsidiary, TPI Distributors, allowing you to receive discounts from most of the company's regular vendors. While you won't be obliged to buy exclusively through the system, "it's an advantageous option," according to Kevin Olson, cofounder of The Pro Image. "Deliveries from manufacturers sometimes take months. And a hot team's product is hard to get a hold of quickly. TPI can increase delivery speed. Plus stores can special order merchandise they don't stock." A computer software program has also been created to let you track inventory and reorder supplies more easily.

Using its affiliations with major mall developers and owners, the company will assist you in selecting a location for your store and participate in the lease negotiation. The sales staff will make recommendations on the size of your facility, and, with layouts planned for efficiency and customer appeal, help you in the merchandising, setup, and design of the store, staying through your opening day.

At the company's Salt Lake City headquarters, you'll attend a four-day training session, learning step by step the process for starting and operating your Pro Center business. The material will cover such subjects as purchasing procedures, financial systems, customer relations, and marketing techniques. Once you're out there running your store, service department representatives will be in touch at least once a month and will make regular visits to your location. The Pro Image also keeps you outfitted with professional advertising and marketing materials, including ad slicks, radio jingles, and TV commercials, as well as supplies and guidelines for in-store promotional campaigns.

The Pro Image's monthly newsletter will help you stay informed about the latest company and industry happenings—new vendors and products, new discounts—along with management tips and creative marketing ideas. Bringing together franchisees and suppliers, annual conventions give you a chance to preview the latest items being offered by team-licensed manufacturers, in addition to attending seminars on relevant issues affecting Pro Image shop owners, like the growing competition from shopping channels and mail-order catalogues. While that has admittedly become a concern, one that the company is addressing with countermeasures, Chad Olson, The Pro

Image's other cofounder, maintains that the merchandising and marketing approaches of the enterprises are so different that each should be able to thrive. "We deal with a lot of impulse buyers—people who browse a mall and happen to walk in and see all of these colorful items. You just can't replace the feeling of being surrounded by team-licensed products and trying on a jacket or hat in front of a mirror."

For further information contact:
  Tom Haraldson, Information Director, The Pro Image, Inc., 563 W. 500 South, Suite 330, Bountiful, UT 84010, 801-292-8777, fax 801-292-4603

Video

Video Update, Inc.

Initial license fee: $19,500
Royalties: 5%
Advertising royalties: 1%
Minimum cash required: $20,000
Capital required: $90,000 to $263,000
Financing: Assistance available
Length of contract: 10 years

In business since: 1981
Franchising since: 1982
Total number of units: 54
Number of company-operated units: 10
Total number of units planned, 1995: 250
Number of company-operated units planned, 1995: 40

This chain of video-rental stores aims to expand both geographically and in the number of its franchises. It seeks new franchisees not only all across America, but in Europe, Australia, and Malaysia.

A typical Video Update store covers 3,000 to 5,000 square feet, and carries more than 4,000 movies. All the company stores have a special kids' section known as "Yippidyland," where kid-size fixtures, a playland, and balloons encourage children to browse. The company will help you select the site for your store and will advise you on exterior and interior design.

You will be trained at your own Video Update store. Instruction will focus on retailing, accounting, customer and employee relations, advertising, and store operations. Later on, periodic visits from company representatives and phone contact with the franchisor will keep you up to date on company policies and programs.

Video Update is dedicated to opening the best video stores in the world.

For further information contact:
  John Bedard, Video Update, Inc., 287 E. Sixth St., St. Paul, MN 55101,
  612-222-0006 or 1-800-433-1195

West Coast Video

Initial license fee: $60,000
Royalties: 7%
Advertising royalties: 3%
Minimum cash required: $80,000
Capital required: $250,000
Financing: None
Length of contract: 10 years

In business since: 1983
Franchising since: 1985
Total number of units: 650
Number of company-operated units: 75
Total number of units planned, 1995: 2,000
Number of company-operated units planned, 1995: NA

The time has long passed when almost anyone could open a video-rental business and automatically expect to make a profit. Intense competition has allowed customers to become far more choosy about the video stores they'll patronize and, in most parts of the country, the market has become so saturated that only a limited number are flourishing. So what has made West Coast Videos one of those successes—successful enough, that is, to have become the second-largest video chain in the nation, with stores throughout the United States and Canada (well beyond the West Coast) serving five million customers monthly, and to have been identified by *Entrepreneur* magazine as America's fastest-growing new franchisor?

To start, West Coast Video was there at the beginning, in business since the concept of video rentals first caught on. As more and more chains and independent retailers got into the act, however, the company recognized that customer loyalty could be counted on only as long as it was nourished with improved services. So West Coast worked to avoid what it saw as the shortcomings of rival operations—limited selection; poor organization, with tapes scattered randomly about the shelves; a sales staff with no knowledge of customer service;

and a general attitude of "if we've got the tapes, you'll rent them from us no matter how we treat you or how messy and dismal our stores are." The difference at West Coast Videos is apparent even in the store design itself, created to convey the excitement of going to the movies when customers come in to rent a video. The decor concept, in a word, is red—not just red carpets but red walls, red shelves, red graphics, red trim, a touch of red, too, in the sales staff uniforms. The effect is, to say the least, vibrant, giving the store a bit of show-biz pizzazz. Then there are the videotapes themselves, an abundance of new releases, classic films, foreign pictures, and made-for-video features, each categorized and displayed in alphabetical order. To make browsing more pleasurable, your store will be clean, bright—brighter than daylight, in fact—and uncluttered.

Like a theater, you'll supply an assortment of snacks for sale— candy, soda, chips, and popcorn—that your customers can devour later on when they're screening their movies. Your store might carry other home-entertainment merchandise as well, such as CDs, audiotapes, Nintendo games, and private label West Coast Video TV and VCR accessories.

While your customers might enjoy lingering over your inventory, watching a moment or two of the film running on the store monitors, and giving their child a quarter for the mechanical rides, they'll want to head home quickly once they've made their choice. Sending them on their way, you'll use the company's custom computer equipment to process the transaction quickly and accurately.

Through its experience in many different cities and markets, West Coast Videos has developed specific guidelines and recommendations for the location of its stores. The real estate staff will participate in site selection and will show you how to use the strength of a nationally known retail chain to your advantage during lease negotiations. Other company officials will provide layout and design plans and supervise the construction or remodeling of your facility.

You and a designated employee or two will attend an initial one-week training session at the company's "West Coast College," located, contrary to where you might expect, in Philadelphia. Both in the classroom and behind the counter of an actual West Coast store, you'll learn about video hardware and software, daily operations, purchasing and pricing procedures, and how to keep track of your entire business, from inventory to customer data, with the computer software.

Special advice is given to absentee or multistore owners, but each franchisee is provided with personal guidance based on his or her needs and experience. "Before I bought my franchise," says Ben Flamm of Hollywood, Florida, "I didn't know a great deal about video. So the corporate folks worked with me to figure out what made the best business sense for my store." The company's movie buying department will assist you in selecting your merchandise and introduce you to the volume purchasing arrangements that West Coast video enjoys with the major video suppliers. Shortly before your store is ready for business and through opening day, a West Coast regional operations manager will work with you, helping with setup, staff hiring, and coordinating your launch event.

With a full in-house art department, West Coast's marketing department takes charge of a variety of programs from which you'll benefit, most prominently, cooperative promotions with Coca-Cola, Disney, Paramount, and other major studios and corporations, featuring membership campaigns, seasonal events, and sweepstakes connected with new title releases. You'll receive bulletins about the upcoming activities, along with the advertising and marketing materials to publicize them. Additionally, the company will send you monthly franchise newsletters, plus complimentary magazines to display in your store, filled with Hollywood news, celebrity profiles, announcements about the movies just out on video, and information on special rental deals.

Meanwhile, ongoing personal contact with the company is hardly limited to occasional appearances by Viddy O. Bear, the West Coast mascot. Your regional manager will visit regularly and you'll get together with fellow franchisees and the corporate staff alike during the annual conventions.

For further information contact:
  John L. Barry, Vice President, Franchise Development, West Coast Video, 9990 Global Rd., Philadelphia, PA 19115, 215-677-1000 or 1-800-433-5171 ext. 281, fax 215-677-5804

18. The Travel Industry

Contents

Hotels, Motels, and Campgrounds

Embassy Suites, Inc.

Initial license fee: $500/suite or $100,000, whichever is greater
Royalties: 4%
Advertising royalties: 3%
Minimum cash required: Varies
Capital required: Varies
Financing: None
Length of contract: 20 years

In business since: 1983
Franchising since: 1984
Total number of units: 94
Number of company-operated units: 51
Total number of units planned, 1995: 150
Number of company-operated units planned, 1995: 80

The "all-suite" first-class hotel has become a highly successful concept in the lodging trade, and Embassy Suites is an industry leader, with more locations—from airports and downtown business districts to suburban and resort areas—than any of its competitors, and more suites than all of them combined. At the same time, the company has also been rated by both *Fortune* and *Consumer Reports* as the nation's best hotel chain.

Embassy Suites claims that customers are so satisfied that over 95 percent say they'll stay at Embassy Suites Hotels in the future. For about the same price as a single room in a traditional upscale hotel, your guests will get an entire 450-square-foot suite offering a separate living room that contains a sofa bed and wet bar with refrigerator, microwave, and coffee maker. The bathrooms are spacious and well-appointed and each lodging is equipped with two color televisions, two telephones, and a king-sized or two double beds. In addition, every suite overlooks an expansive landscaped atrium featuring fountains and waterfalls, where you'll serve free breakfast and complimentary cocktails.

A variety of amenities, including a restaurant, gift shop, and deli, as well as room service and laundry and valet service, will be available at your hotel to accommodate business travelers and vacationing families alike. You'll have meeting rooms and banquet space for companies and organizations holding seminars or conventions, and recreational facilities—a swimming pool with a spa and sun deck, plus an exercise room and sauna—that can be enjoyed by all of your guests.

While these features are consistent throughout the chain, there is no prototype Embassy Suites Hotel. Each structure, rather, is designed specifically for its site and market, with an architectural style that complements the surrounding environment while reflecting a distinctive character. Throughout the planning and building process, the company's design and construction department will provide guidance, referring you to architects, contractors, and suppliers, reviewing the layouts and decorating schemes, and conducting on-site inspections.

You will be invited to attend Embassy Suites' management development course, while your staff can participate in the same instruction program created for the employees of the company-operated hotels. Cross-training personnel in several different service or maintenance jobs, these classes also furnish cash incentives for learning new skills.

Embassy Suites' marketing department and reservations center work closely with travel agents, airlines, and other intermediaries to generate business for the chain, with specialized strategies to target the profitable international, trade, and corporate meetings markets. On a direct level, you'll benefit from the company's extensive telemarketing systems, like the toll-free reservations line linked to your hotel by computer and the Excaliber "front office" software, allowing you to maintain and analyze guest records. Embassy Suites also manages national advertising and promotional efforts, such as the company's "Diplomat" preferred customers club and its TV and print "Fat Cat" campaign starring Garfield as the chain's "spokescat," creating media materials for you to use locally.

Embassy Suite Hotels are currently located in 76 cities, including the key "gateway" markets of New York, Chicago, the San Francisco Bay Area, and Atlanta. The company is seeking to expand its operation in the Northeast, California, and Florida in particular, but also in other areas across the country, along with Canada, Mexico, and the Caribbean. Embassy Suites franchise candidates—usually a group of partners—are expected to have proven development and operating skills, a desire to develop multiple hotels, and extensive financial capabilities. Don't underestimate the expenses involved here—a hotel like this will require several million dollars to build, so you and your partners will have to line up a huge amount of financial backing, and have a considerable reserve of your own funds. But if you can afford to make this kind of investment, the rewards can be appropriately ample as well.

For further information contact:
  Bill Moeckel, Senior Vice President, Development, Embassy Suites, Inc., 850 Ridge Lake Blvd., Suite 400, Memphis, TN 38120, 901-680-7200

Super 8 Motels, Inc.

Initial license fee: $20,000
Royalties: 4%
Advertising royalties: 3%
Minimum cash required: Varies by size of motel
Capital required: $100,000 to $250,000
Financing: Assistance in obtaining
Length of contract: 20 years

In business since: 1973
Franchising since: 1976
Total number of units: 799
Number of company-operated units: 52
Total number of units planned, 1995: 1,200
Number of company-operated units planned, 1995: 100

The Super 8 Motels chain guests know that, wherever in the country the motel is located, they can count on a large, well-appointed room at an affordable rate, with free color television and direct-dial phones.

Starting with a single facility in Aberdeen, South Dakota, the Super 8 Motels chain now has airport and roadside locations in 47 states, Canada, and Mexico, and plans to expand shortly to Europe, Asia, and Australia as well. Even the Middle East may be on the horizon. Super 8 Motels' policy, however, remains the same throughout the system—to provide clean, comfortable accommodations for cost-conscious travelers, businesspeople and vacationing families alike.

Whether customers simply pull into the motel after a day on the road or call in advance for a reservation, franchisees rely on Super 8 Motels' reputation and marketing programs to bring in business. Programs like its toll-free "Superline" reservation system, which handles over three million calls a year, sending you the information by computer and generating nearly 20 percent of your revenues, contribute to this good reputation. The company also encourages repeat business through its VIP preferred customers' club, extending room discounts, guaranteed reservations, express check-in services, and check-cashing privileges. To see that all of the motels maintain the company's standards, the quality assurance department inspects each facility in the system every 90 days. And to inspire superior service, Super 8 Motels runs employee contests—the national bed-making competition is a popular one—and incentive programs.

Most Super 8 Motels feature the chain's familiar English Tudor—style exterior, although other options are available to ensure that your facility is nicely suited to its surroundings. You'll have the choice of constructing a new building from the ground up or converting an existing property—and avoiding the extra construction cost and time.

You might decide to open one of the company's new "Supersuite" complexes, offering a selection of three-room lodgings, some equipped with a kitchenette, along with public spaces like a lobby, breakfast room, and pool and spa area.

Whichever way you decide to go, Super 8 Motels will assist with finding a location for your motel, using in-house market studies and conferring with industry contacts. You'll receive a guarantee in writing that no other Super 8 Motels will be built within a designated range of your facility. Providing construction plans and design specifications, the company will also estimate your budget and introduce you to contractors who do good work for reasonable fees.

Midwest Motel Supply, an independent service company long affiliated with Super 8 Motels, will install your exterior signs and help you coordinate the decor of your rooms, recommending vendors from whom you can obtain furniture packages, wall coverings, and lock sets. In addition, the company will outfit you with a telecommunications system, as well as cable satellite television equipment if you'd like it. Meanwhile, promotional materials, from ad copy to billboard layouts, will be furnished by Super 8 Motels, along with guidance in creating an advertising campaign that complements the chain's nationwide efforts. You'll also be supplied with guest and market trend data generated by the Superline system—including lists of common inquiries and prevalent travel origins—to help you make your marketing programs more effective.

Running a full-time training school, Super 8 Motels will teach you and your staff daily administrative and operations procedures, cleaning techniques, and customer relations, and instruct you on crisis management and motel law. Follow-up training will be offered during national and regional meetings, while you'll also receive manuals and videotapes to conduct on-the-job training for future employees. To monitor your business, management advisory services staff can perform a complete operations analysis through the computer system. Moreover, with the Super 8 Motels' fleet of planes available to enable personnel to meet with franchisees, company representatives will travel to your facility for personal consultation.

For further information contact:
  Joan Ganje-Fischer, Vice President, Marketing and Corporate Relations, Super
  8 Motels, Inc., P.O. Box 4090, Aberdeen, SD 57402-4090, 605-225-2272, fax
  605-225-5060

Yogi Bear's Jellystone Park Camp-Resort

Initial license fee: $15,000
Royalties: 6%
Advertising royalties: 1%
Minimum cash required: $20,000
Capital required: $15,000 to $200,000
Financing: None
Length of contract: 5 years

In business since: 1969
Franchising since: 1969
Total number of units: 70
Number of company-operated units: None
Total number of units planned, 1995: 135 to 140
Number of company-operated units planned, 1995: None

If you think that Yogi Bear is lost on a generation of children who are practically too young to remember the Smurfs, then you just haven't been watching a lot of afternoon television lately. According to a recent survey, in fact, the characters are immediately recognizable to nearly 95 percent of American youngsters and an equal number of teens and adults. Leisure Systems, Inc., the franchisor of Jellystone Parks, believes Yogi makes a superb mascot for a family campground— and a superb way to distinguish it from the competition. When a carload of budget vacationers has the choice between a big field of dirt or a fully equipped facility with an array of recreational features and familiar cartoon figures to greet them, the company reasons, which one are the kids clamoring in the back—and their tired parents, for that matter—more likely to pick?

Communing with nature isn't enough for most camping families these days. The young ones need something to do; the folks need amenities—and something to do with the young ones. That's why Jellystone Park provides much more than a pretty place to pitch a tent or park a trailer. You'll have clean and well-outfitted restrooms with showers, of course, and a laundry room, too. In the "ranger's station" will be a snack bar and general store, where you'll sell groceries, camping supplies, and Jellystone Park souvenirs and gifts.

But you'll also offer a playground, a game room, a video theater showing Yogi Bear cartoons, and a nine-hole miniature golf course— perhaps a swimming and wading pool as well. And you'll conduct a busy program of activities and special events throughout the camping season, from family sports tournaments and sing-alongs to group picnics and campfires, where Yogi and Boo Boo (plucky employees in costume) may make an appearance.

Many Jellystone Park operators simply convert an independent campground that they already owned. But you need neither the property nor the experience to be eligible for a franchise. If you'll be opening a new campground, Leisure Systems, Inc., will help you find a location with space enough for at least 125 campsites near a well-traveled route on the way to a major vacation destination. The company will also furnish prototype designs for buildings and other facilities and pass along a list of qualified engineers and contractors in your area. In addition, you'll receive a catalogue for ordering equipment and supplies.

For both new and converting Jellystone Park franchisees, Leisure Systems runs a training course teaching campground management and maintenance along with merchandising techniques. A company official will also provide field assistance at your facility prior to opening day, and continue to offer guidance and perform periodic on-site evaluations thereafter. Regional meetings, the annual convention, and the Jellystone Park newsletter will be further sources of information about recent trends and profit-making programs in the camping business.

Running ads in trade and recreation-theme periodicals, Leisure Systems publicizes the network of Jellystone Parks and their national toll-free advance reservation telephone line. The company will also outfit you with a local marketing package that includes an advertising kit, press release forms, promotions manual, and activities handbook. And to generate interest from regular campers, brochures for your facility will be displayed at the other campgrounds in the system, located in 25 states across the country and in Canada.

For further information contact:
   Robert E. Schutter, Vice President and General Manager, Leisure Systems, Inc., 6201 Kellogg Ave., Cincinnati, OH 45230, 513-232-6800 or 1-800-345-4173, fax 513-231-1191

Travel Agencies

Cruise Holidays International

Initial license fee: $25,000
Royalties: 1%
Advertising royalties: None
Minimum cash required: $40,000 to $45,000
Capital required: $80,000
Financing: None
Length of contract: 7 years

In business since: 1984
Franchising since: 1984
Total number of units: 103
Number of company-operated units: 1
Total number of units planned, 1995: 350 to 400
Number of company-operated units planned, 1995: 1

It's the fastest-growing segment of the travel industry, and not just be-cause of the popularity of *The Love Boat*. Cruises, simply stated, are no longer exclusively for the retired and wealthy. With the record number of ships and cruise lines that have entered the market over the past few years, the heightened competition has lowered prices significantly and put this holiday option within the reach of many who could not afford it before. Leisure seekers on a budget appreciate the fact that one price pays for almost everything, from the stateroom and meals to the entertainment and, of course, shipboard transport to intriguing ports of call. And working couples with limited vacation time appreci-ate being able to avoid the wasted hours—or days—in an airport and on the plane, commencing with the fun as soon as they climb aboard the ship. Moreover, voyagers who are only now testing the waters, so to speak, are apt to become converts—over 85 percent of first-time cruisers, it's been reported recently, will become repeat customers.

The number of choices available these days can be a little intimidat-ing: excursions to Mexico, Hawaii, Alaska, the Caribbean, through the Panama Canal, Europe and the Mediterranean, Africa, and Asia, too, not to mention programs that cater to singles, families, those who keep kosher, even weight-watchers and recovering alcoholics. That's why many would-be cruisers seek the counsel of experts, namely, agencies that specialize in cruise booking. And Cruise Holidays is the oldest—and largest—of them all.

Your customers will count on you to provide a degree of knowledge and a level of service not available from a general agency. Because the only trips you'll sell are cruise vacations, you'll develop a solid famil-iarity with the different ships and their amenities, with the cruise lines and the special accommodations they're willing to make, with the schedules and routes, learning when the weather is best for cruis-ing, and with the destinations, learning how to distinguish the tourist meccas from the tourist traps. Armed with that intelligence, you'll be able to help your customers, both individuals and groups, select the trip that's right for them.

Cruise lines, including such renowned companies as Cunard, Prin-cess, and Royal Viking, have long enjoyed a close and successful work-ing relationship with Cruise Holidays agents and franchisees (they also are the ones who'll be paying your commissions, but rest assured there's nothing fishy about that). Some excursions and programs that they offer, in fact, are sold exclusively through the agency. And taking advantage of Cruise Holidays' buying power and volume booking, you'll be able to extend discounts unobtainable elsewhere.

Cruise Holidays will grant you an exclusive territory and will assist with site selection and store design. After one week of classroom training, the company takes the "learning by doing" concept to its logical and pleasant extreme—a one-week cruise with on-site training on board. Keep in mind as well that many cruise lines, promoting a new ship or route, are apt to give discounts or complimentary state-rooms to travel agents like you, so the work will come with many opportunities for low-cost travel.

Besides being a lot of fun, that will be an integral part of keeping abreast of the cruise industry. Cruise Holidays' regional meetings and annual conventions provide further ways to stay informed. On a daily basis, you are in touch through your telecommunications package, making reservations and learning about changing rates and space availability, while you'll use Cruise Holidays' computer software for accounting and office management tasks.

Generating sales leads for its agents, the company conducts a national marketing program and helps franchisees create co-op advertising campaigns. You'll also be supplied with brochures and other materials from the major cruise lines, along with Cruise Holidays' customer newsletters and magazines, featuring lightly delivered sales pitches and heavily promoted sweepstakes contests.

Cruise Holidays is now operating in over 20 states and in Canada, although most franchisees are congregated on the East and West coasts. There are still, therefore, many untapped markets across the country with high potential. After all, folks living far inland have even more of a reason to want to take a cruise.

For further information contact:
  Jackie Wessel, Director, Franchise Development, Cruise Holidays International, P.O. Box 23559, San Diego, CA 92193, 619-279-4780

Empress Travel

Initial license fee: $20,000
Royalties: 1.5%
Advertising royalties: 0.4%
Minimum cash required: $70,000
Capital required: NA
Financing: Available
Length of contract: 20 years

In business since: 1957
Franchising since: 1974
Total number of units: 70
Number of company-operated units: None
Total number of units planned, 1995: 100
Number of company-operated units planned, 1995: None

Empress Travel can hardly be considered a fly-by-night agency. Since before the age of jet travel, the company has handled the business and vacation plans for thousands of customers throughout the Northeast, whether it's making hotel reservations, getting airline tickets, booking space on tours and cruises, arranging for rental cars—or any combination of the above.

Both corporations and independent travelers, Empress maintains, are more comfortable using a large, established agency network rather than an independent enterprise. It behooves agency operators as well, the company believes, to be affiliated with a solidly entrenched chain, benefiting from the kind of business volume, organizational structure, and marketing efforts that are unavailable to most solo establishments.

Due to deregulation, prices in the travel industry can now vary widely. Being an Empress franchisee will give you access to the buying power of a large chain, receiving significant discounts that you can pass on to your customers. In addition, you'll be able to obtain higher, "wholesale" commissions for your services, because of the premiums and overrides offered exclusively to multiunit agencies.

Empress will make sure that you have the telecommunications support necessary to run your business, with more than a little help from your industry suppliers. American Airlines, for example, will supply a computer system and ticket printer, giving you instant access not only to their company but also to each of the other major airlines, along with hotels, tour operators, cruise lines, and rental agencies. With this equipment, you'll be able to make reservations and provide your customers with up-to-the-minute information about ticket availability, waiting-list status, and flight schedules.

While you can expect to receive a great deal of repeat business, Empress will help you seek out new customers as well. In particular, the company conducts an aggressive marketing effort directed toward the professional sector, to generate year-round corporate business that eases the off-season slump plaguing most agencies. Empress also runs weekly ads in the travel sections of major newspapers like the *New York Times* and the *Washington Post* to bring in the individual patron, supplying you with direct mail pieces and other materials to use in your own market. As a further promotional opportunity, you'll have the chance to participate in local and regional co-op advertising with your fellow Empress franchisees.

Working with you to select a location for your facility and negotiate the lease, Empress will also advise you on economical choices in office furnishings, equipment, and supplies. The company will assist, too, in the hiring and training of your staff, and lead a one-week workshop to teach you how to operate your agency. Regular follow-up instructional seminars are available for you and your staff to improve your computer operations skills and product awareness, while frequent mailings from the home office will keep you updated on new sales techniques and special airfares, hotel deals, and tour package offers.

Previous travel agency experience is not a prerequisite to become an Empress franchisee. Because you will, however, be required to obtain the proper accreditation for your business, the company will guide you through the licensing process and register your agency with major travel and tourism organizations.

For further information contact:
  Jack Cygielman, Empress Travel Franchise Corp., 450 Harmon Meadow Blvd., P.O. Box 1568, Secaucus, NJ 07096-1568, 201-617-8513, fax 201-617-7579

International Tours, Inc.

Initial license fee: $34,500
Royalties: Fixed monthly royalty; 6-month grace period, $275 per month second 6 months, $550 per month for next 12 months, then $700 for length of agreement; royalty cancellation agreement available after first year
Advertising royalties: None
Minimum cash required: $61,000
Capital required: $70,000 to $90,000
Financing: None
Length of contract: 20 years

In business since: 1968
Franchising since: 1970
Total number of units: 336
Number of company-operated units: 1
Total number of units planned, 1995: 600 to 800
Number of company-operated units planned, 1995: 1

The number of travel agencies has doubled over the past decade, and their average annual volume has tripled. Travel costs less than it used to, so more people can afford to take trips. We have an older population, and older people often travel for pleasure. But the intense competition from airline deregulation has promoted bigness among the agencies as much as among airlines. The discounts available to volume purchasers emphasize economies of scale in the travel business. In this atmosphere, the little guy gets squeezed.

International Tours suggests that travel agents caught in this squeeze, or people interested in getting into the field in the first place, would do well to link their fortunes to the oldest franchisor of travel agencies. But although International aims for growth, it intends to grow under closely controlled conditions. Only in the past decade has the company begun to expand out of the Midwest.

Particular about its choice of franchisees, International prefers somebody with successful managerial or sales experience, although it does not insist on this. More than half of its franchisees owned a business previously, but no more than 20 percent of these were travel agents.

The company's president, Ron Blaylock, says of International's franchise selection policy: "We're looking for quality applicants with financial and business experience who will be successful in running a travel agency. It benefits everyone when we are thorough in our selection process."

If the company does accept you as a franchisee, it will evaluate agency location, grant exclusive territory, find a manager, provide ownership and financial consultation, assist with your bond application (travel agents must be bonded by the Airlines Reporting Corporation), and help you plan your office layout.

The company will also authorize the use of its name, trademarks, and logo, and buy the initial office forms, subscriptions, and operations manuals you'll need to set up your office. It will provide two-week training for you and your manager, recommend an agency budget, set up a six-month accounting system, assist with a marketing plan, and provide on-site management assistance.

International Travel will assure you higher commissions and cooperative advertising. It provides a travel agent training course, technical and grand opening assistance, airline and cruise line agreements, collateral material, and selected travel videos.

You will receive regular communications and updates from the company, and can benefit from its advisory council, automation agreements, national meetings, study trips, continuing education program, and corporate services.

International Tours, Inc., prides itself on being a company with a rock-solid reputation and a policy of steady but conservative growth. Its strength has made it one of only 12 national companies to serve on the Advisory Council of the Airlines Reporting Corporation. It is also a member of the International Airline Travel Agent Network, along with a host of other travel-related associations.

Mary Ridlon, a company franchisee, was recently quoted in a national travel publication as saying, "International Tours, Inc., has encouraged and guided me since I began. I credit much of my success to the Tulsa-based franchisor. The advantages offered by being a franchisee are the difference between really making it and just breaking even."

For further information contact:
  Ron Blaylock, International Tours, Inc., 5810 E. Skelly Dr., Suite 400, Tulsa, OK 74135, 918-665-2300

Travel Agents International, Inc.

Initial license fee: $34,500
Royalties: $500/month
Advertising royalties: $500/month
Minimum cash required: $44,500
Capital required: $100,000 (includes franchise fee)
Financing: None
Length of contract: 15 years

In business since: 1980
Franchising since: 1982
Total number of units: 353
Number of company-operated units: 2
Total number of units planned, 1995: 850
Number of company-operated units planned, 1995: 5

Travel Agents International, Inc., provides individuals with the chance to become part of the exciting world of travel without having to jump into it alone. While owning their own retail travel agency, franchisees can benefit from the experience and resources of the company's international support center in St. Petersburg, Florida.

"Most of our new franchises are turnkeys," states Roger E. Block, president and chairman of the board. "And, most of our new franchisees have little or no experience in the travel industry. It is our job to provide the best support available to make an agency successful."

The company prides itself on the amount and quality of support services available to its franchisees. Services include override (above the standard) commission programs, exclusive publications for leisure and corporate clients, a proprietary 24-hour emergency number for clients, and the Sailaway Cruise Center, which offers discount rates to clients on more than 2,000 cruises a year.

Before you open your agency, the company will help you find a site and hire a manager. A complete interior furniture package, including all necessary printed materials, is included in your initial franchise package.

A two-week training course, held at the company's St. Petersburg headquarters, will get you started in the travel industry on the right foot. Courses highlight marketing and advertising, incentive plans, government regulation agencies, computer training, travel insurance, vacation and corporate sales, and standard business topics such as accounting and employee relations. A complete how-to manual, detailing your preopening tasks and the sequence in which they should be completed, is provided as well.

Ongoing field and marketing visits will furnish you with on-site help for daily operations and promotional activity. Quarterly regional meetings will keep you abreast of new programs. The annual convention gives you an opportunity to achieve camaraderie with other members of the company while learning about sales and operations in the company's many seminars.

A co-op and regional advertising program is provided to franchisees in qualifying areas, and the company will provide assistance in securing advertising dollars from many of its preferred travel suppliers. The company has recently instituted a conversion program that permits established independent agencies to enter the company's system at a reduced fee.

T.A.I. Travel Academy, an affiliated company, provides you with a second earning possibility if you enter their business as well as the company's. Their academies provide travel training for those interested in the travel industry. The complete program and setup can be purchased from Travel Agents International for an additional fee.

"Travel is a 'fun' industry, but it can also be very competitive at times," says company president Block. "We help a person establish and grow in a business in an enjoyable industry."

For further information contact:
  Travel Agents International, Inc., P.O. Box 31005, St. Petersburg, FL 33731-8509, 1-800-678-8241

Travel Network, Ltd.

Initial license fee: $29,900
Royalties: $350/month, going up to $750/month
Advertising royalties: $200/month
Minimum cash required: $40,000

Capital required: $85,000
Financing: Available
Length of contract: 10 years

In business since: 1982
Franchising since: 1982
Total number of units: 181
Number of company-operated units: 1
Total number of units planned, 1995: 750
Number of company-operated units planned, 1995: 1

The travel agency business is a fragmented one, with no commanding brand-name organization. Independent operations predominate, but they have limited resources, run little or no advertising, and possess no individual buying power. So there are automatic advantages to being part of an agency franchise.

Becoming a Travel Network franchisee, however, will bring you additional benefits. A 20-year-old marketing organization serving as a liaison between travel agents and travel suppliers, Travel Network's parent company, SPACE Consortium, will provide you with extensive facilities, background and contacts, and industry clout. Then there are the two affiliated companies in the umbrella organization, TFI Tours International, one of the largest U.S.–based charter operators, offering low-cost flights to Europe, Asia, and the Caribbean; and Space & Leisure Tours, a nationwide tour wholesaler specializing in resort destinations. Through these and other relationships with industry suppliers, you'll be able to extend worldwide savings on airfare, charters, resorts, and tours to vacationers, and be able to get even more extensive allowances for business travelers. "Travel Network corporate hotel rates, airfare quality control programs that guarantee lowest fares, our own . . . air desk, Travel Network 24-hour service, and all of the other corporate travel programs available to us have given us the competitive edge in offering our clients exceptional travel savings and services," report Tampa, Florida, franchisees John and Laura Unger. "We could never have built this business as an independent travel agency."

Due to the combined strength of Travel Network and SPACE, moreover, you'll earn higher commissions for these sales and services. In addition, you'll receive personal travel benefits, from familiarization tours at vastly reduced prices to airline and hotel discounts as high as 75 percent.

Although many Travel Network franchisees converted their independent agencies, a travel industry background is not required. The company will help you find a qualified manager for your business who meets all regulatory requirements, and will furnish further assistance so you can become a properly accredited agency.

Four weeks of start-up training will prepare you for running the office. Beginning with a week of business development instruction at Travel Network's New Jersey headquarters, you'll then attend a seven-day computer course, followed by a stint down at the company's Orlando, Florida, office concentrating on operations, and finishing up with a week of on-site guidance spread over the first 90 days that you are open. Videocassette and audiocassette programs to use in your office will also be supplied, and Travel Network personnel will make monthly visits to sharpen the skills of your employees. Furthermore, ongoing training seminars and meetings are held for you and your staff throughout the year, both at the New Jersey corporate office and in travel spots around the world, giving you the opportunity to expand your knowledge of the industry through firsthand experience.

Advising you through the site selection and lease negotiation process, Travel Network will give you a list of the company's preferred suppliers of furniture and equipment. You'll be under no obligation, however, to purchase materials from these vendors. The company asks only that your office be outfitted with the same fixtures and decorated in the same color scheme as the other Travel Network agencies, to promote a national chain image.

You'll be assigned a Travel Network field representative who will get to know your operation thoroughly, providing regular consultation and problem solving and serving as the liaison between you and the head office. At the same time, the computerized electronic mail service will keep you in daily contact with the company, informing you about upcoming seminars; new airline, hotel, and tour offers and promotions; and fresh marketing opportunities. And your automation package ties you directly to the companies with whom you'll be making flight, hotel room, tour, cruise, and car rental reservations.

Travel Network conducts national and regional advertising and publicity that's affordable because the cost is shared by the entire chain— and often travel suppliers, too. Similarly, the company will prepare materials for you to use locally in newspapers and on TV and radio, along with direct mail pieces including Travel Network's consumer magazine. Registering you to receive important mailings, announcements, and promotional literature from the major players in the travel industry, Travel Network will also sign you up for subscriptions to the leading trade publications.

For further information contact:
  Michael Y. Brent, Executive Vice President, Travel Network, Ltd., 560 Sylvan

Ave., Englewood Cliffs, NJ 07632, 201-567-8500 or 1-800-872-8638, fax
201-567-4405

Uniglobe Travel [International] Inc.

Initial license fee: $2,500 to $48,000
Royalties: 0.5% to 1%
Advertising royalties: NA
Minimum cash required: $55,000
Capital required: $120,000
Financing: Varies by region
Length of contract: 10 years

In business since: 1980
Franchising since: 1981
Total number of units: 900
Number of company-operated units: None
Total number of units planned, 1995: NA
Number of company-operated units planned, 1995: None

One of the top four international travel organizations after only 10 years in existence, Uniglobe accounts for over 2 percent of all retail travel outlets in America. The company has zeroed in on the corporate travel market, pursuing small to medium-sized commercial contracts by using aggressive sales techniques. To date, this strategy has landed as many as 58,000 corporate accounts. The Uniglobe business strategy for the next few years calls for active marketing of its private-label vacation packages as aggressively as it has sold commercial travel.

Uniglobe sells conversion franchises to independent travel agents for a fee of $5,000. For brand new start-up businesses, it charges up to $48,000 and awards you what they coin a "proven business system." The company offers exterior and interior design for your agency and will help you staff your business and obtain all necessary licenses.

You must take the company's four-day management training course, which it holds in Vancouver, British Columbia. Uniglobe encourages you to bring your manager along, too. Your franchise fee covers tuition for both of you. The course topics include commercial and group sales, the vacation market, advertising, image marketing, cash flow, and personnel.

Uniglobe believes in continual training and provides courses several times during the year. To increase your knowledge and skills and that of your staff, the company offers an extensive selection of regional courses on advanced topics in the travel business. These courses cover subjects such as closing commercial sales, vacation sales, employee motivation, promotions, financial management, special incentive programs, customer relations, and budgeting.

Your regional office will provide guidance during your start-up period, beginning with a more than 50-step checklist that will help you systematically do everything you need to do to get off to a strong start. The regional office will also put you in touch with your travel products suppliers and will help coordinate your opening promotion. Thereafter, the regional office will serve as your eight-hour-a-day training and development consultant, just as you and your staff act as consultants to your customers.

Your franchise package includes exclusive computer software, initial office supplies, stationery, and business forms imprinted with your company name. Uniglobe will give you a list of "preferred suppliers" for your future purchases.

Also available is a seven-day-a-week, 24-hour-a-day emergency telephone service, providing your customers with a toll-free number they can call from anywhere in the world. It includes translation services in over 140 languages.

The Uniglobe goal is to become the household name in travel. It hopes to accomplish this by television advertising. The company currently spends about $7 million a year to promote the image of its franchises.

For further information contact:
John Henry, Senior Vice President, Uniglobe Travel [International] Inc., 1199 W. Pender St., Suite 1100, Vancouver, B.C., Canada V6E 2R1, 604-662-3800

Part III

Appendices and Index

Appendix 1

Uniform Franchise Offering Circular Disclosure Requirements

The Uniform Franchise Offering Circular (UFOC) format for franchise disclosure consists of 23 categories of information that must be provided by the franchisor to the prospective franchisee at least 10 days prior to the execution of the franchise agreement. Because this format has been adopted by many states as a matter of law, franchisors are not allowed to reorder the manner in which information is presented, nor may any of the disclosure items be omitted in the document. In addition, many sections of the UFOC must be a mirror image of the actual franchise agreement (and related documents) that the franchisee will be expected to sign. There should be no factual or legal inconsistencies between the UFOC and the franchise agreement, which the franchisee will sign.

Here is a description of the information required by each disclosure item of the UFOC:

Item One: The Franchisor and Any Predecessors

This first section of the UFOC is designed to inform the franchisee as to the historical background of the franchisor and any of its predecessors. The franchisor's corporate and trade name, form of doing business, principal headquarters, state and date of incorporation, prior business experience, and current business activities all must be disclosed in the section. The franchisor must also disclose the nature of the franchise being offered and its qualifications for offering this type of business. This will include a general description of business operations and discussion of the competition that the franchisee will face.

Item Two: Identity and Business Experience of Persons Affiliated with the Franchisor; Franchise Brokers

This section requires the disclosure of the identity of each director, trustee, general partner (where applicable) and each officer or manager of the franchisor who will have significant responsibility in connection with the operation of the franchisor's business or in the support services to be provided to the franchisees. The principal occupation of each person listed in Item Two for the past five years must be disclosed, including dates of employment, nature of the position, and the identity of the employer.

Item Three: Litigation

A full and frank discussion of any litigation, arbitration, or administrative hearings affecting the franchisor, its officers, directors, or sales representatives should be included in this section. The formal case name, location of the dispute, nature of the claim, and the current status of each action must be disclosed.

Item Four: Bankruptcy

This section requires the franchisor to disclose whether the company, any of its predecessors, officers, or general partners, have, during the past 15 years, been adjudged bankrupt or reorganized due to insolvency. The court in which the bankruptcy or reorganization proceeding occurred, the formal case title, and any material facts and circumstances surrounding the proceeding must be disclosed.

Item Five: Franchisee's Initial Franchise Fee or Other Initial Payment

The initial franchise fee and related payments to the franchisor upon executions of the franchise agreement must be disclosed in this section. The manner in which the payments are made, the use of the proceeds by the franchisor, and whether or not the fee is refundable in whole or in part must be disclosed.

Item Six: Other Fees

Any other initial or recurring fee payable by the franchisee to the franchisor or an affiliate must be disclosed and the nature of each fee fully discussed, including but not limited to royalty payments, training fees, audit fees, public offering review fees, advertising contributions, mandatory insurance requirements, transfer fees, renewal fees, lease negotiations fees, and any consulting fees charged by the franchisor or an affiliate for special services.

Item Seven: Franchisee's Initial Investment

Each component of the franchisee's initial investment that is required in order to open the franchised business must be estimated in this section, usually in chart form, regardless of whether such payments are made directly to the franchisor. Real estate, equipment, fixtures, security deposits, inventory, construction costs, working capital, and any other costs and expenditures should be disclosed. The disclosure should include to whom such payments are made, under what general terms and condition and what portion, if any, is refundable. Naturally, this section should be carefully reviewed by the state's loan officer in reviewing the applicant's loan proposal.

Item Eight: Obligations of the Franchisee to Purchase or Lease from Designated Sources

Any obligation of the franchisee to purchase services, supplies, fixtures, equipment, or inventory that relates to the establishment or operation of the franchised business from a source designated by the franchisor should be disclosed. If the franchisor will or may derive direct or indirect income based on these purchases from required sources, then the nature and amount of such income must be fully disclosed. Remember that such obligations must be able to withstand the scrutiny of the antitrust laws.

Item Nine: Obligations of the Franchisee to Purchase or Lease in Accordance with Specifications or from Approved Suppliers

All quality control standards, equipment specifications, and approved supplier programs that have been developed by the franchisor and must be followed by the franchisee must be disclosed under this item. The criteria that are applied by the franchisor for approving or designating a particular supplier or vendor must be included. A detailed discussion of these standards and specifications need not be actually set forth in the UFOC, rather, a summary discussion of the programs with reference to exhibits or confidential operating manuals is sufficient. Finally, any income derived by the franchisor in connection with the designation of any approved supplier must be disclosed.

Item Ten: Financing Arrangements

In this section, the franchisor must disclose the terms and conditions of any financing arrangements that are offered to the franchisee, either by the franchisor or by any of its affiliates. The exact terms of any direct or indirect debt financing, equipment or real estate leasing programs, operating lines of credit, or inventory financing must be disclosed. If any of these financing programs are offered by an affiliate, then the exact relationship between the franchisor and the affiliate must be disclosed. Terms that may be detrimental to the franchisee upon default, such as a confession of judgment, waiver of defenses, or acceleration clauses, must be included in this item of the UFOC.

Item Eleven: Obligation of the Franchisor; Other Supervision, Assistance, or Services

This section is one of the most important to the prospective franchisee (as well as the welfare of the lender to the franchisee) because it discusses the initial and ongoing support and services that are provided by the franchisor. Each obligation of the franchisor to provide assistance must cross-reference to the specific paragraph of the franchise agreement where the corresponding contractual provision may be found. Most services offered by the franchisor fall into one of two categories: initial or continuing services. Initial support includes all services offered by the franchisor prior to the opening of the franchised business, such as architectural or engineering plans, construction supervision, personnel recruitment, site selection, preopening promotion, and acquisition of initial inventory. The location, duration, content, and qualifications of the staff of the training program offered by the franchisor must be discussed in some detail. Any assistance provided by the franchisor that it is not contractually bound to provide must also be disclosed. Similar disclosures should be made for the continuing services to be offered by the franchisor once the business has opened, such as ongoing training, advertising and promotion, bookkeeping, inventory control, and any products to be sold by the franchisor to the franchisee.

Item Twelve: Exclusive Area or Territory

The exact territory or exclusive area, if any, to be granted by the franchisor to the franchisee should be disclosed, as well as the right to adjust the size of this territory in the event that certain contractual conditions are not met, such as the failure to achieve certain performance quotas. The right of the franchisor to establish company-owned units or to grant franchises to others within the territory must be disclosed. A detailed description and/or map should be included as an exhibit to the franchise agreement.

Item Thirteen: Trademarks, Service Marks, Trade Names, Logotypes, and Commercial Symbols

It has often been said that the trademark is at the heart of a franchising program. Therefore, the extent to which the franchisor's trade identity (trademarks, logos, slogans, etc.) have been protected should be disclosed, including whether or not these marks are registered at either federal or state levels, or whether there are any limitations or infringement disputes involving the marks or related aspects of the trade identity. The rights and obligations of the franchisor and franchisee in the event of a trademark dispute with a third party must also be disclosed.

Item Fourteen: Patents and Copyrights

Any rights in patents or copyrights that are material to the operation and management of the franchised business should be described in the same detail as required by Item 13.

Item Fifteen: Obligation of the Franchisee to Participate in the Actual Operation of the Franchised Business

The franchisor must disclose in this item whether or not absentee ownership and management will be permitted in connection with the operation of the franchised business. If the franchisee may hire a manager, the franchisor must disclose any mandatory employment terms or equity ownership.

Item Sixteen: Restriction of Goods and Services Offered by Franchised

In this section the franchisor must disclose any special contractual provisions or other circumstances that limit either the types of products and services the franchisee may offer *or* the types or locations of the customers to whom the products and services may be offered.

Item Seventeen: Franchise Renewal, Termination, Repurchase, and Assignment

This item is typically the most overlooked portion of the UFOC—but it is one of the most important. No one wants to think about how the franchise will be sold, terminated, or assigned if the business doesn't work out or if the franchisor disenfranchises a franchisee. But all these issues are vital and should be discussed with a qualified franchise attorney.

Item Eighteen: Arrangements with Public Figures

Any compensation or benefit given to a public figure in return for an endorsement of the franchise and/or products and services offered by the franchisee must be disclosed. The extent to which the public figure owns or is involved in the management of the franchisor must also be disclosed. The right of the franchisee to use the name of the public figure in its local promotional campaign and the material terms of the agreement between the franchisor and the public figure must also be included in this item.

Item Nineteen: Actual, Average, Projected, or Forecasted Franchise Sales, Profits, or Earnings

Whether or not the franchisor is willing to provide the prospective franchisee with sample earnings claims or projections must be discussed in Item 19.

In 1986, NASAA (National Association of State Approval Agencies) adopted new regulations for the use and content of earnings claims by franchisors. These new guidelines were adopted as the exclusive form of earnings claims permitted by the FTC as of January 1, 1989. Under the new rules, any earning claim made in connection with the offer of a franchise must be included in the UFOC. If no earning claim is made, the following statement must appear:

"Franchisor does not furnish or authorize its salespersons to furnish any oral or written information concerning the actual or potential sales, costs, income or profits of a (*franchised business name*). Actual results vary from unit to unit and franchisor cannot estimate the results of any particular franchise."

If the franchisor does elect to make an earnings claim, then it must:
(a) have a reasonable basis for the claim at the time which it is made;
(b) include a description of the factual basis for the claim; and
(c) include an overview of the material assumptions underlying the claim. If earnings claims are made, then the documents should be carefully reviewed by the state and its counsel prior to extending financing.

Item Twenty: Information Regarding Franchises of the Franchisor

A full summary of the number of franchises sold, number of units operational, and number of company-owned units must be broken down in Item 20, usually in tabular form, including an estimate of franchise sales for the upcoming fiscal year broken down by state. In addition, the number of franchises terminated or not renewed, and the cause of termination or nonrenewal, must be broken down for the previous three years of operations.

Item Twenty-one: Financial Statements

A full set of financial statements prepared in accordance with generally accepted accounting principles must be included in Item 21 as part of the disclosure package to be provided to a franchisee. Most registration states will require that the statements be audited, with limited exceptions for start-up franchisors. The balance sheet provided should have been prepared as of a date within 90 days prior to the date that the registration application is filed. Unaudited statements may be used for interim periods. Franchisors with weak financial statements may be required to make special arrangements with the franchise administrator in each state for the protection of prospective franchisees.

Item Twenty-two: Franchise Agreement and Related Contracts

A copy of the franchise agreement, as well as any other document to be signed by the franchisee, must be attached to the UFOC.

Item Twenty-three: Acknowledgment of Receipt by a Prospective Franchisee

The last page of the UFOC is usually a detachable document that acknowledges receipt of the offering circular by the prospective franchisee.

Appendix 2

"Red Flags" for Franchisees

When reviewing the franchise offering circular and franchise agreement, there are several "red flags" that should be of special concern. Naturally, specific "red flags" will vary from franchisor to franchisor, but overall, it makes good sense to give careful attention to the following issues:

- Unregistered and unprotected trademarks and copyrights.
- Extensive litigation against franchisees for no apparent reason.
- Weak balance sheet of a troubled or start-up franchisor.
- Excessive control by the franchisor over the franchisee in unnecessary areas.
- Contractual provisions that require the franchisee to purchase all or virtually all of its inventory or supplies from the franchisor or an affiliate of the franchisor.
- An excessive number of "hidden fees" charged by the franchisor, such as lease review fees, consulting fees, additional training fees, transfer fees, and commissions on leases on bank financing.
- Franchisors who assume the control of the franchisee's location by serving as the sublessor.
- Extensive and burdensome covenants against competition during and after the term of the franchise agreement.
- Overly stringent conditions to the renewal of the franchise upon expiration of the term, such as excessive renewal fees, a mandatory release form, or an ability of the franchisor to deny renewal for even one notice of breach during the term.
- Absolute discretion being vested in the franchisor in certain key areas, such as approval of suppliers, approval of issuance of securities, approval of a proposed transferee, or allocation of national advertising funds.

- Extremely broad ground for termination of the franchise agreement for virtually *any* breach by the franchisee.
- Provisions that provide little to no assurance of geographic exclusivity being granted to the franchisee (which could result in negative situations).
- Contractual clauses that provide for termination upon the death of the franchisee without the right to transfer the franchise to an heir or surviving spouse.
- An inexperienced management team who know little about franchising or an overly strong dependence on a particular person.
- A very short training program (which may imply a shallow foundation for the system) or a very long training program (which may imply a high degree of difficulty in teaching the underlying concepts).

Alphabetical Index of Companies